VERDI'S

THEATER

VERDI'S

THEATER

CREATING DRAMA

THROUGH MUSIC

GILLES

DE VAN

Translated from the French by

GILDA ROBERTS

THE UNIVERSITY

of CHICAGO PRESS

CHICAGO & LONDON

Gilles de Van is professor of Italian literature and the history of opera at the University of Sorbonne Nouvelle (Paris III). He is the editor of *Guide Verdi.*

The University of Chicago Press, Chicago 60637
The University of Chicago Press, Ltd., London
© 1998 by The University of Chicago
All rights reserved. Published 1998
Printed in the United States of America
07 06 05 04 03 02 01 00 99 98   5 4 3 2 1

ISBN (cloth): 0-226-14369-4
ISBN (paper): 0-226-14370-8

Originally published as *Verdi: Un Théâtre en Musique,* © Librairie Arthème Fayard 1992

Library of Congress Cataloging-in-Publication Data

Van, Gilles de
    [Verdi, un théâtre en musique. English]
    Verdi's theater : creating drama through music / Gilles de Van ;
translated from the French by Gilda Roberts.
        p.   cm.
    Includes bibliographical references and index.
    ISBN 0-226-14369-4. — ISBN 0-226-14370-8 (pbk.)
    1. Verdi, Giuseppe, 1813–1901. Operas.   2. Opera—Dramaturgy.
I. Title.
ML410.V4V2313   1998
782.1′092—dc21   97-46109
                                                                  CIP

⊚ The paper used in this publication meets the minimum requirements of the American National Standard for Information Sciences—Permanence of Paper for Printed Library Materials, ANSI Z39.48-1992.

Dedicated to the memory of
Nives Sanfelice di Bagnoli

CONTENTS

vii

PREFACE

For a long time, for reasons that I examine in the first chapter of this book, many musicians and music lovers thought of Verdi not as a true dramatist so much as a skillful practitioner who pandered to the tastes of a public that essentially wanted to hear beautiful singing. Over the last thirty years this perspective has changed, and the Verdian bibliography has grown, both in quantity and in quality. Today one finds a vast number of books dedicated to the composer's life and personality as well as to his operas—not to mention a profusion of articles on various aspects of his oeuvre, the important work being done in specialized centers like the Istituto Nazionale di Studi Verdiani in Parma and the American Institute for Verdi Studies in New York, and the critical edition of Verdi scores being prepared jointly by the University of Chicago Press and Ricordi in Milan.

Nevertheless, there is no study that examines Verdi's dramaturgy as a logical, articulated whole. This book, a somewhat shortened, reworked version of a study published in Paris in 1992, seeks to fill the gap. No claim is made to replace existing monographs; rather, my aim is to round them out through an attempt at synthesis that is not rigidly subject to chronological order and follows certain methodological choices described in the chapter "Aesthetics."

CHAPTER ONE

Verdi, Dramatist

A HARD-WON APPRECIATION

The nineteenth century was a period of tremendous crisis. Revolution burst out in France and spread across Europe, to be followed by the Napoleonic adventure, and an order that had held for hundreds of years crumbled into dust. These were unprecedented events, and they had grave repercussions: people started to question the modes of living and the values underlying the foundation of social existence. True, this calling into question had begun well before the fall of the Bastille, but it is also true that the upheavals the Revolution brought in its wake throughout Europe—the excesses of some and the ferocious reaction of others—provided a dramatic twist by intensifying conflicts that up to that time had been waged in calmer fashion. The old order gradually disappeared, not without nostalgia or regrets, while a liberal way of thinking arose that was based on the emergence of the individual, on the individual's claim to govern his own destiny free of subjection to a religion-based cosmogony. The relation of the individual to history, to society and its institutions, became the overriding question, and, torn between nostalgia for a long-gone stability on the one hand and the lure of individualism and the dream of new social configurations on the other, nineteenth-century man was racked with anxiety and tensions.

At this time opera became a prominent arena for the acting out of these tensions. This was due not only to its huge popularity throughout the Continent but also to its predilection for clear-cut conflict and stock characters. However much librettists and composers had to avoid offending the powers that be, however eager they were to please the majority and soften any harsh edges, they nevertheless did stage the major conflicts of their age—between the individual and authority, between personal conscience and history, between the desire for freedom and traditional subordination to the law. The inexorable decline, in the first twenty years of the century, of the "happy ending" that resolved even the deadliest confrontations shows how profound these tensions were. The unspoken battle between Figaro and the Count in *The Marriage of Figaro* could still be waged with kid gloves and end with the illusion of complete reconciliation. A few decades later, swords are drawn, and the fighting invariably finishes in the total defeat or even physical elimination of at least one of the protagonists.

Little wonder, then, that this period of contrasting light and shadow lent itself readily to operatic dramatization and that it produced two of the most complex dramaturgies of the operatic repertoire, those of Verdi and Wagner, with a third, Mozart's, slightly preceding them. But note the difference in stature between the first two composers: Wagner was very quickly embraced by the musical and intellectual elites, which, thanks to his musical genius, the theories he expounded, his break with traditional opera, and his innovative librettos, recognized in his work an elaborate dramatic art that expressed the tensions of the time. Verdi, on the other hand, was long seen as a skillful composer who charmed the public but aroused the scorn and even the hostility of the elites. The popular success of his operas contrasts sharply with the coolness of the critics: even leaving aside the notorious attacks of a Scudo, a Fétis, or a Montazio, the press tended to be hard on this music the public adored.[1] Fellow artists, too, were somewhat disdainful of the composer from Busseto: witness Delacroix's punning reference in his journal to Verdi as "Merdi."

It is true that the situation did gradually change, with Verdi, late in life, receiving the homage of a number of fellow composers such as Saint-Saëns, Reyer, and Richard Strauss, who sent him the score of his *Guntram*. There were some startling changes of heart like that of the conductor Hans von Bülow, who, having maligned the composer, wrote him a resounding retraction, which Verdi acknowledged coolly.[2] The premieres of *Otello* and *Falstaff* stirred all Europe. Still, certain bastions held out. In 1904, Siegfried Wagner was asked what his father had thought of Verdi, and the son of the composer of *Tristan* replied, "We did not speak *nor do we speak* of such matters." The Austrian writer Franz Werfel recalled that around 1930 it was blasphemous in German-speaking countries to mention Verdi in the same breath as universally acclaimed composers like Beethoven and Wagner.[3]

Verdi's recognition, indeed, embraced only the later works: if *Otello* fared well, *Rigoletto* was a different matter. It was at the beginning of this century that the tide began to turn. In 1902, Toscanini staged an epoch-making revival of *Trovatore:* "When it was rumored that Toscanini was going to dig up that old mummy, there were hoots of derision. The progressivist Toscanini, champion of the Wagnerians, thanks to whom *Tristan* was such a smashing success?"[4] The Italian conductor in fact played a leading role in bringing about the meticulous, impassioned rereading of Verdi's works, both early and late. Then the critics started to delve into the rediscovery with the writings of Roncaglia (1914), Della Corte (1923–25), Toye (1931), Gerigk (1932), Mila (1933), and so on, while in the 1920s Germany saw the beginning of the so-called Verdi renaissance, to which Franz Werfel lent his fervent cooperation. Little by little, other works besides *Aida, Otello,* and *Falstaff* emerged from relative oblivion.[5]

This turning of the tide was irreversible, but up to the 1960s progress was extremely slow. In 1951, the novelist Dino Buzzati could still say, "Verdi isn't chic, Verdi isn't fashionable; praising Verdi will not ingratiate you with the fashionable sets."[6] The recording world followed this line and neglected Verdi's youthful works.[7] France, for its part, was probably the last country, if not to acclaim Verdi, then at least to recognize him as a leading creator of musical literature: Roland Mancini could still remember in 1972 that "going to see *Rigoletto* just a short time ago was an offense that students of composition committed without saying a word to their professor,"[8] a situation that had scarcely changed by the 1980s. Benjamin Britten personally testified to this resistance: he had always thought of Verdi as a clever but routine composer, devoid of musical interest, until a chance hearing of a performance of *La traviata* made him completely change his mind, launching an ever-increasing admiration.[9]

What stands out in this brief review of Verdi's fortunes is the contrast between the public's approval and the reticence on the part of members of musical and, on a broader scale, intellectual circles. As regards the early works, part of the reason may be the temporary eclipse of a whole tradition, that of the first half of the preceding century, which included the serious operas of Rossini, Bellini, Donizetti, as well as early Verdi. "Technical" reservations concerning a style that was judged poor or primitive have served as an excuse, despite Stravinsky's polemical efforts to rehabilitate Verdi by contrasting the "substance" and "real invention" of *Rigoletto* with the "vociferations" of the Tetralogy, and despite the analyses of certain respected scholars (like René Leibowitz in France) or, especially, recent studies of Verdi's method of composition. Still, the continued misunderstanding the composer has suffered can probably be explained in a more general way by his attitude toward what one might call the crisis of Romanticism.

As the old systems of reference disappeared and the desire grew to develop new ones and set new goals for humanity, art gained a loftier purpose than simply the desire to please or move. The artist became an intellectual, art a way of understanding. Art could now both represent reality and comment on it. The artist could create worlds that mirrored the coherence and unity the age seemed to have lost. As he invoked a freedom at once heady and fraught with danger, the artist became alienated from the old tradition, which he now contemplated with mingled irony and nostalgia. It became necessary to break with that tradition; only then would the artist be able to devise means of expression that would do justice to the new aims of art that Hegel had put forward in his *Aesthetics*.

Wagner was quick to take note of the crisis. Sizing up what was at stake, he made a complete break with operatic tradition, which for him meant the Italian and French styles (although obviously this did not prevent him from continuing to be in their debt). Verdi and the Italians, for their part, appeared to ignore him, or at least not to make much of his actions, and continued to compose operas that delighted the public. Where Wagner, asserting that the artist now had new tasks, destroyed tradition by staging a sort of coup d'état and creating his own genre, Verdi seemed to accept tradition without apparent effort, even if in fact he gradually broke it down to lead opera into quite new directions. This explains why Wagner was promptly hailed as an artist of "modernity," that is, one having a global and problematic vision of man, while Verdi was denied the status of "modern" and, despite the growing admiration for him as a "musician," was neither automatically nor immediately acknowledged as a "dramatist," that is, the creator of a coherent, clearly defined world.

It may be, too, that Verdi's arduous ascent to fame in the highest circles of culture is linked to the cultural and social milieu in which his career developed.

ARTISAN AND ARTIST

The conditions in which an artist practices his profession and the image society confers on him both clearly affect his work and the way he views his art. Still, Verdi's case stands by itself. In his time there were not only two Italys and two societies but two musical cultures, two very different traditions. Thus, the history of Verdi's career traces the evolution of the eighteenth-century conception of the composer as "craftsman" into the modern profile of the artist. The artistic milieu in which Verdi developed has been well documented,[10] so it should suffice to recall the salient points insofar as they affected Verdi's vision of his art.

1. Verdi started his career in a fragmented Italy that had been occupied by foreign powers and ended it in a united country that was entering the rank of great nations. The society of his early years was provincial and strictly hierarchical, whereas the one he left at his death had to a large extent caught up with the other European states.

2. In 1840, opera was the chief distraction for this provincial, compartmentalized world. Penetrating into the tiniest villages,[11] it reached the working classes through a series of town-to-village relays, becoming a truly popular entertainment. Then, after the 1848 revolutions, opera gradually ceased to serve as a social forum; as the municipal and aristocratic structure that had formed the basis of Italian village operatic life was torn down, the small provincial theaters, and sometimes even the big opera houses, began to decline. And, finally, opera became "professionalized," widening the hitherto somewhat narrow gap between the trained and the amateur artist.

3. Up to the 1850s, operatic life enjoyed great vitality. Operas sprang up like mushrooms after rain, but they were short-lived and quickly forgotten, with the result that composers had to work continuously and without security.[12] Around mid-century the modern notion of repertoire emerged. Verdi's hugely successful "trilogy" *(Rigoletto, Trovatore, Traviata)* was largely responsible for the practice of taking up "old" works, with the inherent danger that one day operatic theater would become a museum entrusted with the care of an ever dwindling patrimony.

4. This vitality of operatic life came at the expense of great risk. One opera came on the heels of another; the absence of legal protection of artistic property meant that the composer was forced to produce if he wanted to keep his name in the public eye. Besides this financial uncertainty, there was the "psychological" insecurity of being at the mercy of a fickle public quick to destroy what it had wildly applauded. And there were practical risks: impresarios often went bankrupt; scores were treated with extreme carelessness, with arias added, cut out, or interpolated from other operas as circumstance or the singers' whims decreed. A body of laws established between 1840 and 1882 ensured that composers' works would be better protected, a change that had repercussions for Verdi's rhythm of production by enabling him to write a new opera while living

off the income from the one before. Meanwhile, the publisher gained increasing power, making for more efficient control over opera production and a certain standardization of staging.

In this brief review we have looked at two profoundly different operatic cultures. The one that was established from 1850 on was fairly close to our own; it was based on theaters that relied on a repertoire, increasingly specialized orchestras, singers who were international stars, a more attentive and less fickle audience, a cult of the great composer, and a religion of art. As for the system that held sway in the first half of the century, judgments were conflicting. George Sand and Stendhal were enchanted by the Italians' passion for singing and opera, while Berlioz and Mendelssohn were shocked by the amateurishness of the singers, the rowdiness of the spectators, and the lack of respect shown to the opera.

The special interest in Verdi's situation is, of course, that he lived in both worlds. Beginning his career in conditions more or less similar to those of his predecessors, Rossini, Bellini, and Donizetti, he ended it as a Jupiter of the musical Olympus who succeeded in imposing his will on virtually all areas of opera production. To believe that he alone was responsible for this transformation would be naive since Verdi benefited from a general improvement in composers' conditions throughout Europe; yet it would be a mistake to underestimate the will and determination he showed in taking advantage of, and sometimes even furthering, this rise in the composer's power.

The system Verdi encountered at the outset of his career granted the artist little freedom. The composer was merely a temporary employee of a theater, serving an impresario who in turn had to report to a princely court or theater-owning oligarchy. If he wanted to avoid this situation, he had only two solutions: to create his own system, as Wagner would do, although in a totally different context, or, by dint of perseverance, acquire the power that would allow him to deal with theaters from a position of strength.

This latter was the approach Verdi chose, instinctively and without hesitation.[13] True, he frequently had to retreat or accept compromises, but his tenacity, his way of handling his affairs himself, without intermediaries, and also his growing reputation assured him a position of great power.[14] Nevertheless, the fact that he exerted this power on a daily basis, over every detail of each new opera, shows that it arose not so much from a Romantic conception of the artist as demiurge as from the conviction that the success of an opera could not depend entirely on the quality of a score but called for control of all dimensions of the stage production. The voicing of this will for power could seem despotic, as Verdi himself recognized in a famous letter to Du Locle written in 1869,[15] yet tempering this image considerably is another—that of the man of the theater willing to compromise when it is justified and capable of changing course when he realizes he has chosen the wrong way.

The vision of the artist that emerges from Verdi's long career is a complex, not to say contradictory one, especially when it is compared to the Romantic image of the creative genius blazing new trails for his contemporaries but misunderstood by a mercantilist society. Verdi's youthful beginnings in the 1840s imbued him with the idea that the creative artist was a mountebank selling emotion to the public at the risk of life and limb. Even though his business talents enabled him to transform his small craftsman's shop into a flourishing enterprise, like a captain of industry, he never forgot the cruel law governing the link between artist and public. These were the rules of the game; he not only accepted them but also interiorized them, showing an attitude that shocked many of his contemporaries, a certain cynicism that put its finger bluntly on the venality of the relationship between the artist and his public: "Everything is fine! Ovations and encores mean nothing if the till is empty. If the till is full, that means many people are going to the theater. When many people go to the theater, it means the public is interested in the show. If they are interested in the show, it means that the production is good. That's our goal!"[16] Unreservedly, and without appearing to compromise, Verdi accepted the law governing the exchanging of emotion between the composer-seller and the public-buyer; he accepted his successes without enthusiasm and stomached the failures, mortified but unfrowning.

Having agreed to the rules of this game, late in life he even idealized them, seeing the theater as a fair fight where the composer appears before the public with his talent as his only wealth. So, when a more sophisticated cultural industry came into being, backed by publishers and the press, Verdi was inclined to reject it. Noting the barrage of publicity attending the premiere of *Aida* in Cairo, he wrote the critic Filippo Filippi, looking back nostalgically to the beginnings of his career: "My reaction is simply disgust and humiliation! I always recall with joy my early days when practically without a friend, without anyone talking about me, without any preparation, without the least influence, I presented myself to the public with my operas, ready to be shot at and overjoyed when I managed to create a favorable impression. How much fuss goes into the making of an opera nowadays! Journalists, chorus artists, stage directors, musicians, etc., etc.... each must bring his brick to raise the edifice of

réclame and erect a framework of small miseries that do not add a thing
to the value of an opera but, on the contrary, obscure its real worth. It is
deplorable, deeply deplorable!"[17] He noted with regret how well behaved
the public had become, applauded the gallery audience, which used to be
unruly but spontaneous, and deplored the "ecstatic silence" of Bayreuth.[18]

Even though Verdi came to idealize this law of the theater in comparison with the modern forms of the industry, it aroused in him feelings of
extreme ambivalence, as though it were a yoke he had helped put around
his own neck. To whoever would listen he declared that he hated the
theater and did not see when he might retire, asserting bitterly to his
publisher Ricordi in 1885: "I cannot help passing on a thought that is
rather discouraging for me. In my long career, I have always found impresarios, publishers, etc., etc. who were tough, inflexible, inexorable, always with their rules and regulations close at hand. Their words were
gentle, their actions deplorable. In the final analysis, I have always been
considered an object, a tool to be used as long as it is serviceable."[19]

As so often in his operas, Verdi here strips away appearances to disclose
the real relations between the partners as they face each other, making no
attempt to soften the resulting hurt: "this icy exterior, this impassivity of
feature and attitude," which for the musicologist F. J. Fétis revealed a
diplomat more than an artist,[20] these were an acquired armor rather than
Verdi's true nature. Recalling the failure of his second opera, he accepted
the public's verdict but deplored its lack of consideration for a man who
had been cruelly tested in his private life (he had just lost his wife and,
shortly before that, his two children), and the iron pact he drew up is
based on regret for another kind of relationship, one that had never existed: "But as long as [the public] recognizes the value of these works that
have been heard around the world, we are even. I do not wish to condemn
my audience: I can accept the coldness and the boos as long as I don't
have to give anything in exchange for the applause. We poor gypsies,
charlatans and everything you want to call us, must sell our fatigue, our
thoughts, our ecstasies for gold. For three lire the public buys the right to
hiss or applaud us. Our fate is to be resigned to it. That's all!"[21]

These confessions show a different, more vulnerable Verdi and suggest
a cleavage between the lone creator and the seller of operas. Consider
these soul-baring words, which the composer seems almost to regret since
he ends them abruptly: "Oh no! I adored and I do adore this art! and
when I am alone and am wrestling with my notes, then my heart pounds,
tears stream from my eyes, and the emotions and pleasures are beyond
description. But when I think that these poor notes of mine will be

thrown to creatures with no intelligence, to a publisher who is willing to sell them as fodder for the amusement or mockery of the masses, then, I assure you, there's nothing left for me to love any more! . . . Let's not talk about it." [22]

Thus, behind the composer, moneygrubbing and pugnacious in his business dealings, looms the wistful jester, humiliated at having to sell his intimate life's secrets. Pride in the fight mingles with a feeling of dispossession, and, although the list of successes constitutes a revenge, it also aggravates his sense of selling himself.

The light this ambivalence sheds on characters like Manrico, Rigoletto, and Violetta is inescapable. The trilogy of the 1850s, the mature Verdi's first great success, portrays three characters whose job is to amuse the public. True, Manrico is only marginally a troubadour, but Rigoletto and "La traviata" share a fundamental feature, the one being a court jester and the other a courtesan who has to satisfy the pleasures of the Louis-Philippe bourgeoisie. In both cases, the public buys the right to be amused, indifferent to the private lives of those entertaining them. Hence the profound sympathy between Verdi and his two characters—a jester's fellow feeling. Hence, too, the autobiographical echoes one finds in the great monologue in which Rigoletto describes his master, the Duke of Mantua, whom he has to amuse even when he has no inclination to do so and toward whom he feels a mixture of envy and bitterness.

Where Verdi is concerned, it is therefore legitimate to use the terms *artisan* and *artist:* well into the nineteenth century he continued the role of the composer as craftsman inherited from the century before, meanwhile fighting for autonomy for the creator and due respect for his work. His ties to the world of the early Ottocento and his familiarity with the theater saved him from that rupture with society that characterized the avant-gardes of the second half of the century, yet at the same time he emerges as a solitary artist obeying no law save that of his inspiration. It is a difficult balance, one that Verdi captured in his characteristically vivid language when he declared that the artist must be walleyed—one eye on the public, the other on art.

Questions of Method

THE LIBRETTO

If dramaturgy is defined as the creation of a dramatic universe characterized by certain themes, characters, and situations, as the thinking that organizes and articulates these elements and the combination of techniques governing their realization on the stage, the question arises whether one can legitimately speak of an opera composer's dramaturgy. It stands to reason that the musical techniques that go into this dramaturgy are his by right, but what about the libretto? It is well known that Verdi did not write any of his texts, borrowing them instead from literary sources of various nationalities and epochs and entrusting the task of adaptation to librettists. Is it not inaccurate, then, to speak of Verdi's dramaturgy in connection with *Macbeth?* Should we not rather speak of Shakespeare's dramaturgy, then in second place that of Piave, the librettist, and describe as Verdian only those situations or themes that can be proved to have sprung from the composer's initiative alone?

In fact, this argument about authorship is somewhat pointless. In the vast majority of cases, opera composers work on texts that are written by librettists and almost always drawn from literary sources. Like cuckoos, which deposit their eggs in other birds' nests, they develop their art by assimilating the works of others, which become theirs through inner appropriation. This assimilation becomes a second authorship, and to deny it to composers is to reduce them to mere musical illustrators of texts—a role they have emphatically refused, particularly in the nineteenth century, by insisting on total control over their creations and a status as men of the theater.

This appropriation is all the more evident in that the texts Verdi chose emerged from a forest of librettos or plays that he read and put aside: "I am devastated," he wrote in September 1857, before starting work on *Un ballo in maschera;* "I have read through countless plays (some of them very fine) but none of them suits my purpose."[23] The leitmotiv quickly became obsessive when, from the 1850s on, the composer began to space out his operas and became more finicky in his choice of subjects. Thus, Dumas *père*'s *Kean,* Grillparzer's *Die Ahnfrau,* Byron's *Bride of Abydos* and *Cain,* Antonio Gil y Zarate's *Gusman el Bueno,* Zorrilla's *El zapatero y el rey,* Victor Hugo's *Ruy Blas* and *Marion Delorme,* Shakespeare's *Tempest* and *Hamlet,* not to mention *King Lear,* were considered, in some cases even translated or made into scenarios, then abandoned. Sometimes there was a good reason to reject these plots; in other cases Verdi simply set the play aside or considered the subject foreign to his nature: "Cleopatra is not a subject for me," he declared when turning down the text written by Méry and Du Locle, the future librettists of *Don Carlos.*[24]

Verdi was certainly not alone in this exhausting search for a libretto, if we are to believe what Mozart wrote his father in 1783: "I have looked through at least 100 libretti and more, but I have hardly found a single one with which I am satisfied."[25] Yet this endless quest does tend to lessen the gap between the composer who creates his own libretto and the one who searches for it and actually finds "the needle in the haystack." The libretto then becomes the reward for waiting so long, the fulfillment of a secret, undefined longing. King without a kingdom, the composer at last invades a foreign land, but, when he takes possession of it, it is as though it had always belonged to him. Verdi pinpoints this process of appropriation in a letter, written in French in 1864, to Emile Perrin, director of the Paris Opéra: "I know for certain that if one day I were to write for the Opéra, I should do so only if the poem were to my complete satisfaction, and above all, if it truly excited me."[26]

Consequently, his attitude toward the "poem" he has chosen, whether typified by great faithfulness to the original text or by manipulations, additions, or deletions, in each case acts as a signpost to his dramatic thought. For instance, convinced that *Macbeth,* which was far removed from the Italian operatic tradition, called for particular care, especially where language was concerned, he urged his librettist not to lose sight of his model. His first reactions to the scenario for *Don Carlos* were quite different: he accepted the Fontainebleau act, which has no counterpart in Schiller (it comes from another source probably unknown to Verdi), and called for spectacular scenes like those in Meyerbeer's *Le Prophète,* whence the grandiose finale of the auto-da-fé, which, of course, is not to be found in the German play. On the other hand, the introduction of duets for the King and the Marquis of Posa, the King and the Grand Inquisitor, betrays a desire to stay close to Schiller.[27] These diverse attitudes demonstrate that, once Verdi had chosen a "story," he felt free to treat it as he saw fit.

It is therefore possible to think of Verdi as being fully responsible for his librettos, for better or worse, because of this inner appropriation that is a fundamental stage in an opera's genesis. One can also, of course, take a second look to see whether the composer was faithful to the original or took liberties, even inventing some scenes completely, but it is important to take these librettos quite seriously and avoid those subtle comparisons with the literary source that lead the listener to approve of the music *in spite of* the libretto. In the vast majority of cases Verdi identified with his plots, however questionable they might appear, and used them because they struck him as convincing.

Here we come up against a general cultural problem. Nineteenth-century Italian opera production was based on a reservoir in which all manner of subjects—the serious theatrical repertoire, works for the boulevard theaters, the latest novels—were mixed together indiscriminately, all offering serviceable plots. Verdi's own culture was similarly disparate: although it was founded on the Bible, Dante, Manzoni, and Shakespeare and included such diverse authors as the Greek dramatists, Ariosto, Ossian, Plato, Schopenhauer, Pascal, Darwin, Balzac, Zola, Alfieri, etc., it also embraced popular contemporaries like Sue, Dumas, Verne, and Ohnet.[28] His reading did grow in sophistication with age, but the composer would always have a "penny dreadful" streak, doubtless stemming from the cheap romances, or *romanzacci,* that his biographer Michele Lessona tells us he loved to read in his youth. It is worth remembering, however, that, as Peter Brooks has shown, the works of such novelists as Balzac, Dickens, Hugo, Dostoyevsky, Conrad, and James draw on the same melodramatic techniques that thrilled popular audiences on the "Boulevard du Crime" and that, especially in the case of opera, the distinction between high and popular culture is always somewhat blurred.[29]

A MAN OF THE THEATER

When *Falstaff* was staged in Rome in 1893, a committee of musicians came to pay homage to their country's "greatest composer." "No, no, don't say great composer," Verdi interrupted; "I am a man of the theater."[30] Indeed, in his dealings with librettists Verdi spoke less as a composer than as a dramatist. For him, as for Wagner, opera was above all else a theatrical event, a spectacle intended for the stage, and he deemed himself competent to judge this spectacle in all its aspects—the scenario, its division into scenes, the introduction of the characters, the length of the speeches allotted to them, and so on, not to mention the staging, decor, and costumes. The one area he explicitly declared to be outside his jurisdiction was the literary quality of the versification, that is, the "beauty" of the lines, although he insisted on judging their effectiveness on stage. For Verdi, a libretto was not literature but theater; the librettist answered to him and enjoyed relative autonomy only as regards the final phase of setting into verse.

Further evidence of Verdi's calling as a man of the theater can be seen in his tepid liking for absolute music. His instrumental output is limited to one quartet, while his nonoperatic works consist of solo songs, hymns, or religious music, all of them with words. Thus, Verdi's inspiration invariably arose from a text and never worked in the abstract on a purely musical structure.[31] This attitude shows through in certain key concepts of his language as well as in the way he took possession of a text.

Drama

The new reality that emerged in the nineteenth century, at least in the works of farsighted composers like Verdi and Wagner, was that words and music must yield pride of place to an idea overarching them both, that of drama. Mozart had already tended to go beyond the pointless dispute over the primacy of music or words to come out in favor of total spectacle, although he did state in one letter that poetry should be "music's obedient daughter." In the same letter, he declared that "the best thing of all is when a good composer, *who understands the stage and is talented enough to make sound suggestions,* meets an able poet, that true phoenix."[32] When, in the case of *L'oca del Cairo,* he demanded complete docility from the librettist, Varesco, he gave as his reason not so much the fact that Varesco was a poet where he himself was a musician as that Varesco had "not the slightest knowledge or experience of the theater."[33] Here, Mozart seems to suggest a hierarchy where the words are subject to the music, which in turn is subject to the opera as a theatrical whole. The words have no autonomy in relation to the drama, but music is just as heteronomous in relation to the drama. Thus, the composer divides himself in two, becoming on the one hand a musician responsible for one of the elements of the drama and on the other a dramatist whose task is to manage the spectacle in each one of its aspects.

The same vision of opera emerges clearly from Wagner's theoretical writings. In his work on the aesthetics of Wagnerian drama, Carl Dahlhaus points out the error of those critics who see Wagner as the successor of Gluck in his desire to make music subservient to the text it illustrates: these critics are confusing poetry and drama. For Wagner, neither poetic intention nor musical expression is autonomous: each blends into the single reality, the drama.[34]

Although Verdi never resorted to such theoretical exposition, his operatic practice was inspired by the same principles, long before he became acquainted with Wagner's operas.[35] His directions to librettists and advice to singers always implied the preeminence of drama, whether he referred to it as "action," "position," or, especially in later years, "situation." Like Mozart before him, he never failed to recommend that singers go beyond the words and saturate themselves with the psychological and dramatic situation since only then could they arrive at proper inflection both for declamation and for singing. True, Verdi spelled out this conviction most clearly in connection with his last works, as to Ghislanzoni during the preparation of *Aida* ("Unfortunately, in the theater we sometimes need poets and composers who also have a talent for *not* making poetry or music") and even more strongly to Boito, during the revision of *Simon Boccanegra* ("I believe that in the theater, just as it is sometimes admirable if composers have the talent to not make music, and to know how to *s'effacer,* so also in the case of poets, sometimes intelligible, dramatic words are better than beautiful verse").[36]

Effect

The convergence of the various elements of an opera in a single scenic realization is achieved by means of "effect." Although the term crops up frequently in the writings of other opera composers—Gluck, Haydn, Mozart, Bellini—it has an overriding place in Verdi's correspondence: no emotion without "impression," no impression without theatrical "effect," no effect without a profound sense of naturalness and rightness. Beauty of writing and musical refinement are useless if they don't get across the footlights! Effect may arise from any element of the spectacle: it may be a question of a purely musical process, for instance, the musical use of space in the great apparitions scene in *Macbeth* or the Miserere in *Il trovatore;* or else a singer's general attitude, including vocal style, gait, gestures, etc., as in the sleepwalking scene in *Macbeth;* or a detail regarding the dramatic rhythm, the way musical episodes are linked together,[37] the staging, or the costumes.

Just as he dissociated the "beauty" of the poetry from its theatrical force, so Verdi made a distinction between the abstract value of a line or musical passage, which might be beautiful but "cold" (a damning term with Verdi), and its impact on the stage: "I was, and still am, interested to know exactly what effect the last piece made," he wrote Bottesini, conductor of the first *Aida* production in Cairo. "Mind you, I'm not talking about value, only about effect. If you haven't written me already, do write me extensively about this and be sure to tell me the whole truth. I wish to know about the effect made by the orchestra, by the singers, and above all the total effect and general impression of the whole performance."[38] Verdi's curiosity is understandable: Aida and Radames's final duet relies on diaphanous orchestration and unusual shapings of meter and melody, but also on a particular visual impression, superimposing two simultaneously visible levels—the tomb, where the two lovers are immured, below and the interior of Vulcan's temple, where Amneris stands, above.

Verdi's enemies liked to harp on this dichotomy between value and effect, accusing him of using his artistry to charm the audience with facile tricks. It is true that he never disdained to use devices that might spark the audience's attention; but in this is he any more cynical than Mozart, who wrote about the first finale of his *Entführung aus dem Serail,* "The more noise the better, and the shorter the better, so that the audience may not have time to cool down with their applause"?[39] What this proves is, simply, that the idea of effect has as much to do with theatrical practice, in the most conventional sense, as with the imperative to create characters of flesh and blood and passion and to make them believable enough to touch the spectator.

As a result, a Verdi opera cannot be judged merely by being read, or even listened to, because it comes to life only on the stage. People sometimes make fun of Charles Osborne's excessive indulgence for the operas of Verdi's youth, but one should give the English critic his due for usually pointing out that a particular passage that might seem banal is nevertheless "effective in performance."[40] Similarly, Schumann, seeing *Tannhäuser* for the first time, became aware of the gulf between reading an opera score and witnessing a stage performance. After opining that Wagner could not "think out four successive bars of music," he completely changed his mind when he saw the opera: "It makes quite a different effect on the stage. Much of it impressed me deeply."[41]

A Global Approach

A few rare examples show that, when Verdi took hold of a subject, he saw the opera as a whole and his musical imagination was inseparable from his dramatic understanding. In 1836, F. D. Guerrazzi's historical novel *L'assedio di Firenze* was published, dealing with the popular uprising against the imperial army during the siege of Florence in 1529. In 1849, amid full revolutionary upheaval, Verdi was fired with enthusiasm for this highly patriotic subject and wrote Cammarano, sketching out a number of scenes:

> To start with the banqueting scene: I want it to be handsome, large, characteristic, a mixture of the comical and the serious, etc. I would like Dante and Lodovico seated at the end of the table looking depressed and embarrassed because of the orgy, occasionally throwing suspicious glances at Malatesta. The orgy could be expressed with an unruly chorus with people clamoring, asking questions, answering back, etc., some talking about their travels, some about their amorous

adventures, with nobody listening. A loud voice cries out, "Gentlemen, I'm dead! I've been murdered!" etc. And all the others: "Oh, oh,
he's been murdered!" And another, "Long live Florence! The Republic or death! We'll have both! ... Death ... Republic ... Florence....
Here, cup bearers!" While the wine is being poured and everyone is
drinking, the bell strikes midnight and a gloomy voice is heard calling
from outside: "This is the hour when the lover, wrapped in his cloak,
goes to see his mistress. This is the hour when the dead open their
tombs to torment their murderers. This is the hour of treason.... Ah!
It is Ferruccio, the people's prophet!" Dante, who had exited earlier,
comes back and tells Martelli: "Yes, it is the hour of treason. I saw Baccio talk to a solitary soul." ... "To a solitary soul? I fear Malatesta!!
..." They glance at Malatesta who, unable to sustain their glances,
grabs a large beaker and, toasting the liberty of Florence, pretends to
be drinking as he hides his face.... Lodovico and Dante disappear.
Malatesta removes the cup from his eyes.... "They have disappeared!" Enter Baccio, etc.[42]

This melodramatic scene never saw the light, but obviously these are
the words of a man of the theater, not simply a composer. Verdi defines
the type of scene (a mixture of comedy and tragedy, "à la façon de Shakespeare," he notes a little further on). He aims for an effect of confusion
through the interweaving of the guests' innocuous remarks, asking his
librettist later to come up with "strange, unruly meters, like the situation."
He contrasts the frivolity of the banquet with the apprehension of the
protagonists, who fear treason. He gives fairly precise indications as to
the stage effects and the characters' movements. But where is the music
in all this? In fact, it is already there, in Verdi's wish to set up a sort of
musical conversation like the one he would realize in *Rigoletto* and *Traviata;* in the opposition between the incoherent comments of the guests and
the protagonists' resolute replies; in the way he makes certain strong
words—*death, republic, Florence*—predominate; in the effect of the toll-
ing bell and, especially, the offstage voice with its suggestion of the musical use of space. Verdi even anticipates Cammarano's work when he
makes this voice begin its tirade in regular verse *(settenari).*

REFUSING ANY SYSTEM

At first glance, Verdi's output strikes one as a succession of different kinds
of operas stretching over a long period of time rather than as a well-

structured ensemble: his first opera dates from November 1839, the last from February 1893. Such a long career is not unique (one has only to think of Handel), but only rarely does it coincide with such profound political, social, and cultural changes. Is there any question that Verdi, who was born in Napoleon's time, lived through the wars of independence, followed the process of national unification, and saw firsthand the problems of a young parliamentary monarchy, was profoundly affected by these events?

What is surprising is not that he changed but that he changed so greatly that there is a wider gap between *Oberto* and *Otello* than between this first opera and an opera seria of the 1790s. Massimo Mila correctly notes that Verdi represents that rare phenomenon, the artist who embodies two epochs and two cultures: "The era of the early Romanticism of 1848, enthusiastic, belligerent and revolutionary, with the people making its appearance on the stage of musical creation, and the era of late Romanticism, inhibited and conservative, the Romanticism of the fin-de-siècle, the age of Schumann and Brahms, of Mazzini—and also of Freud, as he begins to explore the abyss of the subconscious."[43] Borne along by his time or marching in its vanguard, Verdi pulls off the near-impossible trick of always being contemporary with his age, thus avoiding the decline suffered by those artists who remain faithful to the inner self and finally lose touch with their time.

Coupled with the length of Verdi's career is the extreme diversity of his output: restrained or ebullient, tortuous or linear, intimate or showy, his operas defy classification. Chronology is of no help in bringing order to this profusion, for the good reason that works of widely different treatment and character can coexist in one and the same period: *Nabucco* and *I Lombardi,* both steeped in politico-religious messianism, are followed by *Ernani,* which deals with strictly individual heroic conflicts, then by the intimacy of *I due Foscari.* Three months separate *La traviata,* called by some the first verismo opera, from *Il trovatore,* which plunges us into the romance and chivalry of the Middle Ages. After the pomp and monumentality of *Aida,* Verdi turns, with *Otello,* to a more intimate framework, one "of Italian dimensions," without excessive changes of scene and without a ballet.

The complex parameters that circumscribe opera add to this diversity and make it difficult to take a purely chronological view of Verdi's works. For example, *Un ballo in maschera,* which is thought of as "classical" in its formal organization, that is, in line with Italian operatic tradition, is based on a dramaturgy that has nothing in common with that same tradition. *Don Carlos* falls perfectly into the mold of French grand opera, a genre that was beginning to go out of fashion by 1867; at the same time the opera goes further than any other in its treatment of a character's inner crisis, the debunking of the brand of heroism that was the glory of the early Romantic operas. One feels, indeed, that each work is a unique experiment that is not to be repeated, so fertile is the residue each leaves behind.[44] After a chance meeting or commission, the composer emerges from his rural retreat and sets a new star in the operatic firmament.

Verdi himself, with his deep-seated pragmatism and dislike of putting forth theories and opinions, is of no help here. No Verdian aesthetics exists if by that one means a complete, coherent exposition, even if the correspondence is rich in pointed comments and vigorous aphorisms that shed light on his vision of the making of art.[45] In fact, Verdi theorizes by reaction rather than systematically, recalling the importance of inspiration when someone mentions schools of influence, evoking the rich Italian vocal tradition when he feels threatened by Wagnerism. His goal is to set up an ideal line of influence rather than to justify his compositional decisions or changes of course. (By the time he praised the cabaletta of Romantic opera, late in his career, he had practically stopped writing any.) Caring little for evaluations or the long-term view, as though he feared becoming the custodian of his own mausoleum, he often showed a certain indifference toward his "old" works: in 1850, he described *Nabucco* (written barely eight years earlier) as "an aged, ancient work" and expressed amazement in 1889 that the public could put up with a tiresome, old-fashioned opera like *Oberto*.[46]

He regarded it as equally trivial to inform the public about the genesis of his works or his technical choices. At times one can even detect in his correspondence an inclination to erase the history of a work, as when he tells Ghislanzoni that there is no overture for *Aida*,[47] whereas he had written one for Milan to replace the Cairo prelude but then discarded it as too weak, or when he insists that all 1853 scores of *Traviata* be withdrawn from circulation in favor of the definitive version of 1854. Similarly, as sure and precise as his judgments were as soon as he started work on a libretto, his impressions on first encountering a text sound more like an explosion of enthusiasm than a critical appreciation: "I'm very busy with *Attila!* What a wonderful subject!" "I couldn't find or imagine any theme that was more beautiful, more passionate and more musical" *(Il corsaro).* "The subject matter is great, immense, and it features a character who is one of the greatest creations the theater of all countries and all times could boast" *(Rigoletto).* "The drama is powerful, extremely vast; I like it very much. I don't know whether the public will like it as I do, but it is certainly something out of the ordinary" *(Forza).*[48]

Behind all these attitudes is what I will call an inevitability of impression. The essential thing in an opera is the emotive shock it produces, the impression it leaves in the soul—all the rest is empty chatter. Hence Verdi's extreme reluctance to voice opinions, which always seem to him to fall short of emotion: "Besides, I'm not familiar with Faccio's talent," he writes about that composer and conductor; "neither do I know his work. And I do not wish to know it so that I won't have to discuss it or give my opinion about it. These are things I detest because they are the most useless things in the world. Discussions have never convinced anyone, and opinions are misleading most of the time."[49] More lapidary still: "In art, opinions are useless and they can be harmful."[50]

It is plain to see that criticism, comment, analysis, are completely foreign to Verdi! In keeping with this attitude, he expects the public to be satisfied with immediate impressions: "The public has no business worrying about the methods an artist uses! . . . Nor should it have prejudices regarding style. . . . If a performance is good, they should applaud, if it is bad, let them boo. That's all! Music is universal. But some idiots and pedants insist on inventing schools and systems! I want the public to judge on a high level, not following the pitiful views of journalists and professional or amateur musicians, but by their own impressions. Do you understand? Impressions, impressions, nothing else."[51] The letter to Perrin quoted above suggests that it is direct impact, above all else, that dictates the composer's choice of libretto, style, or procedure.[52]

There is nothing very original in insisting on the role of emotion in the conception of an opera or in its reception. More original is the fact that Verdi wholeheartedly accepts the implications of this position. Just as he takes care in preparing an opera, so he accepts the public's verdict without question, knowing that its emotion can be irrational, unjust, and unpredictable but that it remains the ultimate arbiter. He takes note of his flops, all the while hoping that time will vindicate him, and is careful not to accuse the audience of incompetence: "It's a bad sign when we accuse the public of not understanding. True, there are publics and publics, yet all of them are qualified and all are touched when there's reason to be."[53] Consequently, a succès d'estime is the worst insult to a creator's pride: "I believe and have always believed 'that when the public does not rush to see a new production it is already a failure!' A bit of charitable applause, a few indulgent reviews as a solace to the *Grand Old Man* cannot move me. No, no, neither indulgence nor pity. Better the boos!"[54] As

Italian audiences eventually became more civilized, less excessive in their opinions, and more inclined to seek "interest" rather than "passion" in opera, Verdi began to lament the audiences of his youth, which may have lacked restraint but not abandon.[55]

If Verdi's relation to art reflects a theatrical experience acquired during the 1840s, it also reflects a temperament whose inclination was in all circumstances—in life as in drama—to aim straight for the hard core of a situation, no matter how brutal it might be, brushing aside any veils that might soften the hurtful aspects of reality. He offers us his works as they are, without adding his theories, as Wagner does. One might see this attitude as a limitation but also as a strength: Verdi lived in the present, which gave him an extraordinary capacity for self-renewal. His lack of interest in doctrine had the advantage that he was never a prisoner of himself or his ideas. Just as the man was clear-cut in character and strong in his ethical principles and convictions, so the artist followed the currents and encounters of life with a versatility rare among creative artists of this quality and with a well-nigh-unique capacity for resilience.

THE PROBLEM OF UNITY

The diversity of Verdi's oeuvre and his indifference to any systematic ordering of his work as a whole inevitably pose a problem, that of the unity of his output and the nature of his genius. The search for what is "Verdian" and what is not has unfortunately led to reductive views whose chief flaw is that they obscure those aspects of Verdi's personality that fail to conform to the suggested definition. The image of a heroic composer brimming over with patriotism and warlike ardor in sympathy with his country's cause ignores his intimate side; the image of Verdi as a hot-blooded conqueror has overshadowed those frequent passages in the early operas born of a dark, disenchanted mood. Those who thought of Verdi essentially as an instinctive melodist, as Bizet did after seeing *Don Carlos*, made the fatal mistake of believing that he betrayed his inspiration when he changed his style. And, recently, Leibowitz still felt the need to defend the parallelism of Verdi's melodic and harmonic development.[56] The idea of nationalism and what was thought of as the essentially Italian nature of his genius helped push his French operas into the background for a considerable time. Nonetheless, it is clear that, if Verdi never denied his native tradition and indeed remained deeply loyal to it, he also showed an astonishing disposition to follow new trails, even if they sometimes failed him. In short, Verdi is to be found as much in the challenges he set himself as in those works of his that gushed forth almost spontaneously—as much in what he did with ease as in what he attempted more ambitiously.

The problem of the unity of an output stretching over more than fifty years is trickier because in this period of time Verdi's attitude toward composition changed perceptibly. In his youth he wrote rapidly and with great frequency, but around 1855 his pace slowed: fourteen operas over ten years, from *Oberto* to *La battaglia di Legnano;* thirteen operas in forty-four years, from *Luisa Miller* to *Falstaff* (not counting the revisions). His attention to the libretto became increasingly refined, concentrating more on detail of expression; his writing was subtler, his orchestration richer; and he grew increasingly inflexible regarding the staging of his works.

What direction did this evolution take? For a time it was thought that what Vuillermoz called a "magnificent technical ascent" was also a "creative ascent" (the term comes from *L'ascensione creatrice di G. Verdi,* a book by Gino Roncaglia first published in 1914) leading up to the masterworks of Verdi's old age. This view, colored as it was by the idea of progress—that of talent marching toward its perfection—had the disadvantage of grading the operas, setting the earlier ones lower than the last, as though *Otello* were superior to *Rigoletto,* which in turn was preferable to *Nabucco.* Insofar as the last operas seemed to approach the concept of unified, or through-composed, music drama and the idea of progress had for decades been embodied in the conviction that German-style music drama was opera's highest achievement,[57] Verdi's evolution tended to be equated with a struggle between conventional, Italian-style opera and music drama.

The critics separated the wheat from the chaff by lauding those occasions when Verdi "broke free of traditional forms" and deploring those when he "yielded to convention." Today, when a plurality of aesthetic forms in opera is taken as an established fact, the problem is not to note the "improvements" the composer made to a conception that has its own inner logic but to understand this logic and see why at a certain juncture it ceased to serve his dramatic thought.

To get away from this monolithic view, the critics next imagined a duality of Verdian inspiration: "We must acknowledge the existence of two Verdis, both supreme, one culminating in the *Rigoletto-Trovatore-Traviata* triad, the other in the *Otello-Falstaff* duo."[58] By this, Massimo Mila simply meant to break up the inevitable hierarchy referred to above;

yet, although presented in a slightly different guise, this argument has often been no more than a variant of the first. When the German critic Guckeisen wrote in 1877 that "Giuseppe Verdi is for the German people the composer of *Trovatore,* for the musical aristocracy the composer of the *Requiem,*" when Paul Dukas posited in 1901 that after being a "maker of operas" Verdi later became a "dramatic composer,"[59] both men set up a false dichotomy since quite naturally one facet of the composer's genius is made subordinate to the other.

This idea of a popular Verdi and a Verdi pleasing to the elite inevitably led to a reaction, where the brutal, unpolished writer of *Nabucco* was exalted to the detriment of the more refined but more anemic composer of *Falstaff.* The most brilliant representative of the trend is Bruno Barilli, who, in a famous book published in 1930, *Il paese del melodramma* (The land of melodrama), made polemical comparisons between *Falstaff*— "this great masterwork, solace and edification of all conductors, where, however, the fire of the great Verdi no longer amounts to more than warm ashes"—and *Il trovatore,* where "genius is positively crackling! There is so much genius that it hits us like a hailstorm."[60] The idea of a popular, neobarbarian Verdi did not disappear with Barilli, and, in 1974, Mila was still attacking those intellectuals, "structuralists and existential philosophers, avant-garde composers and abstract painters," who found Verdi's art all the greater the "more uncultivated and primitive" it was.[61]

Most of these views have no great practical value, but they are interesting from the standpoint of cultural history. Verdi's powerful, complex personality fell victim to all manner of mythological disguises: he could be the fiery bard of the Risorgimento, the "father" of a new Italy who forged a place for his homeland in the European sun, the peasant from the depths of the Italian provinces who won a Continent-wide dimension by the sweat of his brow, the smiling patriarch of the final years, and so on. The appreciation of his oeuvre has called into question the great aesthetic choices of our time: number opera versus music drama, popular art versus art of the elites, art as instinct versus art as construction, barbarism versus decadence.[62] So it is logical that the ideas put forward to explain Verdi's development and place his operas in distinct categories were usually freighted with ideological implications.

There is, clearly, no denying the historic dimension of Verdi's output or the progress that may have taken place from one opera to another. Nor is there any question that, leaving aside certain striking successes, from the 1850s his works took on a subtlety and a depth that were rarely evinced in the early years—a maturation that is, by the way, perfectly normal. Nevertheless, I have chosen to avoid a chronological approach because underlying it, insidious but almost unavoidable, is the notion of continuous progress. The following chapter will explain my methodological choices.

$\mathcal{A}estheti cs$

Wherever people discuss the
real problems of form, one of
life's truths is at stake.
GEORG LUKÁCS

If one wishes to study a composer's musical dramaturgy—the textual and
musical techniques he uses to create a dramatic world—one should first
try to understand the goals he was pursuing and the vision of truth and
beauty arising from his oeuvre, that is to say, the aesthetics that inspired
him, consciously or not, and the human experience on which this aesthetics was based.

As countless critics have observed over the course of its long history,
opera defies common sense. From Doctor Johnson, for whom opera was
"an exotick and irrational entertainment," to Paul Valéry, who compared
it to a picture lit by a stained glass window, critics have seen that every
opera composer faces near insoluble problems to which he can provide
only precarious solutions. The problems are manifold: whether to follow
the words of the text step by step, eschewing any purely musical logic, or
to force them into a musical structure, thereby frequently making them
unintelligible; to choose between creating an imitation of reality, a fairly
difficult matter so far as opera is concerned, or a phantasmagoria, thus running the risk of providing mere spectacle; to opt for the sensuous beauty of
song, which is pleasing to the ear but often censured as mere frivolity, or
for the depiction of passions, insofar as music is capable of portraying
them with any precision. Put another way, it is illusory to imagine that
there exists a perfect or "natural" form of opera against which the forms
the genre has taken throughout its history should be judged.

As a result, opera can function only if it is based on a certain number
of conventions or codes, chosen by the composer and agreed to by his
public, that provide acceptable, if provisional, answers to these problems.
Their function is chiefly a technical one, to make possible the coexistence

of two or even three systems of signs (words, music, the visual arts), each of which works in a different way. These conventions change over time because there comes a point when the public tires of a long-accepted code. A new code is then put in place that, although not superior or inferior to the old one, has the advantage of satisfying a new sensibility—which, in its turn, will change a few decades further on.

These changes entail new technical solutions, but above all they reflect a different way of viewing human reality that causes the public to be dissatisfied with traditional modes of portrayal. For if the image of man is inseparable from representation, at the same time, representation gives him a particular moral and psychological form. Thus, the dramatic and musical choices that an age, or a composer, makes give rise to a conception of human existence that justifies these choices and gives them meaning. If the meaning changes substantially, if it goes beyond merely improving or varying a system, this evolution will bring forth a new aesthetics, which in turn will convey a different view of the world and of man.

Verdi's case is probably unique in the history of opera in that his development was slow and discontinuous yet too radical to be placed beneath the emblem of a single, unvarying aesthetics. His career extended over a period of profound change; moreover he worked against the background of Italian Romanticism, a cultural movement that—less monolithic than is often thought—saw widespread debate over the various methods of operatic representation and their aesthetic and moral implications. Although conservative on the whole, contemporary thought was nevertheless attracted by the innovative currents coming both from native-born composers and from foreign cultures, especially those of France and Germany; it swung between rigidity and change, loyalty to the Italian tradition and susceptibility to suggestions coming from elsewhere.[1] With his powerful personality, Verdi was inevitably looked to as the supreme arbiter of these conflicts. This seems a good moment, therefore, to review the major disputes before proposing a key to the study of the composer's development.

Words and Music

CONCERNING A FAMILIAR "QUERELLE"

Underlying the thorny question of the connection between words and music in opera is an even more difficult one: that of the meaning of music.[2] It is impossible to deal with such a complex problem in a few lines, save to recall certain facts that touch our subject directly.

If we think of music as a mere play of sounds, a combination without any demonstrable meaning, it is undeniable that music arouses in us sensations that we immediately translate into images, however arbitrary and subjective the conversion may seem. Independent of their strictly musical value, it happens that certain themes are more evocative than others since they call up concrete images in the listener, even if these differ from one listener to another. It is impossible to prove that these images have any foundation, yet the hearer does have the feeling of a precise, almost tangible meaning. As T. W. Adorno writes, "Music indicates what it wants to say, and in detail. But at the same time the purpose is always concealed."[3] It is precisely the mark of the great dramatic composers like Mozart, Verdi, Wagner, and Puccini that they created themes that, although not necessarily more "beautiful" than others, "speak" or "show" something that cannot be precisely pinpointed.

Language is of little help in discovering the meaning of these themes—in the end, as Vladimir Jankélévitch points out, the insistence on a verbal equivalent amounts to seeking the truth of music beyond music itself.[4] Rather, the meaning of music is like that of a gesture or a facial expression in the sense that it offers the same mixture of expressive intensity and semantic indeterminacy. The allusion to gesture and physiognomy is all the more apt since for the most part these themes reach us through the medium of a singer who, if he or she is an exceptionally gifted artist, reinforces the music's emotive power through his or her own expressiveness.

This gestural, vaguely referential character of music sets up a kind of double articulation in opera: a musical theme suggests a sense that is at once precise and elusive and that approximates the physical and emotive registering of the melody in the body of the listener, who at once searches his imagination for a verbal or emotional motivation. The second level, the word, assigns a sense and, in turn, directs the gestural content toward a motivation, a series of images, thus suspending the "semanticization" to which the listener would otherwise have spontaneously proceeded.

A perfectly successful completion of this process occurs when the listener finds the semantic content given to the musical theme perfectly appropriate. Yet it should be emphasized that this feeling of appropriateness is both illusory and real. It is justified by our acceptance of the association, our feeling that the musical phrase perfectly matches the textual content coupled with it; but it is illusory if we conclude that the text has revealed the hidden "truth" of the music since the same musical phrase may serve different semantic contents equally well. That the Roman audience, as Stendhal tells the story, imagined it heard in the overture to *Il barbiere di Siviglia* "all the threats and bluster of the elderly, jealous and enamored guardian and all the plaintive sighs of his pretty ward" shows he was convinced that the overture was perfectly suited to the atmosphere of the opera, whereas we know that the music was employed on two other occasions![5]

This mixture of indeterminacy and perfect appropriateness crops up again in the area of gesture and expression. Readers may recall the experiments that L. V. Kuleshov carried out in Russia in the 1920s: he took a close-up of the face of the actor Mosjoukine and showed it to an audience, intercutting it with a series of unrelated images suggesting different emotions.[6] Each time, viewers found that, although it remained unchanged, the face perfectly expressed the feeling evoked by the image. We see the same ambiguity in the way listeners interpret instrumental passages in opera. The beautiful E-major theme of the prelude to *Simon Boccanegra* (1881 version) suggests the sea to Claudio Abbado, nobility and tenderness to Julian Budden; for Massimo Mila it embodies the dignity of democracy;[7] but it is just as possible to see in it one of those dark, tortuous themes that in Verdi tend to connote power and its attendant conflicts. None of these interpretations can be proved, the point being that for each commentator the theme seems to be perfectly linked to the drama it is introducing.

This slight gap between text and music, each element aiming toward the same dramatic reality, calls for caution when it comes to judging the fit between the two. People are often shocked to find the same vocal line accompanying radically different, even opposing, texts, as often occurs in the symmetrical ensembles of Italian opera. One almost farcical example is the first section of the Roberto-Elisabetta duet in act 1 of Donizetti's *Roberto Devereux,* where the same musical strophe describes Elisabetta's memories of happiness and Roberto's despair. The fact is that melody can find its justification over and beyond the text, at a level of expression comparable to that of gesture and open to widely different verbal meanings.

The Italian tradition's opposition to continuous recitative of the Wagnerian type, led by Rossini, can be explained by some reasons that I will take up later, but also by mistrust of techniques that "pack" words and music together too tightly and destroy the suggestive vagueness that is both the limitation and the strength of music. This same desire to allow for "play" between text and music may also account for the modest use that Verdi and the Italians generally make of the leitmotiv, a technique that subjects a musical phrase strictly to a given meaning.

Still, in order to be expressive of the meaning of the text it is commenting on, the musical phrase must be at least oriented toward that meaning. This is achieved by means of analogy, using a set of conventions involving rhythm, melodic pace, harmony, and instrumentation. Direct analogy, as in imitative music (military sounds, suggestion of storms), is rare. Far broader is the area of indirect analogy, which can be defined taking chromaticism as an example. Chromaticism is to the tonal system (which it tends to destroy) what the particular feeling a character is describing (anguish, anxiety, despair) is to his psychic equilibrium (which it likewise tends to destroy). However loose this analogical method may be, it does serve to orient the listener toward a sphere that the words will explain more precisely. Thus, when, in her duet with Don Giovanni, Zerlina replies to his insistent advances, "Non son più forte," the light chromaticism of her vocal line is enough to tell us that she is thrown off balance by her interlocutor, even before the words confirm it.

CROSS-FIRES

It is a common misconception, especially in France, that music's task in opera is to illustrate the text.[8] As a result, the more closely the composer adheres to the language, the closer he is considered to be to the drama, while the more he deviates from the words for the sake of the musical structure or for other reasons, the farther he strays from it. One can imagine the ravages caused when such a conception is applied to a highly formalized tradition like that of Italian opera, with its procession of fixed forms such as arias, duets, trios, and ensembles. Based on a confusion between the *text* and the *drama,* this false perspective leads to the belief that the degree of formalization in the musical commentary is an inverse function of its dramatic truth. However, this view is belied by the Italian operatic tradition, which, from the early 1600s, began to free itself from the initial subjection to the text and became more relaxed.

In fact, until the beginning of our century, the opera composer has tended to oscillate between two extreme approaches to the text that, naturally, left room for several intermediary positions. Starting with the sense of a phrase, its stresses, its tone, and the emotional atmosphere it implied—or, in the terminology of linguistics, with both the signifier and the signified of the phrase—the composer could seek out an arrangement of sounds to inspire him toward a melody. The famous phrase "Lascia-temi morire" from Monteverdi's *Lamento d'Arianna* might be a perfect example of this first approach. Or he might start from an overall perception of a situation and create a melody he felt was appropriate for translating it into sounds, leaving the words to be adapted to it later on. This latter approach explains how a composer would sometimes write a melody without having the text to hand (although usually knowing the general sense of it) or request changes of meter so that the verse would fit a melodic line that had already been formed. In the one case, the composer "musicalizes" the word and arrives at the music via the text; in the other, he "semanticizes" the music and arrives at the text via the melody; either the music issues from the text in some way, or else it becomes one with a text that already exists or is about to take shape. In either case, the overriding consideration is the drama.

Abramo Basevi had these two possible approaches in mind when he noted that sometimes music stretches out the poetry and sometimes the poetry interprets the music.[9] But he equated them with the traditional subdivisions of recitative and aria. The musicalization of the word does indeed suggest simple recitative, while the semanticization of the music suggests aria, with accompanied recitative constituting a compromise between the two. In fact, these three procedures trace back to older subdivisions like the modes of Greek vocal music: the Greeks made a distinction between "spoken or chanted declamation, *melos* or song in the strict sense of the term, and, midway between these two modes, a kind of high-pitched psalmody, *recto tono,* with flute accompaniment."[10] Another forerunner is the distinction in Roman liturgy between *accentus* (the musical pointing of the phrase) and *concentus* (chant).

At first glance these distinctions would seem to correspond to the fundamental division in Italian baroque opera between poetry, predominant in the recitative, and music, which prevailed in the aria. Recitative was based on a combination of different meters (essentially lines of eleven and seven syllables) that ruled out the elaboration of regular melodies and forced the composer to follow the more irregular rhythms of speech; while, for the aria, the poet offered the composer regular verses that could be adapted to a vocal line characterized by symmetry and repetition. In the nineteenth century this bipartition survived in the distinction between *versi sciolti* (free mixing of meters) and *versi lirici* (metered stanzas).

Even with its obvious drawbacks, this rigid overall structure did not prevent composers from enjoying a certain freedom within the structures allotted them (arias and ensembles). The extraordinary variety that Handel achieved in a form as fixed as the da capo aria cannot be explained solely by his melodic genius but is also due to his ability to view the text in different ways: he often uses—in the same aria—pure song, arioso, and even a declamation that is very close to recitative.

Thus, the absolute dominance enjoyed by the nineteenth-century composer should be interpreted not as the absolute dominance of song, defined as subordination of text to melodic line, but as the replacing of a rigid scheme with a far more supple procedure where the composer could decide from moment to moment which strategy to adopt. The gradual disappearance of classic recitative and the simultaneous disappearance of its characteristic meters (John Black has calculated that the proportion of *versi sciolti,* traditionally used for recitative, dropped from 60 to 30 percent between the beginning and the middle of the century)[11] does not imply that the balance between the two approaches described here was disrupted. What it does imply is that the composer now had complete freedom to decide how he would treat the text; in short, the flexibility that had always existed within the narrow frontiers of closed (lyrical) numbers was now extended. Massimo Mila has noted that in *Otello* it is possible to distinguish five ways in which words and music are linked together: the traditional melody of song; cantabile and *declamato melodico,* corresponding to the mixed types of the arioso and accompanied recitative; traditional recitative; and, finally, parlato, an extreme form of simple recitative.[12] The opera unfolds continuously so that there is a constant, imperceptible flow from one form into another.

The same seesawing between the two approaches can be seen in operatic aesthetics. The frequent demands on the part of the literati that music illustrate poetry step by step provoked prompt reaction from other theorists. For instance, in 1753, Charles Avison wrote that the composer "is not principally to dwell on particular Words, in the Way of Imitation, but to comprehend the Poet's general Drift or Intention, and on this to form his Arts and Harmony, either by Imitation (so far as Imitation may be proper to the End) or by any other means."[13] Even more radically, Schoenberg claimed the freedom to distance himself from the letter of the text, the better to appropriate its spirit: "It will be clear that, without knowing the poetic text, what it really contained, I had grasped it in perhaps a more profound manner than if I had remained glued to the surface of the ideas the words expressed."[14] In contrast, Donizetti, who might have been expected to defend bel canto, wrote: "Music is but a declamation accentuated by sounds, which is why every composer must imagine *[intuire]* a song and let it arise from the accentuation of the word."[15] In an inauthentic letter that may nevertheless be revealing, Bellini described his typical working method of declaiming his characters' texts over and over until they gave rise to a melody.[16]

The choice of one approach or the other assumes that the composer is aware of the advantages and disadvantages of each. For, in fact, the ineffability of the meaning of music does not always function in the same way. The musicalization of the word, which corresponded historically to recitative in both its simple and its more elaborate forms, made it possible to follow the path of the meaning, step by step, in its variety and flexibility and to accentuate its affective nuances. This meant that in the baroque and classical periods song and music retreated to the background, leaving declamation in the foreground. In complete contrast is the "closed form" of the aria, where the semanticization of the music is predominant. Here, if the musical choices (rhythm, melodic line, harmony, instrumentation) and the overall sense of the text direct the spectator to a given meaning, the musical structure, dominated as it is by demands for clarity, balance, and symmetry, tends to guide the spectator's understanding in a simple but often univocal direction. Thus, the meaning loses in flexibility and variety what it gains in intensity.

During the nineteenth century the loosening and eventual disappearance of traditional forms, together with the search for continuity in musical discourse and the development of orchestral commentary, made the mechanisms of meaning more complex. The adaptability of recitative tended to influence the closed form, while recitative benefited from the richness of musical commentary. The orchestra became more and more autonomous; no longer was it content to accompany, hence to amplify, song: now it could fill out the text with suggestions, allusions, and meanings that were subsidiary or even contrary to those delivered by the text. The recurrence of musical elements (reminiscences, quotations, leitmotivs), whether associated with textual elements or not, set up a system of signs that was linked to the semantic content conveyed by the text but relatively independent of it. The word, declaimed or sung, ceased to be the sole conveyor of meaning—which is no doubt another reason for the opposition shown by Rossini and the Italians to continuous recitative of the Wagnerian type. Thus, if meaning still functions along the same analogical mechanisms, the form chosen modifies the "message" that the words-music combination transmits to us.

* * * * * * *

The ideal of every composer is to reach a point where the music seems to rise out of the words while the text suddenly seems to speak the music's truth. When Verdi went into ecstasies over one of Figaro's phrases in the act 1 finale of *Il barbiere di Siviglia*, "Signor giudizio, per carità," he recognized "that it is neither melody nor harmony: it is the word, declaimed, exact and true; and it is music."[17] But it is impossible to maintain this balance throughout the two to three hours of the typical opera, and most of the time one of the two elements plays the part of prime mover.

This alternation is no defect since in truth the oscillation between the musicalization of the word and the semanticization of the music is the very life breath of opera. All opera composers know that the quality of a work depends on the diversity of approaches taken to the text, and from this point of view the different national traditions are often closer than they may at first appear. The Italians, usually seen above all as pure melodists, were far more sensitive than is generally recognized to the phonetic and semantic value of the word. The Russians, firm defenders of the musicalized word, seeking, like Mussorgsky, Dargomizhsky, and César Cui, "a melody arising from the language," "a melody motivated by the sense,"[18] did not hesitate to introduce into their operas songs and couplets—closed forms—as though the predominance of one approach had finally proved tiresome and its opposite had to be adopted for relief.

Valid at the macroscopic level of the overall organization of an opera, this pendulum-like movement is present at every stage of an opera's composition, and in many cases the quality of the whole results from a blending of different approaches to a text. Mozart, on whom, it will be remembered, Verdi was nurtured, provides numerous instances of this, but we will take a Verdian example. Readers will recall the situation setting up the famous quartet from act 3 of *Rigoletto:* the frivolous Duke of Mantua arrives at Sparafucile's inn and flirts with his sister Maddalena, who is not insensitive to the charms of the dashing duke even though, as a professional, she is used to such gallantries. Through a chink in the wall, young Gilda discovers the libertine character of the man she had taken for a penniless student and with whom she is passionately in love, while her father, Rigoletto, only finds his suspicions confirmed.

The Duke begins the Andante of the quartet with a sixteen-measure melody that is both splendid and conventional and perfectly suits the seductive, unmysterious tenor. Above all, he *sings:* his melody is more important than the text, a strophe describing an amorous outburst as passionate as it is impersonal (See ex. 1*a*).

At the opposite end is the baritone Rigoletto (the last to join the quar-

EX. 1*a*

EX. 1*b*

tet). He does not sing but *declaims* a text whose stresses and intonations are punctiliously respected ("Be quiet! What use is weeping?" ex. 1*b*). The semitone movement from A♭ to B♭♭ and the lengthening of the note on *vale* have no melodic value but instead perform a purely expressive function, illustrating as they do the jester's exasperation by accenting the word *vale* (what use).

Between the two men, Maddalena and Gilda suggest two further ways of linking text and music. One is tempted to say that the mezzo-soprano *speaks* since her attack (unfortunately barely audible in most recordings) is based on the stylization of a rapid parlato typical of opera buffa (notes of equal value, staccato notes; ex. 1*c*). Rather than illustrating a text, the music describes a tone, a careless, teasing way of speaking. The soprano's entrance, in contrast to Maddalena's, is a model of *dramatic singing,* being based on syncopation and appoggiaturas that suggest inner suffering (ex. 1*d*). The expressiveness of Gilda's melodic line is so striking that one for-

EX. 1c/d

gets that the text is being battered by syncopated notes that break up the words: "in/feli/ce co/re, cor tradi/to per. . . ." As in the example of the Duke, although in a different way, the text comments on the music, whereas the reverse is the case with Maddalena and Rigoletto.

The exposition thus sets up, very vividly, four sharply contrasting characters differentiated by four distinct approaches to the text. Far be it from Verdi, however, to stick to this course. He changes the relation of one voice to another, either enclosing the tenor's and mezzo's badinage within the long melodic lines of the soprano and baritone, with their drawn-out notes, or contrasting Gilda's syncopations and the gypsy's flirtatious laughter. This combination never hurts the perfect comprehensibility of the ensemble, whose dramatic poles have been fixed with extraordinary skill.

In the foregoing example these different ways of connecting music and text are employed simultaneously, yet it is clear that they are used successively just as often. Indeed, this successive use is even relatively codified owing to the respective advantages of the two methods: the musicalization of the word allows for more precise and flexible characterization as well as greater intelligibility of the text, while the semanticization of the melody offers less effective characterization but a greater emotional charge. Hence, it is easy to understand how operatic practice came to pin down a sort of standard progression from one to the other. As has been said, recitative charges the gun, while the aria fires the shot. As opera moved away from the *scena,* usually informative in character, toward the slow and then the fast movements of a double aria, or toward the Andante and then the cabaletta of an ensemble or the Largo and Stretta of a Finale, the connection to the text was progressively diluted, giving way to the emotional crescendo.

Audiences, preferring the deployment of melody, and convinced that

Italian opera consists of nothing else, often neglect recitative and *scene:* in *Norma,* one looks forward to the spell of "Casta diva" and listens distractedly to "Sediziose voci," the preceding *scena,* despite Bellini's admirable attention to the text. We thrill to the cabaletta of the Ernani-Elvira-Carlo trio (in act 1 of *Ernani*), but do we notice the *declamato* before that ("Tu sei Ernani"), which conveys so admirably the King of Spain's impatience and anger? It is true that, as traditional Italian opera systematized the design of the *scena,* moving to the lyrical moment, then toward virtuoso display, the whole procedure became tedious, yet it should not be forgotten that these stages are both complementary and indispensable.

The association of words and music in opera has often been likened to an ideal couple, where the two spouses finally are one, but that is the deceptive, pernicious myth of the androgyne. Each member of the duo in fact possesses an inherent logic and autonomy, and each can, in his or her own way, define the drama and help it along. If we must speak of a couple, it is rather of a "modern" couple, where both husband and wife are autonomous, a couple with a dynamic that lets each one play the role of prime mover, depending on the situation. The essential thing is that there should always be a love story.

Form: What Is at Stake?

THE IDEAL AND THE TRUE

All composers claim by some right or other to offer a certain image of the truth. But which truth? A faithful image copied from real-life situations, or a refashioned image presenting passions and characters in an ideal form? In the eighteenth century, truth was passed through the double filter of idealization and aesthetic stylization. Even if the way a passion was represented was mimetic from certain points of view (i.e., if an attempt was made to imitate it by musical procedures that offered an equivalent of what it would be in reality), the composer strove to attain a purified image of passion, one free of excessive precision, removed from its immediate dramatic context, and meant to be contemplated for its own sake as one of the possible ideal forms of joy, grief, anger, and so on. Alongside this idealization was a stylization in which elegance and virtuosity of singing played a large part and that gave a stamp of beauty and harmony to the passion being depicted. Hence the well-known rhythm of opera seria, which surprises the modern listener, accustomed as he is to continuity of dramatic action. Here, the characters come to life, get excited, act, speak, then suddenly freeze and start to analyze and describe themselves and the feelings prompted in them by the plot.

It is clear that this gradual distilling of the affetti, moving toward the serene and joyous contemplation of the world of passions, is linked to the techniques employed. Those techniques that emphasize the text and its referential ability (recitative in its various forms) allow for a diversified, flexible representation of situations; the closed form, dominated by the attention to musical architecture evident in the da capo, the respect for certain symmetries, and clarity of development, schematizes this representation. Thus, the shifting world of human passions that is traced in the tortuous plots of baroque opera is mirrored by another world—more intense, but also more serene, more balanced, and transfigured by an ideal of beauty.

To be sure, this somewhat rigorous codification presupposes a confidence that the affetti can be distilled and yet offer a satisfying image of humankind. Yet, even when this confidence was in crisis and, impelled by Gluck's and Calzabigi's reforms but also by those of opera buffa, the old form gave way to a less balanced conception of drama and to the demand for a more directly mimetic representation, the conviction that opera must offer a stylized, idealized image remained as a restraint. Mozart, who did so much to move arias and ensembles away from merely representing abstract passions, tying them closely to the context whence they arose so as to draw out their peculiar color, set a limit to any attempt at mimesis. Speaking of Osmin's rage in *Die Entführung aus dem Serail,* he writes: "For just as a man in such a towering rage oversteps all the bounds of order, moderation and propriety, and completely forgets himself, so must the music too forget itself. But as passions, whether violent or not, must never be expressed in such a way as to excite disgust, and as music, even in the most terrible situations, must never offend the ear, but must please the hearer, or in other words must never cease to be music, I have gone from F [the key in which the aria is written], not into a remote key but into a related one, not, however, into its nearest relative D minor, but into the more remote A minor."[19] The clear-eyed realization that mimesis would dictate that music imitate a character's psychic disorder by itself becoming chaotic is counterbalanced by the need for harmony, understood as something pleasing, which leads to a technical compromise (choosing a tonality relatively far removed from but related to the original key).

Faced with a similar situation, Verdi would opt for going further into mimesis, which indicates how far this trend had evolved in the nineteenth century. Commenting on the triple exclamation that Otello utters just before he dies—"morta, morta, morta"—he criticized the German translator's too elaborate rendering and added: "At this point there should be neither a poetic nor a musical phrase. I myself, even I, have had the good sense to produce only some sounds that have almost no tonality!"[20] In short, Verdi accepted the fact that music is no longer to be identified with an ideal of dramatic truth, a truth that Mozart had mitigated for beauty's sake.

* * * * * * * *

The trend toward an idealized representation of the passions regained favor with Rossini, whose ideas carried weight because it was he who established the bases of Italian Romantic opera, his successors working for decades in the so-called code Rossini. Rossini had little faith in the mimetic power of music—a power he acknowledged in the case of language and painting—and much faith in its ideal character: "The art of music is sublime because, not having the means to imitate what is real, it ascends beyond common nature into a world that is ideal, and with its celestial harmony it has the power to move earthly passions. Music, I repeat, is all ideal, it is not an art that imitates."[21] This conviction justified the Rossinian conception of opera as combining poetry's "true" and music's "ideal" expression; the libretto provided the drama, while the music created a "moral atmosphere." It also explains the procedure so commonly used by the composer of *Semiramide:* that of moving from a preliminary "mimetic" phase, anchored by strong, declamatory song to set up the dramatic situation; to another phase, this time consisting of expressive song (still fairly close to a direct expression of passion); and, finally, to a phase that, by exploiting virtuosity and melodic refinement, "consumes" its dramatic subject matter in order to attain the "celestial harmony" that Rossini describes.

In light of the parallelism noted between aesthetics and compositional practice, it is not surprising that Rossini showed an undisguised aversion to the exaggerated extension of recitative and to the tendency to subordinate musical form to the details of the text: "If the maestro chooses to follow the sense of the words step by step, he will compose a music that is not expressive in itself but poor, vulgar, made, I venture to say, like a mosaic, incoherent and ridiculous." In 1868, he again inveighed against "those new philosophical principles that would make the art of music into a literary art, an art of imitation, a veritable philosophical singsong that would resemble recitative—now free, now measured, with various accompaniments of tremolos and so forth."[22] The allusion to Wagner could not be more obvious.

Rossini clearly opposed two conceptions of operatic music that were to vie with each other over the first two-thirds of the nineteenth century: on the one hand the music sometimes curiously described as "philosophical," by virtue of its concern with sticking closely to the text, and on the other the cult of ideal beauty accompanied by a defense of florid singing. In his *Filosofia della musica* Mazzini took issue with the hedonism of song and called for greater fidelity to the drama, with suggestions that strangely anticipate Wagner. In reaction, the conservative front nostalgically invoked the name of Rossini and even eighteenth-century opera; the most outspoken of them, like Giovanni Batista Rinuccini, raged against the "Romantic syphilis" and deplored "the staccato, convulsive, barrack-room style" that had invaded opera.[23] Between the two reefs navigated pragmatic souls who attempted to reconcile the Italian tradition and the new trends. Carlo Ritorni congratulated Bellini on having tempered the excesses of Rossinianism, seeing *Norma* as a model. Abramo Basevi clearly paid attention to Verdi's new style yet complained that the musical world had entered "the wider orbit of philosophical music," which consisted of "relating everything to poetry."[24] The same pragmatism characterized much of the music of the period, but composers too often incurred the wrath of the critics, who either reproached them for their orchestral "Germanism" (a criticism Rossini was not spared), found them too philosophical,[25] or accused them of corrupting bel canto.[26]

The fact is that Rossinian practice, in particular his idea of song (at least up to *Guillaume Tell*), could not long stand up to the new moral climate in Europe or to the aspirations of the young—those "new generations arising in large measure from the pillagings, the barricades and other nonsenses of that type" for whom the composer felt little sympathy.[27] Was it the conflict between his innovative tendencies—to which all the Italian opera composers were indebted—and his traditionalist convictions that drove him to silence?[28] Certainly, from his earliest works Bellini turned his back on the *stile dei fiori,* as Ritorni charmingly put it, in order to devise a quasi-syllabic, spare style and to pay special heed to recitative. Friedrich Lippmann attributes this volte-face to the young composer's desire to break free from the "swan of Pesaro." Still, the new style also reflected a change of dramaturgy, opera having moved from a heroic, noble world to an unhappy, suffering humanity, from the brilliant to the pathetic, from pleasure to tears.[29]

This development did not, however, put an end to the process of sublimation and idealization, although it brought a change of direction. The fact that after his first operas Bellini discreetly reintroduced a certain infusion of coloratura is a good indication of this. The grand *scene* around which Bellini's dramaturgy, like Donizetti's, was built culminate in the aria, which distills a situation in order to reach the sublime. Donizetti frequently roughened the customary musical forms to rid them of their overly balanced quality and thereby benefit the dramatic rhythm,[30] but he remained faithful to the sublimation of passions in song. This spirit of reconciliation is most noticeable in extreme situations, as, for example, in the great mad scenes of both composers. These depict a psychic disorder that makes the personality burst its bounds, and the music describes the disorder by means of extremely free composition (see *Il pirata, I puritani,* and *Lucia di Lammermoor*). Yet the cathartic virtue of song is never sacrificed; dramatic intensity and sublimation complement each other. Lippmann very aptly observes that the slightest detail could destroy the miraculous equilibrium of these moments: too much pathos (accentuating the mimetic tension) or too much fioritura (which would retain only the vocal transfiguration).[31]

* * * * * * * *

Verdi's position is different in that he obeys but a single criterion, that of dramatic truth, thereby abolishing the dichotomy that Rossini had set up between the materiality of the drama embodied in the libretto and its ideal transfiguration wrought by the music. The importance he gives the libretto, the need he affirms to understand it perfectly and be convinced by it, the care with which he supervises its writing, the way he presents himself as a dramatist, a man of the theater rather than a composer, his doctrine of the *parola scenica* (to be discussed in the next chapter)—all this proves that he placed the truth of the drama above the beauty of the music and the literary quality of the lines.

He sometimes goes so far as to abdicate his role as animating spirit in favor of the librettist if the latter is capable of solving a tricky problem, such as the denouement for the new version of *La forza del destino:* "If the poet can find an ending that is good both logically and theatrically, the musical ending will automatically be good."[32] Advising Felice Varesi, who created the character of Macbeth, he explains that the quality of the musical interpretation depends on a good understanding of the drama: "I'll never stop urging you to study the position, the words and the dramatic situation: then the music will come right of its own accord. In a word, I'd rather you served the poet better than you serve the composer."[33] No trace, as one can see, of that division of powers giving the music the task of stylizing, refining, and transfiguring the dramatic material. This credo never varied, even though the character of the dramas chosen and the method of tackling them changed a great deal.

It is probably this drive toward dramatic truth, originally conceived as action, energy, and intensity of the passions, that accounts for a certain clumsiness in the young Verdi's art (setting aside a few brilliant exceptions). Verdi was not so immediately at ease with the structures of Italian opera as were his predecessors Bellini and Donizetti. He was often more conventional. He matured more slowly, and it is only from the years 1849–50 that he conveys the feeling of being total master of his art.

It is clear that Verdi did not aim to the same degree for the emotional sublimation of song. He sought not elegance but the force of the gesture, the truth of an attitude, and it is as though the moment of singing sapped that energy and lessened the power of the performance. Thus, he destroyed the edifice before transforming it, striving to give the "closed form" a sort of urgency so as to prevent the lyrical pause from ever freezing the movement of the drama. To adopt Massimo Mila's felicitous phrase, he captured tradition by storm just as Bonaparte would scatter armies by the suddenness of his maneuvers. Only after twelve years or so, with the help of experience and of contact with other operatic traditions, when he felt capable of finding the right form for each dramatic situation, did he convey a feeling of ease and rediscover the joy of song and its power to achieve sublimation.

Verdi's loyalty to drama implies that the dramatic situation dictates the musical choices: when the situation demands it, he writes Ghislanzoni, "one must not have scruples."[34] Thus, Verdi does not have the same reservations about recitative as Rossini does, and he gives the music far greater descriptive power: the example quoted above of Otello's death shows that he is willing to go much further in musical imitation (here by accepting the near suspension of tonality). The composer's development, the gradual suppression of such traditions as the cabaletta or the stretta of the finale, the considerable importance he gives the *scena* as a free musical discourse, its use in preference to the aria in presenting major characters such as Rigoletto, the slow closing of gaps between the *scene* and the closed forms—all show Verdi tending toward a drama that is continuous and seamless.

His notion of dramatic truth expands to include examples of realism that formerly seemed to be incompatible with "ideal beauty," moments where transcription into music inevitably entailed a rejection of the usual demands for balance and harmony. (Verdi often contrasted *beautiful* and *theatrical* when speaking of a line, invariably showing a preference for the latter term.) In this connection one can do no better than quote the famous letter in which Verdi objects to Eugenia Tadolini as interpreter of Lady Macbeth: "Tadolini has a beautiful and attractive appearance; and I would like Lady Macbeth to be ugly and evil. Tadolini sings to perfection; and I would like the Lady not to sing. Tadolini has a stupendous voice, clear, limpid, powerful; and I would like the Lady to have a harsh, stifled, and hollow voice. Tadolini's voice has an angelic quality; I would like the Lady's voice to have a diabolical quality!"[35] Note how the rejection of a certain type of beauty is accompanied by a rejection of its musical equivalent, a certain type of singing; indeed, in the same letter the composer specifies that the principal pieces of the opera must absolutely not be sung but rather "acted" and "declaimed" in a "somber, veiled" voice.

No doubt the shades of Shakespeare and Hugo (especially his theory of the grotesque) inspired Verdi in this broadening of his dramaturgy, encouraging him to choose ambiguous and deformed characters like the court jester Rigoletto and to break up the uniformly noble tone of the traditional libretto with comic episodes. He derived a certain pride from shocking opera habitués by introducing characters, subjects, even props, that had hitherto been unacceptable: Ernani's horn, Rigoletto's hump, Stiffelio's divorce, prostitution, the importance of money and illness in *Traviata*. "Why is it impossible at your San Carlo," he writes his friend De Sanctis, "to present a queen as well as a peasant girl, a virtuous woman or a whore? Why can't a doctor feel a patient's pulse, why no masked balls, etc., etc.? It's unfair! Why? If a character can die of poison or by the sword, why can't he die of tuberculosis or the plague? Doesn't all this happen in everyday life?"[36]

· · · · · · ·

So we see that the trend to dramatic mimesis that Rossini deflected in the direction of idealization seems to culminate in Verdi. It would be tempting to speak of realism had not Verdi set the limits of this imitation very clearly in another famous passage influenced by Shakespeare, whom he familiarly calls "Papa": "Copying from what is real may be a good thing, but inventing what is real is better, much better. There seems to be a contradiction in these words, 'invent what is real,' but ask Papa. It is possible that he, Papa, had come across somebody like Falstaff, but it is unlikely he ever met anyone as evil as Iago, and never, ever angels like Cordelia, Imogen, Desdemona, etc., etc., and yet they are so real! To copy from what is real may be a good thing, but it is photography. It is not painting."[37] Invention is preferred to imitation; the ideal is replaced not by reality but by representation. Verdi seeks characters larger than life, more true than real, the kind he finds in Shakespeare. He avoids mythic personages and even shows a certain reserve toward Aeschylus, claiming that with him "one is never sure whether characters are men or gods."[38] He wants types that, without exactly corresponding to real human beings, are striking enough by their truth to shed light on our understanding of reality.

This conception of truth as the creator of living models has certain consequences. It constrains musical mimesis, which is accepted, but only up to a certain point (the composer viewed verismo with extreme reservations), just so long as the search for the real in all its complexity is tempered by concern for the archetypal power of the character. In this way Verdi can, while changing its direction, maintain the formal heritage of his predecessors since the "closed form" helps make this archetypal dimension more obvious and palpable. It replaces verisimilitude, understood as conformity with what might happen in real life, with a theatrical verisimilitude that implies an exaggeration of effects. Not that Verdi is careless about the logic of his librettos. He rebukes Piave for chronological incongruities in *Rigoletto,* reproaches Ghislanzoni for mentioning a battle that never took place in *Aida,* deplores an inconsistency in *I due Foscari.*[39] But his dual concern for brevity and theatricality—he refers to the *parola scenica,* not the right or true word—implies that the way to truth is the stage and that it can tolerate rapid transitions and disproportionate effects.

THE AMBIGUITY OF REALISM

It may seem absurd to talk of realism in connection with a genre founded on a convention as unreal as the use of singing instead of speech. Yet the growing importance given in the last century to historical, geographic, and social context as well as to philosophy is also felt in opera. From the early 1800s, people no longer tolerated the careless way the eighteenth century showed bewigged Greeks and Romans; they demanded more historical accuracy and deplored the more blatant anachronisms. It is in this precise sense, in relation to history, that I shall describe Verdi's attitude.

First of all, it should be noted that the word *realism* was not in his vocabulary and that there is every reason to think that he was wary of it; yet he was not indifferent to history, although his attitude was ambiguous and complex. Let us recall, to start with, that, in the case of opera, history served to "de-realize" a plot rather than to make it more real. The elimination of the historical or geographic context was often an elementary precaution to avoid the ire of the censor. It allowed the composer to portray a perfectly contemporaneous ideological and moral world in a faraway past that was vague and unfamiliar. Distance lent dignity. Scotland, Africa, Gaul, the age of the Crusades, the Renaissance—these were faintly exotic frameworks for tragic love stories that reflected and distilled present-day situations.

The development of learning and the vogue for historical painting, on the other hand, ruled out treating these settings too imprecisely. With *Attila,* and especially with *Macbeth,* Verdi took great pains over the historical and geographic background, even though in the case of the former opera he found inspiration in Raphael rather than in available historical documents.[40] *Macbeth* was prepared painstakingly, with research carried out in London,[41] as it was later for *Falstaff.* Mindful of details, Verdi recommended that the impresario Lanari use neither silk nor velvet, these being inappropriate for the time.[42]

These two examples, which are practically from the same period, show the twin motives that spurred Verdi on to greater visual precision: in the case of *Macbeth,* respect for a work that the composer intended to honor in all its aspects (and that, furthermore, included fantastic scenes likely to cause laughter if incorrectly staged); and, in that of *Attila,* the beginning of a taste for the historical frieze developed in contemporary art, notably by Hayez. Thirty years later, *Aida* would undergo meticulous preparation. Verdi carried out the most careful research and asked endless questions of Du Locle, who in turn gathered information from the Egyptologist Mariette. (The latter had meanwhile let it be known that "the viceroy wants a rigorously exact stage setting, and a strictly observed local color.")[43]

At the time of *Otello,* the erudite Boito coached Verdi on the Italian sources of Shakespeare's tragedy. He also strongly recommended that the costume designer study Carpaccio and Gentile Bellini, while Verdi attentively supervised Edel's costumes and Ferrario's stage sets.[44] The so-called production books, drawn up under the watchful eye of librettist and composer, even suggested the duel between Montano and Cassio be overseen by a competent technician "who knows the art of fencing as it was practiced in the fifteenth century."[45] A few years later a miniature theater was brought to Busseto so that Verdi, assisted by Boito and the painter Hohenstein, might supervise the tiniest details of the stage representation of *Falstaff*.[46]

. . . .

Up to this point it was a question of historical accuracy only, insofar as contemporary scholarship allowed. Why not explore further and consider the ethos of each age and its psychological conditioning of people? This is what Verdi was suggesting when the censors proposed that the action of *Ballo* be put back to 1385: "All epochs, as we know, have their particular characteristics. The customs and feelings of people of the fifteenth century were different from those of the nineteenth century. Nor did people of the north look like those of the south. And as for their musical character, they couldn't be more different. Take for instance a Neapolitan and a Swedish song and you'll see the difference. A composer can and must emphasize these distinctions." If the action took place in Florence, then the "Cracovienne" he had written for Stettin would be useless! The censors had made Silvano a hunter instead of a sailor, but, the composer noted, the audience would burst out laughing if it heard "sailor-like" songs coming from a hunter.[47]

Verdi's understanding of the determining power of history was nonetheless extremely flexible. Still apropos *Ballo,* he yielded to the censors' injunctions and moved the action from Sweden to Stettin, in Pomerania, because that was a Celtic region and the people did a lot of dancing! If he preferred the seventeenth century to the fourteenth, which the censors had suggested, it was because the former was "an elegant, chivalrous century" while the latter was "a time of blood and the sword" in Florence.[48] In short, he must find a period that would not jar the somewhat vague ideas the public and the author had of it or contradict the world of the plot. Verdi would prove far more intransigent on the question of the dramatic axes of *Ballo* than on that of its historical placement, which leads one to be skeptical as to the usefulness of certain recent attempts to restore the opera's original setting, the Sweden of Gustav III.

Given these rather flexible principles, the modern critic might be forgiven for questioning the importance of the historical and political context. David R. B. Kimbell reproaches Cammarano for suppressing the historical background of *Il trovatore* that gave rise to the adventures of Manrico and the Count de Luna, the wars of succession that steeped Aragon in blood over the death of Don Martin el Humano in 1410.[49] He also reproaches him for eliminating the character of Don Huillén, Leonora's brother, who personifies honor and aristocratic pride. But would it really have been worth the trouble to keep this confusing context? For one thing, the audience would not have made much of it, and, for another, the author of the Spanish play did not scrupulously respect it since he made de Luna Urgel's enemy when in fact he was one of his followers.[50] The code that enables the audience immediately to grasp the protagonists of this somber story is clear enough that we perceive Manrico as a fringe character in revolt, Luna as a representative of the established order, and Leonora as an aristocrat drawn by love to the rebel—clear enough, that is to say, for our sympathy to go to the "liberal" and not the "conservative."

Simon Boccanegra is a much more overtly political drama, but here too the details of the political and social connections between the Doge and his rivals get lost in the mist. García Gutiérrez's Spanish play is far more explicit in this regard, portraying as it does characters who play a double game and politicians who are at the same time naive and racketeers (Fiesco). But it was not Verdi's aim to depict the confused world of political intrigue: he wanted to pit against each other two giants, a vindictive feudal enforcer of the law, imbued with the privileges of his class, and a leader of men who sacrifices his life to the desire for unity—justification enough for the drama, as it progressed from prose text to draft libretto to final version, to leave vague the practical details of these rivalries.

Don Carlos posed the problem of historical context one last time, and the composer's reaction is significant. When in 1882–83 Verdi was working on the revised four-act version, the ghost of Charles V still bothered him, so much so that he ended up questioning the whole historical basis of Schiller's play:

> Charles V appears robed as an emperor! This is not very believable. The emperor had been dead a number of years. But in this drama, so splendid in form and in its high-minded concepts, everything is false.
>
> Don Carlos was a fool, a madman, an unpleasant fellow.

Elisabeth was never in love with Don Carlos.

Posa is an imaginary being who could never have existed under Philip's reign.

Philip, who among other things says:

Garde-toi de mon Inquisiteur . . .
Qui me rendra ce mort!

Philip wasn't as softhearted as that.

In other words, in this drama there is nothing historical, nor is there any Shakespearean truth or profundity . . . so one thing more or less won't do any harm; and I myself don't dislike the apparition of the old emperor.[51]

We can see from this that Verdi's understanding of history had its limitations, and Alberto Moravia is not mistaken when he writes: "Verdi's conception of history is motionless, static, Plutarchan. If, indeed, we are interested in Verdi's characters even today, it is precisely because they are men and women first and only secondarily men and women of the Middle Ages or the Renaissance."[52] In fact, although his concern for historical accuracy is undeniable, it does not reach the heart of his characters, who remain subject to one great criterion—truth, a truth independent of the passage of time. If Schiller's drama had impressed him as possessing a truth as powerful as Shakespeare's, he would perhaps not have minded its historical discrepancies.

* * * * * * *

The "Cracovienne" in *Ballo* presented the problem of *couleur locale,* which loomed large in Verdi's time, even if authenticity was not always guaranteed. Here, too, the composer's first reaction, a desire for historical accuracy, later gave way to a folklore of his own invention. While writing *Vêpres,* he turned to his friend De Sanctis several times for information: What was the "real" tarantella like? Could he find any genuine sicilianos, not arranged by scholars?[53] He was disappointed with what De Sanctis sent him, and, in any case, the score was already finished.[54] Did Verdi have in mind something for Hélène's "sicilienne" in act 5? Whatever the case, without waiting any longer, he made it a bolero and did not even change the name of the dance.

When he was preparing *Forza,* Piave suggested using seguidillas, and Verdi told him curtly that he had no need of authentic examples (the act 2 seguidilla is one in name only).[55] The problem was obviously insoluble in the case of *Aida*[56] but turned up again in the case of the *Otello* ballet. With his usual impatience, he asked all his friends to find him "Greek-Cypriot" dances, then something Turkish, then something Venetian. With nothing meeting his approval, he finally sent the ballet to his publisher with this facetious comment: "Your doctors of music could find nothing for me . . . but I found a Greek song of 5000 B.C.! . . . If the world didn't exist then, it's the world's tough luck! Then I found a Muranese, composed 2000 years ago for a war between Venice and Murano, which the Muranese won. No matter if Venice didn't yet exist."[57]

This tirade provides a good definition of Venetian local color—an ideal, invented folklore. When the composer Gallignani asked him if he had done any special research to create *Aida*'s "realistic" *couleur locale,* Verdi answered simply, "No, that's the way I imagined it."[58] For a man whose ear had been trained in childhood by the sounds of wandering musicians, it was not such a bad method. In the end, his ideal folklore sounded more genuine than the undoubtedly contrived melodies his learned friends sent him.[59]

* * * * * * *

The ambiguity of "realism," for Verdi and for opera in general, comes through most strongly in *Aida*. It is well known that the composer carefully studied ancient Egyptian history and society before writing the opera.[60] Contemporary Egyptologists respected his research, which was limited only by contemporary learning. One example is the case of the trumpets, which Verdi had specially made; the documentary evidence on which they are based is flimsy since the first Egyptian trumpets did not come to light until 1932.[61]

Yet this vast labor of "Egyptology" is awash in "Egyptomania," to use Jean Humbert's expression: in the mythology, in the evocation of "mysterious Egypt, with its architectural immensities, its alleys of crouching sphinxes, its avenues of obelisks" conjured up by Théophile Gautier.[62] The opera is like an exotic dream embodying what Gautier calls "le Spleen lumineux de l'Orient," and the somewhat conventional visual pomp of many of its scenes overshadows the powerful, somber love triangle.

With *Aida,* Verdi echoed the ambiguity of French grand opera, where an often remarkable documentary accuracy was inseparably coupled with exotic escapism. The historical precision that enchanted the audiences of *La Muette de Portici, Les Huguenots,* or *La Juive* quickly descended into the no-man's-lands of *Le Roi de Lahore* and *Esclarmonde*. Hence, this "Egyptian" opera, where, as Alfred Einstein observes, Verdi for the first time gives a major role to *couleur locale,* is ultimately bathed in an atmosphere no less unreal than those of the wondrous grottoes and other enchantments of baroque opera. Perhaps it was an awareness of this contradiction that caused Verdi to turn away from extravagant stagings, to take care that the historical accuracy of his last operas did not eclipse the emotional and moral themes of the drama.

BACCHANAL AND TRAGEDY

Schiller once wrote that he had confidence in opera and believed in its capacity to rise from bacchanal to tragedy.[63] If it is the paradox of every work of art to give pleasure by representing both joyous and painful realities, opera is indeed the genre that flaunts this desire for pleasure in the crudest, most scandalous way, and Italian opera has probably done the least to try to hide it. From the baroque operas whose fantastic spectacles astonished and delighted their audiences to those of Puccini, who wanted to arouse emotion by portraying "great suffering in little souls," composers have always found ways to touch this Dionysian chord.

In nineteenth-century Italy the public thirsted for strong sensations: a fine opera was "all the rage," provoked "fanaticism." One opera lover, quoted by Carlo Ritorni, declared that he craved music that "moves me, electrifies me, draws me out of myself,"[64] and Bellini, attending a performance of *La Sonnambula* in Paris, wrote with pride, "It was as though everyone's nerves had been charged with electricity."[65] It is not surprising then that part of the public looked askance at the "philosophical" trends of the new school. The orgiastic aspect of opera delighted foreign visitors like Hegel while scandalizing others such as Liszt, Wagner, Delacroix, and Berlioz.

The importance given to pleasure, pure and simple, provoked a muted struggle that permeates the entire history of opera and gives it a sort of zigzag pattern, with oscillation between extremes. On one side was a popular tradition that craved spectacle—discontinuous, above all vocal, physical, and showy. On the other was an aristocratic tradition more concerned that the work have continuity and that pleasure be subordinated to truth. It was, in other words, a conflict between bacchanal and tragedy. Faced with this wild hedonism on the part of the public, the political authorities were divided: sometimes they saw opera as a distraction that had the advantage of diverting minds from other concerns like politics;

other times, as in France in certain eras, they considered opera a "lubri-
cious" spectacle and wanted to make it a "supervised pleasure."[66]

The theoreticians were apt to be distrustful. Counted against the isolated voice of Pier Jacopo Martello, who recognized at once that people
went to the opera to "wallow in pleasure" and that this aim amply excused
the "slavish verses" of most librettos,[67] how many writers tried to put a
stop to this pursuit of pleasure? Whether out of loyalty to the mythical
founder of Greek tragedy, out of pedagogical concern (Mazzini), or else
because they were mindful that the traditional aim of art was to purge
the passions (Ritorni), they wanted the pleasure to be a rational one and
violently attacked the "voluptuous pleasure of the ears," condemning the
excesses of song that pleased the people because "they don't have to think
any further."[68]

* * * * * * * *

The heart of the problem lies, in fact, in the connection between pleasure
and performance. No doubt this pleasure comes essentially from the music and even more from song—indeed, quite simply from the voice, given
the emotional load a voice can offer by its very presence, independent of
the words being sung. In his *Massimilla Doni,* Balzac describes two opera
lovers who go into a trance every night, one over the soprano's trills, the
other over the combination of voice and violin. The opera lover I quoted
above confessed quite frankly that he sought an animal pleasure that did
not call for any study, thought, or understanding on his part.

The pleasure appears to be unmotivated, quite unrelated to any actions
onstage that might be supposed to provoke it. Music, especially song,
"robs" the words of the product of their long journey toward meaning
and plunges the listener into a state of unreasoning enjoyment. One might
go on to infer, as has recently been suggested, that the pleasure of opera
is to be found in the abolition of the rational meaning of the performance.
Yet it is hard to defend the claim that "the meaning of the situation counts
for nothing in the eruption of emotion."[69] In order for the meaning to
disappear, it still must first be presented; otherwise, opera becomes the
product of a monstrous misunderstanding, and it is hard to see why so
many composers—Mozart, Gluck, Wagner, Verdi—expended so much
effort on fitting the emotional power of their art to a plausible story.

On the other hand, Michel Poizat's theory does pinpoint one characteristic peculiar to opera, that to a certain extent music dilutes the meaning
connected with performance and dramatic logic. Edgar Allan Poe ad-

mirably describes this phenomenon, in an essay on poetry: "While the rhythm ... is an essential aid in the development of the poet's highest idea—the idea of the Beautiful—the artificialities of this rhythm are an inescapable bar to the development of all points of thought or expression which have their basis in Truth."[70] The writer observes that rhythm—which in music is combined with color, intensity, and sound intervals—at first assists in the representation of truth by giving it form, then acts as a brake.

In opera, with dilution comes a displacement of the meaning. The lyrical sweep given to a passion draws us from the performance into ourselves, toward interiorization. By the force of its effects, the music moves our attention from the object onstage to the subject, from the spectacle to the spectator, from the epoch represented to our present. Having gone out to see a fiction, we are thrown back on our innermost selves (we listen to music with our eyes closed), and the links binding us to the drama give way as though we ourselves had become the protagonists.

If music has the power to arouse in us sensations and experiences that have nothing to do with performance, emotion also arises from the performance in a way similar to the "trance by identification" studied by Gilbert Rouget—set up by the composer, transmitted by the singer, and induced in the spectator.[71] The story is the point of departure, but the music finally creates a gray area between the opera, which proposes a meaning, the singer, who personifies it, and the spectator, who absorbs it. As Adorno nicely puts it, speaking of sacrifice in opera: "Frequently we may no longer know who is being sacrificed, the work, the virtuoso, or ourselves."[72]

This indistinctness creates a sort of double stage, an inner and an outer stage of the drama, with practical consequences that composers seem to have always been aware of, judging from their concern for dramatic rhythm—in the sense of alternating the phases of introspection and dramatic action. What happens chiefly is that less importance is given to the cohesion of the parts with the whole and of the different situations with the "chain" linking them, with the result that there is a greater tolerance for fragmentation.

In a letter to Verdi, Arrigo Boito shows himself to be remarkably aware of this peculiarity. Having just demolished a rather far-fetched suggestion of Verdi's, he immediately adds: "This is the Critic's reasoning, and it is right. But an opera is not a play; our art lives on elements unknown to spoken tragedy. The destroyed atmosphere can be created anew. Eight measures suffice to revive a feeling, a rhythm can restore a character; music is the most omnipotent of the arts, it has a logic of its own, more rapid, more free than the logic of spoken thought and far more eloquent. You, Maestro, with a stroke of the pen can reduce to silence the most cogent arguments of the Critics."[73]

Boito, who, it will be recalled, was a composer as well as a writer, admits in essence that, through music, opera can tolerate discontinuity and compartmentalization of its various sections more readily than can spoken drama—a tolerance that I believe is connected to the oscillation between what I have called the outer and inner stages. This view explains the endurance of the so-called conventional forms, which springs not necessarily from a conservative, backward-looking tradition but from a perfect awareness of the way opera "breathes."

The survival, against all odds, of the closed form, the disappearance of meaning in song, the liking for simplified characters and the hidden persistence of the aesthetics of the affetti, all can be traced to this inner stage to which opera periodically migrates so that the affective appropriation of the performance can take place. In contrast, with its ambition of realizing total coincidence of dramatic logic and musical discourse, Wagnerian music drama is like a challenge, a leap in the dark, a near-impossible wager. This should be borne in mind when one notes Verdi's hesitations over casting off a heritage two centuries old.

Furthermore, certain procedures tended to formalize the rise of intensity accompanying the transition from one scene to the next, corresponding to the shift of what Rossini called the materiality of the drama to the ideality of the music. The finale probably offers the best instance of this exalting mechanism. Let us take a highly successful example, the act 1 finale of *Macbeth*. This opens with a *scena,* an Allegro agitato during which Macduff warns Banquo, who sees and then calls out that Duncan has been murdered. The chorus thereupon bursts out into curses—"Schiudi, inferno, la bocca ed inghiotti" (Jaws of hell, open wide and swallow all creation in your bowels)—which are treated in a violently declamatory style driven by a vigorously anapestic rhythm (Adagio in B♭ minor).

The purpose of this section is to explain the "situation," the court's horrified reaction to the king's assassination. The following section, in D♭ major, "O gran Dio che ne' cori penetri," brings us to song, a meditative chorus (with soloists) imploring the Lord's aid, utterly different from what has gone before. With the third section, "l'ira tua formidabile e pronta," a Grandioso in D♭ major calling down divine punishment on the head of the guilty one, the mechanism of the finale is unleashed. This affective commingling of supplication and terror is freed by a melodic movement that swings back and forth three times before breaking loose in a leap of a seventh, then swells in a crescendo rising to a high B♭.

These musical articulations closely mirror the divisions of the text—horrified imprecations, prayer and meditation, call for punishment—yet all the while the music is clearly moving toward the third Grandioso section, where the dynamics of song take flight. In the most successful cases, like this *Macbeth* finale, the emotional crescendo does not result in any lessening of the dramatic pertinence of the musical commentary, in other words, its adequacy to the drama. Sometimes, however, this adequacy does diminish as the finale approaches the vocal apotheosis. This gap is surely proof of that shift to interior jubilation, that is, in the spectator, induced by the dramatic situation but now independent of it—an example of the "electricity" Bellini liked to arouse in his audience.

So we see that opera is based on a dual impulse that is both complementary and contradictory: the dramatic impulse that leads us to external fiction and the musical impulse that draws us into ourselves through the intermediate stage of identification and on to the final stage of trance. The first impulse is toward attention, continuity, logic, and verisimilitude, the second toward discontinuity, fragmentation into emotive shocks, destruction of chronology, and the return to an absolute present, that of pleasure. The opera composer is careful not to cross the bounds of bacchanal into tragedy—quite the contrary, he strives to bring the two as close together as he can.

Path of an Evolution

Nella vita quello che si acquista
da una parte si perde dall'altra.
EUGENIO MONTALE

We have seen how Verdi obeyed an aesthetic ideal that implied the primacy of dramatic truth, although a truth conceived as a creation of archetypes rather than the imitation of models to be found in everyday life. Yet one is struck by a curious pendulum-like motion that constantly governs his thinking. Often, when faced with a drama, the composer would hesitate between two opposing solutions. With *Il trovatore* before him, a fairly traditional opera close to melodrama in spirit, he writes to Cammarano: "If operas had no cavatinas, duets, trios, choruses or finales, etc., etc., and if an entire opera were of a piece, I would find it more reasonable and right." By contrast, faced with an opera as unusual as *Il Re Lear,* he calls for strophes, and yet more strophes, in order to create arias, duets, and ensembles and opines that the play does not lend itself to the kind of music he writes.[74]

More striking still are those occasions when the oscillation occurs over a considerable period of time. As long as the tradition appears solid and unshakable, Verdi constantly demands new approaches: original texts, new and untried forms. When it shows signs of weakening (Julian Budden speaks of the period from the 1850s on as "the collapse of a tradition") and young composers harken to the sirens of Wagnerian music drama, he returns to the past and defends the national tradition. He praises the cabaletta, speaks warmly of Rossini, extols the inspiration and spontaneity of the "ancients," and expresses annoyance over "the art of the future."[75]

Some have seen in this indecision signs of a nature at once innovative and timorous, an explanation that strikes me as implausible. On the other hand, it is true that Verdi was fond of holding himself aloof from the crowd, acting the innovator when others were traditionalist and the reactionary when his contemporaries wanted to be seen as progressive. A solid streak of nationalism, and to a small degree of chauvinism, must be taken into account in his stance against German symphonism and the music of the future. We should bear in mind, however, that, if Verdi advocated a return to the past (as in his celebrated formula, "Let's go back to the old ways: it will be progress"), he was thinking not of Rossini or the opera of his early years but of the sources of Italian vocal tradition, of Palestrina.

This oscillation between a generally innovative way of working and the appeal of tradition—an antiquarianism that was often purely ideological and had nothing to do with his style of composing at the time—in fact reveals Verdi's awareness that the profound changes coursing through his oeuvre (as in contemporary opera) represented a gain, but also perhaps a loss. Verdi hesitated between the temptation of complexity that urged him toward music drama and nostalgia for the stereotypes and the plenitude that bound him to a traditional formal universe. He bent the aesthetics with which he had begun, one of sublimation and idealization, toward a more scrupulous respect for the drama, but he drew back when it became clear that pursuing music drama in earnest would bring about the destruction of that tradition.

In general Verdi followed contemporary trends, the gradual loosening of traditional forms and the tendency toward a continuous arioso supported by a highly diversified orchestral commentary. Yet the fact that he belonged to two worlds, two cultures, two artistic traditions, made him peculiarly aware of the significance of these changes. In the musical domain, he weighed the pros and cons of two methods of composition: recitative, with its great analytic capacity but weak synthetic one, and aria, with its greater power of synthesis but lesser subtlety, the one taking us to a multifarious but troubled reality, the other to a simple world, but one characterized by plenitude.

Verdi was perfectly aware of the psychological and moral significance of these formal choices, as is shown by a highly illuminating letter on the subject of *Otello:* "Desdemona is a part where the thread, the melodic line, never stops from the first to the last note. Just as Iago must only declaim and *ricaner* [sneer]. Just as Otello, now warrior, now passionate lover, now cast down into the filth, now as ferocious as a savage, must sing and howl, so Desdemona must always sing."[76] The choice of vocal style is clearly linked to the character's moral nature: to Desdemona, whom the composer conceived as a "type," goes purity of song; Iago is too devious, too far removed from any moral exemplarity to go beyond declamation to song; and, finally, for Otello, the gap between song and the cry admirably defines the gulf between the heroic dream and its disintegration. On a larger scale, one can see that certain operas "sing" better than others: *Trovatore* has more arias than *Rigoletto,* but it would be rash to conclude that one is an opera in the old style and the other more innovative since the choice is based on the dramaturgy of each.

It is apropos of *Rigoletto* that Gabriele Baldini imagines Verdi found himself at a crossroads. In this opera some characters are treated as in *Ernani,* that is, recreated synthetically through aria, with relative indifference to the details of the text, while Rigoletto himself is followed step by step with a new kind of writing, more open and flexible. This produces a crisis, a dilemma between the old musical style and characters and the new-style characters: "Other characters may have gained in depth, but they also lost in substance: the more the subtleties of their characters were made evident and varied, the less one felt the consistency of musical material. . . . The character may have emerged more delicately mastered, but had a corresponding lack of musical life."[77] In short, Baldini says, the composer was faced with a dramatic choice, whether to remain loyal to a tradition that painted the character in bold strokes but with strong musical articulation or to turn his back on it and yield to what the critic calls the "rituals of the word."

It is impossible to agree with Baldini when he speaks of an abstraction in the musical depiction of character after *Rigoletto;* impossible, too, to admit that the choice of style that pointed to music drama amounted to a capitulation of music to text, unless one believes that the music asserts itself only in the exclusive framework of the "closed form"; impossible, in short, to speak of "crisis" for the good reason that Verdi did not abandon one method for another but diversified his style without completely giving up the traditional forms, as we shall see further on. Still, there is justification for imagining that the composer felt somewhat perplexed when faced with the new world of drama he approached with *Rigoletto* (and even well before that, with *Macbeth*).

The Italian critic in fact puts his finger on the coexistence of two approaches to drama that are characteristic of Verdi's development. As was pointed out in the introduction to this chapter, his development was profound, so profound that it cannot be explained solely by the inner growth of a single aesthetics but is more readily grasped if one postulates the existence of two aesthetics, different but each one logical and coherent. Verdi began by telling "stories" in concise, synthetic fashion, keeping to the essential turns of the plot and, rather than reproducing reality in all its complexity, striving to encompass passions, characters, and destinies in a series of significant "gestures." This is *melodrama,* compatible with opera's traditional structure and even arising out of it. Little by little, as his vision grew more analytic, he confronted the complexity these same stories might have been concealing and faced the ambiguity in his characters, adopting a more detached, critical approach. This is *music drama.* Each aesthetics imposed different choices of form and style.

If melodrama dominated Verdi's first operas and music drama the later ones, his originality springs from the coexistence of the two approaches, which fight and nourish each other at the same time. The early Verdi tended toward a musical straightforwardness that was also a moral straightforwardness of characters and situations; force and clarity were his goals. This comprehensibility of the world with its ethical transparency gradually vanished or decayed, and one can understand how Verdi regretted that marvelous clarity and must have felt he had mastered complexity at the cost of plenitude. Nostalgia for tradition then became nostalgia for that firm grasp of reality that, because of the ever greater refinement of dramaturgy, was no longer possible.

My working hypothesis therefore assumes a dual reading of Verdi's oeuvre: it implies on the one hand the mastering of a shifting, contradictory reality and on the other the abandonment of an epic, comprehensive perception of that reality.

Theodor Adorno suggests that Balzac's realism is a "realism through loss of reality":[78] the novelist auscultates the world ever more minutely as it grows alien to him and he has to understand and conquer it anew. Something of the kind occurred with Verdi, always along with the secret desire finally to reach a comprehensive grasp of human beings and situations. Verdi's development was inevitable, resulting as it did from the composer's gradual reconciliation with his age in its context of European culture. We might describe it as a passage from archaism to modernity.

The dichotomy described above will therefore be the key to studying Verdi's evolution. It rests on two poles that I examine in two chapters, "Melodrama" and "Music Drama." Even though the passage from one pole to the other is a chronological one, both poles are always present in Verdi's works because they mark contradictory but powerful aspirations. Between them are intermediate stages: the chapter "Metamorphoses I" describes the fluctuations in the dramatic code the composer was leaving behind. "Metamorphoses II" deals with the discovery of an inner dimension of each character clearly distinct from his or her social self, a Janus-like appearance not lacking in ambiguity or mystery. Next, it outlines the means by which the composer diversified his dramaturgy, heretofore uniformly "serious," avoiding plots that up to that time tended to focus blindly on the concatenation of the passions. Finally, "Unity" attempts to show that Verdi always strove for cohesion in his operas but pursued his goal by different paths: through rhythm, architecture, and *tinta,* or color. But, before that, we must examine what constitutes the basis of every opera—the libretto.

A SYMBOLIC SPACE

Das Zeitalter des Gesanges und
Gesetzes ist nun zu Ende. Welches
Zeitalter aber hat begonnen?
FRANZ WERFEL,
Die Geschwister von Neapel

In conclusion, in order to throw a different light on the evolution of opera in the past century, and in particular that of Verdi, let us dwell briefly on Franz Werfel's phrase, which stands as the epigraph to this section.[79] The Austrian writer sets up a curious parallel between the age of song and that of the law, as though song were encamped directly opposite the law and the disappearance of one should entail the disappearance of the other. Werfel's phrase finds its confirmation in the crisis that struck opera at the end of the last century, one parallel to a general identity crisis of Western man and a crisis of the values on which his psychic equilibrium rested. The age of doubt and questioning that began at that time seemed to deal a fatal blow to song, as it had been fashioned over the preceding centuries, and to open the way to other forms of musical theater, with opera appearing a more and more unlikely genre.

Musically, as an order governing the individual but at the same time restraining him, the law is for the most part expressed by a declamation very close to *recto tono,* that is, to a minimum amount of song, as, for example, the voice in *Idomeneo,* the Commendatore in the graveyard scene of *Don Giovanni,* Monterone in *Rigoletto,* the priests in *Aida,* and so on. The more the voice embodies the law as supreme authority, the more rigid song becomes, confining itself to a solemn, austere declamation that shuns melisma. In short, the law kills song but at the same time serves as its guiding light. The impersonality of *recto tono* is the sign of its absolute power, its transcendent character, and its value as a marker of boundaries, for often, as in the example of the Commendatore, it is linked to the ultimate limit, death—whether real death or metaphoric death since the law calls for the sacrifice of the individual.

At the other extreme is the cry, which expresses the impossibility of articulation, the immediate, violent reaction. Whether a cry of joy, pain, or distress, it expresses the revolt of the body against order—chaos, the pure illogicality of impulse. Granted, the true "cry," such as Don Giovanni utters when he falls into the pit of hell, is rare, but there is a "musicalized" cry that is subject to no rule and that, even if it offers a melodic line, seems to be aimed at capturing the "true" cry as near as possible to its spontaneous utterance. Innumerable, with Verdi, are the outbursts and explosions that can only be called cries, so feeble is the stylization and so transparent the energy of joy or despair.

Song constitutes a juncture between these two mutually exclusive levels. It combines the fervor of the body, of gesture, the immediacy of individual presence, and at the same time the clarity of formulation that is already the beginning of an order; it has periodicity, breadth, symmetry. It represents the individual in tension between the immanence of the cry and the transcendence of order. Between the funereal, marble coldness of the law and the disorderly, impulsive warmth of human experience, song creates a kind of miraculous equilibrium that outlines the shape of the individual but leaves around it an aura of corporality and irrationality.

Song therefore becomes at one and the same time acceptance of the world's law and revolt against it, a celebration of order even in its most painful aspects and the challenge of the individual who cannot be assimilated to any rule. It is the reality of opera, seeking a precarious, precious balance between pure pleasure and horror on the one side and order and the search for form on the other.

In contrast, as soon as the law, as a point of reference, becomes hazy and uncertain or is debased into a purely impersonal order where the individual is no longer recognized, the world becomes darkness and the individual is dispatched to his demons—and he cries or, as Verdi says of Otello, howls. All that remains is the word, which analyzes, describes, and seeks to understand—a word beyond music—and the cry, as a sudden revelation of what cannot be contained by the word. Song, as a compromise, becomes impossible save in quotation, a sort of echo of what no longer exists.

The Miserere scene of *Il trovatore* provides a striking illustration of these registers of expression and their use in a symbolic space.[80] Leonora comes to one of the towers of the Alaferia palace where the condemned men are imprisoned, in particular her beloved Manrico, the troubadour. Suddenly, the strains of a religious choir come from the wings: "Miserere d'un alma già vicina / Alla partenza che non ha ritorno!" (Have mercy on a soul now close to the voyage from which no one returns!). Finally, from a narrow window in the tower we hear Manrico's plaintive "Ah, che la morte ognora / È tarde nel venir / A chi desia morir" (Ah, how slow is death to come to the one who would die).

The prisoners' chorus, a psalmody that is almost *recto tono,* is so liturgical in character that many commentators assume the men are monks.[81] The chorus expresses the fatal nature of death and the necessity for human beings to submit to it and beg for divine mercy. Metaphorically, we are in the sphere of the law, which here takes the form of the ineluctable (ex. 2a).

Death, rendered by an all-enveloping orchestral accompaniment (the orchestra is complete but plays *ppp*) and a traditional funeral-like rhythm, makes Leonora's blood run cold. Her staccato singing is stifled almost immediately; we are here at the closest possible point to the cry, the cry of revolt and distress (ex. 2b).

Only Manrico sings, his vocal line being in complete contrast to those

EX. 2*a*

EX. 2*b*

EX. 2c

of the other characters both in tonality (A♭ major, not minor) and regularity and in its conventional accompaniment; he hurls a challenge at death that is scornful and sublime (ex. 2c).

The three symbolic spheres described above are here present in their full significance.

The great judgment scene in *Aida* echoes this same scheme, although slightly differently. The priests sing as they invoke their god, but they are confined in a sort of *recto tono* when they command Radames to answer their charges. Amneris comments on these charges with one of the most beautiful cries of distress Verdi ever wrote, but Radames sings no more. In fact, it is Amneris who, transmuting her grief into rage, sings when she pronounces a violent curse that crystalizes her rebellious state.

The menace that hangs over song is nonetheless present in both these scenes. Shattered by his betrayal, and incapable of the bravery that Manrico could still call forth, Radames falls silent, and his silence symbolizes an eclipse of song that leaves, confronting each other, the priests' implacable rigor and the individual's suffering. Inescapable, too, in *Trovatore,* is the unreal, absurd, otherworldly quality of Manrico's singing—Manrico who is fixed in his role of hapless hero and tensed in a vain challenge to death, of whose cruel presence Leonora and the prisoners are so keenly aware. Moreover, the opera as a whole, which some have mistakenly considered a traditional work, is probably the one that celebrates most lustrously the beauty of song and its synthesizing power. At once one of the darkest, most oneiric of operas, marked by blood, violence, and disorder, it raises a monument to the glory of this fragile vocal synthesis and at the same time conveys how precarious, threatened, and desperate is its nature.

CHAPTER THREE

Working on the Libretto

A libretto, a libretto and
the opera's made!
GIUSEPPE VERDI

Why Librettists?

We have seen that many nineteenth-century composers refused to observe
the traditional division of tasks that the preceding century had formalized, claiming a dramatist's right to supervise every aspect of an opera.
Why, then, did Verdi not write his own librettos, as Wagner did? "I, too,
have attempted to blend music and drama in my *Macbeth*," he said in
1875 in an interview for a Viennese newspaper, "but unlike Wagner I
was not able to write my own librettos."[1] Indeed, he did not write any
and apparently was not tempted to do so. How was this possible, considering that he believed almost all aspects of the libretto to be within his
province?

A first reply to the question lies in the custom of writing librettos in
verse. Following the tradition inherited from the century before, passages
of recitative (or *scena*) were written in unrhymed lines of hendecasyllables, or eleven syllables, alternating with lines of seven (or five) syllables
(versi sciolti), while arias and ensembles used *versi lirici* of varying lengths,
the most common being five, six, seven, or eight syllables. In the nineteenth century certain hitherto little-used meters were added, such as the
decasyllable and compound lines (5 × 2, 6 × 2). This tradition conformed
to the dignity required of operatic spectacle, too noble for vulgar prose.
It is true that in 1855 Verdi suggested writing *Simon Boccanegra* in prose
"for novelty's sake," but the authorities at La Fenice did not take the
proposal seriously.[2] Irritated by the convolutions of poetic language, Verdi

often declared himself eager to resort to prose. Yet his librettos would
always be written in verse, his prose sketches sometimes including lines
that needed only a finishing touch to be orthodox.[3]

The custom of systematically versifying librettos can be explained by
the dominance of symmetrical four-measure phrases and a relatively constricting isorhythm in the composition of arias and ensembles. This musical regularity implied a textual regularity that only versification could
supply. Not only should the segments of text have the same number of
syllables to correspond to musical units of four or eight measures, but
semantically, too, the words had to match the musical phrase so that there
would be a perfect correspondence between the two elements: note that
Verdi often refused lines that, because of enjambments, disturbed the
clarity of the musical phrase.[4] Obviously, this preparation of the libretto
called, if not for a poet, at least for a technician.

If the composer sought novelty, the subordination of music to prosody
forced him to urge his librettists to employ different formulas and avoid
monotony at all costs: "The more variety there is in the meters," Verdi
wrote to Antonio Somma in 1855, speaking of *Re Lear,* "the more variety
there will be in the music."[5] In the same way, he strove, as much as was
compatible with correct accentuation, to vary the scansion of his meters
so as to escape the banal. Thus, in his patriotic choruses *(Nabucco, I Lombardi, Ernani)* Verdi willingly used the epic decasyllable by taking advantage of the ample, regular cadence of its ‿ ‿ – ‿ ‿ – ‿ ‿ – ‿ line; yet
its strict balance became confining, and he often avoided this meter or
else, in his musical setting, bent it into a rhythm that would break up the
monotony. Examples of this are the Duke of Mantua's "Questa o quella"
in *Rigoletto* (‿ ‿ – – ‿ ‿ ‿ ‿ – ‿) or the soldiers' chorus "Squilli/
Echeggi" from act 3 of *Il trovatore* (– ‿ – ‿ ‿ – – – ‿ ‿).

Logically enough, Verdi's evolution, driving him as it did to reject the
most commonplace formulas and break up regular rhythms and symmetries, made this demand for metric innovation even more pressing, especially since the traditional rhythmic formulas (studied meticulously by
Lippmann) were varied but not infinite.[6] Thus, he attempted combinations rarely found in the Italian tradition, as when he suggested that in
Aida Ghislanzoni mix together lines of varying lengths, in the French
manner.[7] To avoid the overly common *settenari* and *ottonari* (lines of seven
and eight syllables), Verdi often resorted to long lines of eleven syllables
or to regroupings of lines (7 × 2 or 8 + 6), which gave him ample freedom for segmentation of the melody. The collaboration with Boito was a
godsend for Verdi since Boito was a master of flexible and ambiguous

verse forms and could suggest what the composer needed: for example, "rearrangeable" hendecasyllables that could be broken up into lines of five or seven syllables and even rhymed.[8] *Falstaff* would not have its characteristic brio without Boito's metric tightrope walking and his superimposition of meters, all stimulating the composer's invention.

Should we, as Lippmann suggests, see Verdi's development as a gradual move toward prose, a search for what Schoenberg calls "musical prose," and thus as a break with tradition?[9] Probably not, for, while Verdi called for diversification of the system, he never gives the impression of wanting to do away with it altogether. We might remind readers here that, if the poetics of Italian librettos is highly academic on the level of the actual words, it is very flexible on that of syntax and phonetics. Most words can be contracted: a word like *furono* (they were) can be written *fur, furo,* or *furon* or remain *furono* according to the poet's convenience, and the word order in a phrase enjoys almost complete freedom. Furthermore, Italian prosody is fairly free because line length is determined by the placement of the last tonic accent, not by the total number of syllables; a line of six syllables can therefore in fact have five, six, seven, or eight— a considerable advantage when the librettist is working with short lines and can play with different line endings.[10] Finally, the most exalted meters of the poetic tradition are of odd-numbered syllables (seven, eleven), thus avoiding the monotony that threatens a regular line like the French alexandrine. When one speaks of Italian as the language of opera, one thinks of the diversity of stress that makes it singable, yet its ease of versification has contributed quite as much to creating this reputation.

These advantages have allowed Italian prosody to change and still remain intact. Verdi certainly conformed to the implacable isorhythm dominating early Romantic operas, but, even though he did not hesitate to break up a line (e.g., the *ottonario* in the sleepwalking scene in *Macbeth*) when needs of expression demanded it, he was able to achieve great suppleness of melodic line without sacrificing the basic regularity that versification implied. Consider the fluid hendecasyllable of "O terra addio" in *Aida* or of Fenton's sonnet in *Falstaff*. His approach in this area is similar to the one he adopted toward traditional musical forms.

Another reason should be cited to explain the presence of the librettist as verse technician. Verdi regarded poetry as the shortest way to achieve concision, a key goal of his dramaturgy. He berated Piave because his verses for *La forza del destino* did not have the brevity he craved: "Poetry can and must say everything that can be said in prose but using half the words. So far, you have not been doing that." Mortified, Piave promised to do what he could to pull off "this Tacitus-like genre."[11] Verdi used poetry to distill the overly diffuse language of prose and grasp the essence in a few words. Libretto language, however coded and artificial it may strike us today, was thus a first fundamental step toward the *parola scenica*—the word that, by its visual vitality, akin to gesture, fixes an attitude and establishes a character.

Up to this point the librettist had been no more than a technical collaborator, but now he often became a sort of midwife. Indeed, it is a mystery to see how dramatic temperaments like Mozart's or, especially, Verdi's were incapable of inventing a story or situation, their gifts being realized only through the medium of a librettist. Mozart's dramatic genius did not burst into full bloom until he met Da Ponte, who offered him modes of expression scarcely seen before. Put differently, the job of a good librettist was not so much to have genius as to give genius to the composer he served. Verdi was no exception: his inventions were few and far between and generally related to points of detail. He needed a source and in most cases a collaborator who would ensure the transition from the theatrical to the operatic point of view.

It follows that the tyranny that certain composers, like Verdi and Puccini, exercised over their librettists was not so much evidence of an authoritarian nature as a confession of weakness, the display of a certain frustration that they were incapable of remedying on their own. One story tells how Bellini forced his librettist, Felice Romani, to rewrite the last aria of *La straniera* five times yet could not explain what he wanted short of sitting down at the piano—a good illustration of a composer's tendency not to know what he wants while knowing full well what he does not want.[12] Consequently, the librettist played both a subordinate and a leading role; he was required not so much to show independence and originality on the level of dramatic creation as to be able to divine what a composer managed only imperfectly to express. Piave achieved this by subordinating his personality, by mimicry; stronger characters like Somma and Boito—"I am neutral like Switzerland," the latter wrote in one letter—adopted the same approach by choice.

Once the relationship between composer and librettist is seen in these terms, it is clear that Verdi's attitude was more flexible than has sometimes been portrayed. Categorical when a point seemed clear to him, he showed himself open to suggestions when he had difficulty perceiving a dramatic situation, as happened, for example, several times with the libretto for *Il Re Lear*.[13] Even more striking are the equivocations over the denouement of *La forza del destino*. The first version (1862) ends in the same way as the Spanish play: after killing Don Carlo, who has stabbed the heroine, Leonora, the hero, Don Alvaro, hurls himself in despair over a cliff, shouting blasphemies, to the horror of the monks below.

By May 1863 Verdi was obviously dissatisfied with this overly Romantic ending and sought a solution among his circle of friends. "Tell me," he wrote Ricordi in December 1864, "don't you know any poet, any literary friend who could find me a denouement for this opera?"[14] The publishers Ricordi and Escudier and Emile Perrin, director of the Opéra, all got into the act, then the librettists Piave, Achille de Lauzières, and Ghislanzoni; there was talk of consulting García Gutiérrez (author of *El trobador*) and even the Duke of Rivas, author of the play from which the libretto was derived. Finally, in 1868 a solution was found thanks to Ghislanzoni—who was initially excluded—and the revised finale, in which Leonora dies in Alvaro's arms with Il Padre Guardiano comforting them both, began to take shape. It took almost seven years to solve the problem of the denouement, years during which Verdi consulted friends and enemies while his musical invention was blocked for lack of a solution. So it is a mistake to confuse power with the display of power: only the composer disposed, but the librettist proposed, and not infrequently his solutions carried the day.

VERDI AND HIS LIBRETTISTS

The nineteenth century was the librettist's century par excellence. The previous century had been dominated by the figure of the court poet, the "imperial poet" like Metastasio, who achieved a reputation rarely equaled and produced librettos that were set to music repeatedly, sometimes as many as fifty times. The twentieth century saw the emergence of the man of letters, such as Hofmannsthal and Cocteau, D'Annunzio and Calvino, whose collaborations with composers tended toward musical theater. Between the two reigned the librettist, a pure product of the operatic culture of the past century and a scapegoat of the enemies of opera whom it was long fashionable to blame for the absurdities and excesses of the genre.

Who were these librettists? In most cases they were minor writers who found it hard to make a living with their pens and offered their services to a theater. Here they performed various functions, among them that of fashioning librettos.[15] Piave was stage director at Venice's La Fenice theater, where he was responsible for staging operas; Cammarano held a similar post at the San Carlo of Naples. If their talents tended to be modest, they were seasoned practitioners of opera, perfectly accustomed to musical conventions to which they had no difficulty in adapting.

Their subordinate role did not prevent the most gifted among them from deriving a certain pride from their expertise and feeling themselves full members of the world of letters. This is how Felice Romani describes his job: "Do you think it's so easy to reduce a French tragedy or comedy to an Italian melodrama? Render a whole volume in a few pages? Create miniatures of the characters and situations, take a composition made up entirely of dialogues and eliminate the dialogue, its primary element? And then do you think it is easy to satisfy all the musical requirements: to try to meet all the singers' demands, distribute the so-called pieces in such a manner that one party doesn't get angry at the other, arrange the scenes without letting them get monotonous, using sopranos here, basses there, combine poetic inspiration with practical necessity, widen a concept into a particular number of verses and meters, and narrow it down to so many verses of a particular measure? To say everything in a few words and be brief without being obscure?"[16]

Economic conditions were hard for these librettists. If attached to a theater, they suffered at the hand of administrations that were often fool-hardy in their risk taking. When they wrote librettos, they were paid infinitely less than the composer, in contrast to the situation in France, where rewards were approximately equal: for *Ernani,* Piave's remuneration represented around one-fifteenth Verdi's; for *Forza,* the contract provided a sum of two to three thousand francs for Piave, whereas Verdi was to receive sixty thousand, twenty to thirty times more than his librettist![17] Hence the librettists' bitterness and the feeble attraction the craft held for literary talents.

Although Verdi always ran the ship, his relations with his librettists varied considerably. His dramatic intuition could make him authoritarian and peremptory, yet, when he had difficulty controlling a situation, this same intuition made him attentive to suggestions, and he often welcomed them. Understandably, it was his first true collaborator, that unusual character Temistocle Solera (1815–78), who proved the most susceptible to influence. Solera turned out five librettos for Verdi: *Oberto, Nabucco, I Lombardi, Giovanna d'Arco,* and *Attila,* that is, exclusively youthful works. The connections between *Oberto* and a preceding opera, *Rocester,* which never saw the light of day and was written by another librettist, are un-clear,[18] while the denouement of *Attila* was completed by Piave, aided by Maffei. These exceptions aside, the librettos have common features that reflect the librettist's personality.

In general, the plots are somewhat muddled, the incidents piling up with little care for probability and tending to culminate in a grand frieze, like a huge historical painting. The jumble of situations is particularly apparent in the first two acts of *Nabucco,* with its accumulations of coups de théâtre and unexpected entrances. Nor does *I Lombardi* rate any higher on the scale of clarity: in the long prologue we are told a somber story of amorous rivalry between two brothers, but the next acts take off on another love story, that between a Christian and a Muslim. Thus, one of the first steps taken by Alphonse Royer and Gustave Vaëz, who were responsible for transforming *I Lombardi* into *Jérusalem,* was to bring together these two distinct plots. *Attila* suffers from the same structural fault as *Vêpres,* which is based on the foreboding of a massacre that does not take place until the fifth act. In the earlier opera, the tyrant's murder overhangs the action, but the similarity of events produces a feeling of redundancy, as though each act reproduced the same scenario, slightly modified.

The hodgepodge of melodrama in these operas is bathed in a politico-mystical atmosphere that gives them the aura of epic, largely compensating for the incoherence of the plots. Solera's patriotic fervor shows in all his Verdian librettos, whether the theme be the struggle of the Hebrews against the Assyrians *(Nabucco),* the French against the English *(Giovanna d'Arco),* the "Italians" against the Huns *(Attila),* or the Crusaders against the Infidels *(I Lombardi).* Allied with this fervor is a religious zeal that turns a war of national liberation into a divine mission and sanctifies those leading the struggle, Zaccaria the prophet, Leone the aged Roman, or the French heroine Joan of Arc—the same religious inspiration that is to be found in that great figure of the Italian Risorgimento, Giuseppe Mazzini. In the operas, this messianic drive relegates plots concerning private individuals to relative obscurity, as though these minor streams of passion were intended to merge with the great river of national regeneration. Very early on, the last scene of *Nabucco* was cut so that the opera ends with the great hymn to Jehovah, while *I Lombardi* has as its finale the vision of Jerusalem, reconquered at last amid a chorus of praise. Clearly, Solera would have liked to end *Attila* in the same manner, as he stated after seeing the way Piave had patched up its denouement.[19]

There is no denying that the young Verdi's rise owes something to the curious personality of Solera. The passion of his earliest operas, the warlike ardor, the rather confused action, the heroic activism, the quest for a more austere, less hedonistic moral climate—all this can be linked with Solera's librettos. Verdi obviously appreciated him, boasting that he had practically never altered any of his texts and acknowledging that his librettist knew about "the theater, dramatic effect and musical forms."[20] Excited by Werner's play, Verdi first entrusted *Attila* to Piave but ended up giving it to Solera, conscious that the martial pageantry better suited the latter's talents. This Solerian phase did not last very long, however, as the librettist went abroad and soon foundered in a chaotic life, while the composer changed genres, finding in Piave a more reliable companion with whom to explore new paths.

Francesco Maria Piave (1810–76) was Verdi's most loyal collaborator between 1843 and 1867, after which, stricken with paralysis, he lingered on in precarious health until his death. We owe him nine operas: *Ernani, I due Foscari, Macbeth, Il corsaro, Stiffelio* (reworked under the title *Aroldo*), *Rigoletto, La traviata, Simon Boccanegra, La forza del destino,* and the emendations to *Attila.* The intervention of other collaborators (Maffei for *Macbeth,* Montanelli for *Simon* pending Boito's revisions, Ghislanzoni, who prepared the second version of *Forza* owing to Piave's illness) should not disguise the fullness of his participation in Verdi's oeuvre.

At the beginning of their collaboration, the composer obviously had many reservations about his librettist's knowledge of the stage[21]—it is true that Piave was just starting out—and Verdi would always reproach Piave for a tendency toward the verbose, hounding him furiously throughout their association. On the other hand he just as readily appreciated his skills of versification:[22] he defended him on more than one occasion, mocking the public's tendency to find fault with his verses before the fact, even if they were not actually his.[23] Yet Piave's personality, and hence his role, remains somewhat enigmatic. The operas for which he was responsible mark the emergence of the idea of the individual as a solitary entity (not as representative of a group), of strong, simple characters racked with overpowering passions. He wrote for Verdi at a time when the composer was drawn closely to individuals pursued by fate in a trajectory bearing them from passion to sacrifice and death.

But does this development owe anything to the Murano-born librettist? Piave's part in such triumphs as *Macbeth, Ernani, Rigoletto,* and *La traviata* makes it absurd to treat him with scorn or to speak of him as "poor" Piave, as has often been the case; yet there is no proof that he influenced the direction of Verdi's dramatic thought in any way. Verdi browbeat him and often treated him like a factotum, but this brusqueness was balanced by an undeniable affection.[24] Indeed, Piave offers the somewhat rare example of a profound sympathy between his personality and

Verdi's moral and cultural world in this period, and Baldini is not mistaken in rehabilitating him; he even goes so far as to name him Verdi's best librettist because, "offering to cancel himself out completely, Piave became the only one who found his own extraordinary, inimitable style—in reality the literary style of Verdi."[25]

The case of the Neapolitan Salvadore Cammarano (1810–52) is quite different. His collaboration with Verdi began with *Alzira* in February 1844 (however, Verdi had sought him out as early as June 1843)[26] and continued with *La battaglia di Legnano, Luisa Miller,* and *Il trovatore,* in which the young Luigi Emmanuele Bardare also participated owing to Cammarano's illness and death. When Verdi began working with Cammarano, he was the most highly respected librettist in Italy since Romani, with triumphs like *Inès de Castro* and *Lucia di Lammermoor* to his credit, and had written for the greats of the day—Donizetti *(Belisario, Maria di Rudenz, Poliuto, Roberto Devereux)*, Pacini *(Saffo)*, and Mercadante *(La vestale, Il reggente)* among them. Hence, Verdi addressed him in a completely different tone: "I read your *programma* and I'm sure that you, a man of such superior talent and character, will not take offense if, in all humility, I take the liberty of telling you. . . ."[27] The numerous criticisms that follow are swathed in velvet.

Verdi and Cammarano argued as equals, and the composer did not always have the last word. In the case of *Luisa Miller,* Verdi was the first to suggest seeking inspiration in Schiller's *Kabale und Liebe,*[28] but Cammarano quickly produced a long, detailed synopsis, followed a few days later by a plan for the distribution of musical numbers.[29] Cammarano had suppressed the political context by transposing the action to a vague Tyrolean village, thereby giving the opera a semiseria coloration. The composer regretted that Lady Milford (Federica) had become insipid—she is a character who might have been an Amneris before her time—and would have liked to give the role of Wurm a comic touch, but he did not insist. In contrast, he asserted himself in the case of the first Finale, which he wanted less conventional than the one Cammarano had suggested, that is, without the Stretta. For the Finale of the third act, it was Cammarano who took the initiative, using typically Verdian arguments to encourage Verdi to close the act with Rodolfo's famous aria "Quand le sere al placido."[30] When it came to *Il trovatore,* on the other hand, the composer proved more combative, proposing his own synopsis in response to that of the librettist, who in turn vigorously defended his choices.[31]

This more egalitarian relationship can be explained not only by Cammarano's fame but also by Verdi's genuine admiration for his expertise. The proof: it was to him and no one else that Verdi would propose sketching a *Re Lear,* a play complex enough for the composer to turn to an experienced dramatist, not a mere versifier. Cammarano was supremely skilled in reducing a complex story to the reasonable dimensions of a libretto, and his plots are in general solidly constructed: *Lucia di Lammermoor* is one of the best librettos of its kind, and, although that of *Il trovatore* is thought of as absurdly complicated, one need only go back to the original Spanish play to admire the way the librettist has divided up the text. He was a proficient versifier—and was renowned at the time for that reason—although tending toward bombast more than Piave. Finally, Cammarano evidently had a great feeling for emotional situations that place the individual as a victim of society or history *(Inès de Castro, Maria di Rudenz, Maria di Rohan),* and it is more than likely that Verdi's change of direction, from *Luisa Miller* on, toward a more intimate dramaturgy that allowed more room for pathos was stimulated by his librettist's talent.

The last example must be Arrigo Boito (1842–1918). His personality has received varying assessments: whereas at the beginning of this century he was thought of as Verdi's only collaborator of worth, his importance has been more accurately judged of late. His style has dated no less than Piave's, his refinement is often mere affectation, and his thinking is irremediably linked to minor currents of European decadence.

In considering his association with Verdi, one is immediately struck by the quality of a personal relationship built up by a particularly fine correspondence, by the richness of a friendship between two profoundly dissimilar men. This was the first time Verdi had worked with a writer much younger than himself and one from a different moral world than that of Piave, Solera, Cammarano, and Somma. Boito was a well-known composer, a versatile poet, and brilliant critic, a respected figure of Milanese culture and a cosmopolitan (he shared in the French translation of the two librettos he wrote for Verdi and supervised the English translation). His world was that of the fin de siècle, characterized by moral lassitude and the feeling of arriving on the scene too late, divided between the demonic and the angelic, between the temptation of irreverence and nostalgia for the sublime, between Baudelaire and D'Annunzio. The encounter of this world with that of Verdi, with its strong-willed moral foundation and pervasive pessimism, was fertile. In Verdi, the librettist found a steadfastness and an energy lacking in his own generation, and he clung to it like a wrecked ship to its buoy. For his part, Verdi found in Boito an intellectual versatility and finesse of mind that helped him plumb the depths of his creativity and turn his back on the dramaturgy of his youth.

The fruits of their collaboration, the revision of *Simon Boccanegra* and the creation of *Otello* and *Falstaff,* required long discussions between composer and librettist. Yet Verdi's constant supervision in no way detracts from Boito's talent for producing a clear, workman-like libretto—an achievement great enough that some prefer *Otello* to *Othello,* while almost everyone finds *Falstaff* superior to *The Merry Wives of Windsor.* If Verdi's corrections were many and prompt in the case of *Otello,* his structural changes were few.[32] And they were practically nonexistent for *Falstaff,* as is indicated by this resoundingly good report the composer issued to his librettist: "The first act is finished without any change in the poetry, exactly as you gave it to me. I believe the same thing will happen with the second act, except for some cuts in the ensemble piece as you mentioned yourself. We will not talk now about the third; but I believe there will not be much to do in that either." Boito's skill as versifier was formidable, as the example of his "rearrangeable" lines, mentioned above, shows. True, Boito wrote copiously, and Verdi often cut, but this proves not so much Boito's verbosity as his desire to provide a "mass of material" so the composer could "tailor the piece in [his] own way and with greater ease."[33]

Did this priceless help go so far as to color Verdi's dramatic thinking, as some have supposed in connection with certain points (e.g., the elimination of the father character)? Boito's ideological influence would be undeniable had it encouraged the composer to break with his former dramaturgy. Yet, as we shall see, Verdi's last two operas are surely the culmination of a long journey that possessed its own inner logic. The man of letters accompanied rather than led the creation of these final masterpieces.

The fact is that, at least in Verdi's case, Boito wholeheartedly embraced the idea of a librettist being ever on the alert for a thought (the composer's) that was trying to find expression. He defined his attitude very precisely at the earliest stages of their collaboration: "So I have been fortunate enough to provide a suitable form for the concept you were seeking. Now in my handiwork you recognize the thought you dictated to me, which I transcribed, not allowing myself to be troubled by any doubt, not even by the doubts you yourself broached. Working in this way, I showed you I attached far greater value to the feeling that inspired you to speak than to your argued considerations about those feelings." Obviously, their relationship had far fewer disagreements than that of Strauss and Hofmanns-thal. For his part, what Verdi asked of his collaborator was to formulate intuitions that he himself had difficulty in expressing. As he put it: "Try to sense what I have been unable to say."[34]

It turned out that, thanks to his intelligence and culture, Boito was better equipped than others for this art of divination. If, as has been suggested, influence is the nurturing of an existing propensity, then the talent of the best librettists lies in this art of helping a dramatic vision evolve in the direction it already wants to go.

The Stages of the Libretto

SOURCES

As a rule, Verdi's librettos are adapted from literary sources, non-Italian for the most part, and never based on original subjects. The sources are German (Schiller for *Giovanna d'Arco, I masnadieri, Luisa Miller,* and *Don Carlos;* Zacharias Werner for *Attila*), Spanish (García Gutiérrez for *Il trovatore* and *Simon Boccanegra;* the Duke of Rivas for *La forza del destino*), English (Byron for *I due Foscari* and *Il corsaro;* Shakespeare for *Macbeth, Otello,* and *Falstaff*), and Italian (Tommaso Grossi for *I Lombardi*). But the greatest source of librettos, in Verdi's time as in Bellini's and Donizetti's, was France; practically half Verdi's operas are derived, directly or indirectly, from nineteenth-century French texts (the one exception being Voltaire, author of *Alzire ou les Américains,* from which *Alzira* is taken). Sometimes the authors are famous, as with Victor Hugo *(Ernani, Rigoletto)* and Dumas *fils (La traviata).* Sometimes their names have been completely forgotten: *Oberto* (if one accepts that it is the source of *Rocester*), *Nabucco, La battaglia di Legnano, Stiffelio.* In some cases the libretto is a mere reworking of a French one: thus, *Les Vêpres siciliennes* is a new rendering of *Le Duc d'Albe* (Scribe and Duveyrier's libretto, suggested to Donizetti in 1839); *Un ballo in maschera* is based on Scribe's libretto for Auber, *Gustave III ou le bal masqué; Jérusalem* is based on *I Lombardi* but represents a total revision; *Un giorno di regno* is derived from a remote play by Pineau-Duval; and *Aida* comes from a French sketch by Auguste Mariette.

The small number of Italian sources is obviously striking (one Italian for thirteen French). If one goes down the list of librettos that Verdi considered and then discarded, foreign names still predominate: Dumas *père* and *fils,* Byron, Scribe, George Sand, Shakespeare, Hugo, Gil y Zarate,

Zorrilla y Moral, and so on. (One great name missing from the list is Walter Scott, who had enriched the repertoire of the period just before Verdi, between 1820 and 1840.) The preponderance of foreign sources is not peculiar to Verdi: Italian librettists devoured by the dozen the plays packing the theaters of Paris and Madrid and the novels being snapped up by the English public, with "hits" being immediately adapted for one or more composers. This explains the important role that opera librettos played in introducing into Italy European Romantic authors and those, like Shakespeare, who were being reassessed during the period. The first Italian performance of the play *Macbeth* took place in Milan in 1849, that is, after Verdi's opera,[35] and the most widely circulated Shakespearean plays in the first half of the century, if only in Ducis's extremely free versions, were *Othello* and *Romeo and Juliet,* that is to say, works that had grown familiar thanks to the operatic repertoire.

As for the Italian authors, the few popular plays of Silvio Pellico and Marenco did not tempt Verdi, and Manzoni's tragedies did not lend themselves well to translation into opera. When, after *Macbeth,* the poet Giuseppe Giusti reproached the composer for his infatuation with non-Italian literature, he replied that he was only too willing to write from Italian texts but that, "unfortunately, you yourself will agree that if we want something that makes a certain effect we must, to our shame, turn to things that are not ours."[36]

Absent insofar as choice of plot goes, the Italian tradition and its greatest representatives like Alfieri, Foscolo, and Manzoni can nonetheless be felt in Verdi's manner of treating stories and in his style.[37] A great admirer of Alfieri, all of whose tragedies he read when young, Verdi set to music *I deliri di Saul* (1837) and gave his two children the highly Alfierian names of Icilio and Virginia. The liking he would later evince for strong, resounding language that energetically "sculpts" a situation or a passion owes much to this youthful enthusiasm for Alfieri. Well known, too, is the deep respect he held for Manzoni, whose ode "Il cinque maggio" he set to music in 1836 and for whose novel *I promessi sposi* he had unconditional admiration. The gradual emergence of the spirit of reconciliation and forgiveness in Verdi's dramaturgy, the struggle to escape the web of violence woven by rancor and revenge, both are closely tied to the influence of the man Verdi called "the saint."

Alfieri, Foscolo, and Manzoni informed the Italian consciousness of the time, including that of the librettists, even when they had recourse to foreign works. Their texts exemplify the two moral trends that Mazzini identified in Italian literature in the early 1840s, led on the one hand by

Foscolo and Byron and on the other by Manzoni: heroic action, energy, and rebellion and consciousness of the tragedy of history, resignation, and compassion.[38] Aside from the influence of any one writer, the weight of tradition can be sensed in Verdi's search for a compromise between Romanticism and classicism, between rebellion and fury on the one hand and acceptance of order and diffuse religiosity on the other. Writings coming into Italy had their most extreme or provocative features excised (and not only by the censors) so that moral dignity was not offended.[39]

One salient feature of the dramatic repertoire on which Verdi drew is that it belongs overwhelmingly to the first half of the century, even in the case of the later operas. *Simon Boccanegra* and *Forza* are based on plays dating from 1843 and 1835, while *Un ballo in maschera* is a reworking of a libretto of 1833 and that of *Vêpres* one of 1839. The latest source in date is Auguste Mariette's scenario published in Alexandria in 1870, the origin of *Aida,* but its dramaturgy was fairly traditional, as Verdi was quick to point out, except for certain protorealist touches the composer hastily got cut out. Strangely, it was with *Traviata* and *Stiffelio,* inspired by plays dating from 1852 and 1849, that Verdi distanced himself the furthest from the heroic Romanticism of the 1830s and came close to a certain contemporary realism. After that, he relied on authors that were even earlier, although playing a strong part in the development of European Romanticism, such as Schiller and Shakespeare. Thus, his development involved not so much a change of dramatic vision as putting the same vision into a fresh perspective.

Verdi's aesthetic classicism led him to view the rise of verismo, around the time of his last operas, with great mistrust. Mascagni's *Cavalleria rusticana* and *L'amico Fritz* date from 1889 and 1891, Leoncavallo's *I pagliacci* from 1892, and Puccini's *Manon Lescaut* from 1893. The dual thrust toward greater documentary exactness and a more complex, even pathological psychology remained alien to Verdi. He had already rejected the slavish imitation of reality in a famous formula quoted in the preceding chapter: "To copy from what is real may be a good thing, but it is photography. It is not painting." He strongly criticized Alfred Bruneau's *Le Rêve,* had little good to say for *L'amico Fritz,* and found more verismo than verity in Massenet's *Le Roi de Lahore.* In general the objections were musical, but, as always, in the end they all went back to the question of dramaturgy.

One last important point concerns the attitude of librettists and composers toward their sources. Frequently, this has tended to be seen in terms of loyalty and treason. But that is an approach totally foreign to the practitioners of the last century, who in fact were looking for a story rather than an author, a plot that they could adapt to their needs. They cut from, added to, and recast works, now forgotten but many in number, all dealing with the same subjects; the result was that sometimes a huge number of operas would come out, each aping the other, with the connection with the main source becoming diluted in favor of a more general connection with a "tradition."[40] Before Donizetti got hold of it, Scott's *Bride of Lammermoor* inspired Adam (1827), Carafa (1829), Rieschi (1831), Bredal (1832), and Mazzucato (1834), a series of operas both similar and varied.[41] Victor Hugo's *Hernani* tempted Bellini before it became the subject of an opera by Gabussi (1834) and another by Mazzucato, which preceded Verdi's by a few months, while his *Attila* is close in time to Malipiero's (1845).[42]

Among this plethora of works inspired by a given subject, mention should be made of the ballets that, even as late as *Otello*, divided the action or followed the curtain of every opera. Often taken from a literary subject, these ballets were a link between the literary source and the libretto, contributing to the building up of what I have called the "tradition" of a subject. Close to a dozen of Verdi's operas were preceded or (less often) followed by ballets on the same subject.[43] *Macbeth* owes nothing to *Macbetto,* a ballet by Luigi Henry performed at La Scala in 1830. On the other hand, *Nabucco* cannot be appreciated solely by reference to its source, a play by Auguste Anicet-Bourgeois and Francis Cornu (1836). This is because certain moments, notably in act 1, are much closer to Cortesi's historical ballet (La Scala, 1838) than to the French source, while the libretto familiar to us came from a combination of several influences: a French play that was filtered through an Italian ballet and reworked by Solera, with prompt interventions from Verdi, not counting echoes of previous operas like Rossini's *Mosè in Egitto!*

We have seen, with examples taken from *Don Carlos* and *La forza del destino,* how Verdi's behavior was no different from that of his contemporaries. What was new, from *Macbeth* on, was that Verdi was perfectly conscious that beyond the plot there was a dramatic thought that gave sense and validity to the story, a guiding concept that might if need be oblige him to stick to the original text. This meant less fidelity to a text in the abstract than familiarity with the great dramatists—Hugo, Schiller, the Greeks, and above all Shakespeare—who guided his vision and understanding of the world. When he noted the reaction of the Paris press to the revised *Macbeth* (1865), he remembered only one reproach, that of not knowing Shakespeare: "Oh, in that they're completely wrong.

It may be that I have not done justice to *Macbeth;* but to say that I do not know, understand and feel Shachespeare [*sic*]—no, by God, no! He is one of my favorite poets. I have had him in my hands from my earliest youth, and I read and reread him constantly."[44] This meditation on the great authors of the stage repertoire, independent of the themes that might be derived, is without equivalent among Verdi's predecessors.

FROM TEXT TO LIBRETTO

The most ungrateful phase in the elaboration of an opera was the search for a subject; the most fundamental stage was that during which, having chosen his text, Verdi undertook to study it and ruminate over it up to the point where the musical sketch took shape: "Remember," he wrote Piave in 1848, "that I like a very detailed *programma* because I need to make my remarks. Not that I think I am capable of judging the work, but because it is impossible for me to make good music if I haven't understood the drama very well and am not convinced by it."[45] To understand a drama, to be convinced by it, was for him to feel the grand lines of its musical realization—the articulation of the pieces, the search for a tonality, a *tinta,* a rhythm. On the other hand, his musical imagination could not take wing except from a satisfactory dramatic situation, as we have seen in the case of the denouement of *Forza,* in which Verdi's musical invention was blocked until he found an acceptable ending.

The progress from a literary text to a libretto had two stages: the general conception and the versification. The first concerned the elaboration of a scenario (*programma* or *selva*), which could be a simple sketch or a more detailed prose libretto: "I will undertake to put *Gustave III de Suède* into verse," Somma wrote Verdi concerning a scenario for *Ballo,* "from the version that you are sending me with all haste. Apart from the division into scenes . . . it would be useful for the sake of the musical rhythm if you could note down in the margin the form of the verses, the type of line and the number of lines for each verse, so I may the more easily offer you the appropriate poetry."[46] In this precise case, as in others (*Macbeth* and *Simon,* e.g.), Verdi took charge. At times, the poet attended to this side of the work, whether on his own initiative or from the composer's more or less precise indications, and Verdi then meticulously supervised the setting in place of the opera's general structure.

The case of *Ernani* is fascinating, for here we have the composer's first, direct reaction, before any synopsis was sketched, when he undertook a staggering condensation of the French play. Act 1 had to telescope no less than the first three acts of Hugo's drama, while the first act of the original would be condensed into an introduction.[47] Here is proof that Verdi's highly synthetic imagination concentrated above all else on the linking of a number of fundamental situations. The scenario that Mocenigo and Piave drew up represented a more traditional conception and demanded a distinct slowing down of the impetus the composer wanted to give the action.

It might be thought that the second stage, versification, was not so important and fell to the poet alone. That would, however, have perpetuated in a diminished form the word-music division that Verdi precisely wanted to get away from. The composer's desire to take charge of every aspect of an opera implied that he had the power to decide what weight to give the text and the music, respectively, depending on the "moments" of the action. This meant that the importance of the word was strictly dependent on the role allotted it by the overall conception: in a fast aria, in the lyrical effusion of a duet, or an ensemble where different texts would be superimposed, the situation of the character counted for more than the detail of the lines, and the composer might even ask for "any verse whatsoever," as he did for the Finale of *Aida*.[48] In a scene where the word was exposed—in key moments of a dialogue, for instance, or in a narrative aria—the text was often more important than the music, and Verdi exercised close surveillance.

The corrections the composer called for were at times purely phonetic, that is, designed to facilitate the singing,[49] but far more often they were semantic and dramatic. Thus, he reproached his German translator for not having respected Otello's triple exclamation—"morta, morta, morta!"—after he has strangled Desdemona: "A natural and heart-rending exclamation! The translation has produced a phrase neither beautiful nor natural ... 'Sweet dear dead one' or something like that."[50] Even stronger are his recommendations to the French translator for the first-act duet of Lady Macbeth and her husband: "The French translator must stick to the words 'follie, follie,' because it is this word and Lady Macbeth's inner sarcasm that carry the whole secret of the effect of this piece." Here the quality of the acoustic image, the closed vowel *i,* which is propelled by the double liquid consonant preceding it and strongly accented by the music, is combined with the semantic value of the word—madness, nonsense—which conveys the hysterical nervosity with which "Lady" attempts to dispel her husband's anguish after Duncan's murder.[51]

To understand fully the importance that Verdi attached to words, one need only glance through the furious annotations with which he peppered the libretto that the Neapolitan censors sent him to replace the first, rejected text of *Un ballo in maschera;* certain notes have to do with situations, but a large number are aimed at specific words he deemed useless or hollow.[52] Again, one has only to follow the correspondence between Verdi and Ghislanzoni over *Aida* to see how the composer always sought the expression that struck him as the most accurate, psychologically and logically, and the one best suited to the character.[53] True, the importance of the text is most obvious in the mature works; we are also better informed about them. Yet the composer's frequent recommendations to his librettists to model their style on that of the writer they are drawing on—as, for instance, to Piave not to leave out, in *Ernani,* "any of those powerful phrases that are in the original and that always make such a grand effect on the stage"[54]—prove that Verdi was concerned very early on about the theatrical effectiveness of his librettos.

PROCEDURES AND PRINCIPLES

How did Verdi intervene in his relations with librettists? Sometimes he was content to send their copy back to them if he found it unsuitable or had changed his mind about a passage. For example, Amelia's aria in act 2 of *Ballo* was redone three times, in lines of five, then seven, then ten syllables. But it was also common for Verdi to try his hand at writing himself, whether in prose or verse sketches. The act 2 Finale of *Forza,* where the Father Superior welcomes Leonora to the monastery, has no equivalent in the Duke of Rivas's play, and Verdi sketched it in prose that Piave changed into verse. The introductory chorus of *Aroldo* (a reworking of *Stiffelio*) was outlined in a mixture of prose and rough lines of verse; on the other hand, Verdi made a second recasting of Azucena's aria "Stride la vampa" from a first draft by the recently deceased Cammarano, then passed it on to young Bardare for the necessary polishing.[55]

Occasionally, the process was still more complicated, and it is hard to tell which writer was responsible for what. For Lady Macbeth's aria "La luce langue" (in the 1865 revision), Verdi drew inspiration from Shakespeare and suggested a first version in prose, followed four days later by a second version in verse—which crossed in the mail with a third version, also in verse, from Piave, which the composer sharply criticized, not without a certain bad faith. Thereupon, Verdi drew up a fourth sketch in verse that Piave amended.[56] Piave had played, as he often did, the part of mirror or punching bag, allowing Verdi to find the formula he wanted by reacting to the inadequacies of the early drafts for which the composer himself was in part responsible.

Verdi's interventions were governed by two great principles, brevity and theatricality. A single quotation will suffice to show how insistently the first requirement appears. Here are Verdi's first recommendations to Piave when he sent him the sketch for *Macbeth:* "The draft is clean-cut, with nothing conventional, nothing missing, and it's short. Make sure that the verses also are short. The shorter they are the better you'll achieve the effect. The first act is a little too long, but it's up to us to keep the pieces short. In the verses, remember there must be no useless word: every word must say something."[57] Librettists were often hampered by this continual harassment since an opera's rhythm was highly variable, slowing down in lyrical numbers and accelerating in the *scene.* Depending on the situation, the text, to use Verdi's expression, had to "run" or to "sing." In the nineteenth century the librettist lost control over the overall rhythm, whence the many misunderstandings and frictions—more humiliating for the librettist than for the composer, who could use these exchanges to hone his dramatic perception.

Far from being peculiar to Verdi, this exigence is common to most Italian opera. In his study of the libretto, Patrick J. Smith rightly claims that one could offer as a motto for the entire Italian tradition, from Rinuccini to Puccini, Rodolfo's reply in *La Bohème:* "La brevità, gran pregio" (Brevity, it's priceless).[58] This often-repeated imperative originates in structural causes that we would do well to recall: generally speaking, every literary source that was made into a libretto was reduced by half to two-thirds. Marcello Conati has calculated that the 1,600 lines of Hugo's *Le Roi s'amuse* were boiled down to 714 in Piave's libretto for *Rigoletto.* Nor does this calculation take into account the adaptation of long lines (the alexandrine) to short (seven or eight syllables); figuring this in, the proportion is approximately one-third.

Furthermore, Verdi lived in terror that the public would be bored and distracted, which explains why, for him, *long* was synonymous with *boring.* The audience must therefore be kept "awake," and brevity was a stratagem to hold attention. Also, the logic of opera did not function like that of the spoken theater: although the spectator had to understand the motivations of an action, these did not necessarily have to be described as minutely as in the play. Opera was based on predetermined codes, and

simply making a character conform to the stereotype he or she represented rendered any additional explanation unnecessary and allowed for
rapid progress of the action.

Other factors pertain specifically to Verdi. Faced with an opera based
in part on alternating active and static sections (Stendhal held that there
was nothing like a recitative for recovering from the emotion of an aria
and nothing like an aria for ending the monotony of recitative), Verdi
relied on *brevità* to shake up this succession of systoles and diastoles and
impose an overarching rhythm on the whole work. The somewhat frenetic fervor of his youthful operas was his way of counteracting the breaks
introduced by recitatives and the vocal cadences of sung sections. Significantly, he boasted of the economy of Solera's recitatives in *Nabucco* and *I
Lombardi.*[59] In another context, Verdi's recommendations to Piave concerning *Macbeth* show that he saw a link between brevity and dramatic
effect. He remained convinced that for a given situation there was a corresponding natural language and that commentary was superfluous. Thus,
when Piave announced triumphantly that the first *Rigoletto* libretto had
fifty-four fewer lines than that of *Stiffelio,* the composer replied coolly:
"No matter that it has fifty-four lines more or less than *Stiffelio;* sometimes twenty lines is long and sometimes a hundred isn't; in the theater,
the lines that could be shortened are always long: an idea expressed in
two lines is long when it could be expressed in just one."[60] Besides being
an attribute of poetry, as we have seen, concision was therefore a means
of attaining Verdi's second great demand, theatricality.

Verdi formulated his constant requirement with great clarity during
the preparation of *Ballo:* "True, you're saying everything that must be
said, but the word does not sculpt well, it isn't clear enough." This is what
Verdi would call, at the time of *Aida,* the *parola scenica.*[61] The reference
to sculpture or to a purely physical dynamic (elsewhere he writes that the
word does not "spurt," does not "leap out" as it should)[62] proves that
Verdi was seeking not so much meaning, which sets up a certain distance
vis-à-vis the action and evaluates it psychologically and intellectually, as
gesture, an immediate, direct transcription of the dramatic "situation." If
one excludes purely informative passages, the word had to establish a
meaning but reproduce as fully and directly as possible the emotion animating the character.

This somewhat restrictive conception of the word allowed Verdi to
mark the boundaries of his domain. It explains the distinction mentioned
above between the "literary" and "aesthetic" value of a text and its theatrical effectiveness, a distinction that also had the practical advantage of hu-

moring his poets' egos while at the same time making them rewrite dozens of "beautiful" lines. The important thing is that in this way Verdi purged opera of any trace of the rationalist, reflective aesthetics that predominated in the preceding century, where the sweep of a passion would be expressed in pompous arias that shifted interest away from the plot.

In keeping with this approach, Verdi seized on any language that smacked of meditation or generalization, anything that made for opacity or created a gap between action and words: idioms or plays on words, allegories, affectations (which he sometimes had occasion to censure as Boito's pet vice).[63] He tormented his collaborators, urging them to lighten, tighten, and pare down their language so that the meaning would become clear. When, after betraying his country, Radames is surprised by Ramfis, he yields to the high priest, and Ghislanzoni suggested two lines: "Io qui resto, su me scenda / Il tuo vindice furor" (I remain here, on me bring down / your vengeful fury). Verdi preferred the more dramatic "Io qui resto, o sacerdote" (I remain here, O priest), which is very close to the definitive version, "Sacerdote, io resto a te."[64] This is one example among many. Constant pressure from the composer could produce overemphasis or even bad taste, but for the most part it did ensure the direct, effective language of the Verdian librettos.

How did this condensation work? It may be useful to cite an example from *Macbeth*. In the banquet scene, Macbeth is about to sit on his throne when he sees there the ghost of Banquo, visible only to him. The original English lines that were transposed into the Italian rendering unchanged are given in italics (the other characters' cues are given to the chorus):

MACBETH: *Which of you have done this?*

LORDS: *What,* my good lord?

MACBETH: *Thou canst not say I did it; never shake*
    Thy gory locks at me.

ROSS: Gentlemen, rise; *his Highness is not well.*

LADY MACBETH: *Sit,* worthy friends. My lord is often thus,
    And hath been from his youth: pray you, keep seat.
    The fit is momentary; upon a thought
    He will again be well. If much you note him
    You shall offend him and extend his passion.
    Feed, and regard him not. *Are you a man?*

MACBETH: *Ay, and a bold one that dare look on that*
    Which might appall the devil.

LADY MACBETH: O proper stuff!

This is the very painting of your fear;
This is the air-drawn dagger which, you said,
Led you to Duncan. O! these flaws and starts—
Impostors to true fear—would well become
A woman's story at a winter's fire,
Author'd by her grandam. Shame itself!
Why do you make such faces? When all's done,
You look but on a stool.
MACBETH: Prithee see there! *behold! look! lo!* how say you?
Why, what care I? *If thou canst nod, speak too.*
If charnel-houses and *our graves must send*
Those that we bury back, our monuments
shall be the maws of kites. (Ghost disappears.)[65]

Shakespeare's twenty-five lines are reduced to nine; the action and theatrical effects are retained, as are the striking images (e.g., the "gory locks"). The semantic loss is obvious, but on the one hand Verdi chooses to accentuate the relationship of Macbeth and Banquo (the reason Lady Macbeth's words are ruthlessly cut), and on the other he wants the lines he has kept to draw the audience's attention to a dramatic scene that owes its intensity to the music alone.

CENSORSHIP

Any study of the libretto is bound to mention the crushing role of censorship.[66] Verdi was constantly at odds with the censors, and he had to sustain a particularly long and trying fight on two occasions. The first, in Venice, concerned *Rigoletto,* whose libretto was accepted only after lengthy negotiations. The other, in Naples, concerned *Un ballo in maschera,* whose first libretto was disallowed in spite of Verdi's and his librettist's many precautions. One version, thoroughly revised, was then proposed to Verdi, who turned it down. The case had to be taken to court, and the affair ended in a transaction freeing Verdi from his contract.

To understand the power the censors wielded, it should be remembered that their field of action included not only politics (attacks on ruling regimes or manifestations of nationalist feelings) but also religion and morals. Censorship was more or less strict depending on the state—fairly flexible in those states controlled by Austria, more meddlesome in papal Rome and the Naples of the Bourbons. It also varied with the age: the

relatively tolerant atmosphere that prevailed before 1848 became asphyxi-
ating after the failure of the revolutions.

Its presence was felt through endless petty annoyances. In Rome, for
instance, librettos were subject to censorship from three different bod-
ies—the ecclesiastical authorities for religion, ethics, and morals; the government for politics and respect for law and persons; and the municipali-
ties for an examination of the language. Librettos had to be presented in
forty-one copies (understandably, the librettists hated copying out their
work forty-one times!), and the costume designs, maquettes of scenes,
publicity brochures, program, and posters had to be presented as well.[67]

Any allusion to religion was forbidden. God became "a divinity," the
church a "temple," hell Hades, and Lucifer Erebus. Even the first name
Christian was suspect since it included the word *Christ*. Nor was it advisable to show a royal personage on the stage: thus, the king of France
becomes a duke in *Rigoletto,* while the king of Sweden in *Ballo* is demoted
to the rank of duke and eventually simply governor. Finally, freedom of
morals was severely censured. In *Le Roi s'amuse,* when François I arrives
at the inn owned by Saltabadil, whose sister is a prostitute, he asks for
"Your sister and some wine." This reply is replaced in the present libretto
of *Rigoletto* by "a room and some wine," and, since it is easy to guess what
the king-duke is going to do in the room, a revision of the opera refers
simply to "a chair and some wine"! The representation of adultery, a favorite subject of Romantic opera since it sets up a passion-duty conflict,
was highly suspect, so efforts had to be made to attenuate its seriousness
by expedients: an adulterous woman was to have married her lover, but
her family married her off to another, and her passion then became an
unquenchable flame; or the lover had saved the young woman's life, and
gratitude had, in all innocence, turned into love.

In such ways the censors carried out a systematic whitewashing of librettos, choosing expressions that were as neutral as possible and banning
any direct allusion to contemporary reality. Librettists and composers
were forced to put up with pompous, meaningless language, hoping the
audience would be able to decipher it. In fact, as in any oppressive regime,
the public was extremely cunning: there was nothing surprising in the
change from the Lion of Castille in *Ernani* to the Lion of St. Mark, which
flattered Venetian pride, or in the change, in the same opera, of the hymn
to Charlemagne to a hymn to Pius IX, a champion of the hopes of moderate patriots of the time; yet who could have foreseen the incident that
caused *La traviata* to be banned in Rome? When in act 3 the doctor tells

Annetta that "phthisis leaves her [Violetta] but a few hours of life," the Roman audience transmuted the heroine's death agony into that of the papal government, with *tisi* becoming *crisi* (crisis), with the result that everyone was overjoyed to see Violetta die.

The problem was far more serious when the censors wanted to strike at the basic dramatic structure, to refashion the story in some way rather than merely the language. Mario Lavagetto has studied the counterfeit copies of *Rigoletto* that were written for other cities, naturally without the composer's consent. These show how the alterations tended to correct elements of the plots that were considered shocking: for example, a married, freethinking prince who goes unpunished by any earthly or divine power or a grotesque, crippled buffoon who rises up suddenly like a judge to avenge his daughter's honor. In one case, the Duke's licentious character is softened and turned into inconsequential gallantry, while Rigoletto becomes a cantankerous, vindictive plebeian. In another, the Duke of Mantua loses his rank of prince and is made a common seducer who must receive the punishment of man and God: before him rises a Rigoletto shorn of his hump, or, in other words, ennobled and conforming more closely to the traditional image of the father, the guardian of virgins' honor.[68]

Seeing the censors meddle with the structure of his dramas, Verdi rose up in protest and grew uncompromising. A glance at the list of subjects the Naples censorship disputed in the libretto later called *Un ballo in maschera* shows that nothing was left of the original libretto: (1) Amelia's adulterous passion for Riccardo; (2) regicide (Gustav III is assassinated for both political and private reasons); (3) magic (Amelia hopes to extinguish a forbidden love with a magic herb); (4) fate, which appears in Ulrica's prophecy of the protagonist's death, and chance, which aids fate in the lottery scene; (5) the disguises in the masked ball scene, because they hid individual identities; (6) the combination of comic and tragic, which cast a frivolous light on such grave offenses as adultery.[69]

One should, however, give the censors credit for seizing on librettos that effectively questioned certain fundamentals of traditional dramaturgy: in this their blindness was a form of clairvoyance. They should be credited, too, for their stubbornness, which called forth an equal stubbornness on the part of the composer, forcing him to expose and explain in detail the coherence of a dramatic organism whose integrity he was determined to defend. The notion of an "instinctive" composer no longer holds up in the face of the lucidity with which Verdi explains the logic of his thinking. On the other hand, it is impossible to appreciate precisely the most obvious consequence of this ever present censorship—an induced spirit of self-censorship that constrained librettists and composers to avoid situations the censors would not have allowed. We know, for instance, that Verdi, echoing Hugo's play (act 3, scene 2), would have liked to write a duet for Gilda and the Duke of Mantua in which Gilda, locked in the Duke's bedroom, would have been startled to discover that the man she thought was a poor student was actually a rake: "But the priests, the monks and the hypocrites would cry scandal,"[70] and in *Rigoletto* the Duke's bedroom door remains obstinately shut. It is certainly not the only opportunity a composer lost to censorship.

THE LANGUAGE OF THE LIBRETTOS

One way to save librettos was to strip them of all literary dignity and give them a merely utilitarian function, that of providing the spectator with a modicum of information so that he could understand the plot and directing his musical perception toward meanings it did not automatically suggest. This was done by stressing key words—*honor, love, revenge*—even if the details of the text were lost in the flood of sound. In short, once the listener was on track, the libretto's job was done, and it could disappear in a meaningless jumble. As Marcel Beaufils nicely puts it, "without [the key words], the miracle would not take place. Present, they are no more than contrivances."[71]

It should be obvious by now that this expedient was far from satisfactory for Verdi. Librettos were also the foundation on which the operatic convention was built, and their language and style therefore testified to an intimate connection with the genre itself. The truth of opera was conveyed by means of artifice since the aesthetics of melodrama, which as we will see is the very bone structure of Verdi's world, presupposed exaggerated effects, characters that were larger than life, and emphatic gestures. This world of grandiloquence and tension needed an appropriate language, one as alien to everyday realism as music can be. It needed a code where nothing was said simply or in an ordinary way. It should be a sort of Esperanto, a vapid, rather surrealist tongue, as Luigi Dallapiccola has described it,[72] a language absurd when considered on its own but perfectly adapted to its purpose.

It is difficult for non–Italian speakers to imagine what this totally artificial language was really like. To take another example, the parlance of French opera was a middle-of-the-road one that, aside from a few conventional terms and turns of phrase, was not very different, as regards syntax and vocabulary, from that of contemporary novelists or present-day French. Now, such a language did not exist in an Italy where people spoke chiefly dialect and Italian was the language of culture. The librettists resorted to a poetic and erudite language, one far removed from everyday speech. This language, which a Manzoni or a Leopardi made expressive by dint of work and genius, was the basic idiom of the librettos. The librettists adopted its free, elaborate syntax, which abounded in inversions. In this vocabulary, everything had a code name: *house* became *dwelling (la magione);* the *sword,* a *blade (un brando); marriage, Hymen (imene); anger, choler (cruccio),* and so on, if one can make these very rough equivalencies. Money existed only as *gold,* and one told the time only by observing the path of the sun.

Added to this specificity as to vocabulary and syntax, which made the language of opera unreal, was rhetoric: the lake crossed in *I due Foscari* is the "liquid path" (act 2, scene 2), the forest that Zamoro explores in *Alzira* is the place "where the sun's rays rain down less ardently" (prologue); the moon in *Trovatore* is the "nocturnal lamp" (act 1, scene 3), the cannon announcing Charles V's election in *Ernani* becomes an "ignivomous [fire-spitting] bronze" (act 3, scene 1), while the bells in *Battaglia* are "sacred bronzes" (act 4, scene 2). The Homeric epithet is de rigueur: in *La battaglia,* the women are unsuited to war *(imbelli),* the old men trembling *(tremuli),* and the children innocent (act 4, scene 1). In a throwback to the baroque era, in a famous aria in *Traviata,* the fevers of love are compared to consumption. Also favored are brilliant effects, shattering stichomythic lines. As the sensibility of the age called for greater vehemence, no excess was barred; thus, in Cammarano's *Inès de Castro,* Gonzalo's expression is that of a "tiger athirst for blood." Solera describes Attila as follows: "His sword is a bloody comet, / His voice the thunder of heaven. / In the clash of a thousand tempests / His eyes dart the fury of battle" (prologue, scene 2).

To say that this language is beautiful is nonsense, but it is certainly hard to imagine Romantic melodrama without it. Verdi's sketches are not devoid of it—which is all the more striking in that his letter-writing style is one of the most incisive, terse, and unaffected conceivable. Solera even credited him with coming up with a line that is particularly absurd in its naive expressiveness. When, in *I Lombardi,* Oronte tries to convince Giselda that, if she follows him into the desert, their love will suffer from this retreat from civilization, he cries that they will have "only the cry of the hyena as their song of love" (act 3, scene 3).[73]

The standard language of librettos was perfectly suited to nineteenth-century opera, but it was scarcely adaptable to new forms of expression and had almost no capacity for evolution. As a result, any time Verdi strayed from the beaten path of traditional dramaturgy, problems of language immediately arose; he had, for example, the greatest difficulty finding a satisfactory style for rendering the language of Shakespeare's witches in *Macbeth*. When it came to writing *Traviata,* an opera with a contemporary setting and a plot devoid of all heroics, he found—with an amazing sureness of touch—a musical style free of overdramatization or bravado. The libretto should, one feels, have had a language closer to everyday speech as a consequence, but Piave did not follow suit, and expressions that could be tolerated in a medieval context ring false in the Paris of Louis-Philippe.[74]

Verdi's dramatic inspiration changed style with ease, but only rarely did the language adapt in turn, so heavy was the weight of academic tradition and so strong the demand for an exalted stylistic tone. If Piave has recently come back into favor, it is because, for all its faults, his style seems exactly contemporary with Verdi's; conversely, if Boito has lost some of his prestige, the reason is that, despite his excellent qualities, he was caught up in a stylistic conservatism and a concern for "good writing" and so was hard put to keep pace with Verdi's modernity.

$\mathscr{M}elodrama$

A happy life is impossible: the finest
thing that man can realize is an
heroic life.
ARTHUR SCHOPENHAUER,
Parerga und Paralipomena

A Monumental Aesthetics

MAJESTIC AND PASSIONATE

Seeking to define what he calls Verdi's "first manner," covering the decade from 1839 to 1849, from *Oberto* to *La battaglia di Legnano,* Basevi describes it as "majestic." This cult of the majestic, he says, Verdi borrowed from Rossini at the time of *Nabucco* but put to general use where his predecessor had limited it to choruses and ensembles. Acting as a counterweight to the majestic is "the passionate," which, lest it be overpowered by the majestic, must be exaggerated, giving a uniform color of emphasis to the whole work.[1] This view of the young Verdi was largely shared by contemporary critics, whose pens issued forth the same judgments:[2] intensity of passions, grandiosity of situations, epic verve, brutality, crudeness. Although at times admired, this aesthetics was more often derided because the critics tended to confuse majestic with earsplitting.[3] Still, if the young Verdi was the composer of *Nabucco,* he was also responsible for *I due Foscari,* for *Attila,* but also for *Macbeth,* and the notion of the majestic implies amplitude of expression and not necessarily abuse of the brass and bass drum.

Since "the style is the man," it has long been fashionable to see as the cause of these excesses "the dominating force that constitutes the basis of Verdi's genius," to adopt Théophile Gautier's formula. True, the composer was notoriously impulsive by nature, given to sudden rages and extreme reactions. Some recent authors even go further and depict Verdi as a rugged, aggressive savage rising from a land of violence, born of the community of Parma, a "formidable, unruly people" whom Barilli describes, approvingly, as factious and given to brawling.[4]

These extrapolations, obviously inspired in Barilli's case by nostalgia for a "healthy barbarism" that modern civilization has done away with, tend to lose sight of the fact that Verdi was above all a man of order and legality ("I detest everything that is unlawful and out of place," he was wont to say).[5] Conservative from his late thirties on, he hated disorder, was always scrupulously mindful of his promises, and was inclined to be somewhat rigid in his personal life. What is fascinating is not the indisputable violence in his nature but rather its mixture of impulsiveness and control, impetuosity and formality, libertarian thinking and traditionalism. Indeed, one never knows whether it is a case of form, as a discipline, dominating nature (like the barbarian yielding painfully to civilization) or nature trying desperately to escape the constraint of order (the stern bourgeois disciplining his violent impulses to excess).

Nevertheless, a temperament does not explain a style, especially if the latter conforms to an already old tradition and does not actually turn it upside down. As we have seen, opera aesthetics tended at the time toward a certain sublimation of situations and characters that suggested ideals and stereotypes. As Basevi aptly observes, "It is important to note that by its very nature the majestic destroys individuality and personality, transforming them into universals; thus, though a majestic piece may be sung by a single character, it strikes the listener as being expressed by a nation, a caste or an order of people."[6]

From the time of *Nabucco,* the composer's third opera but his first major success, Verdi stands out not so much for any revolutionary techniques as for a new attitude and for the meaning he gives to conventional formulas. The customary arrangement of the drama into arias and ensembles is separated from the process of sublimation, with the result that passions and situations can be projected toward the absolute of an unequivocal gesture by which the character totally fulfills his or her destiny. In order to explain the moral foundation of this aesthetics of the majestic, I shall have recourse to Georg Lukács's analyses in his *Soul and Form.*

Pondering the meaning of Kierkegaard's breaking off of his engagement to Regine Olsen, the Hungarian writer interprets it as the effort to concentrate the significance of a life, its moral value, into an exemplary gesture: "A gesture is nothing more than a movement that clearly expresses something unambiguous. Form is the only way of expressing the absolute in life; a gesture is the only thing which is perfect within itself, the only reality which is more than mere possibility. . . . The gesture is the leap by which the soul passes from one into the other, the leap by which it leaves the always relative facts of reality to reach the eternal certainty of forms."[7]

Why this irrational striving for the definitive gesture that instantly affirms the truth of a whole life? In order, says Lukács, to fight against inconsistency and the wearing away of meaning against everyday reality: "The gesture is the great paradox of life, for only in its rigid permanence is there room for every evanescent moment of life, and only within it does every such moment become true reality. Whoever does more than merely play with life needs the gesture so that his life may become more real for him than a game that can be played by an infinite choice of moves."[8] In describing this quest, Lukács speaks of *monumentality,* and the term, close to Basevi's *majestic,* brings us back to Verdian melodrama and sheds light on its meaning: to depict archetypal characters and situations in order to reach a fullness of significance that everyday reality does not offer with the same clarity. From this viewpoint, excess is necessary so as to attain essence, just as form is needed to arrive at the absolute of meaning.

From his study of the unambiguous, defining gesture, Lukács draws several consequences. The first is the dismissal of psychology insofar as it is concerned with the details of reality: "Where psychology begins, monumentality ends. . . . Once psychology has entered into a life, then it is all up with unambiguous honesty and monumentality. When psychology rules, then there are no gestures any more that can comprise life and all its situations within them. The gesture is unambiguous only for as long as the psychology remains conventional." The philosopher goes so far as to set up an antimony between realism, of which psychology is one of the instruments, and tragedy.[9]

This idea of opposition between gesture and the everyday, between psychology and monumentality, realism and tragedy, is enlightening with regard to Verdi's dramas. It makes it possible to rebut the often-leveled reproach that they lack "psychology," that they schematize characters and portray them conventionally—precisely because of the claim that conventional psychology is an indispensable condition for a monumental aesthetics! Lukács's idea explains the lofty indifference of Verdian heroes for the contingencies of day-to-day life and their way of sweeping aside with a peremptory gesture any objections a literal-minded person might raise. For these heroes, it is enough to exist, to assert the fullness of a passion and the truth of a gesture: an Ernani, a Manrico, or a Duke of Mantua can have just as much dramatic truth as a fully rounded character.

Dismissing psychology, Lukács emphasizes the clarity and total transparency of gesture; this unambiguity conveys the moral unity that must burst forth in the gesture, inasmuch as the gesture sums up a life and gives it meaning. That is why ambiguous, contradictory characters like Rigoletto and even Macbeth would challenge Verdi's early dramaturgy and could only force it to evolve. The kind of dramatization in which each character stakes his all whatever the circumstances, as if every instant were the supreme moment, comes from the asthetics according to which one gesture can state the meaning of an entire life.

We have here an explanation of the relatively narrow range of feelings in Verdi's early works as compared with those of composers both before and after him. To take one example, Mozart "describes" love, and this description takes him to love as passion, love as badinage, love as pride, love as eros, love as tenderness, and so on, enabling him to offer a vast and subtle range of feelings. Verdi, at least at the beginning of his career, does not describe love but presents it as a vindication of existence, with no nuance or alternative, as though the character has no choice but is faced with love or nothing, either fullness of life or nonexistence. In short, the composer's aim is not to depict reality but to proclaim heroism, which relegates specificity of feelings to the shadows. His approach went back to a profound attachment to a world where man forcefully claimed the right to fulfill his destiny to the utmost, even were it to entail his destruction.

MELODRAMA AND "MÉLO"

Although the Italian term *melodramma* has operatic connotations, the English word conjures up not opera but stage melodrama, especially the genre that had its heyday on the Parisian stage between 1800 and 1840 and was linked to writers like Guilbert de Pixérécourt and Caigniez (dubbed the Corneille and Racine of the boulevards).[10] Yet there are precise links between the two genres, for several of these authors inspired librettists. For example, Anicet-Bourgeois, whose play *La Vénitienne* (actually taken from a novel by James Fenimore Cooper) is the source of Mercadante's *Il bravo,* wrote, with Francis Cornu, *Nabuchodonosor,* the origin of *Nabucco.* This same writer was responsible for *La Nonne sanglante* (inspired by a novel by M. G. Lewis), which Gounod set to music in 1854. Adolphe Dennery (or d'Ennery), the author of the extremely popular *Les Deux Orphelines,* discussed a possible libretto with Verdi, while Benjamin Antier is the author of *Rochester,* the remote ancestor of *Oberto.*

What operatic melodrama and stage melodrama have in common is one-dimensional characters that essentially represent great moral categories. The authors of a polemical work published in 1817, *Traité du mélodrame,* who signed themselves A!A!A! (for Abel Hugo, Victor's brother, Armand Malitourne, and Jean-Joseph Ader), put forward a typology based on four characters, although it differs from the one I am about to suggest.[11] As they describe it, one fundamental feature of the technique of *mélo* is to tell all, to leave nothing in the shade; another is that of condensing a life, passion, or moral truth in a telling formula. The authors amusingly sum up a melodrama with a list of emphatic interjections and exclamations, much as people make fun of Italian opera for its key words—*pietà, maledizione, vendetta,* etc.

The book describes certain motifs that were to prove popular in opera, for instance, the lonely spot where secret treasure is hidden (Rigoletto's house), an interrupted wedding ceremony, the return of a character presumed to have vanished, and so on. Certain techniques are also common to both genres: *mélo* usually ends in a tableau, just as opera ends in a grand concertato bringing together all the characters. With typical irony, the authors pretend to applaud this custom: "There is moreover another usage that meets with our approval. At the end of each act, care must be taken to assemble all the personages, making each one assume the attitude best adapted to his state of mind. For example: grief will bring his hand to his forehead; despair will tear his hair out; joy will kick one leg in the air. This ensemble is called a tableau. And we all know how the spectator likes to be able to grasp each character's mood at a glance, yet one more time."[12]

Nonetheless, the resemblances between opera and melodrama are analogies of means rather than ends. Boulevard melodrama, at least up to the 1820s, was an edifying, pedagogical theater (some claim it formed the basis of the morality of the Revolution), one that proclaimed the solidity of the new bourgeois values and showed how they had triumphed over all obstacles. Hence a naive, faintly perverse moralism that preferred to affirm the triumph of virtue by showing the horrors of vice. Operatic melodrama, in contrast, had no pedagogical pretensions, springing as it did from roots that were more classic, dramatic, and tragic. Peter Brooks's highly convincing analyses of the persistence of the spirit of melodrama in the work of major writers like Hugo, Balzac, Conrad, and Dostoyevsky show, however, that such structural analogies between *mélo* and the other arts are valid, not simply a desire to schematize a popular literature.[13] Melodrama's aesthetics of the gesture reflects the need to make a meaning glaringly apparent, to proclaim the unity of a character's behavior as well as its moral significance. In other words, the melodramatic approach seeks to reaffirm, in unambiguous fashion, a commitment, a meaning, and a value that completely fail to come across unless backed up by the expressiveness of gesture.

Grammar of Melodrama

Ever since Shaw's famous epigram—that Italian Romantic operas are about a tenor and a soprano who want to make love and a baritone who won't let them—it has often been said that these operas seem to feature the same characters, even if the names, costumes, and social standing may vary, and that they tell very similar stories in spite of historical and geographic differences. The need for brevity requires the characters to be presented in summary fashion; their scanty background has to be amplified by drawing on a set of conventions linking them closely to a known type so that there is no need to know more about them. In other words, behind each character is the silhouette of a type signaled by voice, dress, and age that can be recognized by the spectator. This same preexisting code made it easy for a play or novel to be adapted to the operatic stage. A minor drama that was doomed to oblivion, having had only ephemeral success, could communicate just as well as an outstanding work of the theatrical repertoire since both plays were based on conflicts and characters common to the operatic world.

Despite the self-evidence of the preceding observations, only rarely has anyone tried to develop them into a systematic study. The most serious and convincing attempt, that of Mario Lavagetto, takes the form of a narrative grammar such as might be drawn up for the novel or the theater.[14] It stresses the logical aspects of the narration and its semantic content rather than its moral or symbolic parameters. For this reason Lavagetto is forced to leave out music, which superimposes its own articulations and logic on the unfolding of the narrative.

In addition, the bond set up between the spectator and a character is very closely tied to the moral value with which he endows that character. In the last century, the spectator thrilled to characters he identified with because of their total transparency: he loved the hero's desperate struggles, suffered with the heroine whose dream of love was unjustly shattered, hated the implacable tyrants or cruel fathers opposing the young lead. In his nostalgic description of the working-class audiences in the Pagliano theater of nineteenth-century Florence, Aldo Palazzeschi gives a graphic description of this passionate fervor: "The center of all aspirations was always the tenor. He was involved in the most exciting and complicated situations. He was also the victim of a most unjust fate, fighting like a lion to his last, dying breath, which usually coincided with or immediately followed that of his beloved—both victims of fatality. He was a gallant warrior, a troubadour or bandit, always displaying well-shaped legs clad in tight-fitting shiny silk hose, his torso encased in splendid armor, a brocade jacket with golden tassels. . . . And then there was always a dark character interfering with his plans, the basso, a vile, preposterous old man who seems to have been born for the mere purpose of driving the tenor to despair by making absurd claims on the soprano or trying to tear her away from him. The basso was detested by everybody, even the lamplighters. Who wasn't ready to kill him with his own nails, this impossible villain who dared interfere in the most abject manner with the great love for which the tenor had endured so much hardship and fought so valiantly?"[15]

Thus, the character asserts himself by his moral clarity and by the way he personifies a fundamental attitude; the more complete the incarnation, the deeper the bond. As Ronconi aptly points out: "Far more than on the stage of the spoken theater, the characters in opera are a kind of collective representation of what the public aspires to at a given time. A character is shaped in conformity with the public's taste, to what it wants to see and listen to and what it expects from certain situations."[16] As in the *mélo* studied by Brooks, they are not so much creatures of flesh and blood as "pure psychic signs" whose connections with one another mark the boundaries of an area of dramatic conflict.

This explains why, rather than a strictly narratological and semantic perspective, I have chosen a grammar based on the moral and symbolic meaning of the characters and the play of conflicts that their attitudes bring about. This typology concerns only the principal characters, not the "utility" parts: in the extremely hierarchical world of opera, minor characters were even more minor than in the theater, having in general to content themselves with a few cues. They performed a very precise "technical" function (e.g., the messenger) or revolved around a leading character (the confidant).[17]

MORPHOLOGY OF CHARACTERS

Types

Verdi's operas are built on four types: the hero, the tyrant, the heroine, and the judge. For the moment, these types are abstract characters, but we will see later on how they take on flesh and blood in the concrete characters of the opera. They are defined, above all, by their moral attitude, an attitude usually associated with a vocal register, a family situation, or a political position.

Attitude should not be confused with actions, even if the one is the origin of the other. In opera, actions are less important than intentions in defining an attitude: on the one hand, a character will often announce his or her intention to act without proceeding to the act itself, the announcement providing a sufficient moral credential. On the other hand, the same action takes on a totally different meaning depending on the character with which it is associated. The heroine may be the victim of an abduction, and, if she is abducted by the hero, the act will appear to be legitimate, an attempt to rescue his lady from a hateful guardian. If the heroine is abducted by the tyrant, the act will appear as an unconscionable abuse of power and, if by a judge, as the wish to punish a rebellious young woman. The attitude is fundamental to arousing the spectator's emotional reaction.

The hero is the type whose heart bleeds for mankind and who "speaks of the universal order as a perversion of the law of the heart and its happiness," to use Hegel's expression.[18] Desire, freedom, and legitimacy are brought into play in his moral sphere. He loves, but it is not love that defines him—after all, other types love no less vehemently—but the fact that his love is shared. This free, reciprocated consent is the basis of his legitimacy (the law of the heart)—a legitimacy that is opposed to other legitimacies (the universal order). To sum up, he personifies individualism as a claim to base all legitimacy on the free consent of individuals, and it is this broad definition that gives him quite naturally a political or national dimension.

The tyrant is a familiar figure in the world of opera, but the character actually evolved over time. In the eighteenth century he was sometimes a powerful, although treacherous, individual, but in most cases he represented a good king led astray momentarily by passion who returns to the path of reason. In early Romantic dramaturgy the tyrant is often confused with a usurper who seizes the lawful sovereign's throne. Nevertheless, the tyrant's sphere is always characterized by force, along with the feeling that the use of this force is evil and illegitimate, even if his political or family situation is itself lawful. If he loves, he uses force to achieve his will since he is not loved in return.

When he carries out his actions in the purely private domain, the tyrant gives rise to a subtype: the male or female rival. Amneris *(Aida)* and Eboli *(Don Carlos)* are rivals who resort to ruse and violence, or at least constraint, to realize their goals.

Properly speaking, the tyrant is a masculine type, but it can apply to women as well: Abigaille in *Nabucco* and Lady Macbeth both try to seize power by unlawful means, the former appearing squarely as the usurper of a throne that is not hers by right. As a political personage, the tyrant is such not by virtue of his power but because he exceeds its lawful limits. He oppresses a people (Nabucco with the Hebrews and Federico Barbarossa with the free Italian communes in *La battaglia di Legnano*) or wields despotic power (Philip II in *Don Carlos*). Finally, there is nothing to prevent a character from exercising the function of both tyrant and rival—in other words, from being tyrannical in both the private and the political domains.

Where the spheres of hero and tyrant meet, there arises a somewhat marginal type, the seducer. There are only three of these in Verdi—Raffaele in *Stiffelio,* who becomes Godvino in *Aroldo* (both secondary vocal roles), Riccardo di Salinguerra in *Oberto,* and the Duke of Mantua in *Rigoletto.* As with the hero, their love is reciprocated (which allows them to be tenors), but they share with the tyrant the fact that this reciprocity has been won by treacherous means: Riccardo lies about his identity in order to seduce Leonora, and the Duke of Mantua passes himself off to Gilda as a poor student. Although the rather prudish nineteenth century had no liking for libertines, it is interesting to note the unique homage Verdi gives Don Juan through the character of the Duke: he does not approve of this "frivolous personage," this "worthless character," but that does not prevent him from being fascinated by his gift of the gab and his cynicism. In the end he gives him three superb solos and makes him a high-class ruffian.

The third type, the judge, is of course the guardian of the law whose actions are dictated by his task of making people respect a law that has been infringed. Even if the means employed to obtain justice seem odious, the validity of this law must not arouse doubt in the spectator's mind. It may be a family law, as in the case of Oberto, who is determined to expunge the insult done to his seduced daughter and thereby his family honor, as well as Rigoletto and Fiesco in *Simon*. Or it may be a conjugal right like the one Stiffelio (and Aroldo) and Otello want to exercise. When his suspicions about Desdemona's fidelity are aroused, Otello reminds Iago, "Otello has his supreme laws," which imply that the guilty will be punished (act 2, scene 3). It may be a politico-religious justice, as in the case of Moser *(I masnadieri)*, Leone *(Attila)*, or Zaccaria *(Nabucco)*: all three have the function of reminding the tyrant of the limits of his power and the threat of divine retribution. Finally, it may be an obligation created by a simple oath that has the force of law: Silva behaves like a judge when, at the end of the opera, he comes and reminds Ernani that the latter promised to die at the sound of the horn. In all these examples, the judge cannot be confused with the tyrant since he only claims his due, and it is this sinister accountancy that gives him his somber beauty.

Establishment of the law and expiation of the offense may take place in a spirit of implacable retaliation or reconciliation. There are thus two categories of judge—the avenger, who ruthlessly applies the *lex talionis,* and the reconciler, who seeks some less bloody reparation. *Oberto* offers both cases: Riccardo has seduced Leonora and is then prepared to marry Cuniza for political reasons. When she learns of the girl's disgrace, Cuniza agrees to give up Riccardo so that he can repair his offense by marrying Leonora (the conciliator). As a good avenger, however, Oberto does not submit to this peaceful solution: "Ben nel sangue lavar dell'indegno / L'onta infame al mio nome saprò" (I will surely wash the shameful stain from my name in the profligate's blood) (act 2, scene 5). The conciliator, extremely rare in the early operas, acquires major importance when Verdi makes an effort to go beyond the bloody chain of transgressions and punishments.

The last type, the heroine, is both the most important, since she is at the heart of the cast of characters (operas that lack love interest are rare), and the most passive, because the heroine is reduced to the role of pawn in a world where women are exchanged, as family interests and politics dictate. It is of course true that, while the heroine can be only a female character, not every female character is necessarily a heroine: we have seen how a woman can be a rival, a tyrant, or even an upholder of the law. She is an object of pleasure for the seducer, an object of conquest for the tyrant, an ornament of the family unit for the judge; only for the hero is the heroine a freely chosen partner. As the term indicates, she is the hero's feminine double, sharing his aspirations of desire, freedom, and legitimacy. Yet she differs from him in that her margin of initiative is extremely restricted: it is true that sometimes the hero, too, is a pawn on the chessboard of interest manipulated by a father (Rodolfo in *Luisa Miller* or the Infante in *Don Carlos*), but he follows his nature and rebels or creates conflict, whereas all action is refused the heroine except deeds that are self-inflicted, that is, sacrifice or suicide. The more active a woman is, the less she is a heroine.

Voices

The spectator becomes aware of the dramatic sense of a character above all through the voice, in accordance with a code that remained perfectly clear throughout the century. The traditional configuration—heroine/soprano, hero/castrato then contralto, villain/tenor—gives way in the first three decades of the 1800s to another configuration: heroine/soprano, hero/tenor, villain/baritone or bass.[19] The common code of these two distributions is simple, at least as far as the men are concerned: the high registers signify youth, purity (both in intentions and actions), loyalty, and spirituality; the voices in the middle range connote maturity, but also strength, and even violence and ruse; while the low voices are associated with the law and greater somberness of character.

With women's roles, the differentiation comes later because the great voices of the first half of the century, *contralto coloratura* and *soprano drammatico d'agilità,* combined a rich, full timbre and a virtuosity that tended toward high pitch. Later, dark color and virtuosity confined to high pitch were separated. Thus, low women's voices came to denote sensuality, ambition, and treachery and high voices spirituality and purity, as witness those famous pairs Amneris and Aida, Carmen and Micaëla in Bizet's opera, Tigrana and Fidelia in Puccini's *Edgar,* and the Princess of Bouillon and Adriana Lecouvreur in Cilea's opera.

The vocal type is determined above all by moral attitude, even if this contradicts the character's age. In his *disposizione scenica* for *Otello,* Boito recalls that Shakespeare's Iago is twenty-eight whereas Otello is over forty, yet the ensign's treachery is entrusted to a low voice.[20] The strength of the code can create optical illusions: for example, Hugo makes Don Carlos and Hernani practically the same age, while Silva is older; yet the vocal distribution leads us to imagine Ernani as a fiery young man, the King of Spain as a man in the prime of life, and Silva a white-haired old man. It is interesting to see how the code is followed when there are several vocal protagonists: in *Don Carlos,* the hero, Don Carlos, is a tenor; Rodrigue, who is also a hero, as we shall see, occupies the next register, that of baritone, relegating to the lower register the tyrant, Philip II (bass), and to darker color the two men of the law represented by the monk and, especially, the Inquisitor (bass). The same pattern holds true in *Attila.*

In this system, the baritone voice acts as a pivot; moreover, a dramaturgy more conflict ridden than its predecessors lent itself readily to expression by this voice. The preference Verdi had for this register and his tendency to stretch it to high pitch, thus creating the Verdi baritone, is well known.[21] The baritone is at the crossing of the ways: close to the tenor because he knows the ravages of passion, he often holds power and through his position as father or leader is familiar with the claims of the law. He is the problematic character par excellence, midway between the other two more fixed types, the hero and the judge. This explains why the category includes both the most odious characters (Iago), the most appealing (the old Miller or Foscari), and, above all, the most complex ones (Rigoletto and Simon Boccanegra).

What is the connection between vocal category and importance in the plot?[22] Usually, the two functions are parallel, but this does not always hold true: Loredano in *I due Foscari,* Walter, Wurm, and Federica in *Luisa Miller,* are only *comprimari,* although they have important plot functions in both dramas. Nineteenth-century opera was based on the classic threesome of tenor, soprano, and baritone or bass, sometimes joined by a fourth voice of any range. Only *Macbeth* has but two leading roles, Macbeth and Lady Macbeth. The first tenor is lacking in just two operas, *Nabucco* and *Macbeth;* the soprano is always present; and the baritone lead is missing in only a handful of operas *(Lombardi, Jérusalem, Oberto).* Twelve operas (or fourteen counting *Aroldo* and *Jérusalem*) have three protagonists, seven include four *(Oberto, Ernani, Attila, Masnadieri, Vêpres, Simon, Aida),* and four have more.

After 1850 there is a noticeable tendency to unlock the stranglehold of this basic triad, leading Verdi, partly under the influence of French opera, to specify five vocal protagonists *(Trovatore, Ballo, Don Carlos)* or even six *(Forza).* Another tendency is to give a key vocal role to a character without dramatic importance: in *Forza,* for example, where two leading roles, Preziosilla and Melitone, exist purely for color. Verdi even wrote that these were the most important parts in the opera,[23] which says volumes about his desire not to adhere strictly to the point of view of the play. Still, the crystal-clear code demanded that certain voices never be associated with certain functions. The tenor is never a rival, tyrant, father, or priest, the soprano never a rival or tyrant. But exceptions prove the rule, as when Verdi uses Abigaille's dramatic register to special effect and insists on the somber, nocturnal color of Lady Macbeth's voice.

Family Situation and Political Position

Analogy plays a big part in opera by setting up a kind of equivalence between the typical nucleus (father and son or daughter) and the political or national community. The equivalence plays both ways. Private conflicts are given a political significance that is perfectly clear to the spectator even if not suggested directly: behind the tenor's claims of love can be sensed the community's aspiration to govern itself freely. In the same way, the judge's persistent efforts cloak the wish to affirm the validity of a traditional order that calls for the submission of the individual. Conversely, political conflicts have more theatrical effect if they are set in family situations, with the result that conflicts are often given such a setting.

To take Bellini as an example, Norma is presented as the daughter of Oroveso and the personification of the rigidity of Gaulish national feeling, which she is not in Soumet's original tragedy; similarly, Mercadante's Vestal Virgin becomes the high priest's daughter, which is not the case in Jouy's original libretto. A simple family setting and a few basic conflicts like love and duty, parental ties and personal conviction, suffice to give the combination a certain variety. In *Les Vêpres siciliennes,* we have a French tyrant, Guy de Montfort, a Sicilian judge, Jean Procida, and a hero and heroine, Henri and Hélène, who side with the judge against the tyrant up to the moment the hero reveals that he is the tyrant's son—a dreadful dilemma for the hero, but also for the heroine! If the situation is logically the same in Scribe's and Duveyrier's *Le Duc d'Albe,* from which the *Vêpres* libretto is derived, it is different in *Giovanni da Procida,* a tragedy by Niccolini (1832): here the heroine is the judge's daughter and the hero the tyrant's son. In Casimir Delavigne's *Les Vêpres siciliennes* (1819), the hero is the judge's son, while the heroine has a certain weakness for the tyrant.

Conversely, the character who, according to the plot, has no family or romantic relationship may risk a certain aridity if he plays only a purely political role: Rodrigue in *Don Carlos,* the exemplary, anachronistic incarnation of a certain liberalism, and Procida, with his rigid, almost fanatic nationalism, test the limits of a character of ideas. Only priests, inquisitors, and prophets elude this rule.

The hero and heroine, tenor and soprano, are potentially son and daughter, if by that is meant a character who lives more or less directly in the shadow of a father. Stiffelio and Aroldo are husbands, but their relationship to their father-in-law places them in a "filial" situation. This is not the case for Otello because of the suppression of the act where Desdemona's father appears. At times the heroine is a wife only, for example, Amelia *(Ballo)* and Desdemona *(Otello)*.

Whether tyrants or judges, the baritones and basses usually belong to the father category, when this parameter has a certain importance. Still, insofar as moral attitude counts for more than family position, we find tyrants who are husbands *(Macbeth)* or sons (Gusmano in *Alzira,* Francesco in *I masnadieri*) and judges who are husbands (Rolando and Renato in *La battaglia di Legnano* and *Ballo*) or even sons (Don Carlo, acting in the place of his murdered father in *Forza*).

TYPES AND CHARACTERS

Let us now examine the relation between actual types and characters in each opera. In order to connect a character to a type, all his or her actions, not merely a single act, must be inspired by the attitude proper to that type. Thus, Amneris "collaborates" with Ramfis, the judge, so as to surprise Radames as he passes on the secrets of the Egyptian army to Aida; that does not make her a judge since her conduct in general qualifies her as a love rival. A character may coincide perfectly with a certain type: Monterone, in *Rigoletto,* is one example of family judge, just as Procida in *Vêpres* or Zaccaria in *Nabucco* personify the political judge. Ernani represents the hero in all his glory, while Nabucco, Attila, or Seid *(Il corsaro)* are tyrants, pure and simple. This total embodiment is convenient because it evokes the memory of the type, associates the character with others that perform the same function in other operas, and so gives the character a sort of chemical purity: the spectator does not really know what the Duke of Mantua has done to Monterone's daughter, but there is no doubt as to the importance of the judge character from his shattering entrance, the Commendatore in person.

The connection of character to type is nevertheless usually more complex:

1. Some characters "await" their function. For two acts in *Ballo,* Renato behaves as a "friend of the hero," watching over his safety like a devoted servant. He thereby enters the hero's orbit like a confidant, even if he is a leading character by voice type. Toward the end of the second act, when he becomes convinced that his wife is deceiving him with his friend, he takes on the austere bearing of the judge. A similar example occurs in *La battaglia di Legnano* with Rolando, the friend of the hero, Arrigo.

2. A character may represent every facet of a type or only certain ones:

Philip II is a tyrant because he suppresses Flanders and denies its people freedom, but he is also his son's rival, taking away from him Elisabeth de Valois, who by the "law of the heart" was intended to be Carlos's.

3. More rarely, two different characters may exemplify the same type: in *Don Carlos,* the Infante takes on the private dimension of hero when he claims a lover's freedom against his father's realpolitik, while his friend Rodrigue, the Marquis of Posa, represents the hero's political side; as such, he becomes the champion of oppressed Flanders and confronts the conservative monarch.

4. Sometimes the character changes function (hence type) during the course of the plot. Up to the end of act 3, Carlo, the king, behaves as Ernani's rival: he attempts to force Elvira to consent, then tries to get rid of Ernani, and finally takes the young woman hostage. But, when he succeeds to the throne, he undergoes a metamorphosis, behaving as a conciliatory judge. He asks Ernani's pardon for his conduct and marries him to Elvira, thus accentuating the opposition with Silva, the vengeful judge who neither forgets nor forgives. Sometimes this change of function is temporary, determined by a subplot. In *La battaglia di Legnano,* Arrigo (hero) and Rolando (hero's friend, then judge) find themselves briefly united as they fight, as political judges, against the tyrant (Federico Barbarossa). But this is only a parenthesis, and in the next act the two characters resume their primary function.

5. Certain characters accumulate functions. The most common example is hero plus judge; if the hero is the defender of the law of the heart, then logically he can become the judge representing this law. When the hero is also a husband, his potential function as judge receives the double seal of social legitimacy and that conferred by the law of the heart—whence the situation of Stiffelio, Aroldo, and Otello. What distinguishes them from judges like Renato or Rolando (*Ballo* and *Battaglia*) is that they remain heroes because of the reciprocity of passion.

6. One character can be answerable to different types, depending on his relation to other characters. In *Trovatore,* the Count de Luna qualifies as tyrant-rival in relation to Manrico and Leonora, but in relation to Azucena he acts as judge because she is said to have killed his brother and, in vowing to have the gypsy burned at the stake, the Count is avenging his brother's and father's memories, in short, his family honor.

7. Certain types are incompatible. The hero cannot be a tyrant, because that would destroy the legitimacy of his claim, or a rival, since that would contradict the fact that his love is returned. In the same way, the tyrant who resorts to force cannot be a judge, who enforces law. Female charac-

ters also give rise to certain incompatibilities. Woman is usually destined to be the object of love, that is, the heroine; by becoming a rival, she is no longer a heroine but does retain characteristics of the type since she tries to assert herself as an object of love or takes revenge when she is refused as such. On the other hand, the role of tyrant seems to be masculine. Thus, when woman is presented as tyrant, she loses her feminity: in *Nabucco,* Abigaille first appears as Fenena's rival in Ismaele's heart, then becomes a schemer bent on seizing Nabucco's crown and destroying the lawful heir, Fenena; from this standpoint, her grand aria (act 2, scene 1) acts as a renunciation of love and by the same token of her feminity.

The judge's function is also by definition masculine; if a woman takes on the function, she must be delegated as such by a man, which excludes her from being a heroine. This is the situation in *Vêpres,* where Hélène must avenge her brother Frédéric of Austria's death at the hands of Guy de Montfort, and similarly in *Attila,* where Odabella's all-important task is to avenge her father. In each case, the character's function as judge stands in the way of her (amorous) situation as heroine. *Giovanna d'Arco* provides the best example of this mechanism in the very free adaptation Solera made of Schiller's play. Entrusted with a sacred mission, that of liberating France, Joan must give up love: "Guai se terreno affetto, / Accoglierai nel coro" (Woe to thee if an earthly love takes root in your heart) (prologue, scene 5). This contradiction is psychologically absurd but symbolically clear: in donning her breastplate and helmet, Joan takes over a male function that makes her unavailable as heroine. The drama arises from the fact that she fails to renounce the status of love object. In other words, although normally destined to be a heroine, the woman who becomes tyrant or judge becomes taboo.

These incompatibilities can be the source of effective dramatic conflicts. Others, by contrast, threaten the coherence of the code. Let us take Rigoletto as an example. As court jester, Rigoletto is the aide of the Duke of Mantua, who is a seducer, that is to say, an erotic variant of the tyrant. He incites the Duke to debauchery, but when, like a faithful disciple, his master seduces the other's daughter, Rigoletto rises up as an avenger-judge and even offers his aid to Monterone, whom he has just ridiculed. But how is it possible to make others respect an order one has oneself continually flouted? The contradiction is a fatal one, and it rebounds on the unfortunate buffoon. Because of both the energetic way Verdi defended the character and the persistence with which the censors tried to persuade him to make it more traditional, the example of Rigoletto proves conclusively that by going beyond conventional types, that is, by creating characters that were ambiguous and problematic, the composer brought about a crisis in the code to which he subscribed.

8. Some characters are harder to classify because they personify a function that circumstances prevent them from fulfilling and are thus reduced to playing a passive role. Massimiliano Moor in *I masnadieri* and the father in *Luisa Miller* are unable to carry out their role as fathers, which would make them judges or tyrants, and are left seemingly helpless victims. Azucena is a unique case in Verdi's dramaturgy, a woman torn between the desire to avenge her mother (judge) and her maternal love, a feeling that does not belong to any type. But this is a rare example; by far the greater number of Verdian characters can readily be categorized by type.

SYNTAX OF ACTIONS

If it is relatively easy to set up a morphology of characters, it is much harder to establish a syntax of actions following fixed models. As we have seen above with the example of the abduction of the heroine, actions are elusive in that there is no criterion allowing them to be attributed to such and such a character type. Aside from the fact that only rarely can an action be attributed to a given type, it may occur at any odd moment of the plot, with widely different results. Thus, a duel, whether initiated by a hero, tyrant, or judge, can either take place at the beginning of the plot, without incurring serious consequences *(Trovatore),* divert the course of the action, without leading to the denouement *(Forza),* or give the plot its final twist *(Oberto).* It should be added that, like the "well-made plays" of Scribe that Stephen Stanton has studied,[24] a good libretto calls for a certain suspense and therefore a measure of the unexpected. In short, as Lavagetto notes, the operas' narrative sequences seem to follow an "open" combinatory logic, mixing together a limited number of actions in an unforeseeable construction.[25]

Naturally, the ideological framework of Romantic operas constitutes the first limit to the indefiniteness of the plots. An opera will allow us a glimpse of the heaven of freedom and love and then suddenly close off the view; rebellion ends in resignation, transgression is invariably punished, and the dream ends in surrendering to all-powerful reality, with the task of rewarding the mourners, oppressed sons, and self-sacrificing women being left to the care of the hereafter. However violent the swings of the plot, they are checked in a way that becomes increasingly systematic as the century progresses. The case of the hero and heroine is the most clear-cut since very often they meet their deaths, but the triumph of a tyrant or judge always leaves a bitter taste. Still, the ideological framework remains vague, setting the course of a plot but never fixing the way it will unfold.

The typology of characters that I am proposing allows us to go a step further. Each type in fact carries with it a dynamic that the spectator expects to see realized more or less completely, as if he were insisting that the character be faithful to his or her "essence" to the very end. Thus, a tyrant must develop his aptitude for violence right up to the moment he meets an obstacle, a force stronger than himself that arrests his course. Sooner or later, the judge-like character must compel the one he is pursuing to settle accounts, whatever the outcome of that confrontation might be. The fact that this "essence" must of necessity be manifest means that all the characters belonging to a type follow a fairly similar course, even if the stages along the way are unpredictable.

Above all, it should be noted that the syntax of opera plots is based not only on the narrative's logic but also on an emotional dynamic that is connected, not to the semantic definition of an action, but to the effect it has on the spectator. Indeed, beyond its meaning, an action possesses a certain emotive force that depends on the circumstances and state of mind in which it was carried out as well as the moment in which it occurs. Striving for this effect implies, in musical terms, choosing a certain tempo, a greater or lesser intensity of sound, and a certain vocal style in order to create what Milan Kundera calls "emotional spaces"; in turn, these emotional spaces are regrouped and made to follow a certain curve that rises or falls, moves forward or is characterized by contrasts, and creates the overall rhythm of a work.

In his *Art of the Novel,* Kundera insists on the close connections between musical composition and the novelist's art. For him, "to compose a novel is to set different emotional spaces side by side."[26] It can even happen that the idea of a certain rhythm, tempo, or dynamic occurs before the situations are invented through which the rhythm is realized; in this case, the imagining of the rhythm leaves the nature of the actions still uncertain, even if it predisposes constraints limiting the field of invention.[27]

If a novelist can admit the priority of a "music" of the novel over the narrative logic, how much more will a composer be preoccupied by this emotional dynamic? Already when he was writing *Ernani,* Verdi affirmed the fundamental importance of the overall rhythm in the success of an opera. Success comes from the "distribution of the pieces," the "calculation of the effects," in short, the general strategy according to which situations are linked rather than the quality of such and such a passage.[28] At times he foresees a dramatic effect before deciding on the semantic content that would lead up to it; thus, in *Jérusalem* he rejects the text of one of Hélène's arias as without interest or "position" since, he says, "I'm still convinced that in that moment Hélène should be moved by a great surprise, something happy and unexpected. Only something strong like that could make her burst into so lively a cabaletta."[29] It was up to the librettist to find a justification for this explosion!

In this way the unpredictability of the narrative can be compensated for by a relatively predictable affective dynamic. However, this dynamic does call for a certain logic of action in order to become plausible. Assuming that it occurs in various operas, the dynamic makes it possible for us to give the same function to actions that differ widely on the strictly semantic level. Luigi Dallapiccola confronts a similar phenomenon in another context, that of the melodic dynamic of the Verdian aria. Drawing on several examples, the composer uncovers a scheme articulated in four phases, the first three leading up to an emotional peak, the fourth constituting the diminuendo. He also gives numerous examples where the same affective rhythm recurs in poetic compositions that are not intended to be sung.[30] It is clear that in these cases the rhythm determines a crescendo that makes it possible to connect very different semantic segments within the same structure. The argument is interesting here on a methodological level because it examines the connection of text to music from the viewpoint, not of how the music fits the words, or vice versa, but of how each is subordinate to rhythmic schemes that are somehow beyond both music and poetry.

My hypothesis is that a similar phenomenon can be seen at the level of the plot, as regards both the curve each character follows and the overarching one of the plot itself; both plot and characters trace a rhythmically accelerating path leading to an emotive apogee that is followed by a fall. In most cases this curve consists of four essential phases, like an echo of those Dallapiccola found in the aria, reaching its most intense moment in the third phase.

The interest of this hypothesis is that it provides an orderly framework for actions that seemed to be linked in random fashion. According to this theory, what the actions consist of is less important than what they do, that is to say, where they are placed at a given moment in the character's progress. Thus, the "perilous initiative," corresponding to the hero's second phase (see below), can take widely varying forms: he may carry off the heroine, or try to do so, or even merely visit her at an inopportune moment; he may fight a duel with his rival or simply challenge or meet with him. The point these actions have in common is that they will arouse feelings of apprehension in the spectator but not of horror, for they will be perceived as perilous but not likely to entail the loss of the hero. Conversely, the duel, as a semantically defined action, may correspond to a certain phase of a character, its significance being established by its position in the trajectory of the opera. Let us now examine those phases—a phase corresponds to one or more actions arising from the same step taken—that mark the path each character type follows throughout the opera, taking one character at a time.

SYNTAX OF CHARACTERS
The Hero

H1. *Unfavorable situation (act 1).* This is certainly the case with Ernani: he loves Elvira but cannot be united with her because her aged uncle and guardian, Silva, intends to marry her; moreover, the hero is in revolt against Don Carlo, the King of Spain, who is hunting him down as chief of brigands.

H2. *Perilous initiative (act 1).* He therefore decides to carry off his beloved but suddenly meets first Don Carlo, who has come to court Elvira, then Silva. Loath to explain the reasons for his visit, Carlo reveals his identity and passes Ernani off as one of his followers. The characteristics of this phase are clearly apparent: it illustrates the hero's daring and courage by neutralizing the risks he might have to face.

H3. *Fatal step (act 2).* Pursued by the King, Ernani takes refuge in Silva's castle, where he learns that the latter is about to marry his ward. Left alone with Elvira, Ernani defies her to explain herself; then they fall into each other's arms. Silva surprises them and challenges the young man to a duel. Considering it disloyal to kill an old man who had taken him in and refused to turn him over to the King, who is still pursuing him, Ernani entrusts his life to Silva. The hero's second visit to Silva's castle is a fatal step because it gives rise to a pact that leads directly to the denouement; the direct link with the denouement is, in fact, the chief characteristic of this phase.

The next act (act 3) is taken up by a subplot in which Ernani and Silva join forces to conspire against Carlo. As a result, they become, temporarily, political judges opposed to the king-tyrant, who surprises their plot but ends up pardoning them.

H4. *The denouement.* Pardoned by the King, who gives him Elvira's hand, Ernani is preparing to wed his beloved when Silva comes to exact the fulfillment of the pact made earlier in the act: Ernani stabs himself, the tragic fate of the majority of opera heroes.

The Tyrant

T1. *Threat (act 1)*. The tyrant has only to appear or be announced for the audience to see at once what a formidable character he is: "Transported with rage / the King of Assyria comes," the chorus informs us of Nabucco (Nebuchadnezzar), King of Babylon.

T2. *First crime (act 1)*. Drunk with power, Nabucco captures Jerusalem and gives orders for the destruction of the Temple and the deportation of the Hebrews.

T3. *Second crime (act 2)*. Dark plots are being woven at Nabucco's court as the people believe that he has been killed in a military campaign, but he returns, to everyone's astonishment, and proclaims himself God: divine thunder crashes on his head, and he goes mad. The manifestation of his most extreme tyranny coincides here with the beginning of his punishment (madness).

T4. *Denouement (acts 3 and 4)*. Nabucco will not die like so many of his kind (Macbeth, Lady Macbeth, Abigaille, Attila, Guy de Montfort), but he will pay grievously for his excesses, mocked by the usurping Abigaille and prostrated by madness. Nevertheless, he is touched by divine grace and becomes a reconciling judge, freeing the Hebrews and worshiping Jehovah (a change of function we have already noted in the case of Carlo in *Ernani*).

The Rival

R1. *Envious inferiority (act 1)*. The trajectory of the rival (both male and female) is logically close to that of the tyrant: Amneris, the King of Egypt's daughter, suspects that the man she loves, the great military leader Radames, is in love with the Ethiopian slave Aida, and this conviction provokes her resentment.

R2. *Harmful step (act 2)*. By a diabolical ruse, Amneris manages to wrest from Aida the secret of her shared love for Radames; she then humiliates her, using her tyrannical power.

R3. *Decisive crime (act 3)*. Amneris and Ramfis, the high priest, surprise Radames just after he has handed over military secrets to Aida, the daughter of the King of Ethiopia who is the sworn enemy of the Egyptians.

R4. *Final defeat (act 4)*. Amneris has "collaborated" with the judge,

Ramfis, but their aims are different: Ramfis wants to punish Radames's treason ruthlessly, while Amneris is determined to try to save him if he will give up Aida. She is forced to resign herself in anguish to the young hero's death.

The Judge

J1. *Proof of transgression (act 1).* Oberto's family honor has been stained by Riccardo, who has seduced his daughter Leonora. The offense demands reparation.

J2. *Plea for help (act 1).* Oberto must explain his misfortune to Cuniza, who is to marry Riccardo that same day, and she decides to help him clear his honor.

J3. *Decisive step (acts 1 and 2).* The goal Oberto has in mind is clearly a duel, and this decisive act is announced in Finale I when he solemnly appears and reveals Riccardo's treachery to the assembly, challenging him. But the duel is interrupted by Cuniza, who suggests a less bloody solution: that Riccardo marry Leonora, whom he has dishonored.

J4. *Denouement (act 2).* Oberto will not give up his vengeance, so the duel takes place. He is killed: his progress is ended.

The Heroine

The definition of the heroine's phases is more subtle. Since opera condemns woman to submit rather than act, she reacts to others' initiatives rather than taking them herself. Still, it is possible to pinpoint the four standard phases:

h1. *Unfavorable situation.* This is a starting point parallel to that of the hero. In *Traviata,* Violetta is touched by Alfredo's love, but the fact that she is a courtesan constitutes a seemingly insurmountable obstacle for that love.

h2. *Preliminary step.* She nevertheless accepts Alfredo's love, and together they flee to the country, far from the gossip of the city. In this case, the heroine's role is active since, contrary to what Germont, Alfredo's father, believes, she is secretly providing the money for their stay.

h3. *Fatal step.* When not resulting from another character's initiative, the heroine's action almost always matches the only one the code will allow her, that of renunciation. At Germont's urging, Violetta agrees to give up her love, even carrying abnegation to the point of pretending to be in love with another man.

h4. *Denouement.* Almost invariably, this is just as catastrophic with the heroine as with the hero. Stricken with both consumption and grief, and despite the tardy repentance of Germont and his son, Violetta dies.

SYNTAX OF PLOTS

The plot is produced by a combination of the trajectories traced by the various types and follows a rhythm that, again, we can divide into four phases: an exposition, a preliminary phase launching the characters into the action, a phase that constitutes the crux of the action and leads to the fourth phase, the denouement.

This four-part division suggests a cutting up into four acts, but this does not always happen. Verdi's oeuvre includes only one opera—*Oberto*—in two acts, a traditional division in the first three decades of the century, and two operas in five acts, both French works, *Vêpres* and *Don Carlos;* the others are split more or less equally into three and four acts. Added to these are those works that include a prologue and two acts *(Alzira)* or three *(Giovanna d'Arco, Attila, Simon):* for the first two of these operas, the indication for a prologue is not given in the autograph.

Although not following a general-purpose scheme, the operas do tend to be divided up in similar fashion: exposition and preliminary phase (one act), crux of action (one act), and catastrophe (one act). The existence of a secondary plot results in another act being tacked on (act 2 in *La battaglia,* act 3 in *Ernani*). On the other hand, in *Aida* each act corresponds to one of the phases of the plot. Before taking up two concrete examples of opera division, I shall point out the distinguishing features that characterize the connection of the plot type with each plot, as I did for those governing the progress from type to character.

1. *The setting.* Each opera is linked to a historical period and to precise places that give it its specific color and provide justification for episodes that are of no importance to the plot but create its atmosphere and give each character his or her particular physiognomy. The links are what are called, in narrative analysis, indices in relation to the functions that advance the plot. Such is the role of the ponderous ritual of the Spanish court in *Don Carlos* or, in *I due Foscari,* the atmosphere of a Machiavellian, secretive Venice, dominated by the all-powerful Council.

2. *The perspective.* Even if an opera includes the four principal character types, the plot gives special importance to one or two protagonists; their trajectory is in the foreground, while the others may be presented more succinctly or follow an incomplete course. Thus, we have hero dra-

mas *(Ernani, Trovatore)*, heroine dramas *(Traviata, Aida)*, tyrant dramas *(Nabucco, Attila)*, and judge dramas *(Oberto)*, while other operas deal with several full trajectories at the same time *(Vêpres, Don Carlos)*.

3. *Accumulation or change of function and secondary plot.* We have seen, speaking of *La battaglia* and *Ernani*, how secondary plots can affect the leading characters and start a new plot curve that may be followed to its completion. The prologue may feature a character who will reappear in the main plot but with a different function. Thus, in act 1 of *I Lombardi* (which actually serves as a prologue even if not so called), Pagano is a rival of his brother Arvino and plays his role through to the end (he tries to kill Arvino). In the following acts he turns up again as a benevolent hermit, a conciliatory judge who tries to quell the conflicts arising from the love between the hero and heroine and also help the Crusaders capture the Holy Sepulcher. His action in the main plot becomes a long expiation of the crimes he committed in the "prologue."

4. *Barriers.* The operas swing between two extreme poles. Sometimes they seem open-ended to the point where anything seems possible and the outcome is theoretically unpredictable *(Ernani, Aida,* etc.); sometimes, in contrast, an opening incident is so heavy with consequences that it bars the action and leaves the character with only an illusory freedom to maneuver *(La battaglia, Don Carlos)*. These blockings come about as a result of assaults on familial or conjugal order. Most typical is the case of *Forza;* when Alvaro unwittingly kills the father of the woman he wants to carry off, this "parricide" is sufficiently serious to forbid all further relations between the hero and the heroine and force each of them, separately, to flee.

5. *Lures.* One can follow Roland Barthes and call *lures* all incidents that tend to give an illusory twist to the action, to divert it from its inevitable outcome, or appear to move prematurely toward the end. Logically, these lures essentially break up the hero and heroine's progress since it is they, above all, who move the spectators to fear or joy. Among the intensifying lures one may cite the hero's attempt at suicide, when he finds that he cannot attain the object of his quest, as, for instance, when Arrigo in *La battaglia* decides to enter the order of the Company of Death so as to meet a heroic end or when Leonora enters a convent on receiving the false news of Manrico's death. Each such action has its corresponding moment of respite, which is equally illusory, as when the heroine tries to dissuade the hero from thoughts of suicide *(La battaglia)* or when Manrico carries off Leonora before she takes her vows.

Along with these artificial plot devices go the false denouements immediately preceding the actual one. For instance, Alfredo and Violetta are at last together under the benevolent gaze of Germont, but it is too late, and La traviata dies. In another example, Carlo Moor is reconciled with his father in *I masnadieri,* but the curse hanging over his life as a brigand proves stronger. These lures should not be confused with those resulting from a character's false beliefs that make him act out of a misreading of his enemy's attitude; thus, Giacomo, Joan of Arc's father, harries his daughter, even handing her over to the English, because he is convinced she has sided with the devil through her love for the King of France and wishes to expunge the stain on his paternal honor. Too late, he comes to understand his error.

6. *Contraction and expansion.* At any moment the composer can expand or contract a phase of the plot, depending on his overall perception of the work. We have a good example in the exposition, which often embarrassed Verdi because traditionally it called for one or more arias that slowed down the action. As was shown above, the very first sketch for *Ernani* provided for a long introduction that would no doubt have presented the leading characters in action, but Verdi stepped back and ended up writing one entrance aria for Ernani (H1) and another for Elvira (h1). In *Ballo,* Somma had written an entrance aria for Amelia (h1); this time the composer preferred to eliminate it, jumping directly to phase 2, where Amelia goes off into Ulrica's cave, since that gave him a chance to include a brief description of the heroine's initial situation. On the other hand, act 1 of *Vêpres* is entirely devoted to the initial situation of the protagonists, Hélène, Henri, and Guy de Montfort, the hero, heroine, and tyrant. This initial situation takes the form of a nascent rebellion that gives an idea of the strength of the opposing forces. It is a typical example of French opera's tendency toward expansion.

Furthermore, the plot often arises from antecedents with which the spectator must be familiar in order to follow what is happening. The librettist may intimate these antecedents in a preface *(I due Foscari);* they may be recounted in an aria (Ferrando's aria in *Trovatore*) or presented in an act or a prologue. Thus, act 1 of *Don Carlos,* the so-called Fontainebleau act, is nothing more than a huge prologue to the main action, which begins in act 2.

Let us take two examples of plots, coded according to my typology. It should be remembered that H = hero, h = heroine, T = tyrant, R = rival, J = judge, and P = plot.

UN BALLO IN MASCHERA

The first setting (P1) shows us the court of the Governor of Boston, a charming hero surrounded by loyal courtiers, and a few conspirators (potential judges but as yet inactive). Riccardo confesses his love for Amelia (H1), a love that is impossible because she is married to his faithful servant Renato (blocking of the action). This latter character, who for now is only a confidant and friend, advises his master not to take any imprudent steps, for he knows that the conspirators are watching.

The second scene takes place in the dwelling of the witch Ulrica, whom members of the court have come to consult. Riccardo conceals himself (perilous initiative that takes the form of an encounter, although it is not actually such), the better to spy on the heroine, who has come to ask the sorceress's aid in helping her forget the guilty love she feels for Riccardo (h1/2, with a contraction, described above). Next, Ulrica foretells that Riccardo will die at the hand of a friend, the first man to shake his hand. To everyone's stupefaction it is Renato, but no one puts much faith in the prophecy (this is therefore a preliminary phase that launches the action but so far without entailing serious consequences). I have not coded Ulrica because her function is to speak, not act, and I will return to this leading character later.

The second act is devoted to the pivotal phase (P3): Amelia goes to pick the herb Ulrica has recommended to help her forget her love (h3: a perfectly orthodox renunciation). Having gleaned information through his eavesdropping, Riccardo joins her and extracts from her the confession of her love (H3: fatal encounter, because it engages the mechanism leading to the denouement). Renato, the faithful friend, comes to announce that conspirators are on the prowl; Riccardo asks him to escort the veiled Amelia back to the city, but Renato thereupon discovers that the woman is none other than his own wife (J1: proof of transgression).

In act 3, Renato considers killing his wife (intensifying lure for the heroine), then decides to turn against his master; he receives the conspirators Samuel and Tom and proposes that they band together to assassinate Riccardo (J2: call for help). In the drawing of lots that follows, Renato is designated the future assassin (J3: Renato appears as the one morally responsible for the denouement even before he is materially responsible). The final scene (P4) shows a masked ball. Riccardo decides to give up Amelia and send her abroad with her husband; Amelia warns him that there is going to be an attempt on his life and that he must flee (lures that mask the denouement). Riccardo dismisses the idea and falls under Renato's dagger (J4, H4).

DON CARLOS

It is logical to take as a second example an opera that because of its dimensions challenges the simple linearity of the code. As we saw, the first act is a huge prologue that constitutes a preliminary plot brought to its conclusion, that is, up to the marriage of Elisabeth de Valois and Philip II of Spain; the marriage puts a definitive end to her relations with the Infante Carlos, whom she was at one time supposed to wed.

At the beginning of the second act (P1), we find Carlos shattered (H1) and tempted by thoughts of suicide, from which his friend Rodrigue, the Marquis of Posa, dissuades him by encouraging him to defend Flanders ($H^2$1: as was pointed out above, the hero as a type is personified by two characters in this opera); majestic and a little threatening, the King of Spain passes by in the distance (T1). The second phase (P2) opens with the trio of Eboli, Elisabeth, and Rodrigue: we note Elisabeth's deep distress (h1) and mark Eboli as a future rival (R1: knowing nothing of the love between Carlos and Elisabeth, she is free of a feeling of envious inferiority, indulging herself in illusions). With the help of Rodrigue, the Infante is assured of a rendezvous with his stepmother, Elisabeth (H2: perilous initiative as inopportune meeting); furious at seeing the Queen on her own, after Carlos has left, the King sends her lady-in-waiting into exile (T2: attenuated form of an abuse of power), then converses with Posa, who pleads the cause of freedom ($H^2$2).

The third act (P3) begins with an action on the part of the Queen's rival, who has granted a nocturnal rendezvous to the hero (R2): chance decrees that Eboli is dressed in the Queen's finery; Carlos, mistaking her, thus reveals to Eboli that the Queen is her rival (H3), and the Princess swears revenge (announcement of R3). During the grand finale, Philip II appears in all his despotic cruelty (T3), and his son Carlos rebels against him in vain (expansion of H3), while Rodrigue calms the violence of the confrontation by intervening. The personality of the tyrant, Philip, is amplified in the next act, through both his great monologue and his meeting with the Grand Inquisitor (a judge who plays a limited role in this plot since he intervenes only to encourage Philip to be stern). Philip's severity is finally revealed in the great scene with the Queen, with the result that phase 3 of the character appears strongly expanded. The accusations that Philip hurls against Elisabeth are, of course, the result of

Eboli's denunciation, her means of vengeance against her rival (realization of R3).

The resolution phase begins with Eboli's aria: condemned to enter a convent (R4), she becomes aware of her cruelty. The phase continues with the death of Rodrigue, whose ambiguous role has gained him the animosity of the Inquisition (H^24). The scene of the people's revolt has no functional value, which is probably why it embarrassed the composer, who shortened it drastically in the Milanese version. The fifth act opens with a false denouement suggested by the last meeting of Carlos and Elisabeth: Carlos vows to fight for Flanders and give up his love, Elisabeth to accept her sad fate. But it is too late, and the King and the Inquisitor arrive to give the denouement a far more dramatic twist (H4, h4, T4). Thus, even though the dimensions of this opera have nothing in common with those of the others, in spite of the spectacular scenes and the expansion of certain phases we still can trace the standard development noted in the preceding works.

* * * * * * * *

This little "grammar" calls for a few general observations:

1. Despite the various accidental happenings designed to fool the spectator and make it hard to tell how the plot will develop, the plot has a framework that is to the drama what musical structure and the four-part organization analyzed by Dallapiccola are to melody. This framework serves as a musical dynamic since it is based on effects of increasing intensity but trickles off into semantic sequences that recur with extreme regularity.

2. The framework accentuates the conventional or, if you will, the ritual nature of opera. We go to the opera to hear a story that we already know, although we do not know how it will be told on this precise occasion; we are going in order to become one with a world of passions that is familiar to us even if it is presented each time in a different guise. This play between the predictable and the unpredictable, the known and the unknown, would clearly be impossible if the syntax were totally random; on the other hand, the code makes up for the deficiency of information, which is reduced to a minimum on the operatic stage.

3. The preceding analyses make it possible to evaluate an opera's plot at its true worth. It is fashionable to say that the plot counts for very little and that only the emotional moments it creates have any importance: "It doesn't matter whether we describe how, when or through what paths,

events or interior processes a character has reached a certain point: what does matter is to show forcefully whether that character is happy or in despair, whether he is jealous, or charmed."[31]

We noted in chapter 2 that opera has a tolerance for discontinuity, a tolerance far greater than that of the spoken theater, but the fact that music periodically breaks the chronological and logical chain does not authorize one to believe that this chain is of no importance. A too radical affirmation of the primacy of the emotional moment brings us back, in fact, to the aesthetic of the affetto in baroque opera, where a character must be by turns furious or bucolic, joyful or loving, with the result that the link between one feeling and another counts for little.

If the syntax that I have just suggested has some foundation, it sets up a correlation between the affective moment and the position that that moment holds in a parabola; the code allows the spectator to pinpoint easily a position in a familiar trajectory. But this reference is still somewhat vague, and to sustain our close bond with the character the "position" should be justified by a logic unique to each opera. The close attention to the drama common to all the great operatic composers, from Handel to Puccini, comes from the conviction that the music loses out if it plays against the logic of the drama or only trusts its own power.

We know that Verdi was supremely devoted to this coherence of the whole and that he never confused an opera with a succession of beautiful "positions." When he turned down Dumas's *La Tour de Nesle,* it was because the text would have made "magnificent pieces of music but certainly not an opera," in other words, not an organic whole. When he boasted of *Rigoletto*'s excellence to Somma, it was not only because of the variety of moods and colors but also because the situations flow out of each other: "All the turns of the plot come from the doings of one shallow character, the libertine Duke: it causes Rigoletto's anxieties, Gilda's passion, etc., etc., producing a series of many excellent dramatic points."[32]

Many people tend to underestimate the plot because they confuse dramatic logic with the verisimilitude that helps make the plot plausible. Yet, from *Così fan tutte* on, we have known that a masterpiece of dramatic and psychological subtlety can be grounded on an entirely improbable idea. Let us take as an example the Finale of act 3 of *Otello,* where the protagonist publicly humiliates Desdemona. Dissatisfied with a first rendering of the action, Verdi envisaged a Turkish attack, an unlikely incident that I shall have occasion to examine at a later stage. In the same letter in which he puts forward this solution, he critiques it, and the order of his objections is interesting: (1) The "situation" is satisfactory from a composer's point of view. (2) Is it satisfactory for the "critic" from the standpoint of probability? No, but that is not a problem since the facts can be arranged so as to make a Turkish attack believable. (3) Is it satisfactory from the point of view of logic or characters? Apparently not, which is far more serious: Boito therefore had no difficulty in convincing him to give up this "brain wave."

The other side of the argument concerning the correlation of the affective moment with the "dramatic connection," on which Dahlhaus rightly insists in his essay on Wagner, is that a moment that is only weakly linked to the context loses its value, however attractive it may be. Thus, the Duke of Mantua's aria "Parmi veder le lagrime" lacks the brilliance of both his ballata "Questa o quella" and the famous song "La donna è mobile," for the simple reason that it does not logically fit the character we have seen, and are to see, represented as a cynical libertine. For Verdi, as for others, a lowering of inspiration was often the result of a false or unsatisfactory situation. The composer was not successful in his reworking of act 2 of *Simon,* which is much inferior to the acts before and after it. In fact it is based on a highly artificial misunderstanding that could be cleared up only by completely changing the plot. The hero, Adorno, decides, as a judge, to assassinate Simon since he believes his beloved's virginity is threatened by the old Doge's lustful desires, not knowing that the intimacy of these two characters is that of father and daughter. His vengeful rage therefore seems a trifle ridiculous.

4. The grammar that I have described is not specifically Verdian since it is to be found in other Romantic operas and, in more general fashion, in the theatrical repertoire from which the composer drew his inspiration. Verdi's originality therefore lies more in the attitude he takes toward these characters and the way he illuminates the plots.

Verdi's preference for the baritone voice is one indication of his tendency to move the vocal axis toward low voices and thereby toward "heavy" characters personifying power or the authority of the law. It is symptomatic that his first opera, *Oberto,* tells the story of a judge, the second (if we disregard his first opera buffa), *Nabucco,* that of a tyrant, and the third, *I Lombardi,* that of a fierce rival who through expiation becomes a beneficent hermit. At this stage, the hero is curiously absent! Must one cite Macbeth, Attila, Rigoletto, Simon Boccanegra, or Philip II as proof of the composer's fondness for mature male characters ravaged by passion, ambition, or desire for revenge? In his *Filosofia della musica,* the Italian revolutionary Mazzini expressed the wish that opera would turn away from erotic hedonism and deal with conflicts that were more austere and more useful to the nation. One can say that, at least in his first operas, Verdi responded to that wish.

Furthermore, the composer establishes a more rigorous balance between action and passion, between dramatic situation and lyrical distillation, so that it is the various phases the character passes through that are thrown into relief, not simply the diversity of his passions. All Verdi's strategy is bent on smoothing the rift between the gesture that creates a sudden change of situation and the affective consequences of this change and ensuring that the singing is still at one with the gesture and the action.

Another salient feature is the priority he consistently gives to the conflict of attitudes over mere description. Verdi "reduces the imbalance, often striking in the previous operas, between the protagonists and the other characters, so that opera is no longer merely the history and development of an absolute passion but the description of a conflict and a transcription of its pivotal points. The relations of the hero with his partners become fundamental, and the composer frequently pays more attention to opposing contrasting attitudes than to delineating personalities in all their brilliance."[33] Thus, it is no accident that Verdi, already famous for his choruses, owed his rapid fame to his ensembles rather than his arias. Nor is it mere chance that the duet is a key piece in his development: this form opposes contrasting attitudes like an ensemble, but it also possesses a mobility that sets these attitudes in motion and makes it possible to follow them as they unfold.

Techniques of Melodrama

Causes are perhaps irrelevant
to effects.
MARQUIS DE SADE

When Verdi began his career, he inherited a firmly established genre that had, however, been significantly reshaped by Rossini in the first two decades of the century—among other means, by absorbing into opera seria techniques that had long been experimented with in opera buffa.[34] The panoply of *forms* (for this and other terms, see the glossary) on which

opera drew at that time was relatively limited: they included the recitative, which around the 1840s ceased to be *semplice* and was usually orchestrated; the *scena,* a freely organized sequence of recitative; the overture
(either a prelude or a sinfonia—i.e., a full-scale, freestanding overture);
the solo for a single character (cavatina, romanza, preghiera, rondò, and
aria in the strict sense of the term); the chorus; the internal instrumental
pieces, often given to the *banda;* the duet or *duettino;* the ensembles (trio,
quartet, etc.); and the finale.

The point at which libretto and musical structure meet is what Verdi
meant by *situation (posizione),* a gesture or series of gestures arising from
a particular moment in the plot; a situation almost invariably corresponds
to a phase in the development of a character or of the plot and, musically,
to the use of a given form. As Verdi observed, speaking of *Macbeth,* writing a libretto meant locating those peak situations of a drama that were
to be articulated musically and linking them together correctly: "The plot
is taken from one of the greatest tragedies the theater boasts, and I have
tried to have all the dramatic situations drawn from it faithfully, to have
it well versified, and to give it a new texture, and to compose music tied
so far as possible to the text and to the situations." [35]

In this task of adaptation, Verdi laid great stress on simplicity: the
characters should stand out clearly; the changes in their fortune or situation should be readily grasped. "Simplicity in art is everything. . . . When
form is intricate, contorted and difficult, there is no emotion, and arousing emotion is the aim of art." [36] Equally important, the situation should
have sufficient dramatic power to make an "impression" on the spectator.
But, once again, this power must be dramatically motivated, for a situation is convincing only insofar as it arises out of strong characters, and
these in turn come alive and acquire substance only through situation.
Verdi was quite conscious of the risks of an empty grandiosity if the link
between character and situation was not adequately established: "After
the powerful effects of Victor Hugo's dramas, everyone strove for effect,
without realizing that, in my opinion, there is always an underlying purpose in Hugo, as well as characters that are powerful, passionate and
above all original. Look at Silva, Marie Tudor, Borgia, Marion, Triboulet,
François, etc., etc. Great characters produce great situations, and effect
follows naturally." [37]

Once it was granted that drama consisted of a succession of situations—and therefore of forms—as logically ordered as possible, all that
remained was for the composer to delineate them musically with certain

characteristics: energy, through the pursuit of tension; conflict, through the systematic use of contrast; and, finally, movement, by giving pride of place to the action.

TENSION

As we saw in the previous chapter, Rossini always aimed for a certain moral elevation of the drama and a musical sublimation of it through song. No matter how dramatic the situations or the clashes between characters, there is always a moment when tension is eased in a lyric release, whether melancholy, heroic, or brilliant. In the text, the same effect is obtained in those abstract, meditative passages where the character retreats into himself and takes stock of his situation.

Without challenging this lyric concretization of the high points of the plot, Verdi's concern to project the decisive gestures that shape a destiny led him constantly to emphasize the situation as a whole and hence the corresponding musical forms; he strove to give traditionally static movements enough energy to counteract in part the lowering of tension that accompanies every lyric pause. Where Bellini stops time to allow the underlying truth of a situation to blossom, Verdi merely suspends it, making the audience feel that it will soon pick up again—much as a statue frozen in mid-gesture can nevertheless give the impression that it is about to complete its movement. The particular appeal of the young Verdi's style comes from this suspended dynamism or temporarily bridled momentum, which Barilli has aptly compared to the vibration of a ship that is motionless but ready to weigh anchor.[38]

Commenting on the act 2 Finale of *I Lombardi,* in particular the phrase "L'empio olocausto" of Giselda's rondò, aptly marked *con slàncio* in the score, Basevi observes that Verdi could be seen as the inventor of such phrases "a grande slàncio" (ex. 3). *Canto di slàncio,* literally "singing with momentum," is, of course, a vocal style that exists in every period, but Basevi rightly notes that no composer before Verdi attained such excesses of impetuosity.[39] The energy of the phrase in Giselda's rondò relies on certain common techniques: an attack, after a pause, on a high note supported by a major triad *ff* in the orchestra; the rising energy of the melody, driven by triplet motion; the appoggiaturas combined with syncopation to create a sense of effort as the melody drives up to the high B, then hurtles down the scale in sixteenth notes, only to take off again even more vigorously.

We can perhaps pinpoint certain characteristics of this energetic, in-

, EX. 3

deed energizing, style, of which only Donizetti offers any analogous examples before Verdi's time:

1. Few composers begin their melodies with as much freedom and
clarity as Verdi. Consider the hammer-blow attacks on strong beats in
Manrico's "Di quella pira" in *Il trovatore.* This opening gesture is all the
more effective in that it is often preceded by a general pause for both voice
and orchestra, as in Ferrando's phrase "Abbietta zingara" *(Trovatore)* or
"Ma noi, donne italiche" in Odabella's entrance aria *(Attila).* It is, however, in *Rigoletto,* in "La donna è mobile," that we find the best example
of this brutal and sudden attack on a strong beat after a caesura separating
the dominant chord from the tonic. Equally dynamic is the attack preceded by an anacrusis, as in the famous main theme of *La forza del destino*
(see ex. *7a* below), or the short anacrusis paving the way for the initial
appoggiaturas of the cabaletta "Or tutti sorgete" in Lady Macbeth's entrance aria.

2. Beyond the opening gesture itself, the composer gives his melodic

EX. 4*a*

EX. 4*b*

lines great propulsive force by creating a sort of balance that ensures forward drive. In the two examples given above, from *Ernani* and *Trovatore* (exx. 4*a* and 4*b*), the first notes work to buttress the melody, which then spins out in a broad trajectory, much as one draws tight a catapult before launching the stone. It matters little that the vocal line then gently descends (the score often specifies *stentando, allargando,* at this point): the blow has been struck.

3. Each of the examples cited above illustrates a process common with Verdi. He uses ornamental notes not so much to sweeten the melodic line and lend it elegance as to give it added energy. Where appoggiaturas often veil the clarity of a gesture, ringing it with a halo of uncertainty, Verdi

instead uses them to suggest single-minded striving toward heroic action. We have a striking instance of this in the cabaletta of Lady Macbeth's entrance aria, "Or tutti sorgete," where the first six measures are launched from an appoggiatura prepared by an upbeat, each on a strong syllable (*tùtti, sorgète, minìstri, infernàli, sàngue, incoràte*). Thus, the composer admirably conveys the energy of a will intent on murder; the seventh measure, on the other hand (*spingète*), begins on a chord tone as though to mark the attainment of the desired goal.

4. Contributing in large measure to this concise depiction of character is Verdi's choice of intervals: when Abigaille (in *Nabucco*) is introduced, we remember less the *terzettino* with Ismaele and Fenena than the brazen recitative "Prode guerrier" with which she reveals herself because of the way it vehemently spans her registral range. Ernani's heroic mood is similarly linked to the prevalence of the ascending major sixth (and sometimes minor sixth, to represent ill-fated heroism): this interval characterizes not only Ernani ("Come rugiada al cespite") but also Elvira ("Ernani, Ernani, involami"), at their respective entrances. Note, too, how the sixth often stretches to a seventh, then to the octave, in a sort of heroic apotheosis.[40]

5. At this stage of Verdi's development, harmony is primarily functional, providing a solid and uncomplicated frame for the melody. Not that Verdi was incapable of harmonic refinement—certain precocious passages like the preghiera in *I Lombardi* indicate that he was—but monumental effects call for simple, four-square harmony, and melodies as beautiful as "La donna è mobile" lose nothing when supported by a banal alternation of tonic and dominant. If one compares the original with some of Liszt's adaptations, one can see how a subtler harmony changes the atmosphere and obscures the theatrical impact of the melodic gesture.

Nonetheless, certain chords do work to create tension. One instance is the six-four chord, so widely used in Italian opera and which with Verdi always signals a dramatic turnaround, an apparition, a sudden revelation or solemn declaration.[41] No example better illustrates this chord's heroic connotation than Otello's last monologue, "Niun mi tema." We are on the dominant of A minor when Otello describes his fall from grace; suddenly a six-four in C major explodes *ff* on the word *gloria,* a brief and belated ray of light after which the bass returns to the dominant of A minor.

More specifically Verdian is the unexpected use of the six-four in keys relatively distant from the local tonic. In this context, the chord suggests a sort of inner wrench or heartbreak: thus, when Alfredo reads Violetta's farewell letter and, devastated with emotion, falls into his father's arms, a six-four chord in D♭ major erupts in the context of F major. A particularly expressive use of the technique occurs in *La forza del destino,* where the chord is heard three times (four times in the 1862 version), associated with the character of Leonora and the idea of suffering and inner constraint. The device is also heard as the heroine bids her father farewell ("ah! padre mio!") at the end of the first scene, but in this context it has no modulatory power since it does not actually lead to the tonality it announces.

6. Rhythm, whether in the accompaniment or in the melodic line itself, is obviously essential to the propulsive quality of the phrase. In this area Verdi did little that was new, instead reaching back into traditional formulas for most of his martial rhythms as well as for specific rhythmic devices like syncopation. Far from disguising the conventional character of these rhythms, he gives them new vigor by stripping them bare, as it were—for instance, by using only a single repeated note in the melody, thereby diverting interest from the melodic line to the rhythmic profile. What could be simpler yet more compelling than the rhythm of "Di quella pira" ♩ ♩ ♩ |♫♫♩ *(Trovatore)* or that of "La donna è mobile" ♫♫ |♫♩ *(Rigoletto),* two of Verdi's most famous melodies? In each case, the rhythm does not vary but rather is repeated with a throbbing insistence that contributes much to the impression of energy that propels the two melodies.

This art of blowing a rhythm out of proportion by giving it a near obsessive character has valuable dramatic applications where it can create a forward motion through entire sections: the relentless rhythms dominating the card-playing scene in *Traviata* (act 2, scene 12) and those of the ball in *Vêpres* (act 3, scene 6) function in this way. In *Vêpres* Verdi managed to sustain a sense of menace throughout an entire opera by means of a simple rhythmic formula ♫♩, a traditional funeral rhythm;[42] the threat is in fact realized by the massacre of the French at the end of the opera.

That this conveying of tension is the result of deliberate planning becomes clear when one observes the thoughtful pacing of most of the melodies that I have mentioned. Verdi always strove for rhythms that were powerful and clearly marked, avoiding those formulas that would make for monotony. He inverted rhythmic schemes, for example, contrasted staccato and legato song, or else modified the melodic orientation. A comparison of the final version of "La donna è mobile" with the early draft in the autograph sketch for *Rigoletto* shows that the composer had settled on a rhythmic pattern from the first but then, after letting himself be guided somewhat by this formula, which then tended to become a bit mechanical, varied it in order to recapture the original effect.[43]

The same sketch contains numerous examples of such systematic labor. The first version of the *tempo d'attacco* of the Rigoletto-Gilda duet in act 1 (beginning as Rigoletto enters the courtyard of his house) is a lively but straightforward melody, much less tremulous than the definitive version, in which trills and syncopations communicate the effusive love between father and daughter. Similarly, the fairly ample vocal line that Verdi sketched for the cabaletta of Gilda and the Duke in their act 1 duet, "Addio, speranza ed anima," is replaced in the final version by a succession of intense, rapid gestures.[44]

This search for tension through a variety of techniques also affects the architecture of the aria. Every composer aims to reach an emotional peak, but, while this peak is usually the result of a slow building toward a culminating point ("Casta diva" from Bellini's *Norma* is an admirable example of this careful management of the emotional crescendo), Verdi piles up the moments of tension to the point where the whole structure seems in danger of toppling. Each phrase is projected as an autonomous vocal gesture, even if it submits to a broader melodic arch. As a result, the aria is borne along on a dual, contradictory current of phrases that aspire to independence while remaining subordinate to the larger structure.

Let us take as an example Elvira's B♭ major cavatina in *Ernani,* "Ernani, Ernani, involami," constructed of four-measure phrases in the pattern a1 a2 b1 b2 a3. The heroine declares her longing to flee with Ernani and follow him wherever fate will take them. In the a1 phrase, the first two measures have the function of a double exclamation, as much musical as textual: the first ("Ernani") leaps a major sixth, while the second ("Ernani, involami") rises to the octave with a sort of dynamic embroidering. The next two measures complete the sense of a phrase that, in fact, is already complete in itself: "Ernani, Ernani, steal me away from his foul embrace!" In a2 the first half phrase is identical; then, just when one would expect a modulation (here, rather unexpectedly, from B♭ major to D minor), the voice braces itself for a new effort ("mi sia d'amor concesso") and climbs to a high A, only to descend again rapidly to low D. In b1, "per antri e lande," and again in b2, the same vehemence with which each melodic segment is projected as an autonomous gesture reappears in the two strongly accented triplets E–F–G–F leading to high G and then, in b2, to high B♭. The climax is reached in a3 ("Un Eden di delizie"), where the leap of a sixth that opened the melody leads to successive flourishes of sixteenth-note sextuplets reaching up to high C. The same phrase is repeated after a four-measure transition and followed by a coda.

This movement is obviously built on a dynamic crescendo in which each phrase has its place (the progression to high C is very clear), but the melody proceeds by thrusts, by vehement lurches forward and lapses back that fragment the melody as if it were trying to escape its bounds. The same phenomenon is again accentuated in Lady Macbeth's wonderful entrance aria, "Vieni, t'affretta! accendere," where the melodic line is broken up into interjections and violent exhortations. Note that this time the agitation of the musical discourse is served by the text, which lends force to these exclamations by conveying the heroine's impatience (Come, hasten, why waver, accept) (see ex. 5).

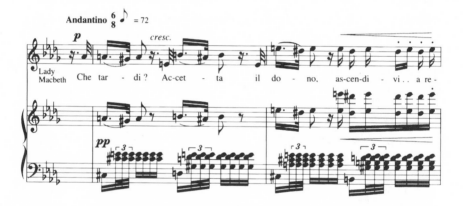

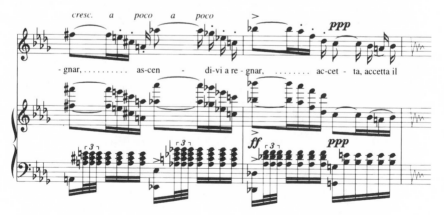

EX. 5

This vocal style certainly did not meet with universal approval, and it earned Verdi the animosity of champions of bel canto.[45] Yet the composer often maintained that, no matter how emphatic his melodies became, they always remained *song* above all: "If only these singers, the women as much as the men, would sing and not shout! If only they would remember that to declaim does not mean to scream! Even if there aren't many vocalises in my music, singers shouldn't take advantage of that and tear their hair out and get excited and shriek as if possessed."[46]

CONTRAST

The grammar of melodrama is based on contrast and assumes that characters' attitudes are defined by their relation to each other. Clear contrast makes for believability in drama, and it is also important in differentiating between the psychological states of a single character. Verdi's earliest operas often do not arouse interest until conflict breaks out. *Oberto,* his first opera, languishes both in the opening chorus and in Riccardo and Leonora's entrance arias and comes alive only with the confrontation of Leonora and Oberto and the trio for Oberto, Leonora, and Cuniza, reaching a climax of dramatic intensity in the act 1 finale.

Furthermore, the Romantic sensibility of the age craved strong clashes of color and atmosphere such as are found as frequently in the historical paintings of the period as in opera. Consider act 1 of *I Lombardi,* with its juxtaposition of the gentle nuns' chorus against the ferocious chorus of Pagano's men, or the opposition between Attila's bloodthirsty soldiers and the virgins and children arriving in a procession from Rome. Basevi notes how this trend in Verdian drama matched the climate of the time: "Verdi often made shrewd use of effects of contrast; he identified the most propitious times for them—for example, when the audience has the strongest need for powerful emotions."[47] How does this tendency manifest itself in concrete terms?

Orchestral Introductions

Contrast is already apparent in the orchestral introduction, but Verdi at first made unsophisticated use of it. The overtures (sinfonie) comprise a certain number of themes that are not developed and often are rather crudely set side by side. One example is the *Oberto* sinfonia, which parades before us four different themes that recur in the course of the opera: a pastoral fiesta theme, a martial theme, and two more dramatic themes connected to the violent events of the plot.

This somewhat hasty, potpourri technique is evident in the overtures of *Nabucco, Giovanna d'Arco,* and *Alzira* and also in some preludes like that of *I due Foscari.* Used more skillfully, it reappears in later overtures, as in *Vêpres, Stiffelio/Aroldo,* and *Forza,* and in the preludes of *Simon* (1857 version) and *Ballo.* More interesting, because here contrast is based on an overall conception of the drama, are those examples where the themes, however abruptly juxtaposed, serve to illuminate the moral breadth of the plot and designate its poles. Thus, the *Ernani* prelude is based on two alternating and opposed themes, one short and dramatic and linked to the death pact between Ernani and Silva, the other ample and lyrical, evoking the love between the hero and Elvira. This same principle underlies some of Verdi's most famous preludes, such as those of *La traviata* and *Aida.*

Arias

The dominant form of the lyric tradition is the bipartite or double aria, made up of a slow movement followed, usually after an intermediate episode known as the *tempo di mezzo,* by a lively movement, the cabaletta. While, in Rossini's era, and sometimes also in later generations, the two movements of the aria had a similar color or even similar texts and metrical profiles, Rossini also initiated a trend, followed by Bellini, Donizetti, and the young Verdi, toward contrasting the movements through various techniques in order to present two distinct or opposing facets of the same personality. This obviously required that the text would be different; the opposition could be further emphasized by a change of meter.

The rigid character of the formula clearly posed textual problems since the switch from one movement to another had to be justified and the justification was often extremely artificial. For example, in *Oberto,* in the Andante mosso of his entrance aria, the young tenor Riccardo sings a hymn of praise to the woman he is about to marry. What could one possibly imagine by way of contrast? As the cabaletta demands, he inveighs against supposed enemies in the Allegro brillante with chorus that follows. Even more preposterous is the organization of Amalia's aria "Tu del mio Carlo al seno" (act 2 of *I masnadieri*): in a lovely Adagio she laments her lover's death; then, when another character rushes in, in the *tempo di mezzo,* to announce that in fact he is alive, she bursts into a jubilant cabaletta.

It would be easy to make fun of all this were there not also examples that succeed brilliantly, in part because the bipartite structure perfectly fits the drama. Thus, Violetta's great aria at the end of act 1 of *La traviata* opens with a slow movement in which she relives her dreams of innocence and love. This is contrasted, after a brief meditation (the *tempo di mezzo*), with a lively movement in which she realizes that her reveries are vain and fate condemns her to life as a courtesan. Here, the double aria reveals different facets or changes within a personality rather than a contrast created by the dramatic action.

More interesting for his future development is Verdi's tendency to set two different sections off against each other in a single-movement aria— a procedure usually inspired by the organization of the Italian romanza, in which one section in a minor key is followed by another in a major key (often the tonic major). We shall meet a significant example further on in Walter's aria in *Luisa Miller,* one movement of which conveys the outrage of a wounded father, the other the longing for a more affectionate bond with his son. The dynamic power of this scheme of articulation is seen very clearly in *Nabucco* in the character of Zaccaria, whose essential nature is presented by this technique. Here, despair is opposed to hope, prostration to desire for rebirth—the very feelings that divide the hearts of the Hebrews.

Zaccaria's prophecy at the end of act 3, "Del futuro nel buio discerno," opens somberly in the key of B minor as he proclaims the destruction of the kingdom of Babylon. Then the prophet collects himself, and the melody changes to B major for the more forceful "Niuna pietra ove sorse." The contrast is all the more striking in that the text suggests no such opposition. Zaccaria's other solos—his cavatina "D'Egitto la sui lidi" and his prayer "Tu sul labbro de' veggenti"—are driven by the same mechanism, which succeeds in conveying the character of the prophet and his role, that of encouraging the downtrodden Hebrews.

Several examples can be found of this method of building up an aria from contrasting movements (AB), one of the last being Otello's monologue in act 3.[48] Here Verdi employs the technique to tremendous effect: the shape of the aria is closely linked to the drama, with contrast in fact becoming a dynamic agent, and the structure is opened up in the absence of reprise—all of which suggests that the method suited him far better than the so-called Bellinian form (a1 a2 b1 a2) and its variants, which are closed on a full melodic arc. More than the two-part aria, this form marks the starting point of a trend, fully apparent in complex numbers like Rigoletto's act 2 "Cortigiani, vil razza dannata," toward basing the aria on movements that are clearly differentiated, even opposed.

Ensembles

The search for contrast is seen most clearly, of course, in the ensembles—duets, trios, and quartets. The main result of this attention to contrast is the gradual abandoning of vocal symmetry, according to which different characters follow the same melodic line in an ensemble. The aesthetic justification for this parallelism has to be the reconciliation of the characters in the transcendence of song. Such transcendence presupposes a gradual distillation of the text that results in the concrete dramatic situation being abandoned for a more abstract, general content appropriate for characters immersed in widely different situations—in other words, a movement from interaction to introspection, to adopt Scott Balthazar's formula.[49] This process soon clashes with the need for dramatic truth, implying that characters should never depart from their "real" situation.

Parallelism survives longer in static movements (the slow middle movement, the Adagio, and the rapid final movement) than in dynamic movements like the *tempo d'attacco* or the *tempo di mezzo* (see the glossary), which are relatively free in conception and can tolerate contrasts. Among the static movements, it persists longer in the cabaletta than in the Adagio, yet the need for differentiation ends up affecting all parts of the ensembles. This symmetrical treatment is found even as late as *Don Carlos, Aida,* and *Otello,* where, however, it is reserved for contexts that justify it dramatically.

Once again, *Oberto* provides a useful point of departure. Of its four ensembles, three devote a major share to vocal parallelism—the three movements of the Oberto-Leonora duet, the three movements of the Riccardo-Cuniza duet, and two of the three movements of the Oberto-Leonora-Cuniza trio. In the quartet, the tenor and soprano confront the bass and mezzo, but after that all the voices gain a certain independence, which, combined with the quality of the melodic attack of this quartet, explains why Verdi considered it "the best piece in the opera."[50]

In *Nabucco,* the act 3 duet between Nabucco and Abigaille is extremely interesting because it is designed throughout to contrast the triumphant arrogance of Abigaille, who has wrested power from the now mad Nabucco, with the prostration of the Assyrian king. The first movement, or *tempo d'attacco,* allegro vivo, which is dominated by a petulant, unsophisticated little theme admirably conveying Abigaille's greed for power, includes a dialogue that is treated as a mixture of recitative and parlante, a fairly common formula in this type of movement. Nabucco is eager to retrieve his crown from the slave Abigaille, but she takes advantage of the King's weakness to force him to sign the Israelites' death warrant, which also includes that of his own daughter, the recently converted Fenena. Then she proceeds under the King's very eyes to tear up the proof of her own illegitimate birth and status as a slave.

We now come to the central section, the Andante "Oh di qual onta aggravasi" in F minor. Here, Nabucco realizes that he is only a shadow of his former self whereas Abigaille is savoring her triumph. Everything in the two characters' music is in total opposition: the tonality (F minor for Nabucco, D♭ major for Abigaille); the King's steady rhythm and the spasmodic rhythm of the usurping slave; the feeble range of the father's song (limited to a minor sixth) contrasted with that of the ill-beloved "daughter," who energetically sweeps the sound space (from its opening first measures, the voice leaps an interval of a tenth). The section a due that closes the movement cleverly maintains the contrast of styles. During the *tempo di mezzo,* the King hears a flourish of trumpets and realizes that the Hebrews are going to their death and that he is Abigaille's prisoner. The cabaletta, a moderately lively number in A♭ major—"deh perdona, deh perdona"—again opposes the pleading Nabucco and the imperious Abigaille, who repeats the petulant theme of the first movement. It is symptomatic that both voices finally meet in this same theme, for the parallelism shows how the ambitious slave has succeeded in bending the powerful ruler to her will and is imposing on him her melodic theme.[51]

Contrast is even more radical in the final duet of act 1 of *I due Foscari.* Here, we have on one side a young woman, Lucrezia Foscari, emboldened by conjugal love and appalled to see her husband unjustly condemned on flimsy presumptions of guilt, and on the other the Doge, Francesco Foscari, who is the victim's father but is helpless to act because of his status as guardian of Venetian law, which forbids him any action that goes against the decisions of the Council of Ten. The contrasts bring into play tonalities (C minor then major, F minor and major), Lucrezia's fiery, vehement style as against the more static style of the Doge, and even rhythm and tempo: Lucrezia's F-minor cabaletta is in three-four time, allegro prestissimo, while that of the Doge is in F major, in four-four time and allegro moderato (see exx. 6a and 6b).

Likewise, the ensembles for three or four characters exemplify this preoccupation with contrast, but the need to present a number of very different characters somewhat slows down the dramatic rhythm.[52] Here, the principle of contrast clashes with the pursuit of movement: the series of "snapshot" portraits had to be enlivened and blended into one continuous movement. Verdi actually acquired this mobility of musical discourse

EX. 6a

early on, with the final trio of *Ernani,* a stage to which we shall return later.

Finale

The conflict that I have just described is even more problematic in the case of the Finale. By tradition, this section reunited all those who had a part in the plot, not counting minor roles or the chorus, with the danger that a diversified presentation of the characters could appear static. Moreover, one of the traditional purposes of the Finale was to set up a giant musical structure: Verdi would never give up this architectural concern,

EX. 6*b*

which produced the monumental constructions in *Aida, Otello,* and *Falstaff,* but linking these grand-scale machineries to the action was to cause him knotty problems, as we shall see.

Verdi's first Finales did not depart from the tradition according to which, although diversification of parts was permitted, the voices were soon combined or else one character with a pivotal role was given a position of contrast to all the others. Thus, in the first concertato Finale of *Nabucco* the Assyrian king, drunk with bloodletting and pillage, occupies the foreground, while in the Stretta all the characters are hurled pell-mell into a frenetic presto. The concertato of the act 2 Finale resorts to the highly classic expedient of canonic entrances *(falso canone)*, which groups everyone together on the same melodic line. The technique whereby a chief character is pitted against the others is found in Finale 1 of *I Lombardi,* where the parricide, Pagano, is set apart, just as is the King of Spain in the first-act Finale of *Ernani* and the tyrant Attila in Finale 1 of that opera.

On the other hand, the act 2 Finale of *I due Foscari* represents an unusual attempt to group together opposing characters: this is the episode in which Jacopo Foscari is brought before the Council of Ten and learns that he has been condemned to permanent exile. The hero, together with his wife, Lucrezia, and their children, tries in vain to sway the councillors' decision. The Finale studiously mixes together the character's diverse vocal styles—Jacopo's defenseless, pleading song, Lucrezia's heated indignation, the anguish of Jacopo's father, the Doge, and the inflexibility of Loredano, the Council's éminence grise.

The trend toward extremely careful differentiation is especially striking in the act 1 Finale of *Luisa Miller.* Eager to put an end to the idyll between his son Rodolfo and the peasant girl Luisa, Count Walter bursts into the home of old Miller, Luisa's father, insults his daughter, and has both of them arrested despite Rodolfo's protestations. The Largo—"Fra' mortali ancor oppressa"—begins by describing each character's reaction to the Count's behavior: old Miller resists his feudal lord with a mixture of awkwardness and pride that is made the more noticeable by the shift away from the traditional four-square form in his entry (three plus two measures instead of the usual four); Rodolfo tries to plead his lover's cause with lyrical fervor; Walter reaffirms his paternal authority in a dryly declamatory manner; and, finally, returning to the four-measure pattern, Luisa expresses the pain of humiliation in a phrase worthy of the future Violetta. The four voices then form a quartet, joined by the chorus, and, supported by Luisa's phrases, which create the fundamental mood of the situation, gradually approach the emotional crescendo that is de rigueur with every Finale.

The care that Verdi took to differentiate his characters' attitudes can be seen in the corrections he made when revising certain operas. For instance, in the duet between Alvaro and Carlo just before the camp scene in the definitive version of *Forza,* the first movement, Allegro mosso, gives Alvaro a cantabile, "Non io, fu il destino," in B minor. In the original version, Carlo takes up this melodic theme, but in A minor. The revision changes the character of Carlo's response, probably because the melodic theme suits Alvaro's vehemence—he wants to convince Leonora's vindictive brother of the integrity of his behavior—but not the sustained rage of the brother, which is more effectively expressed by a nonlyrical treatment. In the Simon-Amelia duet in act 1 of *Simon Boccanegra* (1857 version), Verdi gives the same melody to the two characters in the cabaletta "Figlia! a tal nome palpita," which seems a logical way to express both the father's and the daughter's joy at being reunited; yet the later version gives this melody only to Simon and devises a completely different one to contrast the father's passion and the daughter's gentle calm. When we bear in mind the date (1881), Verdi must have felt both concern for dramatic exactness and impatience with a procedure that by then seemed antiquated to him.

ACTION

In 1843, Verdi spelled out to a possible collaborator what he wanted in a libretto: "lots of fire, a huge amount of action, and brevity." Fire brings us back to the principle of tension, while brevity can be summed up as the desire to rid the text of anything marginal, to limit its task to representing the nature of the action. That same year, in a letter to Piave, the composer set forth very clearly the connection between the preponderance of the action and the necessary brevity: "You know as well as I do that in this type of composition we cannot achieve much effect unless there is action. Therefore use as few words as you can."[53]

The word *action* should not be understood in the narrow sense of "material action" since it can also have to do with an affective or a moral action that simply predisposes an individual to determined acts; it merely rules out any evasion of the drama through thought, meditation, or commentary. This concern for action is totally in the spirit of melodrama since only action allows the character's moral coherence to shine forth in all its brilliance and reveals its grandeur; yet few composers have gone to such lengths to reduce action to a primitive fact, bare of any explanation or justification. One suspects, however, that Verdi's insistence was all the greater in that the genre he inherited was constantly in danger of becoming static owing to the rigidity of forms.

We here come to a problem that is crucial and delicate in every kind of opera, that of form and movement. On becoming a libretto, the action of the drama is changed into a series of situations that are expressed in certain given forms; the combination of the two momentarily freezes the drama, and the larger the scale of this deployment, the more the action seems to come to a halt. Form kills movement as surprise or unexpected change, while movement kills form insofar as it is regular, periodic, and foreseeable. At the same time, without action form becomes lifeless, while without form action is impoverished since, as we have seen, the libretto overly schematizes the drama precisely because it is the task of the music to give it its dramatic and affective texture. This is a problem we shall be meeting throughout this exploration of the Verdian world, although with surprising reversals: from the perspective of "melodrama," it is important to Verdi that the use of forms should not put a brake on the action or weaken the vehemence of gesture; sometimes, as in *Nabucco,* the abundant twists of plot mitigate the opera's monumentality since it comes from the tradition of sacred, biblical opera with its threat of choral stasis. Later, within the perspective of "music drama," Verdi takes care that the advantage of extreme flexibility is not won at the expense of the formal construction of character or situation, in short, at the cost of clarity of gesture. He begins by introducing movement into form and ends up preserving form in movement. The solution of the problem could be found only in a suppler, more diversified handling of traditional forms.

In baroque opera, the alternation of recitative and aria created a duality of tempo, fast for the unfolding of facts as told by the recitative, slow for the lyrical pause of the aria—even slower in that the aria was often based on a maxim or universal truth. From Rossini on, Romantic opera strove to alleviate the effects of this dichotomy, as is demonstrated by Balthazar's study of the development of formal conventions between Rossini and the young Verdi.[54] Balthazar's synoptic tables illustrate how what Philip Gossett has characterized as the "kinetic" or dynamic movements of a number,[55] which previously functioned as a simple preparation for the vocal deployment, gradually acquired textual and musical independence and began to be treated extremely freely.

The *tempo d'attacco,* the first movement of an ensemble, was at first a lyrico-dramatic movement treated in parallel strophes, but, under Donizetti, and more systematically with Verdi, it evolved into a more dramatic presentation. Verdi frequently gives the *tempo d'attacco* breadth by varying the way the characters, tempos, and tonalities are related to one another. For example, in the act 3 duet of *Il corsaro,* Corrado the corsair, a prisoner of the sultan Seid, is visited at night by Gulnara, who is the Sultan's favorite but detests him; she has come to propose to Corrado that they flee together after killing the odious Sultan while he is asleep. Following a prelude and a *scena* in which we see the prisoner bemoan his fate, the *tempo d'attacco,* "Seid la vuole," describes Gulnara's attempts to persuade Corrado. Many different emotional moods come into play in the highly dramatic, flexible writing of this section—the passion of the heroine, who wants to flee Seid out of her hatred of tyranny; her love for the hero, which she quickly confesses; her dismay when she realizes that he loves another; and, on the other hand, the corsair's hesitations as he abandons himself to his fate and begs for death, his revulsion at killing an enemy while he is asleep, and finally his longing for his fiancée Medora.

Often limited to a small chorus or the exchange of a few cues with a confidant or attendant, the *tempo di mezzo* sometimes gives way, in its turn, to a complex development. For instance, in the *tempo di mezzo* of Carlo's aria "Lo vedremo veglio audace," in act 2 of *Ernani,* we have, one after the other, a chorus of Carlo's knights come to search Silva's castle (in vain) for Ernani; a declaration of vengeance of the King of Spain against Silva, who, out of a totally feudal sense of hospitality, has protected a rebel by hiding him; the sudden entrance of Elvira, who bursts in to beg the King not to punish Silva; the King's decision to keep Elvira as hostage; a cantabile on the part of Silva, who implores Carlo not to carry off his fiancée; and, finally, the refusal of the King and the chorus—all treated in widely different styles. Only then does the cabaletta, "Vieni meco, sol di rose," begin.

Nevertheless, the full deployment of these forms is at once massive and predictable: the duet generally consists of five phases in all (see the glossary), and these phases, with which the listener is already familiar, create a feeling of expectancy that is likely both to hold his attention and to weary his curiosity. Despite their growing autonomy, "kinetic" movements often remain merely a kind of preparation for lyrical pauses, which are perceived as the high points of the duet. The composer therefore strove to carry on his predecessors' work and make the traditional forms more dynamic by using certain procedures that we shall now examine in detail.

The Introduzione

The exposition was a delicate phase in opera since it entailed both presenting the characters and giving a brief summary of the background facts of the drama. Added to that were the *convenienze,* which dictated that the singers must, from their first entrance, be given the opportunity to impress the audience. It was difficult, therefore, to avoid a whole string of entrance arias. Thus, Donizetti's *Maria di Rohan* opens with a chorus followed by four arias: the cavatina of Chalais (tenor), that of Maria (soprano), the ballata of Gondi (contralto), and the cavatina of Chevreuse (baritone). A chorus, three double arias, and one ballata, that is, eight numbers, are obviously not likely to give the drama a breezy start.

Verdi's early work often shows examples of such relatively static presentation. *Oberto* begins with an introductory chorus, a double aria for tenor with chorus, and a double aria for soprano. The greater part of acts 1 and 2 of *I due Foscari* is taken up with an introductory chorus, Jacopo's double aria, Lucrezia's double aria with chorus, another chorus, and a romanza for the Doge Foscari. Only then do we reach the fine final duet between the Doge and his daughter-in-law, described above. The same holds true, more or less, for the opening of *Masnadieri*. The composer was palpably uncomfortable in this type of opening scene, as we have observed in connection with the genesis of *Ernani*.[56] A year later he timidly suggested to Cammarano that with *Alzira* he avoid linking three cavatinas in a row.[57]

The same problem arose with the introductory chorus, which was standard (and would remain so for a long time, in both Italian and French opera). Verdi was impatient with it, as this letter to Cammarano, written around the time of *Trovatore,* shows: "I'll tell you, it would be an improvement if in the beginning we could skip the chorus (every opera begins with a chorus) and Leonora's cavatina and start with the troubadour's song. We could blend the first two acts into one single act because to me these isolated pieces that require changing scene with every number seem more like concert pieces than opera."[58] The opera therefore would open with Ferrando's recitative (still accompanied by the chorus), and Verdi appeared to be satisfied, but again he turned up his nose at Leonora's entrance aria (which, to our great good fortune, he would retain): "1st number. The chorus and introductory recitative are fine. We'll cut Leonora's cavatina and have a majestic 2d trio."[59]

The other solution that was traditionally resorted to was the *Introduzione* in the strict sense of the term, a form perfected in opera buffa. Musically, the form made it possible to include solos that were lighter in weight than true entrance arias, and it had the advantage of presenting moments of action and thus being more dynamic. As an example, the *Introduzione* of *Lombardi* tells the story of the rivalry between Arvino and Pagano for Viclinda's love and Pagano's attempt to assassinate Arvino (chorus); then we witness a precarious reconciliation between the rivals (quintet with chorus), and, finally, the characters prepare to leave for the crusade led by Arvino (Stretta of the *Introduzione*).

Verdi made use of this kind of exposition under various guises in several operas (*Alzira, Luisa Miller, Stiffelio,* and, in quite a different spirit, *Ballo*). Still, aside from the fact that the formula did not do away with the ritual of the entrance aria, which was merely postponed, it could appear ponderous when it led to a grand concertato followed by a Stretta, in effect constituting a small-scale Finale. The composer therefore had to try to navigate between Scylla (the chorus or entrance arias) and Charybdis (the *Introduzione*) in order to find a way to integrate the exposition into the drama. The problem began with the libretto: in fact, in this case as in many others, if the originality of the musical rendering was the composer's task, it was up to the librettist first of all to propose fresh solutions.

Macbeth and *La battaglia di Legnano* provide elegant solutions to the problem by offering *Introduzioni* that are self-contained, like independent episodes. Macbeth's first meeting with the witches forms a kind of prologue to the real action, which does not begin until Lady Macbeth's cavatina. Hence, the organization that was chosen—witches' chorus, Banquo-Macbeth *scena* and duet, witches' chorus in the form of a Stretta—reinforces the prefatory character of this moment, necessary for the unleashing of the drama. In the same way, the introduction of *Battaglia* tends to turn in on itself since the series of numbers—chorus, solos of Arrigo, then Rolando, choral oath—are enclosed within a march that is announced by the chorus and concluded by the swearing of the oath: it therefore conveys the feeling of a complete episode rather than a succession of isolated numbers.

A great leap forward was accomplished with the introductions to *Rigoletto* and *La traviata,* which are ample and flexible at the same time. Seemingly, they are close to the traditional *Introduzione,* of which they retain certain elements like the concertato and Stretta in *Rigoletto* and the Stretta in *La traviata;* but in fact they differ from it profoundly in the sense that they set loose a chain of events rather than being organized around the climax of an ensemble and its Stretta. These *Introduzioni* are therefore like vast *scene* in which are set, gem-like, various pieces that seem to emerge out of the flow of sound: the Duke of Mantua's "ballad," the grand ensemble, Monterone's arioso with its Stretta, in the case of *Rigoletto;* and the brindisi, duet, and Stretta in that of *La traviata.* In *I Lombardi,* the elements of the *Introduzione* converge on the great quintet that is its central moment; in *Rigoletto,* Monterone's arrival is surely the high point of this episode, but it comes out of the blue, without any preparation, as if it were just one event after others before it. Furthermore, these *Introduzioni* set up a continuity of sound since each one is based on the pretext of festivity, which opens the way for a seamless succession of dances of various kinds—a continuum from which free, casual conversation can arise quite naturally.

Later on, and here I am looking ahead to music drama, Verdi tried to go to the heart of the matter more directly through conversation. In *Rigoletto,* the first words suggest a conversation that the spectator overhears as the curtain rises: "The Duke and Borsa enter from one of the rooms, chatting," notes a stage direction in the score. *Simon Boccanegra* begins with a question: "Che dicesti?" (What did you say?), addressed by Paolo to Pietro. The first cue in *Forza* is a "Buona notte, mia figlia" from the Marquis di Calatrava, who is obviously ending a conversation; similarly, *Aida* opens with a conversation between Radames and Ramfis: "Sì, corre voce" (Yes, there is a rumor). In all three cases, music joins forces with theater in its claim to raise the curtain on slices of life that somehow catch the spectator unawares. The *Aida* example is especially striking in that Mariette's original scenario provided for a choral introduction in the King's palace complete with officers, scribes, and fan bearers—a conventional solution the composer had discarded.[60]

It is only logical that this quest for animation in the introductory material should detract from the orchestral introduction, which in fact gradually disappeared. Significantly, when he again took up *Simon Boccanegra,* Verdi did away with the potpourri prelude of the 1857 version and replaced it with one great phrase announcing the following scene. Up to *Luisa Miller,* the overtures and preludes (a more flexible, shorter form) were evenly balanced (six overtures and seven preludes). After that Verdi seemed to show a preference for the prelude since we have three overtures (*Vêpres, Stiffelio/Aroldo, Forza* [1869]) as against seven preludes (*Rigoletto, Traviata, Simon* [1857], *Ballo, Forza* [1862], *Don Carlos* [1866], and *Aida*), whereas *Il trovatore* has neither one nor the other. The logical outcome of this development is the suppression, pure and simple, of the orchestral introduction; we can note this in the final versions of *Simon* and *Don Carlos,* and it is even more obvious in *Otello* and *Falstaff.*

Telescopings

Ernani offers several interesting examples of this technique, which consists of fusing together two numbers that would have had far more importance had they been developed fully. In order to avoid giving Carlo an entrance aria, which would have followed those of Ernani and Elvira, the King is introduced in the Bb-major Andantino of his duet with Elvira ("Da quel dì che t'ho veduta"). At the *tempo di mezzo* of this same duet Ernani rushes in just when the King is about to carry off Elvira. The cabaletta that explodes at that moment contrasts the two lovers' defiance and the violent reaction of the King. Verdi thus merges a duet and a trio since the cabaletta of the duet constitutes both the third movement of the duet and the only movement of the trio (the autograph score in fact gives the indication *scena e duetto indi terzetto*): instead of ABC + ABC, we have AB(C) + (AB)C. In this way dramatic continuity is ensured between the conflict of Carlo and Elvira and Ernani's sudden arrival on the scene.

In act 2, the seventh number is entitled "*scena* and trio." The *scena* opens with the hero, who is being hounded by the King of Spain, arriving haggard at Silva's castle and receiving his hospitality; then Ernani's solo, "Quant 'oro ogni avido," in C major, launches the Andante of the trio, which is reduced, for Elvira and Silva, to a short section. Silva goes off to give orders for the castle to be watched, leaving the lovers alone together. Ernani bitterly reproaches his beloved, who is about to wed Silva, and Elvira justifies herself by replying that she had believed her lover dead, whereupon the two are reconciled. This phase corresponds to the first two sections of a duet, the opening section, which is in dialogue form, and the lyrical middle section, "Ah morir potessi adesso." Silva then bursts in violently, furious at finding the two lovers in flagrante delicto, and the brief *scena* leads to the cabaletta in B♭ major, "No, vendetta più tremenda," which combines Silva's thirst for vengeance and the lovers' desperate heroism. Here, the duet is inserted in a trio whose first movement is also extremely light: instead of ABC + abc, we have (A)B + ab(c) + C.

The final example is taken from the next episode, in which the King arrives at Silva's castle and demands that the latter hand over the bandit Ernani, whom he has carefully been hiding. Carlo's aria, "Lo vedremo veglio audace," manages to slip into its coda a dialogue with Silva, "No, de' Silva il disonore"; in this way Verdi was able, without having to write a real duet, to oppose the arrogance of the all-powerful King and the pride of the feudal lord who considers hospitality an inviolable right. The advantage of these telescopings is the establishment of a fast dramatic rhythm compatible with the deployment of *pezzi chiusi*.[61]

Lightening the Baggage

What might be called formal lightening of the baggage occurs when Verdi abandons the obligatory order of succession that usually provides for part X to be followed by part Y. *Oberto,* the requisite starting point since it is Verdi's first opera, includes two tripartite duets (see the glossary), for soprano-bass and mezzo-tenor; one trio in three sections; a two-section quartet; and a grand finale complete with Largo and Stretta. In *Trovatore,* which has justifiably the reputation for being a traditional opera, the Manrico-Leonora-Luna trio of act 1 has only two fast movements;

the duet between Azucena and Manrico also has only two; the Finale 2 consists of merely a concertato (without Stretta); the trio Azucena-Ferrando-Luna is made up of two sections; and at the end of the opera we have, in succession, a one-movement *duettino* for Manrico and Azucena, then a *terzettino* with the two characters plus Leonora that consists of one dialogue movement a due and one lyrical movement a tre in which Azucena takes up the material of her previous *duettino*. Only the Leonora-Luna duet has the more classical makeup of *tempo d'attacco,* cantabile, an Andante con moto, and a cabaletta.

The trend toward reduction is just as clear in the arias. Aside from the tenor's romanza and the mezzo's Adagio, *Oberto* includes four double arias (tenor, soprano, mezzo, and bass) and the soprano's final rondò, also a bipartite aria. After this first opera the rest vary between three and four double arias, but *Macbeth* has only two (soprano and tenor), as has *Battaglia*. *Rigoletto* has but one, and furthermore this tenor aria is very probably a compromise solution. *Simon* includes two, but the 1881 revision brings this down to one. *Ballo* has none. This gradual reduction means not so much a rejection of the form as a refusal to keep it obligatory for every soloist. Verdi retained it for particular occasions, as in *Forza,* which has two double arias; the first concerns the baritone Carlo, who is a conventional character to his fingertips, while the second is given to Melitone and acts as a bravura piece, half buffa.

Logically, it is the cabaletta that bears the cost of this evolution. One reason may well be the change of sensibility on the part of the public, which became alienated from the warlike atmosphere of the 1840s, *cabalettismo* corresponding generally, in Verdi, to a generic affirmation of heroism.[62] Another reason may be the difficulty of justifying the form dramatically once it had become systematic. Moreover, the cabaletta weighed down the aria, which became a massive organism in its complete form (orchestral prelude, recitative or introductory *scena,* sometimes an arioso, a slow movement, an intermediate episode, the cabaletta proper, then the ritornello and reprise). Also, its structure was almost always less interesting than that of the Adagio, even though Verdi periodically attempted to renew it,[63] for it was based chiefly on rhythmic brio.

First the reprise was sacrificed[64] or, more precisely, tended to be integrated into the exposition of the cabaletta: in *La battaglia di Legnano* the cabaletta of the baritone Roland's aria "Se al nuovo dì pugnando" is not repeated, but the last phrase is expanded and then followed by the coda (act 3). The cabaletta of Germont's aria "Di Provenza il mar, il suol"

(*Traviata,* act 2), like that of Stankar/Egberto's "Lina/Mina pensai che un angelo" (*Stiffelio/Aroldo,* act 3), is repeated only in part.[65]

At the next stage the cabaletta was suppressed, yet it is important to note that Verdi did not give up the impulsiveness it expresses but rather strove to integrate this affect into the surviving slow movement. The mechanism can be clearly seen in the revision of *Simon Boccanegra.* In act 1 (1857), Amelia dreams as she gazes at the sea and in a very beautiful Adagio sings of love and the night, "Come in quest'ora bruna"; wondering why her lover, Gabriele, has not come, she suddenly hears him singing offstage a graceful "nocturne," "Cielo di stelle orbato"; her joy bursts forth in a long, virtuoso cabaletta, "Il palpito, deh frena," which has a ritornello, reprise, and brief coda. In 1881, Verdi struck out the short recitative and directly juxtaposed the coda of the Adagio and Gabriele's nocturne, while reducing the cabaletta to two short explosions of joy that retain its meaning. This change led to a beneficial telescoping: in 1857, Gabriele's nocturne is inserted in the *tempo di mezzo* of Amelia's aria, which then runs its course, after which the duet begins; in 1881, this same nocturne and Amelia's outburst directly link her Adagio and the duet that follows.

Two fine examples can be cited of this integration of the vehemence of the cabaletta into the body of the aria. Lady Macbeth's aria "La luce langue," which replaced the original cabaletta of the 1847 version,[66] includes an expressive section in E minor ("La luce langue"), a *scena*-like section ("Nuovo delitto"), and a form of cabaletta in E major ("O voluttà del soglio") that together achieve remarkable balance in a single unit. Similarly, in Eboli's aria in *Don Carlos,* after the cantabile "Adieu reine" / "O mia regina," an Allegro più mosso leads to a brief outburst, "Ah! je me sens renaître" / "Sia benedetto il ciel," which has all the vehemence of a cabaletta. The advantage of these formulas is that the final explosion no longer has anything forced about it but depends strictly on the dramatic situation.[67]

Another obligatory connection that Verdi tends to do away with is that between the Largo and the Stretta of the finale. His first five operas (counting *Un giorno di regno*) include a finale in two movements, but the sixth, *I due Foscari,* in fact has no Stretta but simply a short section *più mosso* taken from the preceding Largo. The allegro ending the first Finale of *Macbeth* is similar to a short Stretta but is joined to the preceding ensemble, while the second Finale does not include a Stretta. *I masnadieri* has no Finale, while *Luisa Miller* has one in act 1, but without Stretta. It will be noted that the innovative operas are those that depart from the grandioso genre and warlike atmosphere, like *I due Foscari, Macbeth,* and *Luisa Miller.* After *Luisa* one still finds Finales in the old style, as in *Stiffelio/Aroldo* and the first version of *Simon,* but Verdi tends to favor a Finale conceived on quite different principles, as we shall see.

We can trace a distinct evolution in each of these examples. It comes from Verdi's wish to get away from the staleness of the old, predictable forms, from his refusal to think of them as obligatory, and his determination to preserve their validity when they are dramatically justified.

The aesthetics of melodrama constitutes the basic framework of Verdi's dramatic world. One can think of it as perfunctory or crude, but undeniably it was an experience indispensable to his growth. Without this assiduous pursuit of tension, contrast, and action, Verdi would very likely not have acquired that surety of melodic line and clarity of articulation and form, that drive that forces the spectator to be caught up in an inescapable mechanism. Furthermore, Verdi adapted this aesthetics but never broke with it or repudiated it, probably because it harmonized with his conviction that man can, even at the risk of death, take his destiny upon himself fully and with pride.

Verdi's attachment to melodrama cropped up curiously at the time he was composing the act 3 finale of *Otello,* in 1880, when he was almost seventy years old. I recalled earlier that, dissatisfied with a first draft that Boito had made, the composer suggested livening up the finale with an attack on the part of the Turks. He described it in these terms (the point is just after the scene in which Otello throws Desdemona to the ground before the people of Cyprus and members of the Venetian senate): "Suddenly in the distance are heard drums, trumpets, cannon fire, etc., etc. . . . 'The Turks! The Turks!!' Populace and Soldiers invade the stage. All are surprised and frightened! Otello recovers himself and stands erect like a lion; he brandishes his sword and addressing Lodovico, says: 'Come! I will again lead you to victory. Venice will then reward me *with dismissal!* . . .' All abandon the stage except Desdemona. Meanwhile the women of the populace, rushing in on all sides, terrified, fling themselves down on their knees, while from off stage the shouts of the warriors are heard, cannon fire, drums, trumpets, etc., all the fury of the battle. Desdemona in the center of the stage, isolated, motionless, her eyes fixed on Heaven, prays for Otello. The curtain falls."[68]

Lovers of Shakespeare will shudder at this coup de théâtre, which is in the pure tradition of *mélo!* It flabbergasted Boito, for whom Verdi's suggestion was "like a fist breaking the window of a room where two people are about to die of asphyxiation."[69] In truth, it was probably Verdi who felt asphyxiated by his hero's slow degradation; even if it meant suggesting a preposterous ending, he wanted to give him a way out—not to survive but to escape that feeling of suffocation. We will see that *Otello* marked the destruction and even proclaimed the impossibility of melodrama. Insofar as this act of destruction was profoundly saddening to Verdi, his suggestion of a Turkish attack is a sudden outburst of defiance, a way of confronting the confused, turbid world that was draining Otello's grandeur, a need to cling one last time to an aesthetics that had accompanied his first steps and that he knew to be condemned.

CHAPTER FIVE

Metamorphoses I

In the previous chapter we saw how the grammar of melodrama is based on certain laws. The first is clarity, or total lack of ambiguity in characters and situations. The second is moral plenitude for each character: this assumes that, even if he is prey to contradictions or contrary feelings, man can be presented dramatically by attitudes that define him in all his fullness. Whether fate deal him failure or success, his changing fortunes cannot alter the clear-cut, compact nature of his personality. The engine driving the action is provided by a third law, that of excess. Melodrama is a world where each character completely fills the space that is allotted him through a kind of latent totalitarianism: there are no gaps, no shadings, since to be larger than life each character must realize his essence to the maximum. Because of this dramatic need, each action encroaches on another character's space; thus, every action is excessive and calls forth a response that is on no less vast a scale.

Verdi's evolution went forward on two levels. At the deepest and aesthetically most important one, it led him to question, not the types and situations peculiar to this code, but the laws governing it: he clouded the essential clarity of melodrama by creating characters that were increasingly complex and ambiguous; he challenged the law of moral plenitude by casting doubt on the monolithic coherence of characters; and, finally, he called into question the law of excess by showing up its destructiveness and absurdity. It is this movement away from a "ritual" perspective toward a more critical one that allowed melodrama to evolve into music drama; thus, the world of melodrama, splendidly epitomized in *Ernani,* becomes totally disintegrated in *Otello.*

Moreover, while still observing the same code, Verdi could change his way of viewing characters, showing them in a different light. The code did not imply a priori a particular perspective, if one understands by that, not the technical choice that favors one character over another, but the way a character is presented to the spectator, attracting either sympathy or rejection. With each type possessing its own system of references, opera shows us contradictory ideologies; thus, from the hero's point of view the tyrant is nothing but a usurper, while the hero is never anything but a seducer in the eyes of the judge.

Verdi took in these various views with a panoramic gaze that changed considerably over the years. To take one example, there is a world of distance from the prophet Zaccaria in *Nabucco* to the Inquisitor in *Don Carlos* or the high priest Ramfis in *Aida*. Yet these are three equally ruthless judge figures: the first is prepared to cut his enemy's daughter's throat, the second urges the King to sacrifice his son for the good of the state, while the third does not hesitate to order the execution of his best general, who is guilty of treason. But the judicial task of these three characters has a different meaning depending on the historical context in which they were conceived. Thus, in 1842, when Romanticism's cry of liberation was resounding, Zaccaria could be made a leader of peoples, one able to galvanize his flock, and the cruelty of his actions could be overlooked. Later, in 1867 or 1871, the disenchanted individualism of the age showed up the oppressive apparatus of the state and of religious ideology. These are fundamental changes that I will here attempt to follow by studying certain major themes and characters.

Revenge and Curse

Transgression—punishment—bang!
Pitiless, pitiless. That's the only way.
JOSEPH CONRAD,
Heart of Darkness

People often make fun of Italian opera's constant repetition of words like *vendetta, maledizione,* and *pietà*. The practice has its roots in the law of excess outlined above. Each character has a "territory" with which he identifies and whose integrity he guards with his honor. For each character type, honor implies physical courage, faithfulness to his promises, and tenacity in his desire to redress wrongs. Yet the ideological content varies considerably depending on the character type—hero, judge, tyrant, or heroine. The judge pursues a personal justice that demands the punishment of an offense and the upholding of a flouted law; the hero claims a legitimate right that is denied him; the tyrant, by dint of force, manifests his blind desire for power and his persistence in clearing all obstacles from his path. Nonetheless, honor always demands the immediate reparation of an offense. Consequently, vengeance appears as the prime mover, if not the essential action of the drama.

We know that the chief characteristic of revenge, as the reaction of honor, is to set in motion a series of actions and reactions that can end only in the death of one of the combatants. As Hegel observed, "There is no end to strife and quarreling owing to the independence of individuals and their inflexible singularity which . . . is implicit in the principle of honor."[1] In *I Lombardi,* Pagano has been rejected by Viclinda and wants to take revenge on his brother, whom she prefers; he attempts to kill him, is banished, but later is readmitted after a period of expiation. His thirst for vengeance has not lessened, however, and he again tries to murder his brother, but mistakenly kills his father. He flees once more, disguising his identity so as to escape from his brother, who in turn must avenge his father's murder. Another characteristic of the spirit of revenge is tenacity, which *La forza del destino* gives us in full measure. Don Carlo di Vargas has vowed to avenge the death of his father, killed by the Indian Alvaro. He pursues Alvaro across Spain, then tracks him down in Italy and challenges him to a duel. The duel is interrupted, and the combatants are separated, after which Don Carlo resumes his search and traces Alvaro to a monastery. This time the duel does take place, but Don Carlo is the one who is killed.

Differences of motivation can be essential to defining the moral aspect of a character, but they carry little weight in the mechanisms of the plot. On the level of the unfolding of the action, base or envious characters like Iago or Paolo Albiani in *Simon Boccanegra* are no less tenacious in their pursuit of vengeance than noble judges. The arguments that Verdi had with Scribe concerning Procida in *Les Vêpres siciliennes* are proof of this: whether he is represented as a fanatic and bigot (Scribe's viewpoint) or as a stern but noble defender of Sicilian independence (Verdi's), Procida still has to carry out his task as political judge to the very end and prepare the Sicilians' revenge on the French.

The curse is an appeal to revenge rather than a true act of vengeance. On the one hand it assumes, implicitly or explicitly, the agency of God, the judge par excellence, gaining solemnity from this appeal to heavenly chastisement. Hence, the curse is almost always pronounced by paternal figures whose actual situation as father, whose status as monarch, high priest, or uncontested leader, or simply whose age or the respect accorded them (as, e.g., Leone in *Attila* or Moser in *I masnadieri*) confers the right to invoke divine aid. A curse also assumes the complicity of the community called to witness the gravity of the offense and representing the social body—hence the judge's practice of soliciting the aid of other characters. As a result of this double implication of divine authority and the mandate of society, a curse often takes on a solemn, public character and gives rise to majestic scenes—Monterone's curse in *Rigoletto* comes immediately to mind. The composer and librettist may even add a curse scene where the literary source has none: for instance, the solemn curse on Duncan's murderer in the act 1 Finale of *Macbeth* has no equivalent in Shakespeare's play.

Another important characteristic of the curse is that it is a deferred revenge, a promise of action that is not a true action. In most cases the curser has no means to wreak his revenge and relies on God, on circumstances, or on helpers. Monterone presents the classic example of the impotent curser when he curses the Duke of Mantua and his jester in the first act, all the while knowing full well that he is powerless against them: "E se al carnefice pur mi darete, / Spettro terribile mi rivedrete, / Portante in mano il teschio mio, / Vendetta chiedere al mondo e a Dio" (And even if you give me to the executioner, you'll see me again, a terrible specter, carrying my own skull in my hand, to ask vengeance of the world, of God; act 1, scene 6). A curse may therefore have absolutely no effect on the action but a considerable impact on the emotional climate: Monterone's curse provides a moment of terror that seizes up the plot, laying a heavy threat on its victim.

The combination of curse and revenge can account for most of an opera's peripeteias: (1) In act 1 of *Nabucco*, the Hebrews are carried off in captivity to Babylon, but the libretto's epigraph at the beginning of the act, taken from Jeremiah, would have us understand that this captivity is retribution for their sins and that therefore Nabucco is merely the instrument of divine vengeance. (2) Meanwhile, we have seen the tenor Ismaele cursed by the Hebrews because he has betrayed them through his love for Nabucco's daughter. (3) In act 2, the triumphant ruler loses his mind and believes that he is a god: he is cursed by Zaccaria, and God grants the prophet's wish by destroying the Assyrian king. (4) Abigaille takes advantage of the situation and assumes power, thus avenging herself for the position of inferiority to which the King had relegated her. After a double expiation, the Hebrews and Nabucco again receive divine grace, but not the ambitious Abigaille, who dies punished for her transgression, murmuring, "Te chiamo ... Dio ... te venero / Non maledire a me" (I call on Thee, O God, I worship Thee, do not curse me; act 4, scene 5).

All-powerful in this political opera, the imbroglio of curse and revenge is no less entangled in a private drama such as *Rigoletto,* which incidentally was at first to have been called *La maledizione.* The jester Rigoletto punishes the courtiers' mockery by urging the Duke of Mantua to carry off their wives; the courtiers in turn have their revenge on the jester by abducting his daughter and handing her over to the Duke. The Duke is a notorious libertine, cursed by Monterone, whose daughter he has seduced. Rigoletto therefore decides to wreak his revenge by having the Duke murdered and, in so doing, takes on himself Monterone's curse, which up to that time has had no effect (act 2, scene 7). But, when he realizes that it is his daughter and not the Duke who has perished under the assassin's knife, Rigoletto understands that the curse of Monterone has come down on his own head.

Certainly, both vengeance and curse are recurrent themes in both Italian and French Romantic opera as well as German (one has only to think of the importance of revenge in Wagner's work with Telramund in *Lohengrin,* Melot in *Tristan,* and Alberich in the *Ring* cycle). Similarly, innumerable other operas feature curses: Spontini's *La vestale;* Rossini's *Otello, The Siege of Corinth,* and *Semiramide;* Donizetti's *Caterina Cornaro* and *Belisario;* and Meyerbeer's *Le Prophète* (to name only a few). But at the same time it is hard to appreciate the real impact of these concepts on the audience. Stendhal believed that the spirit of vengeance was a distinctive Italian trait and proved the strength of the Italian character. Gilbert Maugain's study, now old, shows how easily the Italian nobles unsheathed their swords at the slightest hint of challenge to their honor, but he is describing the customs of the fifteenth and sixteenth centuries. By Verdi's time the code of personal and social honor must have lost much of its force while still preserving a certain prestige, as is the case in societies with a somewhat patriarchal structure.[2]

Whether or not it amounted to a social custom, the ideology of revenge captured the nineteenth-century imagination and touched deep chords in such artists as Verdi. Verdi was notoriously vindictive and a bearer of grudges, as the opera house of La Scala, the conductor Mariani, and others, even Boito, learned at their expense.[3] What is one to make of this violent philippic against the publisher Lucca, Ricordi's rival: "He has been insensitive, mean, demanding toward me. I forgive a slap in the face, because if I can, I'll give back twenty, and then will kill the person who slapped me, even on the altar; but I cannot pardon an insult to which I cannot respond"?[4] Set in verse, this sally could well find a spot in an opera! It is said that art reflects mores, but mores can also reflect art:[5] in his biography of Garibaldi, Max Gallo emphasizes several times how the attitude of the Italian patriot—for whom Verdi long professed deep admiration—was at times worthy of an operatic character.[6]

The same blending of the real and the imaginary turns up again with the theme of the curse. The curse is suited to rural, patriarchal, and hierarchical societies, where fathers ensure the cohesion of the community and hold the threat of curse over rebels and antisocial characters. These authority figures may invoke the image of a vengeful biblical God and compare the one who is being cursed to the biblical victim par excellence—Cain, so frequently invoked in malediction scenes in opera. This patriarchal dominance suffered a crisis over the century but still hung over everyday life. Every solemn oath was coupled with a threat of curse on the perjuror. For example, the members of Giovine Italia, the revolutionary movement led by Mazzini, had to pronounce these ritual words: "I call down upon my head the wrath of God, the scorn of men and the infamy of perjury if I betray my oath either in whole or in part."[7] Consequently, in opera the curse was still felt as a terrible threat: when *Nabucco* was performed for Milanese audiences, scoring a triumph, Emilio Seletti, a historian from Verdi's small native town of Busseto, drew the lesson that "God strikes down the baseness of nations . . . a nation purged by cruel slavery must in the end rise to liberty," a moral that mingles national aspiration and religious messianism.[8]

The curse entered Verdi's life by way of a curious childhood episode. As a young altar boy he was distracted by the sound of music and forgot to hand the priest the vessels of water and wine. The priest, one Don Masini, was exasperated by his behavior and gave him a violent kick, which sent the boy hurtling down the altar steps. Humiliated and furious with rage, Verdi proceeded to call down the lightning of God on the priest's head. Eight years later, lightning did indeed strike a church in the next village, killing two dogs and four priests, among them the famous Don Masini and two lay members. Apparently Verdi liked to tell this story in later years.[9] It is curious, on the other hand, that, when his former pupil and friend Emanuele Muzio was named director of the Théâtre Italien in Paris in 1870, Verdi counseled firmness and equanimity, adding, "Don't nourish either likes or dislikes, and don't be afraid of any curse."[10]

The interweaving of revenge and curse suggests a primitive, ruthless ideology of territoriality, according to which each individual has a sphere that he guards ferociously in the name of his honor. Together, these "spheres" are controlled by a jealous God who punishes transgressors—as Solera writes in the introductory chorus of *Giovanna d'Arco*, "Maledetti cui spinge rea voglia / Fuor del cerchio che il Nume ha segnato" (Cursed be those whom an impious desire hurls out of the circle traced by God). The slightest infraction therefore gives rise to catastrophe, the only recourse being the haste with which hero, tyrant, and judge avenge what they consider slights on their honor. One result of this ideology is that the plot leads inexorably to disaster. Verdi's tendency to seek a balance between action and passion, between dramatic movement and its affective consequences, reveals the ideology as mechanical, implacable, even absurd: faced with this negative vision of existence and history, some artists stressed individual pathos and unhappiness, but Verdi preferred to emphasize the epic, cruel rhythm of reality.

Understandably, some denounced this vindictive spirit and appealed for forgiveness, but they were usually men of the church who encouraged resignation and reminded their flocks that happiness is not of this world. History, as it appears in Verdi's librettos, knows only three types of character—those who blindly enforce political and social laws, those who are its victims, and those who find to their grief that they are powerless over the course of events. As Folco Portinari writes, pardon remains "a hallowed act,"[11] a divine prerogative. With Verdi one continually finds this opposition between God's indulgence and ultimate forgiveness and the ferocity of man, who is incapable of pardon—in *Oberto* (act 2, scene 6), *I masnadieri* (act 4, scene 4), *Battaglia* (act 3, scene 6), and even *Traviata,* where Violetta sorrowfully states that her sin is without remission: "Se pur benefico—le indulge Iddio / L'uomo implacabile—per lei sarà" (Even if God is kind and indulgent to her, mankind will always be implacable; act 2, scene 5).

Unfitness for pardon is admirably described by Milan Kundera in *The Joke,* which is primarily a novel of vengeance: "For people don't know how to offer absolution by themselves, nor do they have the power to do so. They lack the power to annihilate a sin once it has taken place. They need outside assistance. Divesting a sin of its validity, voiding it, rubbing it out of time, in other words making something into nothing, requires a mysterious and supernatural act. Only God—because He is exempt from earthly laws, because He is free, because He can work miracles—may wash away sin, transform it into nothing, and absolve the sinner. Man can hold out absolution to his fellow man only insofar as he founds it on divine absolution."[12]

The impossibility of human forgiveness is made abundantly clear in Romantic drama. The spirit of revenge arises from the memory of the offense, and memory is the thread by which our identity is established and preserved; for an opera character, to give up revenge is to give up his identity, to accept that his integrity has been violated, which he cannot agree to do without running the risk of no longer existing. That is why pardon so often intervenes at the moment of death, the moment when the identity that the character has so stoutly defended is dissolved.

It is true that the code foresees the possibility of pardon by opposing the vengeful judge character and the conciliatory one, but the first always wins out over the second, so much so that often the only effect of the conciliatory approach seems to be to show up the tenacity of the spirit of vengeance—a contrast we find in *Oberto* (Oberto vs. Cuniza), *Ernani* (Silva vs. Carlo), and *Alzira* (Gusmano vs. Alvaro). It is interesting, therefore, to look at those operas in which Verdi tries to present pardon as an act, not simply a pious vow.

Stiffelio, which is taken from a play by Emile Souvestre and Eugène Bourgeois called *Le Pasteur, ou l'Évangile et le foyer,* first put on in Paris in 1849, tells the story of a hero, a leader of the Assasverian sect, who discovers that his wife has been unfaithful to him with a seducer. Stiffelio's father-in-law, a country squire proud of his honor and military past (act 3, scene 1), sees a duel as the only solution, one that is closed to Stiffelio because of his calling as a man of God. Stiffelio nevertheless vehemently sweeps aside any idea of forgiveness and gives in to fury (end of act 2). Stankar, the avenging judge, will manage to kill the seducer, but, in his great act 3 duet, Stiffelio for the first time suggests to Lina the idea of divorce—a totally unaccustomed idea in opera of the time—then realizes that his wife has not really deceived him and that she still loves him. All the interest then is concentrated on the final scene, which takes place in church: rising above the tempest swirling about him, Stiffelio pardons his wife as he reads the lesson of the woman taken in adultery.

Despite this highly original ending, the description of the minister's inner struggle is hastily drawn and the pardon almost brutal.[13] When Verdi changed *Stiffelio* into *Aroldo* in 1857, the pastor became a Saxon knight; instead of talking of divorce, he flees his home and goes off to the banks of a lake in Scotland, where he is joined by his wife and father-in-law and he forgives her. This denouement, which gives rise to a trio and final quartet, is much better handled than that of the first opera, and the pardon appears like the culmination of a painful process, not a sudden, violent about-face. In its original version, the opera is interesting because the year in which it was composed, 1850, saw the beginnings of Verdi's great "trilogy" as well as major changes in his dramaturgy.

La forza del destino plays an important role in this effort to escape the infernal cycle of vengeance. The story line appears to stick to the traditional view contrasting an implacable judge (the Marquis di Calatrava, a role carried on after his death by his son Don Carlo di Vargas) and a compassionate man of the church (Il Padre Guardiano). However, the latter's function is not limited to that of helpless onlooker: not only does he offer Leonora refuge and accept Alvaro, the involuntary murderer of the Marquis di Calatrava, among his monks, but he also plays a fundamental role in Leonora's metamorphosis in act 2, helping her recover inner serenity. Instead of the image of a vengeful father, we have an indulgent parent who soothes away the terrible visions that have been haunting her: "Più non sorge sanguinante / Di mio padre l'ombra innante; / Nè terribile l'ascolto / La sua figlia maledir" (My father's shade no longer rises bleeding before me, nor do I hear him dreadfully curse his daughter; act 2, scene 9).

The 1869 denouement, whose difficult genesis has been described, only accentuates this evolution. In 1862, in the first version, Alvaro receives the full force of the old Marquis's curse and, after killing Don Carlo, throws himself into the abyss uttering horrible blasphemies while Padre Guardiano and the monks' chorus look on helplessly. In 1869, the chorus vanishes, and Padre Guardiano becomes the protagonist of the denouement. The marvelous trio closing the opera depicts a true conversion: at the father's urging, and under Leonora's soothing influence, Alvaro overcomes the temptation of blasphemy and despair and offers himself up to redemption. Opening with a "trio" for Alvaro, Leonora, and the Marquis di Calatrava, the work ends with another trio in which the father who taught vengeance has yielded to a father who teaches forgiveness and sublimation.

This finale lays unusual stress on the effort to go beyond the spirit of revenge and curse. In fact, in the original Spanish play Guardiano has nothing like the dramatic and symbolic role he plays in the opera, one that Verdi clearly intended since he expanded the scene of the meeting with Leonora in act 2 with a finale, writing the text himself.

Yet the most significant opera in this evolution is still *Simon Boccanegra,* in its first and second versions (1857 and 1881). Simon, the corsair, becomes doge of Genoa at the beginning of the fourteenth century, hoisted to power by the people. Twenty-five years later he still encounters the hostility of the patricians, which he answers with clemency. He lifts the decree of exile affecting Amelia Grimaldi's patrician "brothers" (shortly afterward he discovers that in fact she is his own daughter); he treats with indulgence the patrician Gabriele Adorno, who defies and insults him (act 1); he pardons Gabriele for having tried to assassinate him, promising him his daughter's hand in marriage (act 2); and in the last act, when his old enemy Fiesco confronts him while he is in agony, poisoned by one of his partisans, the two are reconciled, and Simon still finds the strength to unite Amelia and young Adorno, to whom he hands over the ducal crown. Thus, to each affront he replies with a magnanimous gesture.

All these circumstances are described in the first version, but the revision accentuates the peacemaking image, both in the suppression of references to Simon as military commander and in the insistence on his role as conciliator. For example, at the beginning of act 3 (1857) Simon has subdued a revolt that had broken out at the end of the preceding act. The chorus celebrates his victory, and the Doge enters: "Brando guerrier nella mia destra splende, / La vostra quel della giustizia impugni" (This warrior sword in my right hand gleams; justice you grasp in yours), he tells the senators, thus inviting them to punish the guilty. In 1881, the act opens with a reminder of the rebellion music of the preceding act, which is restless but not martial; eight short measures of choral song celebrate the victory; then Fiesco, the rebel leader, enters, accompanied by a captain who sets him free and gives him back his sword. No doubt in modifying this introduction Boito intended to correct two inconsistencies of the plot,[14] yet the suppression of Simon's answer and the freeing of Fiesco, his principal enemy, do serve to tone down the Doge's vengeful fury.

The most striking example, however, is the act 1 Finale. In the 1857 version, this was the celebration of the twenty-fifth anniversary of Simon's elevation to the ducal throne. An opening chorus and a barcarole welcome the company to the festivities; then a hymn is heard praising the Doge's warrior-like virtues: "Tu sei di guerra il fulmine / Il sol della vittoria!" (You are the lightning of war, the sun of victory!). This is followed by a dance of African corsairs and a final chorus. In short, what we have is a conventional finale of gala pomp and martial rejoicing. The 1881 Finale retains the action of the original version but changes the framework. It was Verdi who hit on the idea of a session of the Genoese senate, Verdi, too, who remembered the letter that Petrarch wrote in 1352 to the senate and council of Genoa inviting them to end their fratricidal fight against Venice, after having tried a similar approach with the Venetian authorities.[15] So we see Simon warmly approve Petrarch's initiative, confront a popular uprising with dignity, and intervene to prevent the plebeian and patrician councillors from killing one another while each side accuses the other of fomenting agitation. To round out this forceful portrait, a solo for Simon launches the true finale: in the first section, which is firmly declamatory in character ("Plebe! Patrizi!—Popolo"), he inveighs against his fellow citizens and their readiness to destroy each other, while the second section, "Piango su voi" (I weep for you), conveys the longing for an impossible social harmony on the beautiful soil of Genoa. The last phrase of this section—"E vo gridando: pace! / E vo gridando: amor!" (All that I ask is peace, now! All that I ask is love!)—is a sort of refrain dominating the finale to which everyone present responds in his own way.

Simon is a deeply moving opera. However utopian the protagonist and his dream of national reconciliation, one senses Verdi's sadness, deeply grieved as he was to see his country bogged down in the sorry round of scandals, social conflict, and local rivalries. The opera is also a response to a dramaturgy based on the implacable chain of brawls and vendettas. Simon's nostalgia is made palpable in his evocation of the "vast kingdom of the seas," the fatherland that the corsair dreamed of, the freshness of the open sea that gives him a final comfort as he lies dying, victim of his fellow citizens' machinations.

Falstaff marks the end of this long journey, for, although the spirit of revenge plays a major role in the plot, the protagonist uses humor to point a finger at what is the psychological and social basis for this spirit—honor, an empty word, "dell'aria che vola" (some air that flies; act 1, scene 1).

The problem is slightly different as regards the curse. This never disappears from Verdi's theater—one has but to remember Simon Boccanegra's curse on Amelia's seducer, present only in the 1881 version (Finale 1), or Otello's cursing of Desdemona at the end of act 3 ("Anima mia, ti maledico")—yet it does lose its air of sacred rite. Zaccaria, Leone, Moser, and Monterone are characters surrounded with a certain religious aura, living images of an order still formidable enough that any transgression arouses dread. Little by little, Verdi's world becomes secularized, and the social organization loses its religious dimension, that dimension that in the past gave such resonance to the gesture of ostracism represented by the curse; religion becomes a private domain offering comfort and consolation, and, when priests meddle with politics (*Don Carlos* and *Aida*), they are represented as despots. Thus, curse strikes terror in the first operas but later becomes mainly spectacular, an occasion for a "big scene."[16]

To sum up, excessiveness and the spirit of vengeance inhabit Verdi's characters to the very end—*Otello* is an outstanding example—yet their creator becomes less and less at one with these ferocious passions.

The Father and the Sorceress

"Paternal authority is a big word."
FRIEDRICH SCHILLER,
Intrigue and Love

THE FATHER FIGURE

Up to the 1850s, when the system entered a period of crisis, Italian society was generally organized on a patriarchal model based on an extended family, a strong, authoritarian father, and a mother who was attached to the home and stayed relatively in the background but was apt to be stern and austere. The father had extremely broad powers, including that of deciding on his children's professions or marriages, and acts of insubordination were looked on very severely: "A father was still surrounded by a sense of respect bordering on fear, and everyone reverently bowed their heads to his bidding and his words. Thus whenever one of the sons dared oppose his father's will he was held in contempt as a rebel."[17] Indeed, the literature of the age is full of the dreadful consequences, both moral and material, of sons' rebelliousness.

Reinforcing the father's power, the idea of the father figure extended to society as a whole, according to a mechanism that Bossuet admirably summed up in his formula, "Kings take their thrones from God, who is the true father of the human race." The father was to the family what the king was to his people and God to humanity. This meant that any attempt at liberation on the individual's part, whether in the context of family or politics, was doomed to failure since, whatever the arena in which his actions took place, he would come up against a paternal authority to which he had to submit. The three paternal domains—family, politics, and religion—buttressed each other, making any transgression catastrophic. Thus, when Macbeth kills Duncan, his sovereign, he kills his "father" (whence the sterility that strikes his wife, whence in turn the lack, for him, of a consoling family), offending divine majesty and upsetting the political order.

In the 1850s, and even more with Italian unity and the growth of an industrial society, this pattern faded, gradually giving way to the nuclear family.[18] As a result, fearing the mortal danger that they believed the growth of individualism represented for traditional values, the ruling classes tended to perpetuate the old model in an ideology that was conservative, family based, and Catholic, one in which the industrialist became the father of his workers and the constitutional monarch remained the father of his subjects. Seeing his power threatened, the father brandished his authority so as to ensure his perpetual dominion.

Logically enough, opera mirrored this situation, producing countless examples of stern-browed fathers who force their offspring to obey and curb them from freely fulfilling their desires. The fathers' behavior is dictated by their honor, which consists in preserving their rank, their dignity, and their daughters' virginity. What is remarkable is that this latter duty overrides every other moral or political obligation. For instance, Giacomo, Joan of Arc's father, announces in no uncertain terms that, although he is French, he is above all a father; hence, he does not hesitate to side with the English in order to avenge his honor, which has been compromised by the supposed liaison between his daughter and the King of France (act 2, scene 2). This radical choice tends to prove the priority of defense of family honor over political passions.

At times the fathers can be tenderhearted, but usually they are inflexible and even cruel, as in Tomasso Grossi's well-known verse novella *Ildegonda* (1820), from which a dozen operas were derived between 1829 and 1847. Grossi gives us virtually a caricature of the anger of a father furious that his daughter, out of love for another man, is objecting to the husband he has picked for her: "Il padre in sì grand'ira accese / Che corse fulminando come insano / Al letto d'Ildegonda, e un ferro prese, / E la volea trafigger di sua mano: / Se non che la pia madre la difese: / ... Perch'egli con terribili parole / a maledir si volse la sua prole. / E sovra il capo le imprecò l'intera / Terribile vendetta del Signore" (The father approaches in so great a fury that he rushes, raging as if insane, up to Ildegonda's bed, and seizes a sword and would have smitten her with his hand, had not the pious mother defended her ... for with terrible words he begins to curse his child and on her head calls down imprecations, the terrible vengeance of the Lord).[19]

In this example the mother takes part in the scene, but, as she is almost always either dead or absent in opera, the father can use the mother's image as a formidable weapon. In order to obtain forgiveness for her sin (being seduced), Leonora (act 1, scene 3) invokes her mother's pity: "Dal cielo / vede il mio pianto e geme!" (From heaven she sees my weeping and laments). But Oberto replies firmly: "Vede il tuo fallo e freme" (She sees your lapse, and she shudders!). More menacing still, with doubtful taste but to great effect, Amonasro conjures up his wife's ghost to influence Aida: "Una larva orribile / Fra l'ombre e noi s'affaccia.... / Trema! Le scarne braccia / Sul capo tuo levò.... / Tua madre ell'è.... Ravvisala.... Ti maledice" (A horrible form approaches us from the shadows.... Tremble! Its wasted arms are raised toward your head.... It is your mother.... Recognize her.... She curses you; act 3, duet 11).

Paternal violence is to be found throughout all Romantic drama, but the Italian librettists give it particular importance, if necessary departing from their sources. For instance, in Rossini's *La donna del lago,* Douglas wants to force his daughter to marry Rodrigo, whereas in Walter Scott's *Lady of the Lake* this same Douglas has not the slightest intention of holding her to a marriage against her will.[20] In *The Bride of Lammermoor,* again by Scott, Lucia has to stand up to a shilly-shallying father and a mother, Lady Ashton, who is authoritative and ambitious. In the novel's operatic adaptations the mother quickly disappears, to be replaced by the father or, as with Cammarano and Donizetti, a brother who fills the same function, that of marrying off the daughter for the greater glory of the family. If one compares the same episode in Solera's *I Lombardi* and Royer and Vaëz's *Jérusalem,* a French version of the first opera, one can see that Arvino is within a hair's breadth of killing his daughter, the disobedient Giselda (act 2, scene 9), whereas the Count of Toulouse behaves far less violently toward his daughter Hélène (act 3, scene 5). All of this leads one to believe that the pathos of these conflicts appealed to Italian sensibility.

The father is therefore a fundamental character of Romantic dramaturgy, but he takes on a special importance in the Verdian world. From Oberto, who makes a startling appearance in the act 1 finale, proclaiming imperiously that "Un Dio / I passi miei guidò" (A God guided my steps), to Monterone, whose entrance disturbs the gossip of the Mantuan court, or Philip II, proceeding solemnly across the background in act 2 of *Don Carlos,* the father impresses instantly by his somber majesty. There is no father so cruel but Verdi finds attenuating circumstances whenever he defends his honor: Fiesco can sequester his daughter, believing her guilty of a liaison with Simon the corsair (a sequestration from which, incidentally, she dies), he can pursue the Doge with his pointless hatred, but he never lacks the kind of nobility that commands admiration. It is this respect for majestic, unyielding characters, this deference for the values that drive them, that has led critics like Luigi Baldacci to make the father the central character of Verdi's world. He attributes to Verdi a dramaturgy that is fundamentally authoritarian, reflecting the omnipotence of a patriarchal way of thinking that quashes filial rebellion—a "popular, bourgeois dramaturgy" embodying the aspirations of the Italian family.[21] We shall see when we study the hero that this dramaturgy is much more conflict ridden than Baldacci portrays it, yet respect for the father does remain one of its basic component parts.

FATHER AND SON

Even though the same obedience is expected from each one, the father's authority is not exercised toward son and daughter in the same way. It will be observed that the father/son conflict is extremely rare in Verdian opera, not to say nonexistent. True, one can cite the act 3 Finale of *Don Carlos,* where the Infante defies Philip II, or the revolt in act 4 after Posa's death, in which the son inveighs against the father; then there is the brief scene in *Luisa Miller* in which Rodolfo tries to shake Walter's resolve (act 1, scene 6) or again the act 1 Finale in which the hero threatens his father with publicly revealing the crime by which he won his power. Still, these confrontations are rare and brief and never take the form of an articulated confrontation. This is not to say that Verdi was indifferent to this particular conflict; rather, the contrary is true, and it may be that the mixing of emotional bonds and divergence of ideas was too unbearable and painful to be transferred to the stage.[22]

This avoidance is all the more striking in that it involved the suppression of scenes that figure in the literary sources. Act 1, scene 7, of Schiller's *Kabale und Liebe* (the source of *Luisa Miller*) includes a long and very stormy argument between President Walter and his son Ferdinand (later Rodolfo). Walter orders him to marry Lady Milford (Federica), but Ferdinand violently refuses and reproaches his father for his ambition and cynicism ("*Your* good fortune seldom manifests itself except in destruction").[23] Only a pallid summary of this lengthy confrontation survives in the libretto. To take another example, if the somewhat colorless historical figure of the infante Don Carlos has grown to mythic proportions through its literary fame, that is because his story celebrates the myth of the sacrificial lamb, the son devoured by his father.[24] Now, in Schiller's *Don Carlos,* the beginning of act 2 is devoted to a conversation between

Carlos and Philip II: the Infante wants to speak with his father alone, and Philip grudgingly agrees to dismiss his confidant, the Duke of Alba. Carlos tries with moving words to penetrate the King's armor and extract some sign of tenderness from him: "Don't hate me and I'll love you like a child, I'll love you fervently, just don't hate me anymore." Further, he asks his father to be allowed to lead the Flanders army in place of the Duke of Alba, but the King refuses on the pretext of the Infante's political immaturity: "You are a dreamer," the King tells him.[25]

This scene simply vanishes in the opera, even though it was explicitly provided for in the original scenario by Méry and Du Locle.[26] There is an echo of it, in part, in the great encounter between the King and the Marquis of Posa. This is the only great scene setting opposite each other a "father" and a "son" in an adversarial relationship but also as equals, the only time an authoritarian father listens, with a mixture of admiration and astonishment, and hears his son to the end as he defends freedom— the only time a son dares tell the father that his despotism is only leading to death. Yet it is clear that this man-to-man relationship is lacking in the troubling and terrible emotions that can arise between father and son.

A completely different form of the relationship is provided by the one great father-son duet, in *Les Vêpres siciliennes,* in the course of which Henri finds to his horror that his interlocutor is his own father. The Sicilian patriot Henri is fighting Guy de Montfort, the French governor of Sicily, with all the valiance of a hero defending his country's independence and opposing a tyrant (act 3, scene 4), but he suddenly learns that this detestable man, the symbol of "colonial" French occupation, is his father. The discovery paralyzes him: "La foudre est sur moi descendue, et d'épouvante je frémis"/"... arcan funesto Mi si rivela ... fremo d'orror" (A tragic secret is revealed to me ... I tremble with horror!).[27]

The music perfectly conveys the gradual buildup of the father's smothering presence as he slowly stifles his son. It gives a weighty dominance to Montfort, who sings all the melodic material, while Henri is confined to a jerky, halting style as if his position did not allow him any more ample vocal expansion. After a short *scena,* the duet opens with a movement in F minor dominated by Montfort's melody ("Quand ma bonté"/"Quando al mio sen"), which Henri answers with anapestically rhymed asides that betray his terror. Montfort returns to the charge in the same tempo, in D♭ major, with a full, enveloping, and austere melodic line that appears in the overture in G major ("Pour moi, quelle ivresse inconnue"/"Mentre contemplo quel volto"), and Henri continues his panic-stricken interjections. There follows a short, rapid section in A minor where the voices chase each other in overlapping melodic lines expressing Henri's emotion at his terrible discovery and Montfort's reaction to being rejected by his own child. A new Adagio section hands Montfort the advantage ("Quoi, ma tendresse"/"Ah! figlio invano"), while Henri attempts a melodic breakthrough that is immediately strangled ("Si vous m'aimez"/"S'è ver che m'ami").

In the final F-major section, in a highly symbolic kind of shift, Henri takes up Montfort's great phrase from the overture and rushes off ("Ombre sainte que je révère"/"Ombra diletta che in ciel riposi"). It would be hard to express better the melodic muteness that strikes the son vis-à-vis the father, and the choice is musical rather than dramatic since in the first duet with Montfort in act 1, which pitted against each other not son and father but hero and tyrant, Henri enjoyed complete vocal independence. The impression one gets from this duet, actually a quasi monologue on Montfort's part, is that of a love that stifles its object instead of allowing it to live.

FATHER AND DAUGHTER

Schiller, who was wont to give great dramatic importance to parent-child conflict, has Luise say, in *Kabale und Liebe:* "To think that tenderness compels more barbarously than tyrant's fury!"[28] The combination of paternal *potestas* and the demand for love is difficult to live up to for the son but weighs even more heavily on the daughter, except that in Romantic dramaturgy the woman's vocation as victim gives the relationship a less violent tone and can even produce a strangely ambiguous pleasure of self-effacement. Hence an intensity in the relationship of father and daughter that contrasts with the affective coldness of the one between father and son.

The father's attitude toward his daughter, a keystone of his family honor, is well summed up by Capellio in Bellini's *I Capuleti e i Montecchi:* "Sensi de' miei diversi non può nutrir Giulietta" (Juliet could not harbor intentions different from mine; act 1, scene 2). From the very start, the daughter is called on to identify her wishes with those of her father, whence the simplicity of situations deriving from this basic assumption: either the daughter accepts her father's will, with good or not so good grace, like those daughters the father marries off just before he dies (e.g., Lida in *Battaglia*), or she resists and is exposed to terrible punishment. Not only does the father insist on being obeyed, but he wants to be loved as well. And the love of a father and that "consoling angel," the daughter, appealed to that century, so apt to be extremely suspicious of sexuality, for such a love represented an oasis of purity and tenderness.

This theme crops up in the early stages of Romantic opera. For instance, in *Elena da Feltre* (Cammarano and Mercadante, 1838), Elena conjures up her father in the same terms lovers would use to evoke the loved one they would meet again in heaven: "Io corro.... Io volo a te.... / Nell'estasi beata ... / Del tuo paterno amplesso, / Il cielo, il cielo istesso ... / Più bello ... fia ... per me!" (I hasten, I fly to meet you.... The very heaven of your fatherly embrace would be even lovelier for me [she falls in a swoon]; act 3, scene 8). Still, with Verdi the theme has a disturbing ambiguity, suggesting in the end a sort of emotional cannibalism that is most obvious in *Rigoletto,* in the first scene between the jester and his daughter: "After the dissolute whirl of the festivities at the Duke of Mantua's palace, finally there is an eruption of love, but a love that is exclusive, voracious, marked by a suspicious jealousy that forbids Gilda to leave the house save to go to Mass, duly chaperoned; that restricts her from visiting the town where, however, they are apparently staying only a short time, as though they were being hunted down; a love that ends up depriving her of her identity, leaving her in ignorance as to who her father is—'Tell me your name.'... 'Why give me a name? That's useless! I am your father, that should be enough'—in short, a love for which Rigoletto sacrifices everything to his daughter, thereby forgetting 'religion, family, country.' Gilda and Rigoletto are like nomads, fleeing from city to city, or rather like clandestine lovers hiding far from others' eyes a passion that the world reproves; and Gilda yields docilely to this passion, despite the anguish of being unable to cling to anything but the physical presence of her father, despite the irritation this jealousy at times provokes: 'Cielo! / Sempre novel sospetto' (O Heaven! always new suspicions)."[29]

The love between father and daughter obviously cannot infringe the sexual taboo: Rigoletto loves Gilda because of her virginity, but it is precisely this purity that he defends so fiercely that is the object of his desire. When Rigoletto urges Giovanna, Gilda's duenna, to preserve her flower from the fury of the winds—a task of which she acquits herself singularly badly—it is as though he has not the least intention of offering that flower to anyone but means to keep it jealously for himself. This intimate complicity is already present in *Luisa Miller,* when old Miller manages to convince his daughter not to kill herself and the two decide to go away, as if they could find elsewhere some enchanted place, far from contamination of the world and the corruption of society (act 3, scene 2).

The same atmosphere is to be found in *Simon Boccanegra,* although this time the ambiguity is reinforced by the plot. Simon is overjoyed in the first act to find his long-lost daughter, yet he asks her (at least in the 1857 version) not to reveal the true nature of their relationship. Because of this, Gabriele, Amelia's fiancé, believes that she is the victim of the old Doge's lustful desires. The truth is not revealed until the end of act 2. It will be noted that the 1881 revision emphasizes the heavenly sweetness of the reunion: Boito replaced a somewhat neutral quatrain that Piave had supplied with four much more tender lines: "Avrem gioie romite / Soltanto note al ciel; / Io la colomba mite / Sarò del regio ostel" (We will have solitary joys known only to heaven; I shall be the gentle dove of thy regal dwelling; act 1, scene 7).

Verdi enhances the impression of celestial *volupté,* barely suggested in the duet cabaletta of 1857. The F major of the cabaletta is prepared by a long dominant pedal that follows the recognition of father and daughter; its sinuous movement imitates the effusion of two long-repressed hearts. In the cabaletta proper, Amelia's reply, which in 1857 took up Simon's melodic line, changes and becomes more supple, beginning in conjunct motion; the coda is based on a passionate chasing of one voice by the other. In 1857, the duet ends in a *ff* reprise for orchestra of the cabaletta theme; in 1881, this same reprise begins *piano* and *con espressione,* and Verdi draws it out with descending arpeggios (violins, horns, and harps) that exactly reflect Boito's new stage direction: "The Doge remains in ecstasy, contemplating Amelia as she enters the palace." In short, the "faintly military air" that Budden detects at the end of the duet completely disappears in the 1881 revision, giving way to a hazier, more tender atmosphere. So we see that, from *Luisa Miller* to *Simon Boccanegra,* the love of father and daughter—always with the same distinctive features of secrets, isolation, the idyll bathed in tears, chaste embraces—is like a charmed rampart protecting the pair from the harm of this world.

DECLINE OF THE FATHERS

Verdi's dramaturgy by no means shows us only fathers who are triumphant in their glory. Frequently, because of their lack of real power (Monterone) or inferior social standing (Miller), the actions of a wicked son *(I masnadieri),* contradictory impulses *(Rigoletto),* or the helplessness to which their function has reduced them *(I due Foscari),* fathers land in a situation of extreme vulnerability. But these are workings of the plot.

More interesting is to see how their portrayal develops on the emotional level.

If the shadow of pity never touches Oberto, who remains uniformly unyielding from one end of the opera to the other, Verdi's third opera provides us with the first great portrait of wounded paternity. After we have been introduced to a tyrant foaming with fury and pride, act 3 shows us a Nabucco who is haggard and utterly helpless. The first great lyrical moment of the score, more so even than the soprano's aria in act 2, is that in which the mad king begs Abigaille, who has seized power, to spare his daughter Fenena. In his A♭-major Andante ("Deh perdona, deh perdona"), a specifically Verdian quality of effusion appears for the first time, and it concerns an unhappy father. This sympathetic style is all the more striking in that it often has to do with characters who are, by contrast, totally antipathetic. Giacomo, Joan of Arc's father, is stupid and presumptuous in his haste to set himself up as a judge, yet one of the finest moments in the score is his F♯-minor "Speme al vecchio era una figlia" (A daughter was the hope of my old age), which combines the role of the judge and the longing of a father.

Even more striking is the case of Walter in *Luisa Miller*. The rustic landowner is an odious character who sacrifices his son to petty courtier ambitions after he has seized power by criminal means. His contradictions as a father are nonetheless movingly expressed in a beautiful aria, "Il mio sangue, la vita darei" (I would give my blood, my life; act 1). The first section in E♭ minor uses a jagged, declamatory rhythm, accompanied by eighth-note triplets and the imperious battering of thirty-second notes, to express the bitterness of fatherly affection that is repaid with ingratitude. After a pause in the dominant, we pass to E♭ major (the aria is constructed as a romanza on the minor/major scheme), and everything changes: the voice sings rather than declaims, the triplets almost dance, and, although the text bears witness to an absence of love—"Di dolcezze l'affetto paterno / A quest'alma sorgente non è" (For this soul, a father's love is not a source of tenderness)—the music suggests longing for a shared affection. Yet each time, that is, in both the first and the second sections, the voice breaks out in imprecations, hammered out vocally and underscored by arpeggiated chords in the orchestra. All this works to conjure up a mixture of rage and suffering. It is a marvelous musical tableau, and Budden is right in believing that we are on the road leading to Philip II's solitary agony.

A further step along the road is represented by Montfort's aria in *Vê-*

pres, "Au sein de la puissance"/"In braccio alle dovizie," which evokes "power" and "greatness" the better to emphasize emptiness of heart. Moreover, the music stresses the word *vide* (empty) in a remarkable way ("un vide affreux, immense, régnait seul dans mon coeur" [An immense, appalling emptiness reigned alone in my heart]): after setting forth the first four lines (eight measures) in a regular manner, the voice returns to the word *vide,* suspended on a Neapolitan sixth chord, then is carried off in a chromatic whirlwind to high F♯ before coming to rest on the dominant as it prepares for the second part of the aria. The aria shows that by now Verdi was questioning what we have called the law of plenitude, which decreed that characters be made up of strong, unambiguous feelings: Giacomo and Walter are at the same time authoritarian and tormented but without any ambiguity, whereas Montfort's aria suggests a contradiction, not between two sentiments, but between an outward shell, an external appearance, and an emptiness or inner deficiency. This rift or gap between essence and appearance was to extend to other types and affect the very nature of the Verdian character.

The culminating point of this development is Philip II's famous aria "Je dormirai dans mon manteau royal"/"Dormirò sol nel manto mio regal" in *Don Carlos.* The King is describing his loneliness as a husband, but how to separate his feeling of conjugal unhappiness from his situation as an aging man and the suspicions he harbors against his son? Listeners will note, at all points in this remarkable aria, how the orchestra speaks autonomously, aiming not to prepare or round out the melody, like most accompaniments, but to describe what the voice is incapable of expressing, the "profound meditation" into which the King is plunged. Moreover, the voice rises up, dreamlike, from the continuous orchestral flood, gaining assurance only in the aria, then sinking back once more into the melancholy meditation suggested by the reprise of the opening refrain. Everything in the introduction of this scene bespeaks a profound dejection: the plaintive semitone of the first four measures; the melodic line of the solo cello, which descends exhausted to the very deepest notes; the motifs of the strings (m. 14) mirroring the vise of solitude in which Philip's life is spent.

Thus, the ambiguity, or rift, that we seemed to detect in Montfort's aria is here extended to the entire scene, in which a character's capacity to express his soul within the narrow limits of an aria is contrasted with the unfathomable depths of that same soul. For all that, the traditional father does not disappear from the Verdian universe, and Amonasro in *Aida* and Fiesco in the last version of *Simon* are there to remind us of the far-reaching power of paternal right of which Schiller spoke; yet the steady erosion of the father's image is a sign of the weakening of one of the major axes of Romantic dramaturgy.[30]

The Sorceress

No one on earth
is wiser than you;
you know what's hid
in the caves of the night,
what hill and dale
air and water do hold.
RICHARD WAGNER,
Siegfried

The father is an active character who, in the case of transgression, seeks to punish the guilty party either directly or with the help of intermediaries. Still, it can happen that the individual's transgression is itself the source of his trouble and that his passion has a self-destructive power; it is precisely the role of the sorceress to reveal this power, to foretell what is bound to happen through the workings of fate or, more simply, the dynamics of the character's situation. In this sense, the father's principle of transcendence is set against the sorceress's principle of immanence.

The emergence of the principle of immanence, through the sorceress character, is what makes *Macbeth* something new in Verdi's dramaturgy. Such characters were totally alien to the Italian tradition, where the fantastic tended to come down to fairies and the like and act as a sop to the popular imagination.[31] Influenced by Schlegel's interpretation of the witches,[32] Verdi took them very seriously, even tormenting Piave for not finding the right tone and cavalierly going off to seek help from the writer Andrea Maffei, the future translator of Shakespeare. The composer even declared to Léon Escudier in 1865: "The witches dominate the drama; everything derives from them. Shrill and gossipy in the first act, sublime and prophetic in the third."[33]

The witches' job is to say what is going to happen, what is bound to happen. Already in the first act, when they make their triple invocation, Macbeth is staggered (he reacts "in a low voice, almost with terror"); it is a sign that the witches have unveiled only what was within him, although he was unconscious of it. In the third act they merely reveal the dynamics of the actions of Macbeth and his wife. In fact Lady Macbeth dies, destroyed by her crime, unable to wash away the bloodstain that obsesses her; for his part, Macbeth feels his life ebbing even before he battles his enemies: "Eppur la vita / Sento nelle mie fibre inaridita" (And yet I feel my life drying up in my veins; act 4, scene 5). The die is cast in some way, even before the tyrant is killed by Macduff.[34]

Parallel to this appearance of a law of immanence is the eclipse of the "paternal" character in *Macbeth:* Duncan appears only in the distance, accompanied by "rustic music." If this absence can be explained by technical reasons (in opera a king cannot be confined to a few sentences, unlike Shakespeare's character), Verdi turns the restriction to remarkable advantage. The little march in B♭ that accompanies the King is in complete contrast with the preceding scene, Lady Macbeth's cavatina, and with the following one as well, the dagger monologue. Thus, the spatial effect created by the way the music appears close and then fades into the distance gives the impression of a luminous star that approaches but cannot penetrate the dense darkness that then envelops the stage, emphasizing the opposition of two worlds that never touch. The music is relatively trivial, yet its placement at this moment of the drama gives it an eeriness that no doubt explains why Verdi did not touch it when the opera was revived in 1865.

In *Rigoletto* there are no witches, but one may note the coexistence of the two dramatic principles set forth above: the majesty of paternal authority is solemnly affirmed with Monterone, but the curse he utters against the Duke of Mantua is completely ineffectual, and the jester can do nothing to help. The censors' interdiction of regicide on the stage (even if Hugo's François I is now only a duke) is not enough to explain the Duke's impunity from the curse. Only Rigoletto is punished, but Monterone's curse has materially nothing to do with that, for Rigoletto carries this curse within himself, the result of the insoluble contradiction between his status as a jester, which incites him to mock purity and encourage debauchery, and his situation as a father, protecting this very purity. He is caught in his own trap, whereas the Duke, unconcerned with respecting "bourgeois" family virtues, cannot suffer the consequences of a contradiction that is alien to him. Thus, a purely internal mechanism, entrusting to the dynamic of the passions the task of preparing their own destruction, receives the authority of a curse, which usually is destined to strike from outside.

We meet a real witch in the character of Ulrica in *Un ballo in maschera*.[35] She descends directly from Scribe's libretto for Auber, where she goes by the name of Madame Arvedson, "a soothsayer."[36] The gulf that, in the French opera, separates popular superstition and the skeptical rationalism of the Swedish king Gustave III is shifted in Verdi's, which pits opposite one another a frivolous, blinkered court and the mystery of fate. Ulrica in reality merely predicts the catastrophes that are inevitably brought about by the interplay of passions. Beyond her witch's lore, she owes this prescience to the fact that she is a fringe character, living on the outskirts of a society whose intimate workings she can see the more clearly. It is not by chance that the prophetic function almost always falls to marginal figures—madman, innocent, sorceress, gypsy—who penetrate the mechanisms of a world on whose frontiers they spend their lives. In fact, when the setting is switched from Stockholm to Boston, Ulrica is cast as a black (act 1, scene 4), accentuating her marginality.

The atmosphere in this opera is nonetheless profoundly different from that of *Macbeth*. Where Macbeth and his wife succumb to the murderous dynamic that their ambition has set in motion, Riccardo does not so much give in to the dynamic of a passion for a married woman (in any case he renounces her) as fall victim to those risks and unpredictable snags that chance sets in our path and that start the wheel of fate rolling. Destiny now has two faces: a somber, austere face, personified by Ulrica, and another, more frivolous, capricious one, represented by Oscar, Riccardo's faithful page, the instrument of fate who involuntarily contributes to his destruction. The spectacle of passion's implacable workings is now touched by a faint smile.

The same ironic smile extends to the figure of the father. Although there is no actual father figure in this opera, in fact the hero himself is a father, the father of his subjects. In the introduction, which Verdi treats with detached humor, we see a peaceful court, scarcely troubled by the murmurings of a few harmless conspirators. Riccardo enters and straightway declares: "Io deggio / Su' miei figli vegliar, perché sia pago / Ogni voto, se giusto" (I watch over my children and try to fulfill every petition, be they honest; act 1, scene 2). In similar fashion, from the opening chorus Scribe insists on Gustave's "paternity": "You our father, our king." Verdi was forced to abandon the original character of Gustave III because the censors did not want a play about a king who had died not long ago (in 1792), but he energetically refused to make Riccardo a mere "leader." He wanted his protagonist to retain something regal, in other words "paternal," since he needed this solemnity in order to create the paradoxical character of the fallible father who is merely the child of his destiny.

With *La forza del destino* we have a situation that is the reverse of *Mac-*

beth. No longer does the witch pursue the father; instead, it is the father who expels the witch. In the play *Don Alvaro o la fuerza del sino* by the Duke of Rivas, from which the libretto is derived, the gypsy Preziosilla appears in the very first scene, where she is immediately introduced as a fortune-teller: the officer whose fortune she is about to tell prefers not to know what is in store for him. In scene 2 we learn that she has read Alvaro's hand and that his future is not a lucky one; we also learn that Preziosilla's mother predicted from Leonora's birth that she would have just as black a future. Thus, from the beginning of the Spanish play the shadow of ill fortune hangs over the action.[37]

This scene is completely done away with in the opera, and the curtain rises on the Marquis di Calatrava, Leonora's father, who reappears at the end of the act to curse his daughter. Emphasis is thereby laid on the figure of the father, tender at first, then formidable. When we are introduced to Preziosilla in act 2, in spite of her obvious flair for fortune-telling, her role in this scene is more that of a cheerful camp follower, and it is in this capacity that she plays an important role in the great encampment scene in act 3. Verdi therefore practically spirited away Preziosilla's function as "witch," which de Rivas by contrast set squarely in the foreground, most likely because the composer preferred to keep the father figure as an active agent who curses and sees his curse realized, in part, through his son Carlo.[38]

Hence, the father does not meet the witch, Wotan never visits Erda, as he does in the great scene in *Siegfried* (act 3, scene 1), and the father's "will" never encounters the witch's "knowledge." On the other hand, after *Macbeth* we can see developing a dramaturgy based on the destructive dynamics of passion, a dramaturgy that destroys its predecessor, which up to that time was relatively slanted toward the mechanisms of transgression and punishment.

KING LEAR

In the gallery of Verdian fathers one large portrait is missing, that of the most famous of fathers, King Lear. Why did the composer shrink before this figure? Was it out of a kind of deep-seated apprehension? Was it the impossibility of doing justice to the play within the framework of nineteenth-century opera? The long, tortuous history of *Il Re Lear* begins in 1843 and ends around 1865–67. This means that Shakespeare's tragedy accompanied Verdi for nearly twenty-five years, even if it was essentially between 1850 and 1856 that the project was actually laid out.[39]

Why so many missed rendezvous? Gary Schmidgall suggests that Verdi was attracted by the simplicity of *Macbeth* as an opera subject but gave up on *Lear* because of its complexity[40]—yet a complicated plot never made Verdi turn tail and run away! Two other writers, Guglielmo Barblan and Franco Abbiati, believe that the subject of *Lear* had been replaced by *Rigoletto,* another story of a tragic father, but in that case it is hard to see how the main body of work on the libretto was done *after* that opera. Finally, the composer's apprehension about the audience's reaction must have played a certain part since he makes mention of it on more than one occasion,[41] but there are other cases where Verdi fought like a lion when it was a question of insisting on a subject he found "convincing."

Charles Osborne is probably correct in thinking that, "all his life long, Verdi's subconscious protected him from Lear."[42] The problem is knowing whether this subconscious opens onto a more profound unconsciousness, a chasm deep enough for the psychobiographers to fall headlong into it,[43] or whether it is simply the subconscious of a man of the theater, that is, a vague awareness of the difficulty that might arise in reducing *Lear* to opera proportions. Nor can one discount a somewhat mysterious inner block: according to the oral tradition of the Verdi family, the composer had a terror of certain scenes, such as that of Lear on the heath, and of certain characters, such as the Fool, which Mascagni's 1895 testimony confirms.[44] Nonetheless, reasons of aesthetics must have weighed just as heavily, if not more so.

Claus Henneberg, the librettist of Aribert Reimann's *Lear,* created in 1978 in Munich, confesses having initially had the utmost difficulty imagining that music could arise from this text. For his part, the critic Jürgen Maehder observes that nineteenth-century aesthetics made the question of changing the play into an opera extremely problematic: "In 1978, after a tradition of almost seventy-five years of *Literaturoper,* which began with Richard Strauss's *Salome,* and with language having undergone great changes, a musical setting of Shakespeare's text had a large number of dramatic role models to lean on"[45]—models that obviously did not exist in Verdi's time.

In addition, the composer, like the librettist Somma, was appalled at the immensity of the task: "*King Lear* appears at first sight so vast, the plot so intertwined, that it seems impossible to get an opera out of it."[46] If he was immediately attracted by certain aspects of the play that fit easily into the operatic tradition of his age (chief among them being the Lear-Cordelia relationship and the character of the bastard, Edmond, and his relation to Edgar), he did not know what to make of the huge cast of characters (Lear's two other daughters and their husbands, Kent and Gloucester, e.g.), and he made some radical choices (e.g., eliminating the two Gloucester sons). In another connection it is striking to see Verdi, so open at that time to new forms, stumble over the difficulty of cutting up the original text into regular strophes: "With all due respect to your talent," he wrote Somma, "I will tell you that the form does not lend itself well to music. No one likes new forms more than I do, but new forms that are capable of being made into music." And Verdi added: "To make music one needs strophes to write the *cantabili,* strophes to join the voices, strophes to write largos, allegros, etc."[47]

Nonetheless, as Leo Karl Gerhartz has pointed out,[48] the chief difficulty was in the function of the words. In Romantic dramaturgy, and particularly that of Verdi, as we have seen, the word is the prime mover of action; in the English play the word is more reflexive, tending toward a vast meditation on the world. *Lear* is, too, in large measure, a work about the ambiguity of language, as we see in the first great scene, where Lear divides his kingdom among his three daughters but dispossesses Cordelia, the only one who in fact loves him, because she does not demonstrate her affection in hyperbolic language like the devious Goneril and Regan. This essential confrontation clearly embarrassed Verdi, who felt more at ease with incidents like that of Cordelia's departure, a "pathetic," "resigned," "sublime" situation, as Somma put it, that was open to melodramatic expression.[49] Still, Verdi did produce a tragedy about the ambiguity of language, and more generally of signs, that was astonishingly modern—*Otello*—but not until 1887. The means of expression devised for this opera would have suited *Lear* perfectly; however, Verdi preferred to let his former project sleep forever.

The Decline of the Hero

A hero's death!—Meet for worship!
FRIEDRICH SCHILLER,
Die Räuber

In moving from the castrato *primo uomo* to the contralto, then from contralto to tenor, the hero changed in appearance but not in importance or in the role he played. No longer a beribboned, plume-helmeted prince pacing the hall of some Greek or Roman palace or suddenly turning up in a "magnificent place," he is now a troubadour singing beneath the moonlit balcony of a medieval castle or else a brigand haunting some strange, forbidding forest; yet he remains the cynosure of all eyes, the affective center of the actions the opera recounts. As Edward J. Dent observes humorously, "One must never laugh in the presence of a tenor: a tenor is a sacred image before which one takes off one's hat and kneels."[50]

It may be because he is godlike that the hero's epiphany is always a key moment in opera. Whether he is suddenly seen standing on the ramparts of a fort, like Otello calming the storm and resplendent with the triumph of victory, or whether he is hidden and reveals himself with the notes of his lute and a mournful ballad, like Manrico, his nature is such that his appearance is always brilliant in effect. The image of a sun banishing the clouds is suggested by the hero's entrance in Persiani's *Inès de Castro,* written to Cammarano's libretto (1835): "Lightly, lightly, far, far off / there rises a cloud of dust on the plain.... / Who is riding forth on a white charger / enveloped in this cloud of dust? / Now he comes near ... his face can be seen.... / Rejoice.... It is the warrior, your beloved."[51]

The hero's humanity is all embracing. If the nineteenth century slowly abandoned the sexual ambiguity of the hero-castrato, it did not entirely eliminate a certain androgyny that Hans von Bülow summed up when he stated that musical humanity included men, women, and tenors.[52] At the beginning of our own century, Aldo Palazzeschi could still point to this ambivalence, with its powerful hold of fascination on the popular audience: "We could say that in front of the tenor the audience has only one sex, or that he represents a third sex that is nevertheless capable of fascinating the senses. This is the measure of his power over the public."[53] His ambiguity is evident in his ability to combine "feminine" and "virile" qualities—gentleness and violence, sensitivity, even sentimentality, and indomitable courage.

The dominant characteristics of the hero are his moral idealism and his nobility of heart, which imply that he is never prey to base feelings such as envy or meanness. In the last century, this generosity of spirit was personified by the "chevalier sans peur et sans reproche." Is it a coincidence that a figure like Garibaldi, so popular as to be part of the imaginary pantheon of his day, was seen as a knight by the enthusiastic George Sand: "He bears within him the faith of the heroic age, and thus the wonders of chivalry are reborn in our nineteenth century"? This idealism was inseparable from a certain naïveté. When Garibaldi visited London on one occasion, Tennyson thought he had "the divine stupidity of a hero."[54] How many operatic heroes, with their credulousness, their tendency to be manipulated, to believe what they are told without any verification, to flare up in excitement without the shadow of thought, share with Garibaldi this privilege of being both divine and stupid?

If the baroque hero attained serenity by being tested by passion and constrained by duty, the Romantic hero is doomed to unhappiness. In either case, the hero undergoes an initiation, but in the first instance his progress produces a certain happiness that comes from a balance of heart and reason, whereas in the second this same progress is ill starred and leads to defeat and death. Innumerable, among Romantic heroes, are the homeless wanderers, the outlaws, those battling a fatal destiny: "Deserto sulla terra, / Col rio destino in guerra" (Lonely upon the earth, at war with cruel fate), to quote the song of Manrico the troubadour. Whether condemned to be a stranger in his own land or politically condemned by his own people, the hero is relentlessly pursued by destiny, like Ernani (act 2, scene 3), Carlo Moor in *I masnadieri* (act 4, scene 7), Corrado in *Il corsaro* (act 1, scene 2), or Rodolfo in *Luisa Miller* (act 2, scene 9), and believes himself to be the victim of an unjust curse.

INTERPRETATION OF THE HERO

The hero appears, first and foremost, as the personification of individual desire: his nature is both strong and innocent (qualities that rise up uncontrollably from the depths of his being) but also asocial and untouched by the rules of coexistence. The almost constant bond between the hero and love, a love that is above convention and social or moral laws, would seem to encourage this identification, so that one can interpret the tyrant as the one who bends reality to his desire and the judge as the incarnation of social and moral laws. After all, the principle of pleasure, the principle of reality, and the law make a familiar trio! The interpretation is all the more tempting in that it takes into account the childishly regressive aspects of the hero's conduct: the impatience of unfettered desire; the presumption that this is innocent, although society holds it as culpable; naïveté of conduct; the trend toward narcissism.

The hero-child wants everything all at once because his heart so commands, and he learns to his cost the vanity of this hope. Thus, the hero may have the merit of making us return to a time in our development when we indulged in dreams of omnipotence, while his androgyny may mean, quite simply, regression to a stage anterior to the strict separation of the sexes. Seen from this viewpoint, opera reflects our aspiration to a complete, innocent unleashing of our passions, then immediately reminds us that this desire is fundamentally asocial and must be curbed by reality and the law. The hero is therefore a basically anarchic creature, and opera offers us at one and the same time the joy of ephemeral communion with this anarchy we dream of and the awareness that it must be vanquished. The death of the hero, an adorable spectacle as Schiller described it, becomes a ritual sacrifice through which we recognize that our deep-seated aspirations are incompatible with the social and moral order.

This view nonetheless has the disadvantage of isolating the hero from his historic context and erasing the problematic character and political significance that he often had in the last century. Now, we have seen how the hero saw himself as the bearer of a new legitimacy founded on the law of the heart and the individual's claim to autonomy and that this function quite naturally led him to be the spokesman for those groups that wanted to make the same claim (political or national). The hero's "legitimism" appears chiefly in his idea of honor: for him, honor is loyalty to his own word, which forms a pact on the "legality" of which he insists. The pretext for the lengthy storms of abuse to which heroes so often subject their lovers is precisely the reproach of not keeping a promise that was meant to be everlasting.

The hero's political and social significance is illuminated by the contrast with the figure of the seducer, who merely represents the desire for pleasure without the counterpart of commitment. The seducer has the hero's amorous charge, but he does not make the same demands: the Duke of Mantua flits from Gilda to Maddalena without any problem, whereas it is inconceivable that Ernani would break his word to Elvira. How can we interpret this legitimism save as the claim of the individual to make and enact his own law, a law that seems to him to be socially acceptable? Challenging the social space in which he moves, he replaces it with a moral space that is no less rigid, for only the strict observance of its laws guarantees legitimacy.

The hero's claim to legitimacy can be seen before the nineteenth century, including in opera, where it was the moving spirit of traditional buffa, defending the right of nature against established authority. It then became radicalized in the last century, extending to the political and national levels to the point where it seemed to question the reigning order. The hero's aspiration to autonomy became associated with the aspiration toward freedom when confronted with the excesses of executive power, just as it joined forces with the national aspirations of occupied peoples.

The political fortunes of certain operas like *Guillaume Tell* or *La Muette de Portici* leave no doubt as to the political interpretation of personal stories on the stage. The same thing can be seen in Italy, although in a more discreet way owing to censorship: in 1848, the Austrian police and papal government forbade the young to wear a beret "à la Ernani" even though the Milanese rebels sported it that same year.

The hero became a symbolic character to the extent that he was identified with an objective conflict: his enthusiastic aspiration to individual freedom came up against his no less vigorous attachment to the social order and traditional values. Opera provides several examples of the many ways the breath of freedom that the hero personified was resisted; we find countless reminders that individual desire is too unreliable a base for the social edifice to rest on. For instance, in *Traviata,* Germont tells Violetta that, when Alfredo's love cools, there exists no social mechanism that would guarantee a union not "blessed by heaven."

The hero is too self-involved to ensure continuity in the family as a base of society. That may be the symbolic meaning of a topos of Romantic opera whereby the hero is temporarily reported vanished or given up for dead, a misadventure that never happens to the judge! The solitary individual who is not linked to a family line and the duties that it imposes is straightway called an adventurer, a man without roots or country: when Stankar wants to humiliate the seducer Raffaele in *Stiffelio,* he brings up his mysterious origins: "Venturiero, / Che t'avvolgi nel mistero . . . / Nobil conte Raffaello, / tu non sei che un trovatello!" (An adventurer who wraps his life in mystery, noble Count Raffello, you are nothing but a foundling; act 2), in other words, nobody's child. One of the reasons for the Calatravas' hatred for Alvaro is the enigma of his origins, scornfully recalled in the Spanish play from which *La forza del destino* derives: "Nobility an adventurer! Honor, one unknown, without father or family name, a stranger. . . ."[55]

The drama would be limited to a conflict between two opposing forces if the hero did not carry these antagonisms within himself. Indeed, what makes the hero a problematic character is that he interiorizes this conflict in the form of a contradiction between his wish for liberation and his desire to remain attached to a tradition from which he arose. The conflict makes the hero interesting but also causes his political ambiguity since he represents a culture that oscillates between liberal aspiration and an attachment to patriarchal values. The nature of the conflict shapes the evolution of the character of Verdi's hero.

THE VERDIAN HERO

Although logically linked to the figure of the Romantic hero, the Verdian hero has certain peculiar traits that follow from the dramatic choices outlined in the preceding chapter.

Verdi distinctly toned down the elegiac side of the Romantic hero, starting with Ernani, his first true hero, in order to bring out his power and dynamism. Even when doomed to defeat and death, his heroes "stand out because of their extraordinary force of will and the way the music propels them toward action, so much so that we often forget their failures and remember only their furious energy."[56] We have to wait for *Giovanna d'Arco,* with the character of the King of France, and especially Rodolfo in *Luisa Miller* to see portrayed the melancholy, gentle, or languorous aspects of the hero. He is first of all a fighter, and, since Verdi devoted the same care to all the participants in a conflict, he no longer dominates but is a *primus inter pares* who must carry on his struggle like the others.

The composer's preference for combative heroes accounts, I believe, for the minor part that the theme of the curse on the Romantic hero plays in his operas, if one takes that to mean, not the curse uttered by one character on another, but a curse that fate attaches to a single character. True, Ernani, Carlo the bandit, Corrado the corsair, and Rodolfo Miller all admit to being the victim of a curse at one time or another, like so many characters of Romantic opera. Yet the most popular heroes, those who made an impression on the public and still continue to do so, like Ernani and Manrico, are victims not so much of a silent curse as of a proscription from society against which they struggle with all their might.

This shadowy rendering of a major theme of European Romanticism can easily be explained. The curse expresses the impossibility of reconciliation between the hero and the society around him, making all effort vain and doomed to failure. Thus, the curse, which is often a metaphor for the artist's situation as he takes cognizance of his isolation and the impossibility of being integrated into a society that marginalizes him, is in blatant contrast to the political vindication of the Verdian hero, who is determined to see the triumph of an attitude and a morality. The state of total incomprehension characteristic of the relations between Daland and the Dutchman in Wagner's *Der Fliegende Holländer* is hard to imagine in Verdi's case: with him, the hero and his antagonists always have a common language, even if it be only that of arms.

Moreover, the Verdian hero loses his essentially aristocratic status so as to become the spokesman of a rebel group he leads. Through its association with the movement for national unity in Italy, and, in a more general way, through its creator's liberal sympathies, Verdian opera achieved a compromise between the traditional hero's exceptional, superhuman character and the sublimation of the average man, the projection of a bourgeoisie aspiring to power and recognition. This explains how heroes such as Ernani and Manrico became political symbols: whether he sings of love for a woman (*Ernani,* act 1, scene 2), longing for an impossible happiness (*Il corsaro,* act 1, scene 2), love of birthplace (*La battaglia di Legnano,* act 1, scene 1), or nostalgia for his forebears (*I masnadieri,* act 1, scene 2), these pleas finally fuse into the same single aspiration to freedom. The assimilation is perfectly captured by a well-known sequence in Visconti's film *Senso* in which the Venetian audience is fired with enthusiasm when the tenor Manrico sings the famous cabaletta "Di quella pira," the words of which are in no way patriotic.

Nevertheless, the essential aspect of the Verdian hero, the one that traces his evolution, is the inner schism that I described above: the contradiction makes him at the same time *marginal,* outside the society to which he belonged, and *integrated,* linked to that same society either through social adherence or through the values he professes and shares with the members of that society. Since the contradiction remains constant, it gradually changes meaning and becomes reversed, profoundly altering the hero's physiognomy: political at the outset, he becomes an essentially private individual; spokesman for a community, he appears more and more like an isolated character; active and a fighter, he becomes increasingly powerless. The reversal may be summed up in this way: at first marginal, he is ruined by his inner solidarity with the society he is struggling against; later, wholly integrated in the society he lives in, he is ruined by an inner marginality that makes him a stranger to that society.[57]

I shall take as a watershed *La battaglia di Legnano* (1849), essentially because this opera shows a certain dichotomy between the political significance of the hero and his private fate. Politically, Arrigo is Rolando's ally since both men are fighting to free the Italian cities from Barbarossa. In private, however, he is his friend's enemy because he loves the other's wife, and Rolando tries to take revenge in a stereotypical manner. Musically, this dichotomy entails a difference in language, even an unevenness of inspiration that has struck commentators and about which I shall have more to say later on. But this dividing line is significant above all because certain traits of Verdi's first kind of hero appear later in operas that are of the second, political kind.

In most of the operas written before *Battaglia,* as well as in certain ones that come after it, the hero is above all a fringe character in the sense that he is a person excluded. His marginality may be ethnic when he is a member of an oppressed ethnic group. Zamoro, the Peruvian leader in *Alzira,* is in revolt against the Spanish conquistadors; Foresto fights the invader Attila; Arrigo defends his country against Emperor Frederick Barbarossa; Alvaro in *Forza* is an Inca, therefore a native of his land; Henri is a Sicilian fighting the French in *Vêpres.* The exclusion can equally well be political and social and still outlaw the hero from society: Corrado is a corsair, Ernani a brigand, Manrico a gypsy, and Carlo Moor a brigand, a *masnadiero.*

The aim that these characters have in mind is a political and ethical one: they are fighting to expel an invader and recover their national integrity or gain recognition for rights that have been flouted, to see a more just order triumph. By virtue of the universalizing of the hero's claims that is de rigueur in Romantic opera, the "private" struggle generally goes in tandem with the political one. Thus, for Zamoro as for Henri or Foresto, to fight the enemy and win the woman they love is one and the same enterprise.

Still, these characters soon show signs of a deep solidarity with the order with which they are at war, in general because they belong to that order and hope to recover their place in it. Bandit though he is, Ernani is a Spanish grandee, and when the conjuration against the King of Spain is found out, he openly claims the right, reserved for nobles, to die by the axe (act 3, scene 6). Alvaro is an Inca, but he is a king's son, and he proudly proclaims his "royal lineage" (act 3, scene 6), just as in the Spanish play he tries to convince his enemy Calatrava that he is as much a nobleman as is the other. The brigand Carlo Moor is in fact the son of the Count di Moor, therefore heir to his fiefdom and his power; Manrico the gypsy is, without knowing it, the brother of the Count de Luna; and so on. The hero's marginality is therefore inseparable from a deep complicity with the order against which he is fighting.

The important fact is that this unconscious contradiction is the cause of the hero's downfall. Ernani refuses to fight Silva because he is an old man, but why does he have to give him a claim on his life—which Silva exercises ruthlessly—if not out of a deep-seated complicity in the respect for certain feudal values? Ernani has flouted the sacred right of hospitality, and his honor commands him to accept the reparation his enemy imposes. In *Il trovatore,* Manrico is the rival of the Count de Luna, whom he fights ardently, but why, when about to kill the Count in a duel, must his hand be stayed by an incomprehensible inner restraint? A "strange pity," murmurs Azucena, to whom Manrico relates this episode, for she is the only one who can understand the reason for this fatal hesitation, the only one who knows Manrico is actually de Luna's brother. Henri, in *Vêpres,* for his part, prevents the conspirators from assassinating the tyrant Montfort because he knows the latter is none other than his father. Conversely, the brigand Carlo in *I masnadieri* cannot be reconciled with his father and take his place at the family seat because of his crime-laden past, which makes it impossible for him to return to normal life, even though he desires it passionately.

Thus, in one way or another, the hero's dual allegiance is fatal for him, and he pays for the contradiction with his life. He cannot bring about the triumph of the order to which he aspires without violating values that he holds dear and that bind him to the society against which he is fighting. All that remains is for him to die a sacrificial victim, as the hero of Schiller's *Die Räuber* declares: "But something still remains that can reconcile me to the laws against which I have offended, and restore the order which I have violated. They must have a sacrifice—a sacrifice that will make manifest their invulnerable majesty to all mankind—and I myself shall be the victim. For them I must surely die."[58] The hero becomes the spokesman for a revolution that fails because he cannot reconcile his desire for subversion and his respect for traditional authority.

The fact that national struggles succeed in certain operas *(Nabucco, Attila, Alzira)* seems to constitute a glaring exception to this general failure. But in fact it means that, when the hero represents an oppressed minority, having no complicity with the tyrant he is fighting openly, the national dynamic that he represents can end in triumph. Here, too, *La battaglia di Legnano* is a good example: as a national hero, Arrigo is victorious, and the battle for Legnano is a defeat for Barbarossa. But the hero's death—which politically makes a martyr of him—also confirms the impossibility of realizing his passion for Lida. According to the code I have described, the hero has some chance of worsting the tyrant, but virtually none for winning out over the judge. That also means that the hero's libertarian enthusiasm gains a public backing on the question of national struggles (and to a lesser extent political ones) but is shattered when it comes up against the wall of the familial institution.

From *Battaglia* on, the hero's physiognomy tends to change. For one thing, he is now usually a member of the ruling caste: Otello is a victorious general of the Venetian republic, just as Radames is the renowned general of the Egyptian army *(Aida),* while Riccardo is a well-beloved sovereign

(Ballo), Alfredo Germont a member of the solid provincial bourgeoisie *(Traviata),* Rodolfo the son of a Tyrolean squire *(Luisa Miller),* and Don Carlos no less than the son of the King of Spain.

But, lo and behold, this integration, replacing the outer marginality of the first heroes, hides a rift that is very soon revealed in their behavior. Riccardo loves a married woman, Rodolfo and Alfredo a woman banned to them by their social condition, and Radames the daughter of his enemy's king, while Otello has a violent streak that shocks orderly Venetian society. Marginality thus becomes internal, like a secret wound that makes the character a stranger to the society he lives in. Otello's case is pretty much one apart: Schlegel believed that his violence was due to the leveling down of an impulsive, savage nature fitted for the "burning climates" from which he came; his marginality would therefore be ethnic. James Hepokoski recalls, however, that Boito and Verdi firmly corrected this fairly racist interpretation by turning to that of F. V. Hugo, a translator of Shakespeare, who for his part emphasized Otello's honor and nobility.[59] His marginality is therefore that of a soldier outside Venetian society.

Whatever the case, this fault, this inability of the heart to conform to a social order, causes the hero to be destroyed, just as he had formerly been destroyed by his dependence in relation to a society. Sooner or later the surfacing of this inmost self leads the hero to make a false step, for which he will pay with his life; for example, Radames's betrayal, Riccardo's fatal rendezvous with Amelia on the execution field outside Boston, or the last, imprudent meeting of Carlos with his mother-in-law, Elisabeth.

The infante Carlos shows us another feature of this new hero, a kind of inner paralysis that condemns him to inaction. Seeing the woman he loves become his mother-in-law as a result of a political marriage, the Infante can only waver between self-destructive rage and empty threats. The often troubled or forbidden nature of the heroes' desires inhibits their dynamism so that they reel about, incapable of either giving up or rebelling. Alfredo's much criticized cabaletta in his aria in act 2 of *La traviata* ("Oh mio rimorso, oh infamia") bears witness to this development; all in all, it is no worse than many others Verdi wrote, but it is simply misplaced in its dramatic context: Verdi gives Alfredo, a hero of the second type, the vehement accents of a hero of the first. The first hero was a revolutionary manqué, but he died with his sword in his hand; the second is slowly ground down by a society that quashes rebellious aspirations.

At this stage we are not far from the verismo hero consumed by a wicked passion. Yet Verdi would never take that step: he slowly disintegrates his character but does not allow him to exceed certain limits beyond which he would lose his moral stature. To prove the point I shall take a correction that Verdi made to Mariette's original scenario for *Aida*. When the renowned Egyptologist described the scene in which Radames shows Aida the route the Egyptian army is going to take, he portrayed him as an enslaved puppet, a Don José totally love smitten by this Ethiopian Carmen, unscrupulously betraying his country and, what is more, in the presence of Amonasro, his chief enemy.[60]

This behavior, which Du Locle, embroidering Mariette's canvas, only accentuated, did not please Verdi, and he hastened to change it in order, he said, to make the betrayal less odious:[61] Radames unknowingly drops the names of the gorges of Napata through which his army will pass, and it is just after those unfortunate words have been uttered that Amonasro emerges triumphant from his hiding place. Verdi believed it possible for the hero to be destroyed, an end he was to realize fully with Otello, but he was never willing to let any hero lose that ideal aura, that moral nobility that marked the heroes of his early operas. Mariette's choice, by contrast, is typical of an age that made passion into an evil driving force that destroys the individual's moral structure.

We thus see two successive types of heroes. In Verdi's first operas the hero bears within him a utopia of heart and mind, a revolutionary fervor that fails but postulates an ideal state where individual and collective aspirations would be reconciled. The hero of the later operas, on the other hand, represents the utopia of the heart only, insisting on the fundamental innocence of the passions and affirming total opposition between the heart and society. To adopt Marx's terminology, we pass from the public to the private, from the "citizen" to the "bourgeois."

THE RUPTURE OF 1848

How to account for such a change? On this point Verdi conformed to European culture and its evolution from the first to the second half of the century. The disillusions of 1848 constituted a breach that provoked a gradual mutation in Verdi's outlook, as in that of many other artists. Before 1848, the difficulties of everyday living, individual dissatisfaction, intolerance for the traditional hierarchies and those representing a patriarchal order, all were melted into the same lava flow, as if all the barriers preventing the realization of the individual were toppled by the same volcanic upheaval. In Italy, these various needs fused with a common aspiration to national independence, which was felt by a majority of Italians, and encouraged a sort of temporary unanimity that cloaked the differences that the years after 1848 would expose to the light of day. The hero manifested a spirit of rebellion that each individual adapted to his own situation. It was a utopian age, one shot through with hopes, to which failure appeared as no more than sanctioned by the immaturity of the times, the price that had to be paid for a regeneration that could not possibly fail.

Through his immediate family, the man Verdi belonged to the lower fringe of the middle class; through his in-laws (who were like another family for him), he belonged to the commercial middle bourgeoisie. This was a rising class that hoped, if possible without bloodshed or excessive disruption, to enjoy its share of power and attain a certain political autonomy by freeing itself from the hold of the clergy and Austrian protection. Verdi's independent temperament and hatred of any subjection, his desire to appear as the sole creator of his operas rather than the inheritor of some tradition or other—all character traits that had been reinforced by certain episodes of his youth—could not fail to impel him to make certain political choices. Up to 1848 at least, he was nationalist, republican, anticlerical, an admirer of Garibaldi and no less of Mazzini; he assiduously frequented Countess Maffei's nationalist salon, and most of his companions had been involved with the Austrian police.

True, this commitment was more sentimental and verbal than marked by concrete acts; moreover, it was tarnished by the sorry list of dedications of his first works: *Nabucco* to the Archduchess Adelaide of Austria and *I Lombardi* to Marie Louise, daughter of the Emperor of Austria and sovereign of Parma, two examples that evince not duplicity so much as a certain careerism. It is also true that, although the revolution of 1848 drew from him flamboyant nationalist and republican declarations,[62] it did not produce any concrete commitment. This did not prevent Verdi from becoming the spokesman for a desire for national regeneration.

After the failure of the 1848 insurrections, while the country was suffering the heavy hand of repression, Verdi fell silent: "Comments on politics disappear from his letters, as the patriotic, warlike vein disappears from his works."[63] Slowly, his fervent republicanism mellowed into a more realistic politics, one that in his eyes would be represented by Cavour, King Victor Emmanuel's Piedmontese prime minister. Little by little he drew away from the models of his youth, Mazzini and Garibaldi. While his liberal convictions did not really disappear (he sided with France in 1870, declared his hostility to Prussian militarism, and made no secret of his reservations about his own country's colonialist ambitions),[64] his opinions began to move in the direction of a moderate conservatism, marked by paternalism and averse to any form of subversion or radical politics.

It is also interesting to note that the 1848 period is the one when for the first time the composer acquired his "private space." It was most probably in the autumn of 1847 that his liaison with Giuseppina Strepponi began.[65] He spent the summer of 1848 with her at Passy, just outside Paris, and the following year settled in Busseto with the woman who in 1859 would become his wife—a strong pole of attraction for a man whose life since 1840 had been taken up almost entirely by his professional activity. In 1848, too, another side of the man Verdi became apparent, that of landed proprietor. Already the owner of a villa and some land at Busseto, in May 1848—at the height of the revolution—he bought an estate at Sant'Agata, where he settled in 1851, making it his final home. Later, he purchased some more lands close by and became one of the biggest landowners in the region.

Verdi was not the only man for whom 1848 marked a turning point. The period just after the revolutions accentuated divergences in the currents of thought touching the unification of Italy and showed up clear political and social divisions. Those calling for a fairer distribution of wealth became radicalized and broke ranks with other movements calling solely for national liberation or constitutional monarchy. The artist could then choose marginality, which would have made him an outlaw, a rebel having nothing whatever to do with the world around him; this was not the solution for Verdi, who preferred a gradual but clear integration of the artist and society.

The Advent of Woman

Tu sola potrai resistere
nel rogo del Carnevale.
Tu sola che senza maschere
nascondi l'arte d'esistere.
GIORGIO CAPRONI

In his biography of Mozart, Wolfgang Hildesheimer observes, with humor, that in *The Magic Flute* the composer had his revenge on the narrow

Freemason misogyny of the libretto by creating those superb characters the three ladies, Pamina, and the Queen of the Night.[66] We shall see a fairly similar attitude with Verdi. The narrower the setting in which the female character moves, the more it is girt about by iron laws, the more she takes her revenge in the area of inner richness, flexibility, and complexity. What the composer denies the hero he almost invariably grants the heroine—subtlety, sensitivity, inner development, a sense of reality, a capacity for suffering, intelligence of the heart—as though the hero personified man's tenseness and rigidity of will while his female counterpart embodied his soul. The apportioning of traits becomes less absurd when we note that the century liked to see its tragic consciousness reflected in the doomed lives of romantic women, from Norma to Aida, from Anna Bolena to Desdemona, and sometimes those of their interpreters, such as Maria Malibran (today it is Maria Callas). The hero, for his part, is almost always inhibited by his obligatory valor and at times by an arrogant stupidity: not until Otello do we get a searching, step-by-step description of a hero's inner evolution, whereas in the heroine's case it is given as early as Luisa Miller and Violetta. The triumph of the women in *Falstaff,* who are always more cunning, more clear thinking, less subject to illusions than the men, merely acknowledges a gradual development in Verdian dramaturgy in which woman has a privileged connection with reality that is denied the hero, with his naïveté and lack of realism.

IDEOLOGY

The ideology of the feminine that prevailed in the nineteenth century is common knowledge.[67] Alexandre Dumas *fils* defined it with extraordinary brutality: "Woman is born for subordination and obedience: first to the parents, then to the spouse, later to the child, always to duty."[68] She had not the slightest autonomy, and in everyday life she came up against countless legal obstacles. Opera generally reflected this situation through the theme of forced marriage; it is not unusual for a father, *in articulo mortis,* hurriedly to marry off his daughter to some suitor or other as though, fearing a legal gap, he wanted at all costs to ensure the continuity of guardianship.

Those women who apparently escape this dependency are assigned a very precise task and are thus subject to another dependency that temporarily robs them of their femininity. I have already noted the convention that governs Joan of Arc and prevents her from being both woman and warrior. Just as clear-cut is the case of Odabella, in *Attila,* who in her obsessive desire to carry out her father's vengeance cries out as she plunges the dagger in the tyrant's heart, "Father, O my father, I sacrifice him to you!" (act 3, scene 5).

Conversely, the female character who, whether through ill will or ambition, usurps man's active function tends to lose her feminine quality and become an asexual dragon, as we have seen with Abigaille in *Nabucco*. It has also been pointed out that Lady Macbeth's ambition leads her to repress her femininity in an almost hysterical tension of will. Her case is nevertheless more complex since her entrance cavatina has a powerful sexual charge: the scarcely ambiguous words she hurls at Macbeth (Come! Hasten! I want to set on fire that cold heart!), the surges of the melody as it insistently and stubbornly drives the phrase forward ("T'affretta, che tardi, accetta"), the repetitions one after another of "che tardi" (why do you wait), all suggest the confrontation of a lukewarm Macbeth and a "Lady" harshly summoning her man to virility. Yet, far from illustrating her seductive powers, the aria shows that Lady Macbeth has distorted her femininity into a frantic lust for power; the sense is "be a man," but with the sole purpose of furthering the couple's political ambitions.

Her total lack of autonomy dictates woman's way of behavior, which is sacrifice. This is in fact what the heroines of the eponymous operas have in common, all of whom sacrifice their love for a cause or person: Giovanna d'Arco, Alzira, Luisa Miller, La traviata, Aida. Nor is there anything to prevent this first sacrifice from being followed by a second, even more radical one. For instance, Leonora in *Il trovatore* sacrifices her love by offering her hand to the Count de Luna in order to save the troubadour Manrico but immediately poisons herself so that she will not actually be his. In short, sacrifice is woman's "natural" vocation. It is also more radical than in the man's case. For the hero, sacrifice is punishment for a moral or social transgression, but his emotional spontaneity is not actually affected, whereas for the woman sacrifice lies at the root of her desire because, to paraphrase Lacan, she must give to another the cause of her desire.[69] Man is punished for his desires when they do not conform to society's laws, but the subordination demanded of him is mainly external, while the heroine's subordination must penetrate to the very core of her being since her nature as object of exchange prevents her from following her own inclinations.[70]

As compensation for this total abnegation, woman is enthroned as guardian angel and gentle presence at the hearth. Woman, "saint of the future and of purification," as Mazzini defines her in his *Filosofia della musica,* points out to man the way of sacrifice and achieves the paradox of being already in heaven while still alive on earth. This is no doubt one reason for the strange absence of the mother in Romantic opera, so small is the step from moral effacement to absence, pure and simple.

Although absent, the mother is constantly evoked, as, for example, Bravo's mother in the opera of that name by Mercadante (act 1, scene 2), Elvino's mother in Bellini's *La sonnambula* (act 1, scene 5), and Pamira's in Rossini's *Siege of Corinth* (act 2, scene 1) as well as so many Verdian mothers, from Leonora's in *Oberto* to Aida's. The one actual mother of the Verdian theater is Azucena; we can regard the motherhood that Lida describes briefly in *Battaglia* or Amelia's in *Ballo* as negligible.

Her role as guardian angel justifies the frequent occurrence of prayers to the mother. A good example of this is *Stiffelio:* going to meet her seducer in a secret rendezvous, which takes place in a cemetery, Lina passes her mother's tomb and implores her help in overcoming her dangerous situation: "Ah dagli scanni eterei" (act 2, scene 1). The prayer theme was so popular that in the case of another opera, *Vêpres,* it was added even though the libretto did not provide for it: going from Scribe and Duveyrier's French libretto (published by Michel Lévy in 1855) to the score and then to the Italian libretto, the opera gained a prayer of Henri to his mother, at the end of the Henri-Montfort duet in act 3. It was probably added at the composer's urging.

There are no grounds for thinking that Verdi disavowed this ideology since he declared late in life that he did not at all approve of women taking courses of study and saw no other profession for them than medicine, "But only to tend women."[71] A somewhat austere man, very secretive as to his private life, he gave no sign of having the least sympathy for either rakes or fast women even if, after his wife's death, he chose to share his life with a singer whose past was not irreproachable in the eyes of the strict morality of the day and whom he defended nobly and with firmness.[72] In his works, which have with some justification been called sexophobic, the heroines are fiery, passionate, self-opinionated, and jealous, but they never have the languorous, heart-stopping appeal of a Leïla, a Carmen, or a Lakmé. It is not until *Aida* that Verdi pays any attention to a woman's sensual appeal, in that superb phrase of Amneris's at the beginning of act 2—"Vieni, amor mio, m'inebria." Only then do we see him hint at a voluptuous abandon worthy of Delilah.

VIOLETTA

La traviata is probably, together with *Carmen,* the greatest feminine myth of nineteenth-century opera. The parallel is not a new one, the Marquis Monaldi having established it in 1925—totally in favor of Verdi's heroine since he contrasts Carmen's "sensual frenzy" with Violetta's desire for redemption.[73] Yet Marguerite Gautier, "la dame aux camélias," could have been another Carmen if Dumas had been at all faithful to the real-life inspiration of his novel, that strange creature whose intelligence and culture fascinated Franz Liszt and Jules Janin. The enigmatic personality of Marie Duplessis often reminds one of Mérimée's and Bizet's gypsy because of her assurance, the offhand way she ruined her lovers, her mixture of gaiety, insouciance, and deep melancholy, her indifference to the values of the society she lived in, and her capacity to turn a humiliating situation into a challenge.

Some trace of her free and easy ways, her mixture of greed and indifference to money, can still be seen in the novel but completely vanishes in Dumas's play. Yet the novel already had a subtle, hypocritical infusion of moralism and libertinage that is accentuated in the play, a way of mirroring the attractions of lust while at the same time proclaiming the superiority of virtue, of courting the devil and worshiping God—in short, a somewhat dubious marriage of innocence and vice, purity and pleasure.

When Verdi got hold of the story of Violetta,[74] he did away with the ambiguous link implying a complicity in sin between the courtesan and her client, and he did not show the slightest desire to evoke the prostitute's sensual charms. He cut to the heart of the matter: either Violetta is a whore, in which case she interested him not a whit,[75] or she is a *traviata,* a prostitute, certainly, but above all one who has gone astray, a "poor sinner"; then he finds her infinitely touching. No ambiguous seductiveness must mar Violetta's inner purity. This basic innocence is seen very clearly in her first aria, "Ah fors'è lui," in the way it knits together Alfredo's love and her childhood dreams: "A me fanciulla, un candido / E trepido desire / Quest'effigiò dolcissimo / Signor dell'avvenire" (When I was a girl, an innocent and timid desire depicted him, the lord of my future; act 1, scene 5). In this way, the social corruption in which Violetta participates through her profession becomes quite alien to her.

Verdi thus violently rips apart what Dumas had mixed together with a certain gratification; indeed, the composer paints the party at which Violetta shines as hostess with crude, almost savage colors. Dumas redeems Marguerite but at the same time condemns her, marked as she is by the fever of an attractive but wicked sensuality. Once it is admitted that Violetta became a prostitute only because she was unable to escape the corruption of the big city, Verdi absolves her without another thought. This clear-cut choice raises Violetta to mythic stature and makes her a classic "fringe" character. Such a moral attitude, in the end less moralistic than that of the French dramatist, can probably be explained by the context in which the composer places his heroine, one about which I will have more to say a little farther on.

It is true that Violetta's dignity is gained through sacrifice, yet here sacrifice does not have the same meaning as it does for the other Verdian heroines. They sacrifice themselves *because* they are women, whereas Violetta sacrifices herself *in order to be* a woman—to obtain that recognition that Barthes held to be Marguerite Gautier's guiding motivation.[76] With this difference, Violetta is one of the purest sacrificial figures of the Verdian theater: she sacrifices her liaison to the reputation of the Germont family; she sacrifices her image of a woman passionately in love so that Alfredo will fall out of love with her; and, finally, she withdraws before the "chaste virgin" she imagines will one day be Alfredo's wife (act 3, scene 7).

Is it by coincidence that the libretto piles up the signs of this death sentence? Marie Duplessis died on 3 February 1847, at the height of Carnival; in the novel Marguerite Gautier dies during the night of 19–20 February, but Carnival time is over. The play, for its part, has her die on 1 January, a switch that gives rise to an unbearably sentimental diversion since New Year's Day is a family holiday closely following Christmas. Verdi and Piave reinstated the tragic coincidence between Marie's death and Carnival, even to the extent of emphasizing it: the bacchanal procession that passes below the dying Violetta's windows celebrates the triumph of the fattened bull, a ceremony that very probably came down from an ancient sacrificial rite. In the same way, in the Finale of act 2, why do matadors come to Flora Bervoix's salon if not to recall that they are the ones responsible for carrying out a solemn ritual killing?

MUTATIONS

The rigidity of the setting in which the female character evolves is compensated for, as I have pointed out, by the greater subtlety with which she is portrayed and the more careful way the composer deals with her development. Verdi's heroes often have several facets, which incidentally present concrete problems of vocal distribution. It is obvious that a good

Manrico must have both a melancholy streak and heroic verve, but these are contrasting sides of the same personality rather than successive states of mind. The woman, by contrast, can suffer a sea change between one end of the opera and the other. The reason is that conflict and adversity make the hero stiff and inflexible whereas in the heroine's case they serve to mellow her, thanks to the age-old familiarity with grief that opera has always associated with woman.

As a result of the difference between the two, there is an almost constant psychological contrast between the soprano's prescience and the tenor's blindness: the heroine knows all along that the drama will come tumbling pitilessly down on her, whereas the tenor gets bogged down in dreams and the illusion of escaping fate. Consider Riccardo's charmingly carefree air when he comes to see the fortune-teller Ulrica in *Un ballo in maschera* and his mocking incredulousness, so different from Amelia's apprehension. The music tells us clearly that the young woman has understood that her feelings for Riccardo have unleashed the mechanism of fate; moreover, the theme announcing her entrance onstage (at the beginning of the scene and trio 10) is amazingly close to that of *La forza del destino* (ex. 7a): it has the same dramatic forward movement conferred by the anacrusis, the same semitone oscillation, as if the one were an inversion of the other (ex. 7b).

The cruelest example of this contrast is to be found in *Aida*. In act 3, Radames arrives, prancing like a juvenile lead and heralded by a theme of quite Siegfriedian valor: he is convinced that he will be able to get out of marrying Amneris and persuade the King to let him wed Aida. With the ferocity often characteristic of him, Verdi lets the tenor drown himself in his vain hopes, underlining their poignant absurdity with a cut-and-dried martial accompaniment reinforced by sharp trumpet blasts ("Nel fiero anelito"), until at length, by cajoling him, Aida overcomes his resistance and incites him to treason.

The capacity of woman to grasp, indeed to anticipate the drama can be seen in the care with which Verdi depicts the growth of her personality. One can spot this even in certain female characters from the early operas, such as Lucrezia in *I due Foscari,* Joan of Arc, and Lida in *La battaglia di Legnano.* At first her evolution is sketched in strongly contrasting arias that pinpoint the successive stages of a personality. The most striking example is clearly Lady Macbeth, whose entrance aria is a cavatina vibrating with the energy of a will tensed toward power, whereas her final aria, the so-called sleepwalking aria, paints the breakdown of a personality consumed with remorse. The transition between these two extremes

EX. 7a

EX. 7b

would be found in 1865, when the deeply nocturnal aria "La luce langue" replaces the cabaletta of the first version, which was close in style to the entrance aria.

So far as the young girl character goes, her development is still somewhat crudely traced in *Luisa Miller*. Luisa is introduced rather conventionally as an innocent, fresh village maiden; her song with its staccato notes and limpid melody is close in style to the one Bellini and Donizetti used for *La sonnambula* and *Linda di Chamounix* (see ex. 8). Bitter experience quickly matures her, and her second aria, "Tu puniscimi o Signore," which follows the scene in which, to save her father, she is forced to give up her love and pretend to love the odious Wurm, is in complete contrast with her entrance aria. Far more refined, even at that early stage, is Gilda's metamorphosis in *Rigoletto*. Her first aria, "Caro nome," shows us again a carefree, daydreaming young girl, albeit in a style very different from that of Luisa; her second entry in her duet with Rigoletto, "Tutte le sere al tempio," is equally youthful and spontaneous but tinged with melancholy, while in the quartet and trio of act 3 she acquires the tragic dimension of a Violetta or a Leonora of *Trovatore*.

The mature operas give us a concrete, step-by-step representation of

EX. 8

the heroine's change, which is traced in certain great duets such as that of Violetta and Germont *(Traviata)* and Leonora and the Padre Guardiano *(Forza)*. More than duets, these are in fact long monologues in the presence of an interlocutor, in that all the interest is concentrated on the female character. Despite his growing benevolence, Alfredo's father still insists on sacrifice, and the duet illustrates Violetta's gradual, painful acceptance of that fact. The Padre Guardiano remains, throughout the scene, the worthy representative of an institution that finally welcomes a soul in pain, whereas Leonora begins in a state of profound confusion and ends her consultation at peace, almost joyous. These two male characters thus serve as catalysts to the sopranos' inner transformation, bringing them from anguish or rebellion to relief or resignation, each stage being clearly marked by a development of vocal style.

La forza del destino provides another example of this focusing of the drama on the heroine's gradual inner growth. The Duke of Rivas's play was entitled *Don Alvaro o la fuerza del sino,* thus linking the central theme of the force of destiny with the figure of the male protagonist. Verdi and Piave removed the name *Alvaro* from the title and emphasized the role of Leonora; furthermore, the overture is essentially centered on her, for four of its five themes recur in the second tableau of act 2, which is entirely given over to Leonora, with the most famous, the so-called destiny theme, surging forth from the very first measures. Alvaro has only one theme, a theme in A minor (m. 51) that is heard again in the last duet of Alvaro and Carlo di Vargas. When he changed the prelude of the 1862 version into the overture of the definitive version, Verdi did away with the only light note in this introduction (a quotation of the rhythmic motif that occurs at the opening of the inn scene in act 2), with the result that the overture that we know today points immediately to the central axis of the drama: the shock of fate, the suffering it creates, the struggle to break free of it, the attainment of inner peace, in short a résumé of Leonora's story.

The importance of the heroine's evolution is attested by the greater flexibility given to the writing of her part and the fact that her arias are almost always freer and more innovative than the hero's: nineteenth-century opera's gradual mastery of movement and transition happens, with Verdi, essentially through the female role. The most original aria of the youthful operas is undeniably Lady Macbeth's sleepwalking aria; in *Luisa Miller,* the limpidity of Rodolfo's aria "Quando le sere al placido" (two strophes ab and coda) contrasts with the agitation of Luisa's aria "Tu puniscimi o Signore" quoted above, where Verdi abandons the traditional four-measure phrasing when he reaches the second phrase.

The contrast is accentuated in the operas of Verdi's maturity and last years. *Forza* gives Leonora three arias, all of them varying widely in treatment: the mobility and diversity of tone of the romanza "Me pellegrina ed orfana" are of a different order from those of Alvaro's aria, a very beautiful one incidentally, in act 3. The simplicity of Carlo's romanza "Je l'ai vue et dans son sourire"/"Io la vidi e il suo sorriso" is the pendant of Elisabeth's romance "O ma chère compagne"/"Non pianger, mia compagna," but it cannot be compared in richness with his great act 5 aria, actually called a *scena* in the original score. Finally, in *Aida,* it is interesting to compare the transparency of Radames's romanza "Celeste Aida" (a1a2b a1a2 coda) and the complexity of "Ritorna vincitor," with its alternating regular and free sections, which is also called a *scena.* It is as though, from being relatively constricted by the tenor's psychological conventionality, Verdi's writing broke away to soar freely only when the soprano intervened; only the baritone or bass occasionally rivals this originality of expression.

Verdi knew perfectly well how this orientation tested his singers' dramatic gifts and not merely their voices. That is why, for roles like Lady Macbeth and Violetta, he always insisted on the soprano's acting talents and praised singers who, like Piccolomini, Spezia, or Boccadabati, had "small voices but great talent, deep feeling and a sense of the theater."[77] In 1877, he wrote an enthusiastic eulogy of Adelina Patti, whom he had heard in London in 1862. Curiously, when he described her interpretation of Gilda, he remembered not her vocal execution (which was judged perfect, by the way) but the manner in which, in the scene just before the act 3 quartet, when her father shows her her lover in the tavern and asks, "And you still love him?" she answered, "Yes, I love him": "There is no way to express the sublime effect of those words as she said them," he wrote.[78] What we have here is a modest recitative, punctuated by a very ordinary major chord; it must have been that with those simple words— "Io l'amo"—faintly murmured, la Patti succeeded in expressing the painful experience that separated the Gilda of the last act from the Gilda of "Caro nome."

FALSTAFF

Verdi's last opera crowns this evolution, creating a polarization between women's foresight and wisdom and men's folly. True, comedy was always the arena where women got their revenge for the humiliations they suffered in tragedy, but this triumph is particularly striking in *Falstaff,* even at the cost of some unfaithfulness to Shakespeare. In the original play, *The Merry Wives of Windsor,* Ann Page (renamed Nannetta) wants to marry Fenton but comes up against the opposition of both her father, who wants her to wed Slender, and her mother, who would have her marry Doctor Caius, while Mistress Quickly, Dr. Caius's servant, plays the rather dubious role of go-between and promises to make everyone happy. In other words, Ann and Fenton cannot trust their own devices to surmount the obstacles to their love. In the libretto, on the other hand, only Nannetta's father wants to marry her off to Caius, and the women (Alice Ford, Meg Page, and Mistress Quickly) band together to help the young people be united. Thus, the cleavage that with Shakespeare separates the young and the old divides Verdi's characters into two distinct camps: the men on one side and the young, aided by the women, on the other.

Thanks to this change of perspective, the women become the prime movers of the plot. It is they who set up the farces, devise the ruses intended to thwart Ford's plans, and stage-manage the final phantasmagoria, they who, as Verdi put it, make the pot boil and make fools not only of Falstaff but of Ford and Caius as well. This reshaping of the play was essentially the work of Boito, who also took his inspiration from *King Henry IV,* parts 1 and 2; but after he had read the original texts Verdi enthusiastically approved the new orientation and always insisted on the importance of Alice Ford, even going so far as to make her the principal character.[79]

It is the music's task to differentiate the men and the women, and it does so by emphasizing the latter's verve. The first tableau, where only men appear, is dominated by a measure in $\frac{4}{4}$ time so that, when the women come on, in the second tableau, their characteristic $\frac{6}{8}$ time should appear more piquant and sparkling; the lovers' entrance is underlined by $\frac{3}{4}$ time, as if to emphasize their solidarity with the women. The grand ensemble winding up act 1 opposes the women's group and the men's and, in the same way, their $\frac{6}{8}$ time ("Quell'otre, quel tino") and the masculine $\frac{2}{2}$ time ("È un ribaldo, un furbo, un ladro"). In act 2, the "Merry Wives of Windsor" refrain is heard, also in $\frac{6}{8}$ time, while the arrival of Alice's husband, at first pretend and then real, takes us back to $\frac{2}{4}$. During the great screen scene, the men's brusque sixteenth notes contrast with the elegant eighth-note triplets of the women. There is nothing systematic about these rhythmic variations, but there are sufficient indications that the women are made to seem constantly light and tripping and the men abrupt and clumsy.[80]

The women's controlling power is clearly seen in the contrast they present to the illusion under which most of the menfolk live. For instance, Ford disguises his inner insecurity as jealous rage and imagines that he can still exercise full paternal power; Bardolfo and Pistola flaunt a respectability that their lives deny; and Falstaff, the burlesque version of the hero, fancies himself an irresistible seducer, forgetting that he is too fat and a graybeard. Not that the women escape the charm of illusion, but the difference is that they know how to master it; there is a certain melancholy in Alice's great flights of fancy as she reads Sir John's prose, but a huge burst of laughter dispels the slight nostalgia. The most magical moment of the opera is the great invocation of the Fairy Queen, that is, Nannetta, but this superb nightly fairy revel beneath the oak of Herne has been organized by the merry wives. The men are the playthings of illusion, while the women are the players. Shakespeare's solid womenfolk become, in the hands of Boito and Verdi, delicate, crafty creatures who know how to surrender to fancy's charms without becoming its victims. They organize the carnival but are never its dupes.

First Balance Sheet

FROM LAW TO ORDER

Verdi's dramatic evolution can be traced chiefly in the changes affecting the major characters of his theater, but it can also be seen in a change of atmosphere that I will attempt to define by basing my examination on certain themes.

The presence of God, as guarantor of the law, dominates the early dramaturgy and gives a sort of eternal authority to the judge figure. Oberto claims that a God guides his steps; Nabucco is only the instrument of God when he leads the Hebrews into captivity, while the prophet Zaccaria shows them the road of expiation and redemption. Attila is the scourge of God, and Monterone has the statue-like grandeur of a Commendatore. It matters little whether this sacred aura surrounding many characters is the sign of a genuine belief, the result of a religious feeling prevalent in the Italian culture of the time, or merely a metaphor for the respect of tradition: in each case it confronts the individual with social rules that have the majesty of divine law, while often giving the drama the whiff of a religious epic.

In the next stage, God gradually returns to heaven and no longer stands surety for human actions; the law is secularized and becomes no more than an order, constraining, certainly, but marked with social and historical features. In spite of all his grandeur, Fiesco pays the penalty of this evolution: in the great duet in which he stands face to face with the Doge, Simon, he tries in vain to pass himself off as the mouthpiece of an avenging God—"Tua sentenza la mano del nume / Sovra queste pareti vergò" (The hand of God has written your sentence on these walls; act 3, scene 3). He soon realizes that his vengeance may have been no more than the result of an unjustified, long-held grudge. In *La forza del destino,* God is not on the side of Calatrava, who curses his daughter in the name of a feudal notion of filial obedience, but on the side of Il Padre Guardiano who offers her a peaceful refuge, far from worldly turmoil. Did Verdi later come to question religion in favor of the purely human element? It certainly appears so when one sees how in *Don Carlos* and *Aida* the law as dispensed by the church is often no more than the brutal expression of a repressive conservatism.

In this evolution, *La traviata* occupies a particularly interesting niche in that the plot is contemporary with the era in which the opera was created ("around 1850," according to the libretto). Lacking a historical disguise, the father-judge loses much of his majesty and becomes a laughable, worthy father of a family who is afraid of gossip, while the inflexible law that used to call for daughters to sacrifice themselves is now merely the pompous mask of bourgeois order. Moreover, Piave and Verdi felt that they had to enhance this character's prestige by giving him a solemn intervention in the act 2 Finale.

All this has prompted some commentators to see the opera as a work of social polemics, especially since the choice of a contemporary setting (the worldly society under Louis-Philippe) and the featuring of certain themes rare in opera of the time (money, gambling, sickness, the presence of a woman who has lost her social position and is rejected by a pleasure-seeking but orthodox society) herald the dramaturgy of the fin de siècle. In this view, Verdi seems to point a finger at a hypocritical society that called for gratuitous sacrifices, and Germont becomes the personification of this pharisaism.

Yet the reality is a little more complex. Verdi never shows Germont as a hypocrite, and the character appears as a man who is, if not imposing, then at least sympathetic.[81] The fact is that he does not belong to the same world as the Vicomte de Létorières, Baron Douphol, and d'Obigny, those pallid minor characters who attend Violetta's or Flora's soirees. Moreover, it will be seen that, where in Dumas's novel Armand's father (Germont) lives in Tours (near Paris), Verdi and Piave banish him to Provence, a warm, sun-drenched land that is as far as possible from the capital. This factual detail makes it possible to suggest an opposition between two societies—that of Paris, frivolous, cynical, and pleasure loving, and another peaceful, provincial society personified by Germont, the image of a world that is doomed to disappear. This world is that of semiseria opera, an intermediary genre between tragedy and opera buffa that includes operas such as Rossini's *La gazza ladra,* Bellini's *La sonnambula,* and Donizetti's *Linda di Chamounix.* In this idyllic world, which perpetuates the atmosphere of sentimental comedy, we find good people who in spite of their moral conservatism are basically likable; we see the obstacles that virtue and innocence must surmount before they can triumph, and the general atmosphere suggests the peaceful harmony of a provincial, traditional way of life grounded in honesty and hard work.

Verdi never wrote any semiseria opera, although he was tempted by this intimist vein.[82] Yet, because of its simplicity of tone, its melodic fluidity, and its refusal of heroic rhetoric, *La traviata* is linked in part to this genre, while at the same time we can see its unfittedness for Violetta's tragic story. Germont and, partly, Violetta herself belong to this world: his good-hearted, provincial background makes Germont a moralist who can summon arguments, but he is not a whited sepulcher; while Violetta, with her dreams of peace and happiness and her nostalgia for childhood, suggests a Linda di Chamounix who would have gone bad had she succumbed to the pleasures of the big city, making her return home both impossible and something passionately longed for.

The opera is thus at the point where two antinomic worlds touch, the bourgeois idyll based on a conservative morality (of which the law I described earlier is the heroic transfiguration) and the reality of the great metropolis (where the law is merely that pure appearance that Offenbach ridicules so wittily in *Orphée aux enfers*). We are no longer quite in the sphere of the first and not truly in the domain of the second. Germont's world no longer has the power to bring back its lost sheep, any more than the world of Parisian society has the moral coherence to call for the sinning woman's renunciation, which makes Violetta's sacrifice peculiarly ambiguous—at the same time a necessary expiation and a gratuitous death sentence. Thus, *Traviata* occupies a pivotal position between the calm good faith of semiseria opera and the guilty conscience of verismo opera.[83]

PEOPLE AND NATION

The protagonists of Verdi's first operas usually stand out against the background of a group, either a national group (Hebrews against Assyrians, Lombards against Infidels, Indians against Spaniards) or a marginal one (brigands, pirates, gypsies). The self-contained nature of the group is illustrated in the many choruses that are found in these works and that earned Verdi the nickname *papa dei cori;* if some of them have an ancillary function, such as the choruses of "camp followers," "companions," or "comrades in arms," the best known conjure up the image of a strong, united community, in short a nation. This is the case with "Va, pensiero" *(Nabucco),* "O signore dal tetto natio" *(I Lombardi),* "Si ridesti il leon di Castiglia" *(Ernani),* and so on, up to the choruses of *Battaglia* and *Vêpres.*

The evolution of the choruses is quite striking, for they diminish quantitatively and change qualitatively. The fact that they diminish can be explained by the chorus's conventional function of beginning an opera or an act. Verdi evidently tired of this choral ritual quite early on, asking

Cammarano (all of whose serious librettos begin with a chorus) to avoid opening *Il trovatore* in this way.[84] Qualitatively, one can sum up the evolution by saying that the chorus ceased to be a nation and became a people, a crowd, even a rabble. Musically, this process involved a greater "social" characterization of the chorus. For example, the last act of *Aroldo* starts with a triple chorus contrasting the songs of shepherds, hunters, and gleaners. Almost all the operas written after the 1850s present us with motley groups—the lively crowd of customers at the inn at Hornachuelos or the even more variegated one of the camp near Velletri in *Forza;* the throng of woodcutters and their womenfolk in act 1 of *Don Carlos* (original version) or the people's revolt at the end of act 4; the din of an uprising that reaches the hall of the Grand Council in act 1 of *Simon* (1881 version). The people disappear as a nation, a group welded together by a common ideal, giving way to a mass that is both better characterized and more anonymous. As the ultraconservative Boito writes in the finale of *Simon:* "Quest'è dunque del popolo la voce? / Da lungi tuono d'uragan, da presso / Grido di donne e di fanciulli" (Is this then the voice of the people? From afar, the thunder of the tempest, from nearby the cries of women and children; act 1, scene 11).

One can discern this change by comparing the two choruses of homesick Scots in *Macbeth* (act 4) in the 1847 version and that of 1865. The second, with its rich choral texture diversifying the vocal groups (sopranos 1, 2, 3; tenors 1, 2; basses), the subtle harmonics creating plays of appoggiaturas,[85] the atmosphere of desolation suggested by the refrain that opens the chorus and closes it *ppp* on an open fifth, is one of the most beautiful of the Verdian choruses. By comparison, the first, with its anapestic, heavily stressed rhythm, its disposition of the voices first in unison, then almost constantly parallel for the same group, its form based, with little respect for the text, on the minor/major scheme, is handled like the old patriotic, nostalgic choruses and seems more primitive. Still, it does conjure up a homogeneous community rising up from despair to the hope of revenge, whereas the chorus in the later version merely shows the people, the eternal outlaw. In 1887, in *Otello,* the people end up as simply one huge confused din, climbing the ramparts of Cyprus to acclaim their hero (act 3).

WAR, FESTIVITY, AND POMP

Verdi's first operas resound with the noise of battles and duels: heroes, tyrants, judges, sometimes even heroines, all are brimming over with warlike ardor; only *I due Foscari* is an exception to this rule of martial uproar, which is expressed by vibrant cabalettas, hymns, or marches given over to the *banda*. *La battaglia di Legnano,* which was written for Rome, was performed during the brief period of the Roman republic (January 1849), and describes the struggle of the Italian cities against Barbarossa in the twelfth century, is the last of Verdi's operas to give full expression to this combative mood. In the later works war does not vanish from the stage, but it loses importance and essentially acts as a backdrop. At a staging of *La forza del destino,* which does in fact include a "battle scene" and a vast crowd scene in a soldiers' camp, Verdi reproached the conductor, Mariani, for making the brass ring out in the overture, reminding him that "the warlike element is the most episodic you can find." [86] One might say the same of *Aida* (where Radames's triumph is mainly ceremonial) or *Otello.*

In the next operas it is festivity that predominates, festivity intended as a ritual affirming the cohesion of civilian society freed of its obsession with war. Already present in *Macbeth,* it plays an important role in *Rigoletto* and *Vêpres,* even becoming a fundamental theme in *Traviata* and *Ballo.* Still, the spirit presiding over the representation of festivity undergoes profound change. That the banqueting scene in *Macbeth* is painted in crude, violent colors is understandable since it illustrates the ostentatious tastes of the parvenu Macbeths and their wish to assert their newly acquired power, but in the operas of the trilogy festivity is presented without any charm or grace whatsoever.

In *Rigoletto,* if the faintly parodying minuet that the Duke of Mantua dances with the Countess of Ceprano or the Duke's own ballata are relatively elegant, the fete is still basically rough and vulgar. The rapid, mechanical succession of five themes played, allegro con brio, by the *banda* makes this unmistakably clear: the melodies are nervous, a little frenetic; the conversation is lively but staccato; and the whole has a feverish quality that makes this festivity graceless and devoid of charm.

With *La traviata,* festivity takes center stage since it dominates the first act, returns in the act 2 finale, and reappears, at least in echo form, in the bacchanal of act 3. Here, too, in spite of a few moments of abandon, linked to the relationship of Alfredo and Violetta (a tender little D-major theme when Gaston introduces Alfredo to her and the waltz swirling around their duet in act 1), what strikes one is the relentless rhythmic propulsion that marks the fete from the start, driving it into a sort of unstoppable whirling eddy. The same rhythmic pressure dominates the gaming scene (act 2), with its whip-like acciaccaturas energizing this perpetual motion. Striking, too, is how abrupt, violent, almost disjointed, are

EX. 9

the themes opening the fete—the one in A major in act 1, that in C major in Finale 2. Finally, there is the stroke of genius of the four measures separating the prelude from the first scene, which give the precise impression that Verdi is unlocking an enormous mechanism that, subsequently, nothing will be allowed to stop (see ex. 9).

This constant feverishness denotes a rush toward pleasure that the libretto enhances by frequent allusions to the passing of time: "Dell'invito trascorsa è già l'ora. . . . / Voi tardaste . . . ," "Giacommo da Flora, / E giocando quell'ore volâr," "la notte che resta / D'altre gioie qui fate brillar . . . ," "E la fuggevol ora / S'inebri a voluttà," "fugace e rapido / È il gaudio dell'amore," etc. (The time of the invitation is already past. . . . You are late. . . . We were gambling at Flora's, and as we played those hours flew. . . . You make what's left of the night shine with other joys. . . . And let the fleeting hour intoxicate itself with pleasure. . . . Love's joy is quick and fleeting). This highly negative view of partying should not be surprising in an austere, provincial man such as Verdi was at the time: "In this Paris," his wife Giuseppina wrote in 1866, "life is just a violent, rapid, exhausting fever that bears one panting towards the grave."[87] Where war welded together protagonists and chorus in a common outburst of heroism, festivity opposes the emotional world of these same protagonists and the artificial exteriority of a pleasure-seeking society.

Un ballo in maschera, where festivity is given a grace and delicacy it never had before, is here an exception. What Verdi took from Scribe's original libretto was, above all, the elegance and gaiety of the Swedish court and the characters of Gustav and Oscar, "tailored in the French style," all of which he made an effort to retain despite the historical and geographic changes called for by the censors.[88] Without worrying over-much about chronology, he re-created an ideal atmosphere that combined the delicacy of Gustav III's late eighteenth-century Sweden and the verve of Offenbach's Paris (clearly evoked in the Stretta of the introduction, "Dunque signori aspettovi"). Here, festivity has a quite different function: instead of forming a contrast with the characters' inner feelings, it defines the very nature of the hero, a likable and worldly ruler, and the cleavage between festivity and drama no longer divides the characters and society but goes through the very heart of the protagonist.

After *Ballo,* festivity loses its importance and becomes more than anything a diversion, as in the lighter scenes of *Forza,* the fete following Otello's victory, and the *Don Carlos* ballets. What stands out in the last operas is ceremony, the heavy ritual of official celebration. The short but majestic procession of Philip II and the Spanish court to the monastery of St.-Just is a good example. Carlos and Rodrigue sing a heroic cabaletta in the old style, which is interrupted by the solemn royal cortege; one reality banishes another, with the new pomp of state drowning out the revolutionary cheers of the Risorgimento. The grand finale of the auto-da-fé in act 3 of *Don Carlos* and Radames's impressive triumph celebrating not so much war as the glory of ancient Egypt exemplify this new atmosphere, which replaces the warrior fervor of the nation with the pomp of the modern state.

POLITICS

The parallelism of certain themes that we have just studied—on the one side the law, the people-nation, and war and on the other order, society, and the state—suggests a profound change in the composer's relation to society and politics, which must now come up for questioning. Verdi's oeuvre is in fact one of the very few in the world of opera to give a completely clear field to political passions. Yet it must be said that these are expressed within relatively narrow limits: because Verdi's highest priority was to create an emotional atmosphere, there is little room left for the discussion of ideas, but a huge affective resonance is given to attitudes that, even though not explicit or even at times very clear, enjoyed the consensus of the public.

Verdi's political fortunes were linked in large measure to the fact that the man became the symbol of the national struggle for unification and independence. His nationalist sympathies, modest origins, and personal rigidity and austerity gradually built up the myth of a Verdi who represented the new Italy. His name became intertwined with nationalist propaganda—as witness the famous slogan "Viva V.E.R.D.I." that appeared on city billboards from 1859 on—and he was chosen to present King Victor Emmanuel with the results of the annexation referendum of his province and became a deputy of the first Italian parliament in 1861.

Still, it is clear that Verdi's mythic stature went well beyond politics, beyond his personal commitment (which, as we have seen, was somewhat modest), beyond his political convictions, and concerned the man himself. Just as his operas presented onstage "the rugged Italian of Dante and Machiavelli," as Massimo Mila recalled, so the man appeared, strong, both aristocrat and peasant, rock hewn—in a word, just like the image that the new Italy wished for itself. As he grew older Verdi became a sort of "patriarch," "a tutelary divinity of the fatherland."[89] As Mila wrote in 1951, "Speaking of Verdi, for us Italians, is like speaking of our father."[90] This means that what we should look for in his operas is not so much a ringing political message as a moral climate with which every Italian could associate his own convictions.

Nabucco provides a good example of the limits within which the political meaning of Verdi's operas should be understood. First performed at La Scala on 9 March 1842, the work was a triumph, and we know, from the mound of testimony, that the Milanese truly felt that they were hearing a new kind of music. Yet the political significance of the plot is ambiguous, to say the least: the Hebrew-Italians certainly were prisoners of the Assyrian-Austrians, but they do not free themselves from their oppressors or the tyrant who rules over them. It is Nabucco who, by converting to the religion of his "captives," sends them back to their homeland (act 4, scene 4). The denouement celebrates the reconciling of opposing peoples beneath the sign of one God, and the ideology of the libretto is in fact moderate, recommending that the rulers shun the excesses of absolute power and that the occupying forces have more respect for their subjects' values. There is nothing here, in short, to foster nationalist, let alone republican propaganda.

That is not the core of the opera, however, for the central axis is not political but ethical and religious, founded on the notions of expiation and redemption. As is shown clearly in the libretto's epigraphs for the first two acts, taken from Jeremiah, the Hebrews expiate their sins through the vengeful fury of the Assyrian king; later, Nabucco in turn is punished for his excesses and his folly; later still, Fenona prepares to atone with the Hebrews, and Abigaille pays for her ambition and felony by taking poison. Peoples and individuals take parallel paths in this journey sanctioned by the redemption celebrated in act 4—the redemption of an individual through conversion and that of a people through liberation.

The novelty of *Nabucco* therefore is the dynamic that turns tragedy into a form of testing that can lead to moral resurrection rather than despair. This is the driving force that gives the prophet Zaccaria his true worth: no longer is he that stock opera character, the just man mournfully proclaiming that history is the source of every turpitude and that man is doomed to suffer; rather, he is an activist who changes grief into trial, prostration into hope. The opera breaks with the disenchanted pessimism of Verdi's predecessors, according to whom individuals are the victims of an unjust, cruel fate and tragedy is ineluctable; instead, it sets up a dynamic of renewal, struggle, and regeneration. It is nonetheless clear that the importance of this affective climate, however innovative it may have seemed at the time and however great its moral impact, lay not so much in the ideas that might be derived from it as in its ability to bring together in one sweep moderates and extremists, monarchists and republicans.

The dynamic of regeneration thus defines the political Verdi of the early operas, leading one to forget the circumstances of the plot from which each arose. For instance, when we hear "Si ridesti il leon di Castiglia" (Let the lion of Castile rewaken) in *Ernani,* we do not remember that this hymn of vengeance is sung by embittered feudal lords bent on bringing down monarchic power and soon thereafter the might of the future emperor Charles V; similarly, when Ezio, in *Attila,* sings "Avrai tu l'universo, / Resti l'Italia a me" (To you the universe, Italy is enough for me), we forget that in fact the general is proposing that the King of the Huns make a sordid bargain with him. The revolutionary vein is exhausted with *La battaglia di Legnano,* the period of the crisis of 1848 when Verdi muted patriotic themes in his operas.

Yet the political dimension does not disappear from his oeuvre. As a result of the 1848 crisis and the public-private schism that I have described in connection with the hero, the libertarian fervor of the earliest operas vanishes, the warlike ardor of the characters grows dim, and the problematic of power moves to the foreground. Where, at first, the political arena is a place of combat and heroics in which the moral stakes are clear and death does not necessarily mean defeat, it now becomes the scene of purely personal conflict. The tyrant figure is a key witness of this development: as political characters, Nabucco, Attila, and Frederick Barbarossa are two-dimensional and uniformly fierce and bellicose. Seen from outside, they appears as blocks of brute strength whose path can be deflected only by a superior force. Gradually, we move from the "external conflict" to the "conflict of the soul," and the figure of the tyrant becomes equivocal, while the political conflict is echoed by a family conflict that gives it a more human feeling.[91]

I described above Guy de Montfort's great aria, in *Les Vêpres siciliennes*, in which he contrasts his power as absolute ruler with his feeling of profound inner emptiness. This schism is both "private," in that the father has been rejected by his son Henri, who is faithful to the memory of the mother, once brutally seduced, and "public," in that Henri is spokesman for the Sicilian patriots who detest the French governor representing the occupying power. Montfort's only weapon is force, stripped of all legitimacy, political, moral, or affective. He therefore attempts to fill this inner vacuum by trying to win his son's affection and reconcile the French and Sicilians. Even though these steps come too late to stop the avenging mechanism set in motion by Procida, the political judge, within the space of an aria we have become acquainted with the distress and solitude of a man of power.

In this survey, which brings us up to Verdi's last political operas, *Un ballo in maschera* does not seem to me to have a place, even if certain critics have seen it as proof of a conservative shift on the composer's part.[92] Verdi's rallying to the Piedmontese monarchy and his abandonment of all sympathy for the republicans is beyond doubt, yet there is nothing in his correspondence to indicate that he was interested in the opera's political dimension. Scribe's original libretto set up, on opposite sides, not an absolute sovereign versus republican conspirators, but on the one hand feudal lords cheated of their privileges by the King and on the other Gustave III, who in 1772 in Sweden set up a regime of enlightened despotism; the French libretto portrays an "Orleanist" ideology favorable to a modern monarchy and hostile to the reactionary spirit of the conspirators. Actually, by eliminating those episodes that showed the King's "enlightened" nature, Verdi concentrates rigorously on the private plot linking Riccardo, Amelia, and Renato, treating the conspirators Samuel and Tom as somewhat stiff puppets whose motivations are hazy in the extreme. If he was explicitly opposed to the idea of abandoning the ceremony of the Stockholm court, it was not because of its political significance but because of the atmosphere of elegance and spectacle that it represented. To sum up, Verdi deals with political passions or characters never in a playful tone but always in an intense, somber style. Philip II, Fiesco, Simon, and Posa are serious, even austere characters, miles away from the careless elegance with which Riccardo dispatches affairs of state.

As Verdi aged, his view of politics was expressed in two operas, *Don Carlos* and *Simon Boccanegra,* and five characters, Philip II, the Marquis of Posa, the Grand Inquisitor, Simon Boccanegra, and Fiesco. The Grand Inquisitor—like Ramfis in *Aida,* by the way—portrays the decline of the figure of political judge. The prophetic political and religious fervor that inspired a Zaccaria, or a Leone in *Attila,* gives way to a spirit of repression that is blindly insensitive to all humanity, the incarnation of a relentless fanaticism that totally subordinates politics to the power of the church— in short, an imposing but odious figure. Fiesco provides a more subtly drawn image of the judge, both because he is at once a political and familial judge (he wants to have his revenge on Simon because the governor seduced his daughter) and because he represents not absolutism so much as a rigorously hierarchical feudal system. In this capacity he earned Verdi's respect since the composer was always indulgent toward men who were steadfast and principled. Nevertheless, in 1881, when the last version of the opera was produced, and in light of the Doge Simon's liberalizing ambitions, Fiesco comes across as the old-fashioned defender of an outworn system. At the other extreme is Rodrigue, the Marquis of Posa, a zealous but naive revolutionary who seems to personify the spirit of the Risorgimento—but two centuries premature in relation to the period of the drama and twenty years too late in relation to the period in which the opera was produced. Verdi, who found him anachronistic, is even said to have considered suppressing the character and to have got out of the situation by dismissing it as an "episodic and purely singing role."[93]

We must therefore turn to Simon and Philip II to get an idea of Verdi's political vision, but it must be said that it is a dark, disillusioned one. The corsair Simon, who has come to the throne almost accidentally, after a people's revolt in 1339, exercises absolute power to the extent of appearing like a tyrant; however, he at once uses this power to try to move beyond the partisan struggles to which he owes his position and, through a systematic desire for pacification, to set up a lasting peace between the various social groups in his city. Still, his generosity does not succeed in disarming either his enemies (Fiesco) or even his allies, for he is poisoned by one of them; the designation of Adorno as his successor looks very much like an example of wishful thinking! The failure of his utopian ideal widens the chasm between the political ideal of national concord and unity and the reality of power that consists in endless fighting. The Doge-corsair's moving farewell to the sea before he dies is equivalent to a rejection of politics (one that is perfectly explicit in García Gutiérrez's original drama).

Does not exhaustion in the face of his task also dominate the character of Philip II, King of Spain? Verdi strongly deflected the personality of Schiller's king toward greater humanity, but he also sent it in the direction of greater uncertainty. In his famous scene with Posa he indulgently listens to the Marquis's liberal speech but obviously remains quite unconvinced and strongly upholds a policy of pure repression. In the scene with the Inquisitor he does try to defend his friendship with Posa and his fatherly love but nonetheless ends up yielding to the old priest, who wants Posa's head and urges him to be severe with Carlos. As this scene, which is placed toward the end of Schiller's drama (act 5, scene 10), is brought forward in the libretto (to act 4, scenes 1 and 2) to a moment in the plot where the King is faced with important choices, one has the feeling that he is abdicating before the demands of the church. Other episodes confirm this submission: it is the Inquisitor who quells the people's rebellion (act 4), not the Duke of Alba, as in Schiller, just as it is the Inquisitor who eliminates Posa and not Philip II; the finale of the auto-da-fé, which does not exist in the German play, demonstrates the Inquisition's omnipotence. The King of Spain thus appears like a hostage to the temporal power of the church while sharing in its blind intransigence.

The dynamic of Schiller's drama opposes the spirit of freedom of the Enlightenment and the intolerance of despotism. Verdi rejected religious absolutism, but neither did he believe in the liberal utopia, and the result is the image of a monarch enamored of generous sentiments but unable to escape the spiral of violence, a sort of Verdian Wotan pursued by a death wish. Even if we know Verdi was troubled by historical inaccuracies in Schiller's play,[94] this did not prevent him from expressing his perplexity regarding power through the character of Philip II.

The schism between a duty rigorously carried out and a nature in which solitude and confusion are palpable gives the character its modernity. As George Steiner writes of Schiller's monarch (yet it is even more true of Verdi's king): "Behind him, in the shadows of the Escorial, seem to wait John Gabriel Borkman and all the other characters of modern drama in whom there has occurred the death of the heart."[95] Hence the importance of his great aria in act 4: out of a brief monologue, touched with melancholy, that quickly gives way to the spirit of decisiveness (Schiller, act 3, scene 1), Verdi fashioned a fundamental scene that exposes to the harsh light of day the contrast between the outer shell of authority and prestige that protects the King and his inner melancholy, which makes him long for death.

The contrast is shown no less clearly in *Aida*. Paradoxically, this opera, where so much is sacrificed to the attractions of ceremony, is the one that best illustrates its oppressive side. The constant presence of ritual—the consecration of the sword in the first act, Radames's triumph in the second, the prayer to Osiris in the third, the judgment scene in the fourth—confines the individuals within a prison. Spectacle, all too present in this opera, ends up disguising its other side, that of an intimate drama centered on the tragedy of a few individuals lost in the monumental ostentation of ancient Egypt. Where, in former times, political and social rules bonded the protagonists to the collective group, now these same rules have become alien or even hostile to them. Where politics was an ideal or at least an enthusiasm, now it is merely power.

"OTELLO" AND THE AMBIGUITY OF SIGNS

One can think of *Otello*, on the first level, that of melodrama, as the story of a jealous man who, under the influence of the treacherous insinuations of his ensign Iago, gradually becomes convinced that his wife Desdemona is deceiving him with Cassio and, ravaged by jealousy and faithful to his code of honor, decides to kill her. One can also, at the second level, think of *Otello* as an opera about the crisis, or failure, of melodrama. Melodrama implies characters that are easily grasped and substantial in some way, each one representing a clearly defined moral attitude. It presupposes an unambiguous language that indicates plainly what is true and what false. In the view of traditional melodrama, Otello is a hero who changes to a judge and punishes his wife for committing adultery, but, since he has been duped by Iago, her murder is no more than a tragic misapprehension.

This view is obviously not wrong, but it fails completely to take into account the modernity of the opera. In actual fact, we never know exactly what is true and what is false because of the knowing way Shakespeare and his protagonist confuse us and also because of the coexistence of two levels—an actual level, of which we know next to nothing, and a fantasy level, built up entirely by Iago, which colors reality and orients it in a predetermined direction in order to set in motion the mechanism he wants to activate. It is in this sense that the opera is also concerned with the ambiguity of signs and the tenuousness of our perception of reality.

One of the indications of this double level is in the well-known question of the play's chronology: the sequence of events does not actually leave room for Desdemona's supposed adultery to take place—an inconsistency that some have solved by suggesting that Shakespeare used a "double time," a historical, real time and a dramatic time.[96] In the libretto, the omission of act 1 of the play simplifies the question, without, however, clarifying it completely. It is possible, in fact, to assume in the first act of the opera that Otello and Desdemona have just arrived in Cyprus, where they will spend their wedding night: Iago urges Roderigo to provoke Cassio so as to "turbar la prima vigilia d'amore" (disturb happy Othello's first night of love). In the second act, which seems to follow close on the first, the day after Otello's wedding night, Iago prompts Cassio to beg Desdemona to intervene on his behalf with Otello, adding, "È suo costume / Girsene a meriggiar fra quelle fronde" (It is her habit to stroll among those trees at noontime). In that way Cassio could perhaps get back his former rank and return to his lovemaking with Monna Bianca (act 2, scene 1).[97]

How did Otello's wife have the time to get into this "habit" if she had reached Cyprus just the day before, and how did Cassio have the time to hatch a plot *before* being demoted by Otello if he was seen leaving the boat with his general in the first act? It looks very much as though Otello and Desdemona were in Cyprus "before" the first act: why then did they have to wait for their wedding night? Either that, or Desdemona was in Cyprus alone, which is highly unlikely for a young bride and does not settle the Cassio question. It also looks as though a considerable length of time has elapsed between the first and the second acts: why, then, would Cassio, who was very much affected by his punishment, wait so long before asking Desdemona to intervene? These chronological vaguenesses are not very important except to highlight the way Iago seizes time and creates perspectives that have no connection with reality.

The plot itself places deceit and illusion at the core of the play. Iago dupes Roderigo, he dupes Otello by making him believe that his wife is deceiving him with Cassio, he dupes Cassio, and, in the play, he even dupes Desdemona. The result is that the drama becomes, to quote P.-J. Rémy's formula, "the ballet of four dupes and one duper."[98] Still, Iago's art consists not so much in saying the contrary of the truth, an inversion compatible with the spirit of melodrama, as in confusing vision and duplicating reality: he makes Cassio drink to blur his sight; he repeats Otello's words like an echo, in such a way that even the Moor notices ("He makes himself the echo of my words!"); in short, he behaves like a prism that muddles a reality that up to that time had seemed clear and luminous.

Iago's subversive powers are shown most fully when Desdemona appears in the gardens, surrounded by women and children. The sweetness of the apparition is suddenly struck with ambiguity by Iago's sotto voce commentary, suggesting the falsity of this vision, which the music describes as one of paradise ("Non parlo ancor di prova" [I do not yet speak of proof]). Since Boito and Verdi cleverly shifted Desdemona's only solo to the last act—the entrance aria being traditionally the time when the character is presented as he or she "really" is—a feeling of doubt is conveyed to the spectator as to Otello's wife's true personality. The fact that Cassio and Desdemona have known each other before, both being part of the gilded youth of Venice—a world to which the Moorish general is naturally quite alien—only accentuates this uncertainty.

Iago systematically builds up his art of doubt. Shakespeare's character frequently has the opportunity to insist on the fragility of appearances. He portrays himself as a critic ("For I am nothing if not critical"; act 2, scene 1, line 119) and introduces himself with these words: "I am not what I am" (act 1, scene 1, line 64). He knows that he can count on the Moor's credulity: "The Moor is of a free and open nature,/That thinks men honest that but seem to be so" (act 1, scene 3, line 405). Therefore, his aim, or at least the consequence of his action, is not just to make him jealous and point him toward vengeance but to destroy him by making him lose all sense of bearings, by plunging him into a world of mirrors.

Within the framework of opera, with its history of powerful, bombastic tragedies, and in the dramaturgy of a composer whose characters were always intense and of a piece, this clash between two personalities, one devious and the other loyal and naive, is far from being a simple psychological conflict; rather, it sounds the knell of a certain world. With Verdi, as with Shakespeare, Otello is a simple man, habitually straightforward because of his profession as a soldier and his "barbarian" origins, which make him a stranger to the delicate refinement of Venice. He is, in short, a hero of melodrama, in the best sense of the word, and now suddenly this man gets sucked into a confused, indecipherable world, put out of joint because of the deception that Iago conjures up expertly each day.

It seems as though Verdi perfectly understood what was at stake with this opera: Iago prevents Otello from being faithful to his "nature" and his heroic qualities; concretely, he prevents him from singing save when Otello's nature inexorably takes him in the direction of violence and destruction. Consider, for example, the superb first scene between the general and his ensign (act 2, scene 1): Iago draws Otello into a conversation full of hints and rapid innuendos that inflames Otello and makes him explode in a great chromatic phrase ("Nel chiostro dell'anima"). After this outburst, the hero tries to get hold of himself, and the short six-measure arioso in which he orders Iago to tell him the truth, in other words to speak "his" language, has a vibrant, clear accompaniment in the old style that one could imagine in a cabaletta (see ex. 10 on p. 212).

This break in style is no coincidence. Certain sections in the opera—Otello's solo "Ora e per sempre addio" or the duet with Iago "Si, pel ciel marmoreo giuro"—have often been interpreted as relapses into an old-fashioned style, unworthy of the modernity of the work. Yet these are poignant passages where Otello is remembering a former world now gone from his grasp, and how would he do that if not in a style that evoked "dreams of glory," "brave warriors," a "noble standard," "songs of triumph and cries of war"? Otello is in fact constantly out of sync: he is no longer in control of the reality surrounding him, being either beyond it, looking back to a world of grandeur that now is just the stuff of dreams, or within it, confronted with a cataclysmic explosion of passion.

From this standpoint, Iago's motivations—social envy and sexual jealousy according to Shakespeare, homosexual impulses according to some psychoanalytic interpretations—become blurred, leaving only a destructive power quite out of proportion to the reasons that provoked it. In the same way, we forget the more or less futile reasons for Otello's jealousy and are caught up in horror as we witness the hero's slow disintegration—a disintegration that is also that of melodrama's world in which the characters are archetypal and the passions forceful. The confrontation of these two worlds—the world of melodramatic stereotype and the confused, fleeting world of everyday life, of Iago's modernity and Otello's timelessness—may perhaps mirror a certain disenchantment that Verdi felt when faced with a new age in which politics on an epic scale were replaced by subtle, precarious parliamentary balances; what is certain is that it implies the disappearance forever of a dramaturgy based on the grandeur and abundance of emotions.

According to the interpretation of *Otello* given above, Iago represents a new dramaturgy, sweeping away the values of the old with their fragility and basic uncontrolled violence, and is seen primarily as a small, petty creature; but this view conflicts with Iago's satanic aspects, as revealed in his Credo. Both Iago's Credo and Desdemona's Ave Maria were Boito's additions, owing nothing to Shakespeare: they suggest a sort of triptych,

Dun-que sen-za ve - la - mi t'e - spri - mi e senza am-

-ba - gi. T'e-sca fuor dal-la go - la il tuo più ri - o pen-

-sie - ro col - la più ri - a pa - ro - la!

EX. 10

close to the heart of the creator of *Mefistofele,* in which man (Otello) is torn between the angel (Desdemona) and the devil (Iago), between the mire and the ideal. The problem with this satanism is that it does away with Iago's modernity and makes him a symbol, the embodiment of a metaphysical principle—whence the virulent critiques to which the Credo has been subjected.

Still, the importance of the Credo should not be overestimated simply because it has become a baritone's warhorse. Even though he was the instigator, Boito distrusted the diabolical interpretation, writing in the *Disposizione scenica:* "The grossest, most vulgar error for an artist who claims to interpret this character is to portray him as a kind of man-demon! to give his expression a Mephistophelean grin and make him roll big satanic eyes,"[99] which quashes in advance the sarcastic cackle that so many baritones have tacked onto the end of the Credo. Finally, it was almost inconceivable not to give such a prominent character a solo—even though, as Gary Schmidgall rightly points out, Verdi turned down an early, less "demoniac" version. This was not because of its content but because it was in *versi lirici,* suitable for song, whereas he did not want to have Iago "sing," preferring an irregular prose form that would call for declamation.[100]

Verdi very explicitly gave his approval to the "Villainous Credo,"[101] even if there were later indications that he felt only lukewarm enthusiasm for an idea for which he shifted responsibility onto his librettist.[102] Nonetheless, when he conjured up the character of Iago in his mind, he in no way saw him as satanic. In 1880, that is, well before the Credo, he congratulated his friend the painter Domenico Morelli for having pictured Iago as a "just" and "honest" man—Verdi even uses the word *priest* (we would say *Jesuit*).[103] A year and a half later he described his vision of the character in detail: "For the type of figure of Iago . . . you would like a small figure, of (you say) underdeveloped limbs, and, if I have understood correctly, one of those sly, malignant faces. I would say *pointed.* Very well: if you feel him like that, do him like that. But if I were an actor and had to play Iago, I would rather have a long, thin face, thin lips, small eyes set close to the nose like a monkey's, broad, receding brow, and the head developed behind; an absent, *nonchalant* manner, indifferent to everything, incredulous, witty, speaking good and evil almost lightheartedly, and having the air of not even thinking of what he says; so that, if someone were to reproach him: 'What you say is vile!' he could answer: 'Really? I didn't think so . . . we'll say no more about it!' . . . A personality like that can deceive everyone, and even up to a point his wife. A small, malicious figure arouses everyone's suspicion and deceives nobody!"[104] His description is not so much one of demonism as of ephemeral, everyday mediocrity.

Verdi crowned his oeuvre with a comedy, a genre that throughout the ages has had as one of its tasks that of parodying the world of tragedy. In fact, jealousy, honor, and fatuity as attributes of the hero are all targets of ridicule in *Falstaff*. Nevertheless, *Otello* calls this world into question no less radically, for it constitutes a poignant reflection on the fragility of appearances. What is a hero? A noble general obsessed with idealism and integrity or an obtuse brute who falls prey to inconsistent suspicions and abuses his wife before strangling her? What is a villain? A fiend or an extremely ordinary man distilling his paltry, narrow vision of reality with elegance, even charm? What is greatness? A heroic dream or an unjustifiable madness that is shattered in pieces when tested by everyday existence? The profound sadness emanating from *Otello* perhaps comes from this feeling that an irremediable dissolution has taken place of the grand passions on which an entire dramaturgy once rested.

CHAPTER SIX

Metamorphoses II

The previous chapter described the changes affecting the character types and major axes of the melodramatic code on which Verdi's early dramaturgy was founded. What brought about these changes?

First, certain external factors should be noted, such as the influence of public taste, which was fickle and sent styles and aesthetics quickly out of fashion. In 1847, Muzio heard Jenny Lind in London and made this critical judgment of the "Swedish nightingale": "She has an unmatched agility, and generally, to show off her bravura technique, she exaggerates in too many *fioriture, grupetti* [turns], and trills, things that were pleasing to audiences in the last century but not in 1847."[1] Verdi's loyal pupil, doubtless influenced by his teacher's taut, dramatic songwriting, saw that the public was turning away from vocal virtuosity as no longer in keeping with the aesthetic climate of the age.

Again, in 1857 Muzio had these sharp words to say about a libretto abounding in warlike marches and battles: "That's a false genre! In our day those things aren't interesting any more: passion, emotion, that's what people want."[2] This was tantamount to a death warrant against the style of opera inspired by the Risorgimento, a genre Verdi had abandoned several years earlier in favor of more intimate plots.

Verdi clearly cared enough about the success of his operas not to continue down paths that no longer held the public's interest. Similarly, at a time when composers were turning out more than fifty works a year, the forms governing lyric opera rapidly became outmoded, finally estranging both the composers and their audiences. Verdi's reaction with regard to the chorus is one demonstration of this.

The reasons for an artist's development may also be looked for in a man's inner experience, in the way he matures, in his encounters, his loves, his travels. This is the biographer's task and lies beyond our range here. So far as this study is concerned, the main impetus toward change must be sought in the composer's response to a text; Wagner observed in 1851, in *Opera and Drama,* that in opera the task of renovating the old edifice falls to the librettist rather than to the composer. One should not therefore underestimate the importance of Verdi's "encounters" with the writers accompanying his evolution: Hugo, Shakespeare, Dumas, and Schiller. Sometimes he immediately fell in love with a play—*Hernani, Macbeth, Le Roi s'amuse, La Dame aux camélias*—and took charge with a clear-eyed recognition of his aims; sometimes he was reticent about a literary source or even perplexed by it—*Ballo, Aida, Don Carlos*—and it was the libretto that helped him meet the challenge. At this point the librettist in a way moved into the limelight since he had a stake in the presentation of the opera, and we can see how he responded to the pressure Verdi placed on his collaborators, badgering them to come up with forms that were "new," "original," "bold," "bizarre," but that they could not always supply.

The need for novelty does not, at first glance, seem to call into question the tradition of melodrama in which Verdi participated; rather, it appears to be simply an attempt to diversify that world, to enrich it with dramatic and formal solutions that were not inscribed in the tradition. Only when these experiments have come to an end can one tell that the aging facade of melodrama has been completely renovated.

Interiority

THE INNER STAGE

An essential moment in Romantic opera is clearly the one when a character expresses his inmost heart. Although Verdian melodrama focuses most of all on the characters' motivating energy, on the tension driving them to action, it is obvious that more passive sentiments such as melancholy and despair are also to be found in the early operas. The choruses, which contributed in large measure to the young maestro's reputation, often express warlike rage, but it is no coincidence that the most famous of them all, "Va, pensiero, sull'ali dorate," in *Nabucco,* is the song of the homesick Hebrews in exile. Since Romantic opera seeks a balance of alternating dramatic and intimate phases, after a first act devoted to launching the action the second will often open with a moment of reflection and meditation. This custom, which Verdi observes in many instances, can be found in *Oberto* (Cuniza's aria), *Nabucco* (Abigaille's aria), *I due Foscari* (Jacopo's prayer), *Macbeth* (Lady Macbeth's aria), and so on.

Moreover, the youthful operas are by no means saturated with a warlike atmosphere. Alongside saber-rattling ardor we find black melancholy, hope of liberation alternating with despair. A work as bellicose as *Attila,* in which several critics see the climax of Verdian *cabalettismo,* opens with a particularly somber prelude that seems to contradict the riotous heroics suggested by the plot. A flamboyant, chivalric opera like *Trovatore* is also one of the darkest, with its themes of death and the solitude of human beings immured in their passions. To those who deplored its tragic denouement, Verdi countered: "They say that this opera is much too sad and there are too many dead people in it. But after all, everything in life is death. What else is there?"[3]

Nonetheless, such moments of affective pathos, however violent, count for less with Verdi than they do in Donizetti's or Bellini's works, which tend to be dominated by the character of the victim of family or political conflicts. In keeping with the pessimistic image these composers had of history, pride of place is given to characters who suffer its ravages, whereas Verdi's first operas are based on a messianic vision of history that disappears early on but leaves its mark in a more positive conception of commitment to action. The composer thus lays less emphasis on scenes where the individual's passions cut him off from his community. A good example is to be found in *Nabucco:* the opera ends in the death of Abigaille, who, in an Andante, publicly expiates her sin of ambition and begs to be forgiven. This scene was cut after the first performance so that the opera could end with the great hymn to Jehovah celebrating the reconciliation of all the characters in a common acceptance of God's will.

Yet, even in those works where a character's sense of himself is linked to a forbidden or unacknowledgeable passion, this interiority is merely the gap separating his social function (his duty) from his inmost desires. For a time, this inner face is known only to the spectator and a few other characters (confidants), but sooner or later the inner and outer faces must be made one and the character's interiority, that which constitutes his apartness, appear in broad daylight. The public revelation of this hidden face is a moment charged with emotion since it is accompanied by an expiation that, ideally, reintegrates the character into the community from which his sin should normally exclude him. The classic example of this expiatory rite is the finale of *Norma.*

The character's inner face thus corresponds to a feeling that is perfectly transparent; at the most it marks a temporary separation of two worlds that must eventually be united, even if the character has to pay for this reintegration by expiation or death. His interiority has neither mystery nor substance; in extreme cases, it is the sign of nonconformity rather than profound alienation. For melodrama seeks the kind of clarity where characters' feelings are as readily perceived as happenings, in the sort of single dimension analyzed by Erich Auerbach in *Mimesis*.[4]

With *Macbeth* we meet another, more disturbed inner self, which the character discovers with horror, as if his demons were suddenly revealed to him—an incommunicable interiority no collective ritual of expiation is sufficient to absolve. True, Macbeth and his wife meet their end, as they must, yet they carry away with them a secret the other characters never comprehend. The final reestablishment of order cannot wash away the impression arising from this murky world, a region so dark that when light enters at the end of the drama the dissipation of the darkness is no more than an illusion.

Verdi was perfectly aware of the novelty of *Macbeth,* and, although he made concessions to certain tradition-sanctioned rituals,[5] he gave all due weight to the characters' inner conflicts, to their gradual descent into a spiral of crime and their vain efforts to control the dynamic of their ambitions. The importance he always gave certain sections, in particular the great act 1 duet between Macbeth and his wife and the sleepwalking scene,[6] shows beyond doubt that he preferred to emphasize the scene of conscience rather than that of the outside world, psychological drama rather than epic conflict, the twilight within souls rather than clarity of actions.

It should be remembered first of all that *Macbeth* is the only opera that has two protagonists but no antagonist: Banquo *(comprimario)*, Macduff *(comprimario)*, and Malcolm (second tenor) are secondary roles, and in 1865 Verdi vehemently protested the idea of strengthening the role of Macduff.[7] That is a sign of his determination to shift the interest from the exteriority of the conflict between tyrant and judge toward the inner torment of the tyrant alone. The protagonists are seen by themselves, without confrontations; they can only engage in dialogue with each other or in monologue with their consciences. The eclipse of the father figure already referred to and the emergence of a principle of immanence according to which passions carry within them their own destruction find a translation in this absence of a true antagonist.

The punishment of the "guilty" therefore takes on a totally different guise from the one it had in the other operas. Macbeth and Lady disappear unconventionally, without any accusing chorus, swallowed up in a black abyss. The final aria of the original 1847 version that Macbeth sings before his assembled enemies—"Mal per me che m'affidai"—disappears in the definitive version of 1865: Verdi found this muted death, as provided by the original play, more Shakespearean and more true to life.[8]

The theme of murderous ambition called for a nocturnal tonality. Metaphorically, this is rendered by the important theme of light and darkness, as witness the storm that blackens the sky in the opening scene, Lady Macbeth's invocation of night in the cabaletta of her entrance aria (act 1, scene 7), the wish that the sun might never rise on the day Duncan has to go (act 1, scene 8), Macbeth's evocation of the darkness of crime in his monologue (act 1, scene 11), and the description of the owl (act 1, scene 12) as well as the admirable night poetry of Lady Macbeth's aria "La luce langue" (act 2, scene 2).

To find a vocal equivalent of this darkness, Verdi systematically asked for a "nocturnal" way of singing, which he describes minutely in connection with the act 1 duet and the sleepwalking scene in the famous letter already cited: "It is absolutely necessary that these pieces not be sung. They must be acted, and declaimed with a dark, veiled voice, otherwise the scene can't have any effect. The orchestra must be muted. The stage must be extremely dark."[9] This explains the frequency in the score of indications calling for a "low, somber voice" on the part of the singers. In fact, Verdi modulates the voice extremely precisely according to the psychological mood, alternating "day" and "night" phases. For example, the act 1 duet with Banquo should be sung with a different voice at the moment when Macbeth becomes aware of the witches' prophecy, which awakens dark ambitions in him and terrifies his moral conscience. In the monologue, before the great duet with his wife, the voice must expand only at the end—"È squillo eterno"—when he decides to kill Duncan and therefore to move to action.

Thus, entering the world of night destroys song: song renders a soul transparent and confers on it a certain nobility, two conditions that Macbeth and his wife fulfill only rarely (nearly forty years later, in connection with Iago, a no less murky character, Verdi would speak of this same impossibility of song). By yielding to their demons, Macbeth and his Lady become, radically, strangers to other people: they see what others do not and fail to see what others do. As the horrified doctor and lady-in-waiting observe while witnessing the sleepwalking scene, even though she is holding a lamp and her eyes are open, Lady Macbeth sees nothing (act 4, scene 3). At an early point in the opera, the private scene is projected onto the public scene: in the act 2 finale, Macbeth sees a ghost that is visible to none of the crowd of guests at the banquet.

The dark crucible where desires, ambitions, and cupidities are all melted together is given form in the witches, whom Verdi, following Schlegel's *Lectures on Dramatic Art and Literature,* interprets as incarnations of the world's enigmas. Verdi gives them an "uncanniness" (in the Freudian sense of the expression) that actually does not appear until the third act: it is they who, when they first meet Macbeth, make him aware of the criminal goal to which he is mutely heading without acknowledging it to himself, they who reveal to him what lies in his path. Close, too, are the links between the witches and Lady Macbeth, who pours all her will and energy into accomplishing the prophecies they uttered in the first act, so much so that some stage directors are led to suggest that she is conjured up and fabricated by the witches[10]—a dependence that finds its justification in certain curious musical analogies.[11]

Macbeth's "long night" challenges the usually clear, vigorous language of traditional melodrama, an idiom inept for translating the visions and fantastic apparitions that same night yields up. The first version of the opera occasionally manages to create the eerie atmosphere Verdi sought so assiduously, but there is no better way to understand his quest for a new musical speech than to compare the first Florentine version and the definitive one of 1865, written for Paris. In essence, the revision concerns musical numbers relating to the "inner stage": the duet between Lady and Macbeth in act 1; Lady's aria at the beginning of act 2; the passages in the act 2 Finale where Macbeth sees Banquo's ghost; part of the witches' chorus at the beginning of act 3; the ballet that was written for Paris but that, because of its scenario and its principal character, Hecate, goddess of the night and sorcery, is incorporated into the final version; the apparitions scene.[12]

The revised version was aimed at finding music that was dramatic and spectral; hence, the accompaniments are less conventional than in the first version, and the voice becomes less mobile and is often fixed in a *recto tono* declamation, as in the appearance of Banquo's ghost (see exx. 11a and 11b). Like the apparitions scene, the ballet gives rise to little themes that create an eerie atmosphere, for example, the one accompanying the apparition of the crowned child—*un fanciullo col serto dei re.* The instrumentation is more refined, the harmony more adventurous, as at the very beginning of the procession of the eight kings (exx. 12a and 12b).

As a result of this concentration on the "inner stage," the gap separating it from the public one is deep, so deep that the two can no longer

EX. 11*a*   (1847 Version)

EX. 11*b*   (1865 Version) *concluded on overleaf*

meet and the sort of one-dimensional plane peculiar to melodrama disappears. In the original version this opposition can already be perceived in the witches' double aspect, "trivial" in the first act and "prophetic" in the third, or in Finale 2, which contrasts Macbeth's vision and the arrogant drinking song "Si colmi il calice." Still, the definitive version certainly

chio - me   scrol -lar   t'è con - ces - so,   fa -

EX. 11*b*   (1865 Version) *concluded*

EX. 12*a*   (1847 Version)

EX. 12*b*   (1865 Version)

accentuates these contrasts; it includes both those contrasts provided for in the original and others connected to the changes in writing between 1847 and 1865.

One result is that there are compositional disparities—sometimes bothersome for the critics, who have explained them away by noting that the opera was written on two occasions. It is striking, nevertheless, that those passages most typical of Verdi's youthful style—the march accompanying Duncan's arrival, the assassins' chorus at the opening of act 2, the first witches' choruses in the introduction—were not touched when Verdi came to revise the work, which might indicate that he was not afraid to use these contrasts and might even have sought them. In fact, the differences in style have the effect of distancing these "exterior" passages from the actual substance of the drama. The final battle, somewhat flat in the first version, is replaced by a fugue that Verdi chose for its mimetic value since "the running and chasing of the subjects and countersubjects and the clashing sounds may express a battle scene fairly well."[13] This change accentuates the distancing effect in relation to the external event by giving it an objective, impersonal, even slightly ironic consistency: after such a drama, the final hymn with its elegant construction and the liturgical flavor of the chorus's last cadence might well appear ironic—at last order has been saved![14]

It is therefore legitimate to see a turning point in *Macbeth,* the beginnings of a dramaturgy of interiority that does away with the superb transparency of traditional melodrama and marks Verdi's new awareness of the aura of confusion and ambiguity that can inhabit the human soul.

RIFTS

The experience of working on an opera based on the story of two consciences grappling with ambition and crime drew Verdi away from any too perfunctory or external representation of political passions. It even created a rift between the depiction of an individual's private life and his participation in public life. This rift can be seen in *La battaglia di Legnano,* an opera that was never popular except at the time of its first performance, in January 1849 in Rome, when political ferment was at its height.[15] After that it was judged with some severity as an occasion piece, dictated by the exhilaration of the events of 1848.

Indeed, when, in April 1848, Cammarano suggested that Verdi adapt J. Méry's *La Bataille de Toulouse* (1828) to an episode in the Italian cities' struggle against Emperor Frederick I of Hohenstaufen, he pronounced himself convinced that "this kind of subject must move every man with an Italian soul in his breast."[16] The anti-Germanic and nationalistic resonances of the text are obvious, and the libretto approaches Epinal's imagery with many of its themes: national solidarity, the urge to drive the foreigner out of the country, the need to overcome internal divisions, determination to fight to the death, the primacy of political duty over private interests, etc.[17]

Verdi, the "master of choruses," misses no opportunity offered him: an entrance chorus, the pact of unity of all Italians, an oath for defense of the motherland, another oath of the Company of Death, a final hymn of victory, not to mention the vigorous finale pitting the emperor Barbarossa against the representatives of the Lombard League. Yet none of these pieces captures the patriotic ardor of the greatest Verdian choruses.

Massimo Mila has pinpointed the problem, noting that *Battaglia* has a double plot that is both private and political and that, paradoxically, the private plot is the more inspired and successful of the two.[18] The political plot we know. The private plot is conventional enough: Lida has, against her will, wed Rolando, although she loves Arrigo, who was believed to have vanished but returns very much alive; their love is therefore impossible, but their meetings are enough to unleash the jealousy of Lida's husband, who is convinced that he is being deceived. The paradox of the imbalance Mila points out comes from the fact that, for the first time in his career, without having to get around the censors, Verdi was able to give full expression to his attachment to the national cause. Yet there is no trace here of the epic fervor one finds in *Nabucco* or *I Lombardi*.

From this Mila concludes that the opera shows the limitations of "committed" art. But there is no proof that *Battaglia* was merely an occasional piece, for Verdi's letters show that he took an active part in the libretto.[19] Written in the summer of 1848, the work was not composed with any particular hurry: attentive analyst that he is, Julian Budden even believes that, "in purely musical terms, it is the most consistently accomplished that Verdi has yet written."[20] It does in fact include some very fine pages and reveals a certain number of innovations that give it a secure place in the composer's development. Finally, it is clear that up to 1858 the composer expressed the desire to give the opera a new lease on life by changing certain historical facts that were impossible to retain in the repressive atmosphere following the failed revolutions of 1848, which at least proves his attachment for this opera.[21]

Still, it cannot be denied that the plot fails to link the two poles and that the private pole is far more interesting than the political turns of events. Yet this problem of linkage also occurs in most of the operas before this one—*Nabucco, Lombardi, Attila, Giovanna d'Arco, Alzira*—and Verdi almost always solved it in clumsy fashion. However, whether the private plot is carried along by the revolutionary fervor driving the opera, whether the same feelings of excessiveness and heroism recur in each sphere, in these operas the dynamism of the whole causes one to pay little attention to these awkward passages, whereas in *Battaglia* one senses that a private story and a patriotic epic have merely been placed side by side.

The attitude of the man and his attachment to the national cause are not in question here, simply Verdi's capacity as an artist to express it in an inspired way. Most likely the failures of 1848 and the experience of *Macbeth,* which was beyond doubt fundamental, broke the epic spring of his inspiration. On the one hand there was the disappointment of the events of 1848, certain repercussions of which Verdi witnessed just as he was staging his opera—the defeat of the Piedmontese by the Austrians at Custoza in July and the recapture of Milan, again by the Austrians, in August. This disillusionment would push Verdi toward a more "realistic" solution to the Italian problem and toward a certain conservatism. From that point on he displays a great mistrust of revolutionary fervor, and, when it reappears in *Don Carlos,* it is tinged with nostalgia.

Furthermore, the experience of *Macbeth* brought Verdi face to face with a completely different vision of the relation to power, one less naively epic, more ambiguous, and more dramatic. It explains how the composer's portrayal of political passion would always henceforth be colored with a certain disenchantment, a somber, even funereal atmosphere. It is no accident that one of the best "political" moments in *Battaglia* is the great scene of the Company of Death (act 3), the daredevil band that the hero, Arrigo, joins. The vehemence of the oath *Giuram d'Italia* erases neither the impression left by the austere prelude in A minor nor that of the no less austere choral introduction "Fra queste dense tenebre," which throws a pall over the guerrillas' patriotism. We might be at the monastery of St.-Just. The work shows a certain schism, of which we have indicated the probable reasons: no longer is there one uniformly heroic atmosphere to weave the threads of the plots into one skein; the individual as creator of his own story has now split off from the citizen as member of a group.

MARGINALITY

The schism between the individual as exemplary representative of a community and the citizen as member of a group deepens with the development of the theme of marginality, or apartness from society. Marginality is a central theme of Romantic dramaturgy because many operas feature characters whose desires set them in opposition to their surroundings and to their personal links with those surroundings (familial duties and ties). This alienation, along with the political and social aspirations it implies, is often represented for the hero by his choice of a social group—pirates, gypsies, bandits—which he comes to personify. In fact, it becomes apparent that the "exile" no longer completely belongs to the milieu he left but is not yet quite part of the one he has chosen.

This is, in a nutshell, the drama of Carlo, the hero of *I masnadieri*. His idealism and spirit of revolt lead him to break with his family and become chief of a band of brigands, yet, in his entrance aria, he sings of his "father's castle" and its "eternally green hills" and hopes to leave his "perverse" companions. This same opera shows the impossibility of returning to one's original surroundings, for Carlo has grown too closely bound up with the crime and pillage personified by his band of brigands to go back to the castle. Nonetheless, the drama ends on this apparent impossibility rather than stressing the psychological consequences for the hero; that is, it ends with the downfall of an individual, not a citizen in society. In the "trilogy," on the other hand *(Rigoletto, Trovatore, Traviata),* marginality is shown in relation to a defined social space, and exclusion then becomes solitude and the impossibility of attachment to any group whatever.[22]

The trilogy is centered on three marginal characters who, as I have said, stand as a metaphor for the artist. Manrico the troubadour no more belongs to the aristocratic world of his brother, the Count de Luna, than to that of the gypsies and his "mother," Azucena, yet the social space in which he moves remains vague because Verdi stresses the connections between individuals. In the other two operas the connection with a social milieu is, in contrast, essential. Because of her profession, Violetta lives in a world of pleasure that she enlivens with her feigned gaiety but that is alien to her since she is haunted by a long-lost purity that makes her innocent in her inmost being. It is obvious, however, that, for her, purity is now merely a dream, such as is expressed in her great aria at the end of act 1. The dream does materialize briefly and in a totally artificial way in act 2, in the little country house outside Paris. Thus, Violetta does not really belong to the frivolous Parisian world that she inhabits, yet the world to which she aspires is lost and can never be re-created—save ideally at the end, through the sacrificial rite described earlier. Her true destiny is illness and death, which radically exclude her from both worlds.

By being a buffoon, Rigoletto, for his part, has to amuse a society of pleasure that is alien to him and that he loathes. The proper, bourgeois world he dreams of materializes in his home, which is more substantial than Violetta's bucolic dream but no less threatened by the outer world—

in this case, the courtiers who want to abduct his daughter. His home is a sort of protective bubble in which Gilda is held prisoner and that the protagonist tries in vain to guard against all attacks. For Rigoletto, the sign of his exclusion is his hump—a physical deformity that corresponds to a basic bitterness and spitefulness that make him a creature both maleficent and sublime, in the same way that Violetta is both pure and corrupt. For one reason or another, both characters are strangers in the world with which they have contact.

In either case, the character's complex nature is refracted onto the structure of the opera, which forms clearly differentiated spaces. The first act of *Rigoletto* in fact comprises two large contrasting blocks corresponding, in the first instance, to the Duke of Mantua's palace and, in the second, to Rigoletto's house; the first is dominated by laughter and dancing, while in the second the father protects his daughter with warmth and affection. The father's world comes into violent contact with the court through Monterone, while the court invades Rigoletto's secret domain no less brutally by carrying off his daughter. Between these two we have the street, an anonymous place, and two major scenes: the meeting with the assassin Sparafucile, which takes place in a sort of structural no-man's-land, like a floating scene unconnected to either block, and Rigoletto's monologue in which he reveals his twisted nature, his hatred of the world, his regret not to be able to weep, and his jealousy of the Duke.

In the second act Rigoletto comes to court looking for his daughter, whom the courtiers have abducted so as to hand her over to the Duke. The character then appears in his dual nature of father and jester: the two antinomic worlds of the first act confront each other. In this respect the Duke's aria does not fit the large-block structure, for the simple reason that it most probably was a solution by default since Verdi would have preferred to open the act with a duet between the Duke and Gilda that the censors would not have permitted. The third act, by contrast, is perfectly homogeneous. Both topographically and symbolically, it sets up the mysterious night landscape, the no-man's-land presaged in the scene with Sparafucile and the monologue. We leave the clearly defined environs and enter a wasteland—Sparafucile's dilapidated inn, the deserted banks of the Mincio—where the characters appear one after the other. This is where Gilda dies in her father's arms: whereas Victor Hugo had peopled the stage at this point with diverse characters, Verdi leaves the protagonists quite alone, without any protecting space.

La traviata bears strong structural analogies with *Rigoletto*. Here, too, three spaces are suggested: the Parisian party setting at Violetta's and Flora's, the country retreat of Violetta's sentimental dream, and, finally, the space of solitude and death represented by Violetta's apartment, empty of her guests. The greater part of act 1 is taken up with the milling crowd of party goers who have come to amuse themselves in Violetta's apartment. In this extensive episode, the duet between Violetta and Alfredo forms an intimate enclave, surrounded on all sides by the party. The second act is strictly divided into two: the first, intimate, part takes place in the country house with Violetta, Alfredo, and his father Germont; the second, which is at Flora's residence, is devoted to the card scene and the great finale. By contrast, the third act is intimate, centered on Violetta's death in her apartment; this time it is festivity, in the form of the crowd of merrymakers, that creates an enclave (the bacchanal that the dying Violetta can hear below her window). A mirror image is thus formed, which can be clearly seen if we give each act the codes of festivity (a) and intimate area (b): AbA + AB + BaB.

The special function represented in *Rigoletto* by the duet with Sparafucile and the monologue is seen again here in Violetta's great act 1 aria. This, too, has a floating position, in an empty space (the apartment in the small hours, after the guests have left); it is suspended between two worlds, both of which are conjured up in the aria—dreams of love in the Andantino, Violetta's fate as a courtesan in the cabaletta. Just as in act 3 of *Rigoletto* the storm sweeps across the riverbanks announcing drama, so solitude and the icy chill of death invade the stage in the last act of *La traviata:* from far off can be heard the sounds of the indifferent merrymakers, just as the uncaring Duke of Mantua moved across the stage, protected by the glass bell of his famous song. One may regret that for the last scenes Verdi followed Dumas's play and not the novel, in which Marguerite dies abandoned by everyone and practically alone. Yet Germont's and Alfredo's return does not really undermine the impression of solitude that marks Violetta's destiny as it did that of Rigoletto.

LOVE

For all that love is a virtual sine qua non in the making of an opera,[23] the expression of amorous feeling in the nineteenth century had to forge its narrow way through the extremely strict limits of a ferocious puritanism. Under the eagle eye of not only the censors but also prudish librettists, the language of love was invariably vague, culled from a general-purpose collection of formulas, and often descended to the absurd. For example, when Joan of Arc is being pressed by the King of France, she begs him,

"Deh, rispettami qual pria!" (Pray respect me as before); then, in an allusion to the illicit character of their love, her language unwittingly becomes almost obscene: "Ch'io non sugga il suo velen!" (So that I do not suck your poison). Exasperated, Carlo protests, "Ma l'amore è santo, è puro" (But love is pure and holy), and insists, "A Dio lo giuro! Sol lo spirto mi concedi, / E all'incendio basterà" (I swear before God! But give me your soul, and it will be enough for the flames; act 1, scene 4). However full of chaste emotions and holy embraces the love duets may be, the music is marked by passion but very little by pleasure; sensuality is absent, as are the doubts, the swoonings, and the agitation so dear to Mozart or Strauss.

If Verdi's predecessors were familiar with the vehemence of passion, he himself tended at first to describe the way love can inspire aspirations to independence and freedom rather than stressing the feeling itself. Love is identified with strong self-affirmation, of which no too precise description is required. More austere than Bellini and Donizetti, Verdi has not the same indulgence for his characters' amorous effusions. Even Violetta's shattering cry "Amami Alfredo" comes across more as an appeal for help than as a passionate outburst, as the demand for recognition on the part of an individual threatened by death and rejected by society.

Furthermore, in Verdi's plots love finds expression most readily if it is unrealizable; it is a far cry from inspiring badinage. Ernani and Elvira fall into each other's arms only because Silva is about to burst through the door; at the end of the opera they are looking forward to being united forever when the horn sounds, summoning the hero to his engagement with death. In the vast majority of the operas, the threat of danger is always hanging in the air or embodied in a character lurking in the shadows, giving the love duet a feverish, pressing quality. Alfredo and Violetta have only two duets in *Traviata:* in the first (act 1) the time has not yet come for them to be united, and in the second (act 3) it is too late.

The only duet that seems to escape this rule is that between Otello and Desdemona since they are not faced with any danger. Yet the vague menace hanging over the drama—"Tale è il gaudio dell'anima che temo, / Temo che più non mi sarà concesso / quest'attimo divino / Nell'ignoto avvenir del mio destino" (Such is the joy of my soul that I am afraid . . . that I will not be granted again this divine moment in the unknown future of my destiny)—or possibly the weight of memory in the passage, casts a veil of sadness on this admirable love scene. We must wait for *Falstaff* and Nannetta and Fenton's duets to find more serene outpourings (true, we are in comedy here); no more free of supervision than their predecessors, these two find time to steal kisses and tease, and the ire of an authoritarian father disturbs them as little as the threat of the Feld-marschal's sudden arrival prevents the Marschallin and Quinquin from abandoning themselves to passion at the beginning of *Der Rosenkavalier*.

On the other hand, well before *Otello* and *Falstaff* we see emerging a feeling of love conceived as hurt, weakness, disorder, or vertigo. There is a first trace of it in *Vêpres*, in the act 2 duet between Henri and Hélène, and even more in that of act 4.[24] However, this is only a small sign, and passion as intimate wound does not really appear until *Un ballo in maschera*. Riccardo easily falls prey to love since he is free of the obligations of heroism (Baldini even considers him a comic character). In the opening scene, simply reading Amelia's name on a list of guests causes him to lose his balance, a reaction conveyed by the sudden switch from major to minor as well by a theme carried by the oboe, followed by a brief agitated passage in the orchestra. After this flurry the Governor collects himself, returning to his normally carefree manner in his aria. In the last act, when Riccardo has given up Amelia and the chorus seems to have launched the masked ball, Verdi hit on the superb idea of repeating a phrase from the overture and the prelude of his romanza ("Si, rivederti Amelia"), which also has the effect of an unexpected explosion of love.

Nonetheless, it is in the great act 2 duet that we discover how love is eating away at the Governor's seemingly frivolous soul. In the first move-ment (allegro agitato), Amelia confesses her astonishment and confusion at finding Riccardo in the gallows field, a sinister spot to which she has come alone to pick an herb to rid her of her fatal passion. The second movement (allegretto un po' sostenuto) opens with an admirable all-enveloping, sinuous phrase for Riccardo that reveals a new lyricism, "Non sai tu che se l'anima mia"—new because the phrase's undulant rhythm is totally lacking in that willful tension native to the Verdian tenor. It is in fact more murmur than song—mezza voce, the score specifies—a confession of desperation rather than a declaration of love. It is new, too, because, instead of closing on a complete melodic arc of four-times-four measures, the phrase nonchalantly unwinds before twisting in on itself (passing to the minor key), then unfurls and takes off in a veritable cry, climbing up to high B♭. More reserved, Amelia keeps her distance, re-sponding in D♭ major to Riccardo's F major, and reaffirms her attach-ment, if not to a person, at least to the marriage bond.

The surprise comes at the close. Formally, the duet seems to have ended, as indicated by the cadence in F (the tonality of parting) and the way the meter is broken up: three strophes of six decasyllables, each with the same rhyme scheme. The new meter, the *ottonario*—"La mia vita,

EX. 13

l'universo"—seems to prepare the shift to the intermediate dialogue section, the *tempo di mezzo;* yet the music lingers on in a superb, baffling coda that melodically takes up the vocal line of the first movement and harmonically settles on a dominant pedal. Riccardo begs for a confession of love, with the pedal creating an impression of uncertainty while the internal chromaticism conjures up an atmosphere of sorrowful tenderness (see ex. 13). Another surprise is that, instead of returning to the tonic, the coda migrates to the key of A major, in a highly *Tristan*-like atmosphere—tremolos in the strings, with the cellos having the melodic theme—appropriate to the sought confession. The effect of these highly unusual passages is of escaping from the traditional dynamic of the duet for a brief moment of ecstasy.

Riccardo then exults with joy in a few measures of recitative, and the duet's cabaletta, "Oh qual soave brivido," would appear more straightforward and conventional were it not for the delicious delicacy of the orchestration—harp arpeggios, punctuation of the bassoon, flute, and clarinets, soaring violins—which adds a liquid quality to this moment of happiness. In the ritornello leading to the reprise of the cabaletta a due, the confession of love bursts out afresh, but this time in E major.

This is a totally new emotional climate, a mixture of abandon, love, and suffering, and it reappears in such later operas as *Don Carlos, Aida,* and *Otello*. Here, we again see the tendency to enclose emotionally intense moments within formally neutral passages. For instance, in the first duet between Elisabeth and Carlos in act 1 of *Don Carlos,* we find the E-major episode—"Bois dépouillés, ravins, broussailles"/"Sparì l'orror della foresta"—separating the exposition and the reprise of the cabaletta "De quels transports"/"Di qual amore." Similarly, in the same characters' second duet we see how the great strange, ecstatic phrase given to the clarinets and bassoons—"O prodige, mon coeur déchiré se console"/"O prodigio, il mio cor"—divides two presentations of a major theme of the opera ("O bien perdu"/"Perduto ben"). It is a typically Verdian technique, the finest example of which is the Miserere scene in *Il trovatore*—a technique that consists in shaking off the yoke of conventional forms by exploiting movements that are traditionally more freely structured. Yet it is even more striking to see this relatively austere, if not puritanical, dramatist open himself so joyously to the frailties of the heart.

DREAMS

Visions, hallucinations, and ravings are common currency in Romantic opera, but only rarely do they manage to suggest anything more than an exacerbated subjectivity, let alone create a different reality and give it literary or musical consistency. They are usually intended to make us aware of a character's distress or his or her agony or longings: for example, Abigaille's regrets for lost innocence in her first aria, Germont's dream of Provence, or Azucena's vision of the mountains when she is a prisoner of the Count de Luna; or else Azucena's memory of the stake where her mother was burned to death or Jacopo Foscari's hallucination as he suddenly sees before him the condottiere Carmagnola, unjustly condemned by the Republic of Venice, as he himself soon will be (act 2, scene 1). Sometimes the dreams have a premonitory quality, like the one Attila relates in his aria "Mentre gonfiarsi l'anima," which becomes reality not long afterward (act 1, scene 3).

Mad scenes are the only ones that can conjure up not only the disintegration of personality but also an unreal, translucent world. A prime example is the famous one in *Lucia di Lammermoor,* to which Donizetti strove to give an eerie quality by using a solo glass harmonica (later replaced by the flute). However, mad scenes fell out of fashion in the 1840s, apparently causing Verdi not the slightest regret, for, in his theater, madness—Nabucco's or Lady Macbeth's—arises from tension or depression rather than true derangement. When Cammarano proposed making Manrico's mother mad, the composer formally turned him down.[25] Verdi's concern that the character take his destiny upon himself with complete lucidity explains this distrust of madness.

Once again, however, it was *Macbeth* that encouraged the composer to explore further, to evoke a different world that was strange and mysterious. The apparitions and the protagonists' visions may well personify their hallucinations, but they are of an insubstantiality that suggests a quite other, supernatural reality. Here Verdi starts down a road that gives greater musical weight to his characters' oneiric world.

At first sight, Gilda in *Rigoletto* seems to fall in the tradition of the fresh, innocent young girl represented by Amina in *La sonnambula,* or Linda di Chamounix in the opera of that name, or Verdi's own *Luisa Miller.*[26] Yet in Gilda's case there is no peaceful provincial reality or village idyll as there is in the semiseria operas. Her dreams of love have nothing to do with either the world of the Duke of Mantua's court or the stultifying family cocoon imposed on her by Rigoletto; they arise simply from her reverie. Hence the unique character of her famous aria "Caro nome," where she describes the supposed student with whom she is in love. For one thing, the form is an unusual one, the only example of its kind in Verdi. The melody itself is devoid of virtuosity, but great delicacy is needed to bring out the elegance of the variations. The orchestration is just as delicate, with its diaphanous quality fully displayed in a magical coda as the young girl murmurs her beloved's name, Gualtier Maldè: the underlining by the strings is of the utmost discretion, reinforced by feather-light beatings of two solo violins and a chromatic passage for flute and bassoon. The courtiers who have just arrived and are getting ready to carry Gilda off suspend their work of revenge, hypnotized, as they gaze at the creature who can be only "a fairy or an angel." Curiously, the style of this coda is presaged in certain earlier operas, but it is only in *Rigoletto* that it manages to create fairyland.[27]

Another instance of this enchanted atmosphere occurs at the beginning of act 1 of *Simon Boccanegra,* where its charm is all the more potent because of the way it contrasts with the uniformly somber aura of the prologue. The sun is rising over the horizon, and Amelia is lost in a melan-

EX. 14

choly reverie inspired by the "smile" of the sea and the stars. The 1881 revision accentuates the descriptive aptness of the orchestral prelude: trills of the violins over a rocking motion of thirds, a pentatonic melody for the violas (taken from a theme in the original version, of which Verdi kept only the first measure), rapid arpeggios for piccolo, flute, and clarinet (see ex. 14). Two of the three sections of Amelia's cavatina mirror this marine atmosphere in the accompaniment: pizzicatos for divided strings and arpeggios for flutes, piccolo, and clarinets. Just as refined is the coda, which also dates from the revised version.

One could regard this as just a descriptive piece of scoring inspired, like others, by allusions to the sea and the moon if the theme were not so closely linked to the dramaturgy of this particular opera. What Verdi, who usually had little inclination for symphonic description, is evoking here is a utopia of the heart—the sea, so different from the city, where patricians and plebeians vie for power, and from the ostentatiousness of the palazzos, which the young woman explicitly rejects. Amelia shares this utopia, which is part of her childhood, with her father, Simon, a man of the sea and a corsair. In the act 1 Finale (revised version), Simon deplores the fact that the great Genoese families are at each other's throats "while the broad kingdom of the seas invites [them] to glory" ("Mentre v'invita estatico / Il regno ampio dei mari"; act 1, scene 12). Before he dies, devoured by poison, he once again evokes the freshness of the sea (act 3, scene 3). Thus, landscape makes its entrance in Verdian dramaturgy to the precise extent that it is the materialization of a dream of peace and happiness.

The more oppressive society becomes, the more seductive this mirage of an unattainable homeland appears. In *Aida,* exoticism, understood as escape to a land of one's dreams, is developed on two levels: for the spectator, the whole opera is exotic and represents the magic "other country." For Aida, and later for Radames, on the other hand, Ethiopia represents the dream of an unrealizable happiness. The hero conjures up the land in his first romanza, "Celeste Aida," the middle section of which, "Il tuo bel cielo," in B♭ minor, clearly establishes the link between the slave girl and her country: "Il tuo bel cielo vorrei ridarti, / Le dolci brezze del patrio suol" (I would like to give you back your lovely sky, the gentle breezes of your native land). A sinuous melody on the oboe paints what Budden calls the "Ethiopian" color of the opera: it curls in on itself, in the third around D♭, underlined by a flute trill.

In act 3, aptly named the Nile act, this haven of peace and sensuous pleasure shimmers from the first measure to the last. In the brief prelude evoking the Egyptian night on the banks of the Nile, the G that is repeated over four octaves by the first violins and supported by a tremolo in the second violins, together with the staccato of the violas and the flute melody outlining an open fifth, evokes a motionless, mysterious landscape. Here, too, what tempted the composer was not so much the descriptive picture as the effect of contrast between a nocturnal, all-enveloping world and the pomp and ceremony of the preceding act.

On the banks of the river Aida dreams of her lost homeland, and her romanza "O cieli azzuri" again provides the Ethiopian color that Radames had suggested in his: the introductory melody of the oboe, turning and turning again around a pivotal note, the tonal uncertainty of the beginning, followed by the flute trills and the wave-like motion of the accompaniment in the reprise, all combine to suggest an idyllic, faraway atmosphere (see ex. 15 on p. 236).

Amonasro is less convincing when he conjures up the "fragrant forests" and "cool valleys" of Ethiopia at the beginning of the duet with his daughter since for him Ethiopia is no dream, yet in the next duet, in the course of which Aida extorts from her lover the secret her father needs to know, another oboe melody, very similar to the first (at the beginning of the Andantino launching the second movement), again takes us on a

EX. 15

journey. Aida proposes that they flee to a new country—"La, tra foreste vergini"—and three flutes gliding voluptuously through a succession of thirds and sixths conjure up the charm of the "virgin forests" and the perfume of flowers. As we know, this disturbing exotic dream is brutally ended at the close of the Nile act with Radames's arrest, which brings us back to the drama.

The last expression of this kind of enchantment must be sought in the third act of *Falstaff,* in the delicate love madrigal of Fenton's sonnet and especially the airy invocation of Nannetta, now Queen of the Fairies. The nocturnal phantasmagoria in Windsor Park certainly has a dramatic function, that of playing one last trick on the fat knight, but it is also a final pretext for evoking the labile, ephemeral world of dreams.

In more general fashion, Verdi's comedy sets up an original connection between reality and dream (or in this precise case illusion) since it turns the traditional view of opera buffa on its head: this form of opera pokes fun at characters who, through folly or passion, deviate from the everyday norm, from "nature" and good sense (even if in actual fact some composers, such as Rossini, tended to praise this folly). *Falstaff,* too, seems to dispel mirage, but Verdi's relation to dreams or illusions is more subtle: on the one hand it points up their excesses and dangers while on the other celebrating their ability to enliven the monotony of day-to-day life. With his excesses and presumptuousness, Falstaff, that degenerate image of the hero, is the great loser of the story, but he is also the great winner: railed at, ridiculed, plagued, and humiliated, he nevertheless knows it was he who brought a touch of fantasy into the gray lives of those good citizens of Windsor: "Son io che vi fa scaltri. L'arguzia mia crea l'arguzia degli altri" (It is I, it is I who make you clever. My cleverness creates the cleverness of others). The reverse of Rigoletto, he becomes the final metaphor for the artist, a ridiculous, derisory figure whose "ravings" give rise to dreams and chase away the banality of so-called normal life.

❖ ❖ ❖ ❖ ❖ ❖ ❖

The growth of Verdi's concern with the interior life of his characters has one essential consequence: it breaks with the superb objectivity of melodrama and replaces its one-dimensional unfolding of events and feelings with a duality of planes, the one simple and clear-cut and the other more indefinable. What these various revelations I have just described— inner stage, dreams, love, and so on—have in common is that they suggest a "beyond" that transcends the dramatic function of the feeling or situation from which it arose. Instead of appearing in a single block, like a living statue, the character is ringed with a halo of mystery that is suggested not so much by song as by the orchestra.

In fact, it is the orchestra (through harmony, orchestral themes, choice of instruments) that is given the task of suggesting this inner dimension, involving as it does an enriching of the orchestral idiom and a more complex connection between words and music. G. Tomasi di Lampedusa, the well-known author of *Il gattopardo,* reproached Italian opera for being too *explicit;* his reservations arose from the conviction that "truth cannot and must not reside in words alone but *behind* the words, in a background of hints and allusions."[28] It is precisely the increasing autonomy of the orchestral idiom that made it possible to suggest this background behind the words. This meant that the function of the music was no longer to illustrate words or express the meaning of a speech by synthesis but rather to signify, alongside the words, what they suggest but do not clearly say (even if it is hard to tell where the musical commentary of the text ends and its autonomy in relation to the text begins).

The evolution of recitative is significant in this connection. In the beginning recitative simply served to explain the point of the situation tersely and forcefully, completely externalizing intentions and motivations. Often, the revision of an opera provided an opportunity for a change of perspective, and the character on the inner stage would suddenly be revealed. Let us take as an example the recitative in which Carlo di Vargas appears at the convent of Madonna of the Angels, where his enemy Alvaro has taken refuge, in act 4 of *La forza del destino*. In the original version the music is spare but states clearly the essential facts, nothing more: that Carlo is still alive and eager for vengeance (only the words *vivo* and *vendetta* are underlined by chords). In 1869, the text is lengthened but says nothing more of any importance. It is the orchestra that conjures up the neurotic fixation of Carlo's thirst for revenge (a tonic pedal), the dark subsoil of his soul (oscillation of the low strings on *viltà*), the bitterness he carries within him (strident accents on the passing notes), and the character's violent nature (imperious thrusts at the end of the passage).

In *Simon Boccanegra* the whole role of Paolo suddenly becomes consistent thanks to this enrichment of the musical speech. Paolo is only a *comprimario,* but his Iago-like wickedness and cupidity fascinated Verdi, who at the time he was revising the opera was already engaged in writing *Otello.* The scenes he gives him in the second and third acts have great intensity, in particular his monologue at the beginning of act 2, in which he decides to murder the Doge. Here again, a comparison of the two versions is instructive. At issue is Paolo's ambitious profession of faith in the prologue: "Aborriti patrizi, / Alle cime ove alberga il vostro orgoglio, / Disprezzato plebeo, salire io voglio" (Detested patricians, I, a despised plebeian, am determined to rise to the heights where dwells your pride). The original version of 1857 stresses Paolo's determination in the vocal line, which climbs ponderously up to high F. In 1881, the vocal line "freezes" on the high C of the key of F, but the accompaniment repeats, *forte,* fragments of the phrase on which the short prelude is based. The first version translates the passion of ambition into song, while the second shifts to the orchestra, which suggests the dark, turbid depths of frustration that are the inner foundation of that ambition.

Another important consequence of conveying these feelings is that the dramatic rhythms are diversified. Verdi is known for never dragging his feet and for moving his plots forward. Yet one notes how the composer gives increasing importance to passages where the tempo is slowed: this usually occurs when the inevitable disaster is close at hand, whereupon an eerie peace settles on the scene, a kind of timelessness that is the "time" of consciousness temporarily wrested from the constriction of tempo. The third act of *Luisa Miller* may be the first example of a large-scale use of this slow rhythm, especially in the astonishing scene just before the final duet-trio. Verdi gives this moment great intensity by searching out unaccustomed tonal connections, by the simplicity of the vocal line, by employing stretches of silence, a sober but intense orchestral commentary, and contrasts between extremely slow passages and brusque accelerations.

In *Rigoletto* and *Traviata* we find these rhythmic contrasts elevated to a principle, with a careful differentiation established between those "tempos" marking the opposing interior and exterior worlds. In the last scene of *Ballo* Verdi achieves real refinement in these contrasts. After the frenetic entrance chorus on a rather rough polka rhythm—"Fervono amori e danze"—he gives the onstage orchestra a seemingly interminable slow waltz. We know that this is a dramatist's trick to delay the denouement, when Renato must murder his master, and to make the stabbing all the more intolerable; yet it is also an extraordinary moment of peace and languorous abandon totally lacking in the urgency of the lovers' meeting in act 2. The reason is no doubt that the imminence of death makes any kind of haste pointless, as it does any effort to escape the inescapable.

Variety

THE SEARCH FOR A NEW AESTHETICS

Verdi attempted quite early on to unclamp the vise in which he used to lock his dramas and to give them more variety of action. He went about this in three ways: by developing the spectacular dimension, culminating in the creation of grand friezes; by integrating with the main action episodes that alleviated the weightier scenes; and by adopting a light tone that could be tinged with humor or irony.

If the search for spectacle quickly bore fruit, Verdi's art was slow to welcome badinage or diversion. We should remember that his dramaturgy developed in a cultural milieu that professed a rigorous respect for the separation of genres, which is no doubt the reason he left out lighter episodes appearing in the source texts of certain librettos. For instance, Victor Hugo's *Hernani* includes some jocular replies and even whole scenes that are comic or bantering, yet Verdi simply ignored them. The censors might be partly to blame for this omission, yet the composer never seemed to envision giving his drama the slightest comic tone. Similarly, the comic episodes in the original *Macbeth* are left out. Souvestre and Bourgeois's play *Le Pasteur, ou l'Évangile et le foyer,* from which *Stiffelio* derives, includes light social scenes in at least two acts, of which there is not a trace in either that opera or its revision as *Aroldo.*

Around 1848, however, signs of change multiplied. In July of that year Verdi informed Piave that he wanted to write an opera based on Guerrazzi's novel *L'assedio di Firenze* and made these recommendations: "Be very careful to avoid monotony. With subjects that are by nature sad, if we're not very careful we'll end up having a first-class funeral, as for example *I due Foscari,* which has a tint, a color that is too uniform from the beginning to the end."[29] (Note the first signs of self-criticism as regards his earlier works.) In March 1849, when he was sketching certain scenes from the novel, he said he wanted the banquet scene to be based on a "mixture of the comic and terrible (in the manner of Shakespeare)" so as to relieve the monotony of several scenes. To this end he suggested finding inspiration in a motley scene in Schiller's *Wallenstein,* which he wound up using as the encampment episode in *La forza del destino.*[30] In that same year, 1849, he asked Cammarano—who did nothing about it— to give a comic tinge to the character of Wurm in *Luisa Miller.*[31]

Slowly, Verdi ruminated over this need for variety, finally setting forth his ideas a few years later, in April 1853, in a famous and important letter to Somma that makes a clean break with his previous dramaturgy: "Long experience has confirmed the ideas I have always had as to theatrical effect, though in my early days I had the courage to reveal them only in part. (For example, ten years ago I would not have risked doing *Rigoletto.*) I find that our opera is guilty of excessive monotony, and therefore today I would refuse to set subjects in the genre of *Nabucco, Foscari,* etc., etc. They provide interesting scenes but without variety. It is all on just one note, lofty if you like, but still always the same. I will make myself clearer: the poem of Tasso may perhaps be superior, but I prefer Ariosto a thousand, thousand times more. For the same reason I prefer Shakespeare to all other dramatic authors, not excepting the Greeks."[32]

It will be noted that, in order to justify his wish for variety, Verdi goes back to literary models, not musical ones: the humor of Ariosto is set against the pathos of Tasso, the protean genius of Shakespeare against the tragic purity of the Greeks (curiously, for all his efforts to further the mixing of genres, Hugo is not even mentioned). Surprising, especially from such a somber, austere man, is the reference to Ariosto, the author of *Orlando furioso,* who treats his characters with benevolent irony; yet he would repeat his admiration for the "divine" Ariosto in 1874. In any case, these declarations show a desire for taking his bearings that is the key to his search for variety: no longer does Verdi intend to adopt only one character's point of view or to be at one with the plot, willy-nilly: now he is determined to think out the drama from a higher viewpoint, in all its diversity and contradictions. Moreover, the example of *L'assedio di Firenze* with its reference to Shakespeare and, even more, that of *Luisa Miller* show that the "comic" cannot be separated from the "terrible." Variety is designed not to weaken the strength of the drama but, on the contrary, to enhance it;[33] in this way, he says, a comic touch would make Wurm's evil nature stand out all the more.

The letter quoted above places *Rigoletto* at the starting point of this new dramatic vision: in it Verdi praises the dramatic value of the opera but also its variety, its mixture of pathos and brio. Actually, when it was first performed, the opera surprised audiences, with critics going so far as to speak of a semiseria work (i.e., one belonging to an intermediary genre between drama and opera buffa): in other words, they did not find that it demanded nobility of style in the same way as tragedy.[34] Thereafter, *Rigoletto* tended to receive a more ponderous stage interpretation, one characterized more by pathos, yet Alberto Savinio acutely observed that this meant departing from the tone chosen by the composer: "It is about time to restore the mysterious, subtle and playful character of Rigoletto, a precursor to Falstaff, something Verdi himself may not have been aware of."[35] The public was surprised, even shocked, because the opera struck a blow at the sacrosanct separation of genres: the habitués of La Fenice feared that Rigoletto's hump denigrated the dignity of Venice's most renowned theater. Incidentally, in 1842, as the actor Gustavo Modena tells it, the audience was taken aback by the first act of Shakespeare's *Othello*: Brabantio's appearance at a window, having suddenly been woken up, and Iago and Roderigo's remarks struck them as coming straight out of Goldoni or Gozzi, not a tragedy.[36]

Does this mean that all the post-*Rigoletto* operas observed the *programma* outlined in Verdi's letter to Somma? The composer's concern to avoid monotony, not to risk those "funerals" he referred to in connection with certain youthful works, is palpable in all his scores, but the techniques employed vary widely. All the same, there are exceptions. The most notable is *Simon Boccanegra,* which gave its creator no end of trouble. On two occasions he said that he found the opera dull and uniform; in 1880–81, he undertook to revise it in the hope of giving the work the variety it lacked but had to recognize that, even in its amended form, it was interesting but sad.[37]

Dullness, uniformity—these terms are indeed damning in the perspective opened up by the letter to Somma. Yet the original Spanish play contained comic episodes, none of which was transferred to the libretto. Essentially, these have to do with the character of Lorenzino Bucchetto, a pusillanimous, timorous, wealthy merchant who plays a double game between Fiesco's patricians and Simon's plebeians. An entire act—act 2 of the play—is in fact devoted to him, whereas in the final version of the opera he is no more than a name and the victim of a murder (he is killed by Gabriele Adorno, as described in the act 1 Finale).

Why did Verdi get rid of him? Was it because the light episodes in the original were mediocre? Was it that the character of Lorenzino, ridiculous rather than comic, did not enhance the "terrible" quality of the situations but would in fact have tended to diminish it by making Fiesco, a leading figure, look like a paltry, corrupt politician, and that Verdi did not want to hurt the nobility of the conflict opposing him and Simon? These may well be the reasons for Lorenzino's removal, especially in a drama as much about politics as about emotions. The fact is that Verdi's irony found expression far more readily in plots taken from the private domain and pruned of their political implications, like that of *Un ballo in maschera,* than in political dramas:[38] despite its episodes of *couleur locale, Don Carlos* remains an extremely dark opera. Political passions were too weighty to be tempered by humor of any sort.

Nevertheless, nothing is altogether the same after the trilogy. Even those late operas closest to Verdi's early style are treated with a lightness of touch that is the first form of distancing. The exceptional success of *Trovatore* bears this out. The story is one of wild-haired Romanticism and lends itself easily to caricature: the author of *El trovador,* García Gutiérrez, himself wrote a short parody of it in dialect, while Offenbach proposed a skit of the play at one of his soirees, and in Italy the opera gave rise to several satires.[39] Still, Verdi entered wholeheartedly into the spirit of this world of larger-than-life passions and, as we have seen, even gave it a sinister, nighttime coloration. Yet the opera shows an amazing lightness of touch; resembling a sort of sinister fairyland, it has the fluidity of a dream or a "faint delirium," to adopt Baldini's apt expression.[40]

THE ENCOUNTER WITH FRENCH OPERA

Among the reactions provoked by the novelty of *Rigoletto* is that of a Turin critic, who noted in 1856: "The conscientious critic must confess, however, that this type of music is quite French in character: except for the charm, the softness and the spontaneity of melody that one looks for in vain in foreign works, *Rigoletto* is the true 'opéra comique,' and even the melodic line shows a style not entirely in keeping with our tradition."[41] Whether considered a semiseria opera or a French grand opéra, *Rigoletto* certainly did not seem to be a pure product of tradition!

In his pursuit of variety, as we have seen, Verdi turned to writers, not composers; yet the three aspects of opera in which this aim was realized—spectacle, diversion, and the mixing of genres—were features of French opera, notably the grand opera of Auber, Halévy, and Meyerbeer. Whether these elements actually served to produce a pleasing entertainment, as was the hope of Véron, the manager of the Opéra, or were designed more ambitiously to create a "total drama," the genre nevertheless did offer Verdi models that he did not find in his own tradition and that he could exploit in his own way.[42]

For some years now, the importance of Verdi's acquaintance with French opera has been fully recognized.[43] True, the Italian composer's fascination with Paris can be explained by financial reasons (although in Verdi's case they should not be overestimated)[44] as well as by the pursuit of the prestige that would come with consecration in the French capital.[45] Yet with Verdi these motives should not obscure the particular aesthetic benefit he could hope to gain from an encounter with French opera and with Meyerbeer, its chief representative—that is, an expansion of his dramatic palette.

In spite of his acid criticisms of Meyerbeer's commercial acuity, Verdi, like many of his contemporaries, truly admired Meyerbeer. He appreciated his powerful characters like Fidès in *Le Prophète* and Valentine in *Les Huguenots,* his art of mixing the real and the fantastic in *Robert le Diable,* and more generally the German composer's dramatic force and sense of theater.[46] In Italian cultural circles Meyerbeer was held in high esteem: in his *Filosofia della musica* Mazzini did not hesitate to place the character of Bertram on the same level as Mozart's Don Giovanni, and critics argued seriously over his works.[47]

Verdi probably got to know Meyerbeer's work in 1834, when Pietro Massini, the director of the Teatro Filodrammatici in Milan, proposed staging *Robert le diable,* conducted by Verdi.[48] He also followed with interest the widening popularity of the German composer's works in the Italian peninsula from the 1840s[49] (especially since Giuseppina Strepponi performed one of his operas in Verona); at the very beginning of 1845, in his critique of *Giovanna d'Arco,* Muzio claimed that the choruses of that opera could rival those in *Robert le diable.*[50] When Verdi signed a contract with the Opéra in 1852, the starting point of *Vêpres,* it stipulated that he would have as his librettist Scribe, the chief artisan of grand opera texts, and that the work would be staged "with all the pomp that the action will demand and that the antecedents of the Grand-Opéra render indispensable."[51]

In July 1852, he wrote in French to Scribe: "I should like, I need a subject that is grandiose, impassioned and original; a *mise-en-scène* that is imposing and overwhelming. I have constantly in view so many of those magnificent scenes to be found in your poems, among others the Coronation in *Le Prophète.* In this scene no other composer could have done as well as Meyerbeer; but then, too, with such a spectacle and above all with a situation so original, grandiose and at the same time so charged with passion, no composer, however devoid of feeling, could have failed to produce a grand effect!"[52] Similarly, at the time of *Don Carlos,* he at first deplored the lack of spectacular elements; there, too, he made explicit reference to Meyerbeer, more precisely to the skaters' scene and the cathedral scene in *Le Prophète.*[53] Clearly, then, Verdi sought a confrontation with the German composer!

Verdi's fascination can probably be explained by the fact that truly grand opera, in the person of its most famous representative, was an indispensable link with music drama as "total work of art." The variety of modes of expression—poetry, music, ballet, the visual arts—and styles—grandiose or simple, tragic or comic, realistic or fantastic—represented, in approximate fashion, an image of the goals that Verdi and Wagner were aiming for, each in his own way. Weber's hope, expressed as early as 1809, that Romantic opera should be "a work of art forming a whole, where all parts and contributions of the twin arts therein employed become fused and eventually disappear," was realized in grand opera, even if this last sometimes presented only a degraded, commercial form of his ideal.

The venture was not without risks, a fact of which Verdi was perfectly well aware. His criticisms of *Guillaume Tell* and what he called "mosaic operas," together with the reproaches of irrelevance he addressed to Meyerbeer himself,[54] show that he was weighing in his mind how much the expansion of opera into myriad episodes might compromise its unity. The existence of several versions of *Don Carlos,* among them the original French version, that of 1866–67, and the much shortened one of 1884, shows the composer hesitating between two equally tempting paths.

The French experience was nonetheless a decisive one, felt even in the operas not written for Paris. *Un ballo in maschera,* composed for Naples and first performed in Rome, with a libretto taken from Scribe, is haunted by the mirage of a certain French elegance. *La forza del destino,* which premiered in St. Petersburg, abounds in characteristic scenes. *Aïda,* written for the Cairo opera and considered typically Parisian in scale,[55] seizes every occasion for spectacle.

Yet the balance sheet is indecisive. The period of the greatest French "hits" was between 1830 and 1850, a highly turbulent time in European history but one with a solid political and social axis. Against this axis, such themes as religious fanaticism (*Les Huguenots, La Juive*) or social tensions (*La Muette de Portici, Le Prophète*) could be portrayed in strong relief, with the component parts of spectacle being welded together and a dialectical link forged between the protagonists' fate and the course of history. Grand opera, or "social" opera as Heine called it, appeared at the time to realize fully the ideal of Romantic drama as formulated by Schlegel, Hugo, Stendhal, and many others. Unfortunately, it soon started to disintegrate until it often consisted of little more than a plot padded with diversionary scenes and spectacular settings that lacked any basic coherence.[56] Verdi, who had the breadth necessary for these huge syntheses, threw himself into the fray too late (as Budden notes, at the time of *Vêpres* and even more *Don Carlos,* the genre was showing signs of running out of steam, although the time was not far off when Gounod and Bizet would revive the tradition). As we shall see, Verdi had tremendous difficulty mastering French opera's variety of forms.

FRIEZES AND TABLEAUX

There is no question that the development of spectacle in Verdi's work, together with the composer's attention to staging, received a hefty impetus from the contact with French opera. In 1848, Verdi was greatly impressed by the care lavished on stage settings in Paris: "You know they have six, seven and even as many as eight months of rehearsal here, but don't think that's unnecessary. I myself used to think so, but now that I have had the experience I see that it is very necessary indeed. We can say that a good part of an opera has to be done onstage, during rehearsal. The *mise en scène* is perhaps the most important thing and many operas survive because of it."[57] Verdi exercised control over the staging of his operas largely through the *Disposizioni sceniche,* which were inspired by the French *Livrets de mise en scène.*

Nevertheless, it would be a mistake to underestimate the influence of other arts like painting, especially large-scale historical works such as those of Francesco Hayez, with which Verdi was very familiar. This artist's great friezes often dealt with subjects or characters found in opera, for instance, the doge Francesco Foscari, the Sicilian Vespers, the Jerusalem crusades, or Imelda de' Lambertazzi, Caterina Cornaro, and Mary

Stuart, all characters that inspired Donizetti. The paintings are thronged with scenes or secondary figures to provide a veritable feast for the eyes, a combination fascinating for a composer.[58]

If we compare some of Verdi's sketches, we can see that these influences did not just concern minor aspects of opera but affected the basic plan leading up to the finished work. Take, for example, the composer's first reaction to *Hernani:* "Tomorrow I shall write a long letter to Sig.ʳ Piave with all the scenes of Hernani that I feel are adequate. I've already seen that the entire first act could be condensed into a magnificent introduction and we could end the act with the scene of Don Carlos asking Silva to hand over Hernani, who is hidden behind his portrait. For the second act we could use the fourth act of the French play, and we could end the third act with the magnificent trio and the death of Hernani, etc."[59] Clearly, it is movement that predominates in this vertiginous condensation of Hugo's play, the dynamic that leads from the introduction to the final trio.

Now let us look at the sketch of *Attila,* an opera inspired by *Attila, König der Hunnen,* a play by Zacharias Werner written in 1808: "In my opinion it should consist of a prologue and three acts. As the curtain rises we should see Aquileia in flames, with a chorus protesting the Huns' domination. The people are praying, the Huns threatening, etc., etc. Then there should come Ildegonda's aria, then Attila's, etc., etc. . . . and that's the end of the prologue. I should open the first act in Rome, and instead of showing the festivities onstage, I would have it backstage while Azzio is onstage pensive, meditating the events, etc., etc. . . . I would end the first act with Ildegonda telling Attila about the poisoned chalice. Attila believes that she did it out of love, while she only sought revenge for the death of her father and brothers, etc., etc. In the third act it would be magnificent to have Leo's entire scene on the Aventine Hill while the battle is going on down below. This may not be allowed, but we must mask the situation so carefully that we do get permission. The scene must be exactly as I described it."[60]

Here, it is the idea of historical frieze that predominates: the King of the Huns' triumphant arrival in Aquilea, a city in ruins, and next Ildegonda's (Odabella's) challenge, Azzio's (Ezio's) meditation in the foreground, and the majestic meeting on the Aventine Hill of Attila and Pope Leo the Great (who for reasons of censorship would become simply "an old Roman"). Later, another tableau would be added of the sunrise over the lake in the prologue as well as one of the night banquet in Attila's camp (act 2 Finale). The importance of the visual element in the conception of the work is shown by the fact that Verdi inquired about Raphael's frescoes, in Rome, depicting the meeting between Attila and Pope Leo and arranged with the excellent stage designer Giuseppe Bertoja for the sunrise and Attila's camp to be successfully incorporated in the Venice production.[61]

Thus, what we have here is a dual preoccupation, the one tending in the direction of movement as a succession of happenings scarcely hampered by musical formalization, the other concerned with the tableau, which expands in the dimension of time what painting at one stroke renders in space. These two trends were not unknown in the Italian tradition, although the second predominates in French opera. The very idea of a Finale suggests painting (one is reminded of the final "tableau" of stage melodrama described earlier) since the Finale is a painting that unfolds in time whereas painting is a Finale that is suddenly fixed. The word *dramatic,* to which criticism often attaches different meanings, also reflects this dual polarity: sometimes it indicates the sense of rhythm, that is to say, the ability to link rapidly a succession of plot twists, and sometimes, by contrast, it simply means emphasis, the "pictorial" or "sculptural" intensity with which an otherwise static situation is treated.

In any event, the spectacular component quickly became part of the attraction Paris held for Verdi, for the Opéra would enable him to shine in all his brilliance. So it is no surprise to find the composer, as he embarked on *Attila,* dreaming of staging it in the French capital: "Wouldn't it be wonderful to do *Attila* for the Paris Grand Opéra! I would have to add only a few things and all the rest would do quite well as it is."[62] Nor was this dream unfounded since the publisher Escudier had suggested that Verdi rework one of his operas for the Paris stage. In the end it was *I Lombardi* that was taken on, an opera that also lent itself to adaptation to French aesthetics; after heavy changes, and renamed *Jérusalem,* it was staged at the Opéra in November 1847.[63] The need for spectacle can also be seen in plans made for other operatic capitals: in November 1848, in connection with negotiations with Naples's San Carlo, Verdi asked Cammarano if *Ettore Fieramosca,* a novel by Massimo d'Azeglio, contained "well-defined characters, passion, movement. It must have pathetic scenes, and above all it must be grand and spectacular. Otherwise it can't be successful in a big theater."[64]

What effect did this search for a frieze-like effect have on Verdi's conception of drama? It enabled him to include in the plot grandiose scenes like those at the beginning of act 4 of *La battaglia di Legnano,* which, not coincidentally, was composed in Paris. One of the chief innovations in

Jérusalem, the French version of *I Lombardi,* was the great scene in act 3 in which Gaston, unjustly suspected of murder, is disgraced before the Crusaders' army at full strength—a scene created especially for Paris that was a stunning success. But the composer's new departure can be seen most clearly in the transformation of the finale, which Verdi now tended to conceive as an independent, self-contained tableau, "closing" the musical form in on itself by repeating at the end of the episode themes that were used at the beginning. This technique has the effect of replacing the traditional slow-fast dynamic of the finale with an arched structure that at the end brings us back to the point at which we started.

This is how the finale of act 2 of *Vêpres* is put together. An Allegro tarantella in E minor celebrates the betrothal of twelve Sicilian couples. Some French soldiers arrive (the French are occupying Sicily) and stand watching the dancing; the "judge" Procida, always on the lookout for a provocation that might launch a revolt against the French, reminds them that womenfolk are the property of the conquerors. A double chorus in C major opposes the French, celebrating war and conquest, and the Sicilians, who decry the cowardly practice of attacking defenseless peasants. With a return to E minor, the French soldier Robert abducts the Sicilian girl Ninnetta. Next comes a reprise of the double chorus in E major with coda, still with a tarantella rhythm.

The French then leave, taking the women away with them, and a brief orchestral passage leads to a grand ensemble in F$\sharp$ minor, "interdits—accablés—et de honte—et de rage"/"Il rossor—mi copri!—il terror—ho nel sen," consisting of three sections. In the middle section, which contains more dialogue, Hélène and Procida incite their fellow citizens to revolt; there follows a faster, more varied reprise of the first section. At this point a graceful barcarole is heard, sung a cappella and contrasting with the preceding ensemble (F$\sharp$ major, not minor, $\frac{6}{8}$ time instead of $\frac{3}{4}$ and then $\frac{2}{4}$); it emanates from a boat bearing French officers and Sicilian ladies to the Governor's ball. Procida decides to take advantage of the ball to assassinate Governor Montfort, and the act ends with another ensemble combining, in F$\sharp$ major, the Sicilians' concertato and the barcarole.

Here we find the traditional elements used to engage the mechanism of the Italian-style Finale. First, a dramatic episode, the abduction of the Sicilian brides-to-be, leads to the slow-paced ensemble; another episode, the passing of the barge, is justification for a second ensemble. But the Finale is expanded by the important preliminary section (the betrothal celebration accompanied by the tarantella), and after the central ensemble comes not a Stretta but a reprise that hardly differs from the foregoing ensemble, creating the effect of "closing" referred to above.

The same phenomenon can be observed in the striking act 3 Finale of *Don Carlos,* which we know Verdi wanted to make into a spectacular grand opera. The first Finale consisted only of a regal ceremony including the petition of the Flemish deputies, oppressed by the Spaniards, Philip II's refusal, and the revolt of the infante Carlos. Later, Verdi added an auto-da-fé complete with inquisitors and heretics condemned to be burned at the stake.[65] Thus expanded, this Finale provided Verdi with all the advantages he could hope for—a wide variety of "colors," with a jubilant populace, the sinister monks of the Inquisition, the royal court, the protagonists, the Flemish deputies, even a heavenly voice encouraging the condemned men to resignation. Moreover, it is a strikingly balanced and homogeneous composition that ends, as in *Vêpres,* with a partial reprise of the introduction.

This approach reached its apogee in the act 2 Finale of *Aida,* which offers an expanded version of the earlier Finale. With a little perseverance one can trace the old form: a festive choral introduction, a dramatic peripeteia (the arrival among the Ethiopian prisoners of Amonasro, who is instantly recognized by Aida), a slow concertato for the soloists and chorus, another incident (the King gives his daughter's hand to the conquering general, plunging Aida and Radames into despair), and a sort of Stretta in the episode "Fa cor, della tua patria," devoted to the various protagonists' reactions to the announcement of the marriage of Radames and Amneris. Yet over this interweaving of themes hangs the leaden cope of celebratory pomp that accentuates the trend to symmetry and reprises as in the *Don Carlos* finale.

The *Aida* Finale attained a degree of monumentality—and conventionality—that inevitably provoked a reaction. The act 1 Finale of the new version of *Simon* is far less static than that of 1857, while retaining the dramatic twists that justified it in the original version. Verdi eliminated the four purely celebratory pieces of the first Finale (chorus, barcarole, hymn, and dance), replacing them with a lively scene in the Council Chamber where Doge Simon first tries to calm his councillors' animosity, then faces up to a popular uprising. Spectacle is not sacrificed, but dramatic movement regains its rightful place.

For *Otello* Verdi took precautions, announcing loud and clear that this would be an Italian opera, of Italian dimensions.[66] The act 3 Finale gave him enormous trouble since he was determined to avoid the obligatory celebratory Finale even though the dramatic situation (the arrival of representatives of the Venetian senate) made it almost inevitable. The Finales in *Falstaff* are quicksilver, recapturing, although in a quite different style, the devilry that was the joy of the Finales of the eighteenth century and of Rossini.

Late in his career, when he was writing *Falstaff*, Verdi reached the point where he spurned what he had once, if not adored, then at least sought tenaciously: "Ah! So Franchetti likes spectacular *mises-en-scène?* I hate them more than anything. What's needed, and nothing more. With huge *mises-en-scène* you end up doing the same thing all the time . . . big drum . . . impressive crowd . . . and farewell drama and music! They become secondary matters."[67] Clearly, Verdi did not lack the ability to revise his opinions!

BADINAGE

Criticizing the first version of the chorus that opens act 2 of *Aida*, Verdi wrote Ghislanzoni: "The first chorus is cold and insignificant. It tells a story any messenger can deliver. I know very well that there is no action, but with a little *adresse* we can still do something. There is no action in *Don Carlos* either when the ladies of the court stand around the garden outside the convent waiting for the queen. Yet with that small chorus and the snappy, characteristic French song we did get a nice little scene. Here, too, we must create a scene with a sweetly lyrical chorus as Amneris is being dressed by her maids and a group of little Ethiopian blackamoors dance for her."[68]

In his reference to *Don Carlos*, Verdi was alluding to the second tableau of act 2 in which the ladies-in-waiting are sitting on the grass, whiling away the time as they wait for the Queen, who has gone with her husband to meditate over Charles V's tomb at the monastery of St.-Just, where the ladies are not allowed to go. It is a pure genre scene: the chorus "Sous ces bois au feuillage immense"/"Sotto ai folti, immensi abeti" has the rather careless grace of one of Winterhalter's paintings, and, despite its discreet allusions to the plot, Eboli's Veil Song is a genre piece with touches of flamenco. What strikes one in Verdi's commentary is that it amounts to a recognition of the genre scene by a composer who twenty years earlier rejected everything that did not directly benefit the action: he is finally admitting the possibility of introducing into the drama an episode whose value lies simply in its grace or characteristic atmosphere.

Although totally accepted in French opera, this worldly, frivolous strain is not found in the Italian tradition, probably because it derives from an "everyday" style and not from the elevated style characteristic of lyric drama. Thus, librettos taken from French plays tended to excise all the characteristic scenes, as, for example, in the case of *Stiffelio,* which was performed in 1850 minus the first two acts of the original play.[69] Both these acts portray rather self-satisfied provincial bourgeois who hang around Lina and her father-in-law, Stankar, dreaming of a brilliant, worldly existence. Piave completely eliminated these conversations and opened the opera with act 3 of the play, retaining only the drama of love, revenge, and forgiveness.

Conversation certainly plays an important role in *Rigoletto,* in *Traviata,* and in the dance scene of *Vêpres,* but it lacks the free charm of chatter and is instead straitjacketed by a relentless rhythm that gives it a staccato, feverish quality. In contrast, the episode of the French soldier Robert, in the introduction to act 1 of *Vêpres,* is much more carefree as he totters about drunk, with the music attempting to ape his movements. In the fifth act of the same opera, the waltz chorus, Hélène's sicilienne (actually a bolero), and Henri's melody act as genre scenes, but they are not well suited to the characters (at least in Hélène's case) and are not integrated into the plot. The somewhat weak structure of this fifth act comes from the misunderstanding between Scribe, who wanted to exploit the occasion of Hélène and Henri's marriage and the reconciliation of the French and Sicilians, and Verdi, who was loath to lose the thread of the drama and dispel the menace of a general massacre.[70]

The introduction of characteristic scenes comes off far better in *Don Carlos,* essentially because they take place early on in the opera, that is, up to the second tableau of act 3, after which the drama takes over and rules out all frivolity. One cannot think of the opening woodcutters scene (cut before the first performance) as merely a genre tableau since the vision of tragedy and poverty that arises from it hangs heavily over the plot and over Elisabeth's decision to marry the King of Spain; on the other hand, Carlos and Elisabeth's first duet deals with a situation unique in Verdian theater—the first meeting of lovers, Elisabeth not knowing Carlos and he having just seen her for the first time. The first and second sections of the duet, up to the scene of mutual recognition and the cabaletta "De quels transports poignants et doux," show Verdi trying his hand at delicate badinage: the Infante's manner is both timid and eager, while the French princess displays a girlish coquetry that completely disappears when she is Queen of Spain.

Returning to the tableau of the ladies-in-waiting, this genre scene is perfectly integrated into the unfolding of the drama since it provides a contrast with the much more austere scene just before it at the monastery of St.-Just and serves to lighten the atmosphere before the dramatic encounter between the Infante and his mother-in-law. The scene that follows, with the Marquis of Posa's ballata, still retains this atmosphere of worldly conversation thanks to the exchanges between Posa and Eboli concerning the French court: "Que fait-on à la cour de France, ce beau pays de l'élégance?" asks Eboli. Posa speaks of tournaments and praises the elegance of French women, all the while gallantly courting Princess Eboli. True, this scene does mask a more dramatic situation since Posa has just passed on to the Queen a letter from Carlos asking her for a rendezvous, which she hesitates to accept; nevertheless, the rather hip-swaying character of the D-major theme that serves as the accompaniment to the conversation, its dance-tune charm, and its frequent repetitions (six times) suffice to establish an atmosphere of badinage that the plot will shortly dispel.

In this area, Verdi would never achieve the elegant, flowing conversation of a Massenet or the subtle coloring of a Strauss, mixing together bland remarks, confessions, allusions, and agitation. Yet, without these experiments, would he still have been able to convey in so masterly a way, in *Otello,* the ambiguity of worldly sophistication? In the period of *Traviata* and *Rigoletto* the composer had no intimate acquaintance with worldliness, which he evoked without pleasure through conversation hurried along by a convulsive rhythm. In *Otello,* by contrast, the conversational elegance, the appearance of worldly courtesy characterizing social relations, the affectation of Iago, who always behaves like a good host, in short the veneer of refinement and elegance are at once stunningly brought off and disturbing, for elegance may be a cover for perversity, suavity may disguise deceit. In order to conjure up the world of pretense he had to undergo an apprenticeship in frivolity, which was achieved as a result of the experiments described in this chapter.

DIVERSIONS

La forza del destino is the opera where Verdi shows himself most intent on detaching the marginal episode and integrating it as a structural element. One can see this desire plainly in the ample development of the encampment scene in act 3 (drawn from Schiller's *Wallensteins Lager*) and in the importance he gives such roles as those of Preziosilla and Melitone, who have nothing to do with the plot.[71] From the start the play struck him as "extremely vast," and the opera could therefore be no less so.[72] In the end, when supervising the publication of his opera, Verdi insisted on distinguishing *Forza* from traditional operas made up of cavatinas and duets, and he defended his "intentions";[73] most likely he suspected that the marginal scenes and characters might be dropped to focus on the protagonists and that the opera would not be judged as a totality. However clear the composer's intentions may have been, they did nevertheless create delicate structural problems. I shall examine two examples, one where the problem is not really solved, the other where it is very satisfactorily overcome.

Two-thirds of act 3 is devoted to the plot and a good third to an extensive *couleur locale*. The plot brings together Carlo and Alvaro, who are warring in Italy under false names. They strike up a friendship and save each other's life; but Carlo sees Alvaro as his mortal enemy, the one who murdered his father, and he challenges him to a duel. The episode is given over to a humorous, colorful description of the military camp that is its setting and presents Spanish and Italian soldiers, camp followers, peasants, the gypsy Preziosilla, the peddler Trabuco, and the friar Melitone. How to combine these two facets of the act?

In the 1862 version, the camp scene is inserted at the point where Alvaro, whom Carlo has saved, is nevertheless wounded and his adversary has to wait for his recovery before challenging him to a duel. The duel therefore takes place at the end of the act, which finishes with an aria for Alvaro (first version), who, convinced that he has killed his rival, decides to retire from the world. This splicing is logical since the plot is interrupted at the moment when a pause has to be observed, yet the pause is so long that it is difficult to take up the thread of the story.

The 1869 version consolidates all the numbers relating to the plot, but the duel is interrupted by a camp patrol, and the two enemies depart, each going his separate way. For the period when Alvaro recovers, Verdi introduced a ravishing *ronda* sung by one of the night patrols. The end of the act is entirely taken up with the camp scene: suddenly, we have two self-contained blocks, the first dealing with the plot, the second constituting an act within the act. This seemingly arbitrary form of musical structure has given rise to frequent changes and cuts at this point of the opera: as one commentator observes, there was a time when, at each performance, the spectator wondered which numbers he was going to hear and in what order.[74]

Clearly, Verdi never found the overall viewpoint that would have allowed him to bring together very different spheres and link up the minor characters and the protagonists—as is achieved in Russian opera, where episodes that are at the same time light and dramatic combine to paint a vast vision of national history.[75] However brilliant the camp scene numbers may be, they come across as miniatures, amusing but perfectly autonomous; they are too far removed from the main action for the "comic" quality of the diversion to show up the "terrible" quality of the plot.

Quite different is the inn scene in act 2 of the same opera. The brilliant success of this section comes on the one hand from the skillful way the plot and the scenes of *couleur locale* are blended together and on the other hand from a superb mastery of structure. The tableau takes place in the great hall of an inn in the village of Hornachuelos. Leonora, whose lover has unintentionally just killed her father, decides to take refuge in a monastery; disguised as a man, she stops at the inn but does not go and dine with the guests since among them she has recognized her brother Carlo. The latter has in fact been hot on her tracks, intent on avenging his father's memory and killing both her and her lover; he shows up at the same inn, pretending to be a student called Pereda,[76] and dines with the guests. Quite soon, however, he is obviously intrigued by the mysterious guest who sits apart from the company at table and who he suspects is his sister. The characteristic elements include a dance of the muleteers, casual conversation such as can arise around a dining table at an inn, Preziosilla's song, and a pilgrims' chorus.

It should be pointed out that the corresponding scene in the Duke of Rivas's Spanish play (act 2, scene 1) is quite different. No pilgrims' voices are heard; the nearby monastery is simply celebrating its jubilee, thereby attracting a crowd of people; Preziosilla does not appear, her presence in Hornachuelos and Italy being a Verdi-Piave innovation; Leonora is at the inn but is never seen; and the student actually is Pereda, a friend of Carlo di Vargas's. There were obviously some excellent reasons for all these changes, but the tableau ends up being completely original, the invention of Piave and especially Verdi.

In the opera, the tableau may be divided into seven phases corresponding to the musical numbers:

1. *Coro-ballabile.* The first one begins with the twice-repeated three Es already heard at the start of the overture and the beginning of act 1. They are a solemn reminder of the threat of destiny, but the skipping verve of a "fake" seguidilla in A minor, danced by the muleteers, quickly puts these doom-laden notes out of mind.

2. *Scena.* The Alcade (village mayor) announces that all will go to the table. The student (really Carlo) tells us in an aside that he is looking for

his sister and her lover, then blesses the meal in Latin. Leonora catches sight of her brother and retreats to her room, while the guests chatter against the background of the muleteers' dance.

3. *Recitativo e canzone.* Enter Preziosilla, a young gypsy, part fortune-teller and part recruiting sergeant. She announces that war has broken out in Italy and that there are promotions to be won. Her song "al suon del tamburo" celebrates the "jollities of the squadron." She addresses the assembled guests, including the student, whose identity she immediately detects and whose subterfuge makes her roar with laughter.

4. *Preghiera.* From offstage is heard a chorus of pilgrims on their way to Rome, to the jubilee. The guests kneel and pray to heaven. Dominating the group is the voice of Leonora, who has left her room and begs God to save her. There are strong analogies between the ensemble theme in G major, "Su noi prostrati e supplici," and one of the overture themes, also in G (D–E–F$\sharp$–B–A–G in the song as against D–F$\sharp$–B–A–G), a theme that turns up again in the following tableau, in Leonora's aria, linked to her hope of salvation. Note also the cadential formula associated with this same character (on Leonora's first "Pietà signore"). Because of these reminiscences, the "absent" Leonora (i.e., unseen by the assembly) is present at the heart of the ensemble.

5. *Scena.* The pilgrims have drifted off, and both the conversation and the meal continue. The student is intrigued by the guest who did not come down to dine, and he questions the muleteer Trabuco repeatedly until the latter finally goes off in exasperation.

6. *Ballata.* The Alcade wants to protect the anonymity of the mysterious guest and in return asks Pereda to reveal his identity. The latter does so in an elegant, carefree ballata in which he dupes the guests by passing himself off as the student Pereda. He does not, however, deceive the listener, who has been alerted by certain coincidences: the accompaniment of the section "là e dovunque narrâr" is obviously a reversal of the well-known destiny theme that opens the opera!

7. *Scena, coro e ripresa della danza.* Preziosilla, for her part, is not taken in, and her laughter rings out once more while the Alcade suggests that all go to bed. The muleteers' dance, a few measures of Pereda's ballata, and a few more laughs from Preziosilla make a dazzling "coda" to the tableau.

This description shows that Verdi composed a tableau that is rich in color but without once losing sight of the themes of the plot, which in places are recalled by a musical allusion. Even though it includes a certain number of *pezzi chiusi,* the tableau is extremely homogeneous, unified as it is by the key of A, which opens it (in the minor) and closes it (in the major). The different phases of the scene echo and balance each other within a rigorous structure: the overture and conclusion (phases 1 and 7) match each other with the muleteers' dance; phases 2 and 5 are linked through the pretext of the meal; Preziosilla's song (phase 3) and Pereda's ballata (phase 6) echo each other, especially as they share the same *rondò*-like form. At the very center of the structure, in the eye of the storm as it were, is the preghiera (phase 4), which is justified by an external event (the procession of pilgrims) but at the same time brings us to the heart of the drama by highlighting Leonora and her hope of fleeing "the force of destiny." In this case, the counterpoint of the comic and the terrible, of the genre scene and the pursuit of the drama, succeed perfectly.

AMBIVALENCE AND IRONY

One wonders at times whether certain military marches of Verdi's, and in particular certain spirited choruses in which brutal killers tell of horrors—for instance, the chorus of hired assassins in act 2 of *Macbeth*—are intended to be comic. The staccato way of singing that characterizes these choruses and that is already to be found in Rossini, who in turn took it from opera buffa, is a choice of style the composer uses to distinguish the noble high register of his heroes from the middle or low register of men of action and soldiers; nevertheless, the effect is frequently hilarious.[77]

The comic element is not so involuntary in *Rigoletto,* as can be seen in the sprightly chorus the courtiers sing as they make ready to carry off Rigoletto's daughter, "Zitti, zitti, moviamo a vendetta"; with its pianissimo effect (the chorus must be sung in a low voice), its lively rhythm, the delectable effects of the coda where the repetition of *zitti* and *cheti* produces an effect of verbal comedy worthy of Rossini, it is impossible to take the courtiers' malicious trick seriously. Yet it is this farce that is about to launch the drama. We have here an example of the ambivalence of a situation that is at the same time worthy of a vaudeville and yet tragic.

Occasionally, an entire opera is based on this subtle double play, as happens with *Un ballo in maschera.* When Verdi took up this story, which was invented by Scribe and had already been set by composers like Auber, Gabussi, and Mercadante, he at once emphasized its conventional aspect: "It's vast and grandiose; it's beautiful; but it too has conventional things in it like all operas—something I've always disliked and now find intolerable."[78] Clearly, he had no particular desire to work on the plot, but he would be forced to do so by the terms of a contract he had signed with the San Carlo in Naples. Paradoxically, this opera, which he took on without enthusiasm, is the one he was to fight for so tenaciously when it was ripped to pieces by the censors.

How, then, did he make acceptable to himself what had struck him as unacceptable? On the one hand by treating the "serious" aspects of the opera with great intensity: love, which we studied in the preceding chapter and which is treated quite matter-of-factly in Scribe's original play; Ulrica's prophecy, which Verdi comments on with an austere solemnity that only Mercadante comes near achieving; and Renato's revenge, a sentiment that he had not the least difficulty making into something to be dreaded. And on the other hand by treating the conventional episodes with a light, even playful touch.

One of the basic tints of this opera is in fact festivity, which Verdi decides to treat here in a Gallic manner. This style can first be clearly seen in the character of the page Oscar, a traditional figure of French opera whose numbers (the ballata of act 1 and the song in act 3) are written in strophic form *à la française* and in a light, sparkling style. As regards the protagonist, Riccardo, Verdi's correspondence clearly shows that he perceived him as a ruler who was French in spirit, although Swedish by nationality, referring to "the rather French character of Gustav."[79] The Stretta of the introduction and particularly the phrase "Dunque signori aspettovi" certainly conjure up the Paris of Napoleon III and Offenbach rather than the Sweden of Gustav III (or Riccardo's America!).

This time badinage is omnipresent, lending the music a free-and-easy grace that can be seen in numerous orchestral themes (as in the C-major theme accompanying Riccardo's entrance). In this theme as in many others one is struck by the "frivolous" use of the ornamental notes—among others, of acciaccaturas (see Oscar's ballata and song, Riccardo's song, etc.). This ornament, which in *Rigoletto* and *Traviata* implies urgency and helps create rhythmic pressure, here conveys insouciance. Similarly, the appoggiatura, often used to drive melody forward and give it more energy, here conveys a certain nonchalance. This pursuit of suppleness and *sprezzatura* lends almost all *Ballo*'s melodies an elegant, jaunty air, even if they are describing sinister happenings, as in Oscar's part in the quintet "È scherzo od è follia" (see ex. 16).

Humor is another method Verdi adopts to distance himself from convention. He employs it in two ways: by treating certain situations in a deliberately conventional manner, to the point where they approach cari-

EX. 16

cature and have an ironic tinge, and by simultaneously retaining the comic note sounded in Scribe but eliminated by Verdi's predecessors.

Nowhere is irony as evident as in Verdi's treatment of that ultracon-ventional form, the *introduzione,* which, in its customary handling, is the model of good behavior: chorus, the tenor Riccardo's *sortita,* the baritone Renato's cantabile, the ballata of the soprano Oscar, and Stretta. The vari-ous planes are clearly drawn: the courtiers' respectful, dignified "chorale," the conspirators' tortuous fugato, the tenor's elegant reverie, the bari-tone's rather gauche apprehension, the soprano's impulsive vivacity. The effects of the mixed voices (fugato and "chorale," soloists and chorus) fail to cloud this clarity. Nor does the prelude disturb the elegance of the arrangement since it is in the same key as the introductory chorus (B major) and its four themes are all repeated in the introduction.

If one recalls that at this very time Verdi was attempting to transform the *Introduzione* (in ways already described), this classicism would be sur-prising were it not necessary to interpret it as an ironic use of the form. Budden observes, moreover, in connection with two passages from this opera, that Verdi makes use of "the distilled essence of the traditional forms rather than the forms themselves."[80] To use a conventional form with almost exemplary diligence shows a distancing that implies a certain irony. In fact, this *Introduzione,* which transports us to a royal court out of operetta, is merely a deception, as is the "Governor's" calm assurance.

The comic note is essentially found in the act 2 Finale, where the con-spirators laugh at the expense of the mortified Renato. However, because it is combined with the slightly mocking conventionality and festive at-mosphere of the ball scene, contrasting so strongly with some intensely dramatic moments, the comic element has the effect of creating constant ambivalence. Yet the "mix" is very different from the one we examined in *Forza*. There, the "comic" rubs elbows with the "terrible"—they are *juxtaposed,* and humor arises from the overall perception. Here, the comic and the terrible are one—they *overlap.*

The dramaturgic thinking of *Ballo* is ambivalent to start with because Verdi is telling us in the same breath a tragic story and a light comedy, presenting us with an operetta "king" who is also a vulnerable, torn man. Amelia is the only one who escapes this atmosphere since throughout the opera she is conscious of the dreadful implications of her adulterous love. At the heart of the story is fate, a fate that is extremely ambiguous because it is at one and the same time the dark crucible where our lives are plotted and capricious chance; it is Ulrica, with her ponderous, austere song, terrifying all who observe her satanic rites, and Oscar, the unwitting messenger of tragedy. Oscar is the one who encourages Riccardo to visit Ulrica; he who brings Renato the invitations to the masked ball, giving the conspirators an opportunity to murder the Governor; and he who unknowingly becomes Renato's accomplice by revealing to him the mask that is Riccardo's disguise.

Verdi creates ambivalence both by playing on the ambiguities of the connection between text and music and by piling up reminiscences and internal echoes, in which this opera is particularly rich. When Oscar describes Ulrica in his ballata in the *Introduzione,* there is a constant divergence between the brilliance of the music and the sinister reality the words describe: the page's most startling phrase is the one recalling the pact between the sorceress and Lucifer, "È con Lucifero d'accordo ognor." In his cantabile, also in the *Introduzione,* Renato, the Governor's loyal friend, reminds him that because of his imprudence he is running the risk of compromising his "splendid future." Immediately a clarinet, bassoon, and horn play a rhythmic element ♪.♪♩ that is perfectly anodyne. However, this is a rhythm we will hear again, announced by trombones, trumpets, and timpani, accompanying the words *Eri tu,* the opening of the act 3 aria in which Renato decides to turn against his master. Usually confined to the trumpets and trombones, this rhythmic figure threads through Ulrica's scene, beginning with her invocation (in the reprise at number 8), where it underlines the words *nulla, più nulla.* The premature sounding of this element is an ironic comment on Riccardo's "splendid future."[81]

In the next act the connection is reversed, the dominant note being dramatic, but not without a tinge of mockery. After the lovers' duet, and at the very beginning of the trio, Renato enters to tell his master that the conspirators are approaching. The phrase he uses to begin the *tempo d'attacco,* "Per salvarti da lor," is close, both tonally and melodically, to Riccardo's when he begins the second movement of the duet "Non sai tu," as though Renato's fervent desire to save his master was unequaled save by that of Riccardo's to "take" his secretary's wife. When Renato explains that the men have seen him in the company of an "unknown beauty," the orchestra plays a discreet reminder of that same duet ("Ciel pietoso"; ex. 13 above, p. 231); each time the phrase is heard on a dominant pedal note of F.

After the trio, when the conspirators pounce on Renato and the veiled Amelia, their aggression is immediately neutralized by a mocking pedal note ("Scerni tu quel bianco velo"), which turns up again at the end of the quartet. Incidentally, in this opera Verdi makes frequent and appropriate use of the pedal, whose anticipatory quality gives it a certain ambivalence, as though it were impossible to tell whether it is heralding drama or farce. The final quartet, by contrast, makes the two spheres perfectly equal again by opposing Samuel and Tom's comic style (note the derisory acciaccaturas in the orchestra) and Renato's enraged and Amelia's despairing commentaries. Opening with one of the most intensely dramatic preludes Verdi ever wrote, the act thus closes with a scene out of vaudeville.

The last act is rich in effects of the same kind. I will quote only one, taken from the beginning of the quintet. Oscar has just shown up at Renato's home, bringing invitations to the Governor's masked ball. He opens the quintet by praising the splendor of the ball in his customary style. Amelia follows, utterly crushed, for she senses that the ball will be the occasion for a murder to which she feels she is an accessory. The two phrases are very close and at the same time totally different in feeling, like two facets of the same situation (exx. 17*a* and 17*b*).

It is striking how, of all Verdi's operas, *Un ballo in maschera* is the one where love and irony are depicted the most forcefully. Love becomes an inner fissure, a vertigo; irony sees the individual falling in love and recognizes that he must pay the price—it is the awareness that these two parameters, interiority of passion and social exteriority, will never be one. Some have called *Ballo* Verdi's *Tristan,* insisting on certain harmonic affinities between the love duets of each opera. No less significant are the differences: with Wagner, Romantic interiority is the stronger and leads to the longing for the negation of the world, for night and death. With

EX. 17a

EX. 17b

Verdi, reality is the stronger, and it is the world that destroys innocence and passion. Irony consecrates this division and attempts to make it bearable.

The logical culmination of the ironic use of form I described above is its use in quotation, like some nostalgic echo of a world gone by. The procedure is often found in late nineteenth-century opera (just as one finds imitations of past styles), and quite understandably it crops up constantly in *Falstaff*. This "lyrical comedy" that had to wait so long to be born is in certain respects a play on a tradition at once near at hand and far away, both as regards the source of the plot (the old dandy cruelly mocked) and the musical writing. For example, while he was preparing the opera Verdi amused himself by writing fugues, even a comic fugue he did not know where to place (it was to conclude the opera);[82] he built up the first scene of act 1 in sonata form;[83] he made frequent, lightly parodic use of the perfect cadence;[84] at times he employed the most classical forms, as in the aria "Quand'ero paggio del duca di Norfolk," which describes Falstaff's former life by means of a form suited to the opera of the past. Ford and Falstaff sing a "madrigal," and the final double wedding is accompanied by a graceful minuet. Nor did Boito lag behind: his sonnet for Fenton is characterized by archaic phrasing and has a refrain that descends straight from Boccaccio. Nannetta and Fenton's love sparrings swing between Pre-Raphaelite preciosity, courtly metaphysics, and baroque speech.

Verdi's last opera has another claim to a place in this chapter. It is founded on a few great dramatic themes of the Verdian world: honor, jealousy, revenge, the larger-than-life "hero." True, impassioned violence is ridiculed, but the lightness of touch leaves no room for belly laughs or ribaldry, and the gaiety is often tinged with nostalgia. Drama and pathos are never very far removed, and they touch each other in Ford's jealousy and Falstaff's humiliation. Thus, for a second time we find a convergence of the serious and frivolous spheres: in Verdi's tragedies the many-colored spectacle of the world is contrasted with the vehemence of passion, the better to demonstrate the ravages it can cause; in comedy good sense wins the day, and Verdi now smiles at passion's vehemence, yet the triumph is not devoid of melancholy.[85]

It is therefore not hard to understand why this work came into being so late. In 1850, if Verdi's biographer Monaldi is to be believed—that is, just when the composer wanted to add variety to his dramaturgy—Verdi's thoughts turned to comic opera, and he spoke of it often as a possibility; yet the matter was not clinched until July 1889. After the somewhat unfortunate attempt of *Un giorno di regno*, Verdi could not write his own *Don Pasquale* and was obliged to bide his time before confronting a new genre. What is more, he confessed to Monaldi that he had to wait a few dozen years before he found, with Boito's help, a work "that resembles no other," that would be a "lyric comedy" and not an opera buffa.[86] It is a work that bids farewell to a lifelong dramatic experience, taking up its principal themes but with the faintly melancholy humor of old age, an opera that, as Alfred Einstein has so aptly put it, "throws a light back over all of Verdi's previous works."[87]

* * * * * * *

All the procedures I have grouped under the heading *variety* certainly arose from Verdi's need to diversify his dramaturgy, which, as we have seen, he considered too monotonous. Yet they are by no means limited to that purpose and in many ways mark an essential step along the road to music drama. Far from signaling a lighter tone of Verdian dramaturgy, these new procedures accentuate its dark nature, for by giving his characters' passions an aura of frivolity, festivity, or pageantry he emphasizes their isolation, their excesses, and their folly. These passions now seem like the product of an illusion or weakness—moving, to be sure, but ultimately disastrous.

One further step along this road is taken through what I have called the ironic use of form. Its significance seems to me to be the following: at first, form, as a regularly recurring structure, encompasses the character and fixes its gesture completely. Form is the truth of the character. If, because of the character's complexity, the form expresses the character only partially or inadequately, or if the creator harbors doubts as to the aptness of the gesture and hence of the form best suited to define a character, form becomes merely an empty shell, seductive but deceptive. This step raises doubts as to the character's identity: what is he if he is not exactly what he seems?

The mixture of genres that the composer sought so assiduously leads to this same doubt. Commenting on Victor Hugo's claim of a union of the grotesque and the sublime, expressed in his *Preface to Cromwell* (1827), Anne Ubersfeld aptly points out that this presence of the grotesque is "the essentially humorous questioning of the unity and permanence of the self, the incoherences and inner contradictions of which, if they do not make us laugh, provoke both our smiles and our compassion."[88]

If we recall Verdi's enthusiastic description of Triboulet (Rigoletto), that "creation worthy of Shakespeare"[89] (the supreme compliment), we can see how this character, which is precisely a union of the grotesque and the sublime, must have represented a revelation of the ambiguity of the human soul. The character thus becomes an enigma, no longer the dazzling presence typical of melodrama, and in order to explore this new reality Verdi would need other instruments, tools he had patiently been perfecting.

CHAPTER SEVEN

Music Drama

Life is an anarchy of light and dark:
nothing is ever completely fulfilled in
life, nothing ever quite ends.
GEORG LUKÁCS

Gesture is the sign under which I placed the fourth chapter, "Melo-drama," because gesture possesses clarity and the power to communicate; it claims to encompass a whole life and unambiguously define a moral choice. This chapter I will place under the sign of mobility because mobil-ity conveys the variousness of reality, its richness as well as its transitory nature, its abundance but also its power to destroy gesture. For the gesture that embraces a life to the utmost soon comes to seem an illusion and a challenge, even as it conveys a demand for freedom and control. In Lu-kács's essay on Kierkegaard to which I referred earlier, the philosopher insists on the unreliability of the gesture that sums up a destiny: "But can there really be a gesture vis-à-vis life? Is it not self-delusion—however splendidly heroic—to believe that the essence of the gesture lies in an action, . . . rigid as stone and yet containing everything immutably within itself?"[1] The gesture builds "a crystal palace out of air" that resists media-tion and disregards the ambiguity of reality, only to suffer reality's de-structive power.

It is true that movement is present in melodrama, but it is present as action, that is to say in its outward form, as a concatenation of events that shatter the superb loftiness of gestures and force characters to compose others; in this way, the whirlwind bearing the characters off toward the denouement does not fundamentally impair their coherence or sculptural fixity. Little by little, this epic world where the force of gesture and the weight of reality and the law were rigidly opposed opens up to nuance, ambiguity, and contradiction, offering itself to a more detached and ironic gaze.

We can seek to understand this evolution by studying a number of developments: first, the confrontation of two characters, otherwise known as the duet, a form to which Verdi gives increasing mobility; next, on a more abstract level, the permanent conflict between two contrasting principles, the quest for movement that breaks down the self-contained, closed character of traditional forms, and the coherence of the form that resists movement's fragmenting power through a process of diversification and miniaturization (in Lukács's terms this is the dialectic of "psychology" and "monumentality"); finally, the development of the composer's melodic style, which reveals an imbalance between the lyrical stasis that freezes an attitude and the fluidity of musical speech that reveals its metamorphoses.

Dialogue

Conversation is the best means of bringing a drama to life, the best way to give it real mobility and to convey developments arising from the interrelations of the characters. On the musical level, as we have seen in the *Introduzioni* of *Rigoletto* and *Traviata,* it is also the best means of interpenetrating the musical blocks formed by the numbers and bonding them together. It was in order to introduce the vivacity of dialogue, indispensable for comedy, that eighteenth-century opera buffa adopted partly dialogical forms like the *Introduzione* and the Finale, which under Rossini would become standard practice in opera seria.

The effort to present situations in the form of dialogue can be clearly seen in certain revisions to the librettos. The very beginning of act 2 of *Macbeth,* in which, after Duncan's assassination, Lady Macbeth sees the need for another murder to ensure her power, had initially been conceived as a monologue delivered while she writes a letter to her husband counseling him to kill Banquo, his companion at arms. At first Verdi dismissed the idea of the letter; then he suggested to Piave a version in dialogue of the same scene. The change was made easier because in her monologue Lady Macbeth is in fact addressing Macbeth: thus, it was a simple matter to bring him back onstage, and the situation gained intensity because of the troubled and conflict-ridden relations between the two protagonists. Likewise, the first version of the act 2 Finale initially provided for a chorus of praise to Macbeth and his wife, which was replaced by a rapid dialogue among Macbeth, his wife, and the guests.[2] A similar change can be noted in *Alzira,* where one chorus is replaced by a "dialogue" between the chorus and the soloist.[3]

Such conversation is naturally more difficult in ensembles since there are several soloists and each one usually comments on the situation in an aside. Verdi was occasionally embarrassed by this inertia of the ensemble and tried to liven it up by introducing sections of direct exchange. For instance, while he was working on the first version of *Simon Boccanegra* in 1857, he criticized the strophes given to the characters taking part in the last Finale: "The characters never address a single word to each other, and that makes the scene cold and lacking in feeling."[4] In 1881, when he was changing the first Finale of that same opera, he asked Boito to make corrections for similar reasons: "As a rule I dislike asides because they force the artist to remain immobile; and I would like at least Amelia to [address] Fieschi."[5]

THE GRAND DUET

A true psychological confrontation is nonetheless possible only in the duet, which avoids the problem of conversation scattered among several characters. This explains its fundamental importance to Verdi and Wagner, who favored duet as a way of following the sweep of the drama, which changes depending on the relations between characters. In the solidly constructed form perfected by Rossini and further developed by Bellini and Donizetti, dialogue sections—usually concentrated in the *tempo d'attacco* and *tempo di mezzo*—most often use the flexible technique of parlante (see the glossary), to which Abramo Basevi gave a precise definition.[6] The advantage of this technique is that the voices are no longer constrained by regular melody and can move freely while the orchestra, no longer obliged to accompany a melody, has an autonomy that allows it to play a real dramatic role.

We saw in chapter 4 how Verdi continued the evolution his predecessors had begun by systematizing the opposition of characters, abandoning parallel melodies when they were not completely justified, and attempting to get around the monumental quality of the grand "Rossinian" duet by such devices as overlapping, telescoping, and lightening the baggage. I will now follow the further liberation of the form by looking at a few examples.

Let us begin with the duet of *I due Foscari* (act 1), in which I have already stressed the constant differentiation of the two characters. It is also interesting to note the way the duet is constructed: the systematic opposition of the Doge and Lucrezia stretches to the breaking point the links connecting the numbers given either party, with the result that these give the impression of being autonomous sections. For instance, Budden points out that within the usual tripartition there is a structure based on smaller sections: the *tempo d'attacco* corresponds to three sections, the Adagio to two, the cabaletta to three.[7] The interesting thing about this formula is that, without doing away with the traditional articulations, it offers a more flexible structure by means of directly linked sequences. The method is typical of Verdi, who did not want to deprive his listeners of their traditional frames of reference but at the same time wanted to give himself greater freedom to maneuver. These advantages can be clearly seen in the great Violetta-Germont duet in act 2 of *La traviata*.[8]

The duet opens with a *scena* (1) in the course of which Violetta learns that Alfredo has gone to Paris (she does not know that it is to get money as her lover has suddenly realized that his stay in the country with Violetta is putting a financial burden on her shoulders). Germont, Alfredo's father, enters and in very harsh terms reproaches Violetta for having bewitched his son and brought him to financial ruin. She tells him that it is she who is bankrupting herself so as to ensure their life together far from Paris. Germont is surprised at this generosity but nevertheless asks her to give up their love. Written in *versi sciolti,* this passage is treated as a recitative with two short orchestral commentaries and one great outburst in which Violetta haughtily asserts that her love has effaced her past way of life.

To bolster his demand for renunciation, Germont then sings an ample cantabile in A♭ major, "Pura siccome un angelo," based on twelve lines of *settenari* (2). The regular (3 × 8 measures), fluid melody has a rather pompous placidity depicting the irreproachable good conscience of a family man defending his daughter's honor; he points out that Alfredo's conduct runs the risk of compromising his sister's marriage. In a more loosely structured passage (3), to a faster tempo, Violetta understands without really understanding since she agrees to separate from Alfredo for a time; Germont becomes more pressing and explicit, provoking a cry of despair from Violetta: "Giammai, no mai." The next section in C minor/major (4), "Non sapete quale affetto," constitutes her reply to Germont's cantabile: it crystallizes Violetta's rebellion in a regular (5 × 4) but breathless melody. The melody loses its regularity when it braces itself in C major in a violent declamation that grows ever more animated, finally abandoning itself to the chaos of the cry when the voice reaches a fortissimo high B♭.

In a sort of vacuum emphasized by a long pause Germont is silenced, but he resumes the attack with a melody that quickly becomes a regular section in F minor (5), "Un dì quando le veneri." In order to convey the fragility of loves not sanctioned by society, Germont goes back to the calmly reasoned and recurring pattern of "Pura siccome un angelo." This denunciation of illicit love is answered, without a transition, by Violetta's sorrowful Db-minor passage (6), a muted, funereal version of the great love theme "Di quell'amor ch'è palpito" heard in the first act. Where the first proclaimed the universality of love, the second recalls its impossibility for the woman who has sinned. For the first time, Violetta addresses this bitter statement to herself and not to her interlocutor. In 2 and 4, the opposition of the two characters depends on Germont's melodic fluidity and Violetta's confusion; in 5 and 6, the father's staccato singing is contrasted with the young woman's unrestrained, lyrical gesture.

The Andantino "Dite alla giovane" in Eb major begun by Violetta marks the midpoint of the duet (7). After her rebellion, despair, and prostration, it has a sort of lucid resignation thanks to the extreme simplicity of the melodic line, which climbs from the mediant to the tonic in conjunct motion: Violetta agrees to sacrifice her love to the bourgeois peace and quiet of Germont's daughter. In spite of the difference in the vocal lines and modes (major for Violetta, minor for Germont), one can see the rapprochement of the two characters in the speed with which they reach a due singing: Violetta has exchanged her freedom as a "lost" woman for a "filial" subjection that causes Germont to adopt an almost "paternal" attitude.

The following section (8) concerns the question of settling the practical problems posed by Violetta's choice: how to make Alfredo accept it without his suspecting that Germont had a hand in it. The passage is handled like a *scena,* accompanied by a feverish orchestral commentary that we will hear again, in part, in the cabaletta of Germont's aria "No, non udrai rimproveri." The last section (9) matches the cabaletta of the duet and is a sort of break for Violetta: the first phrase in G minor ("Morrò! ... la mia memoria") shows a certain emphasis, extremely rare in this opera, which systematically avoids the so-called noble style; yet as soon as the music moves to Bb major we hear a profoundly melancholy phrase, "Conosca il sagrifizio," confined within a narrow range. As in the Andantino, Germont and Violetta sing together, their statements symmetrical and the vocal lines often parallel since now there is basically nothing to keep them apart. The sound of footsteps—"Qui giunge alcuno"—prevents a true reprise of the cabaletta, which merely repeats the phrase "conosca il sagrifizio," sung almost unadorned, like a sad echo.

Verdi defended the length of the duet, saying in 1855 that it was like his other duets in its "idea" but superior "as to the form and sentiment."[9]

What in fact strikes one in this duet is on the one hand the feeling of great homogeneity of inspiration: moments that are vocally essential and passages that either are informal (1) or act as "transitions" between two movements (3) are both treated equally well. On the other hand one has the impression of perfect continuity, with the music tracing Violetta's development while at the same time marking the main moments of high emotion. Concretely, this continuity is achieved by a linkage of shorter movements, which is why I have broken up the duet into small rather than large sections.

Nonetheless, critics have defended the duet's orthodoxy, that is, its conformity to the traditional mold. Harold S. Powers has analyzed it in the light of the usual subdivisions,[10] finding a *scena* (1), a *tempo d'attacco* (2, 3, 4, 5)—longer than is customary since it includes a cantabile (2) (Germont's)—a transition (3), Violetta's reply (4), a second cantabile (5) (Germont's), Violetta's reply (6), a central cantabile (7), a *tempo di mezzo* (8), and a cabaletta (9). According to this analysis, the duet follows the traditional conception of the form both on the dramatic level (two lively phases, the *scena* and the *tempo d'attacco,* two lyrical phases, the Adagio and cabaletta, separated by the rapid dialogue of the *tempo di mezzo*) and on the musical level (the three regular parts end in a more or less extended a due).

If this analysis is meant to serve as a reminder that Verdi never intended to break with *la solita forma* and the listener's customary frames of reference, it is perfectly convincing, as is Philip Gossett's polemic against those who depict a Verdi impatient to wipe out the "traditional forms."[11] However, a reminder of this loyalty to tradition should not obscure Verdi's pursuit of flexibility, achieved by the breaking up of large movements into a chain of shorter sections. The traditional structure is very clear in Gossett's analysis of the duet between Amneris and Radames in act 4 of *Aida,* whereas it is less evident in other duets in that opera.

The reason for these discrepancies has to do with the drama. In Amneris and Radames's duet we have a frozen situation capable, with slight shifts of the text, of showing at most three different sides of it (1, 2, 4): (1) Amneris reminds Radames that death awaits him because of his treason; she urges him to exculpate himself and promises to help him. Radames rejects her help, fully aware that he is condemning himself by his refusal: he does not consider himself a traitor and longs only for death *(tempo d'attacco)*. (2) In despair, Amneris confesses her love, although this has no effect on Radames's determination (Adagio). (3) In a very animated exchange, Amneris tells Radames that Aida is still alive and that he can be saved if he gives her up; the hero refuses, calling once again for death *(tempo di mezzo).* (4) Amneris then explodes with rage, and Radames repeats his claim of indifference to death and vengeance (cabaletta). This situation, where the two characters stick firmly to their respective positions, is admirably suited to the Rossinian duet presenting three aspects of a conflict that can be complicated by a sudden revelation or turn of the plot. If the situation is more fluid and concerns a character's gradual change of position, it entails a miniaturization of the principal movements, albeit within the customary framework.

This problem turns up again in the great act 2 duet between Leonora and the Padre Guardiano in *La forza del destino,* which also serves to convey a profound change of character. Leonora comes to the monastery of Madonna of the Angels; her father has been killed, her lover is gone, and she believes that if she takes refuge there she will be able to escape her father's curse and her brother's pursuit of her. She hopes to find peace with the Father Superior, who greets her affably, although somewhat sternly. She wants to exchange a terrifying father, her actual father whose shade is haunting her, for a spiritual father who can offer her protection. As in *La traviata,* a relatively static character (Germont or the Padre Guardiano) is contrasted with a character who, on contact with the "father," undergoes a slow, painful change that eventually leads in the one case to resignation and in the other to peace. Here, too, Verdi's intention was to show the gradual blossoming of a new personality, Leonora's.

We can analyze the duet in *Forza* as follows: It opens with a *scena* (1) in which Leonora meets the Father Superior. Then follows an Allegro agitato in F minor, "Infelice, delusa, rejetta," where she begs for his help (2). In a short arioso sostenuto in G major (3) he promises her the aid of faith. A long phrase from Leonora (4), "Più tranquilla l'alma sento," shows her divided between hope of regaining peace of mind and fear of the past. The Father Superior then warns her of the danger of hasty vocations (5). This first part ends in an a due in E major (6), marking a kind of pause. In a short recitative introducing the second part of the duet, the Padre Guardiano advises Leonora to enter a convent. Leonora is in despair at being refused entrance to the monastery and repeats her intention (7). A final section in F major, "È questo il porto," very quickly introducing the a due section (8), informs us that the Father Superior is at last giving in and that Leonora is emerging from her agony. The next passage (9) allows the Father Superior to assure himself that Leonora's decision is irrevocable. The concluding movement (10) in E major, "Sull'alba il piede all'eremo," winds up the episode with Leonora giving thanks to God and the Padre Guardiano making final recommendations.

Here, as in the example from *La traviata,* we can trace the major articulations of the duet: the *scena* (1), *tempo d'attacco* (2–6), central Adagio (7–8), *tempo di mezzo* (9), and cabaletta (10). The division is justified musically by the fact that the three main parts end in an ensemble a due and by the way the drama presses forward, from one vivid, contrast-filled movement toward more lyrical phases. However, what is most important is miniaturization, achieved by the accumulation of tiny sections that mark, with far greater precision, the stages of Leonora's inner journey.

This duet also offers us integration within a larger unit (the second setting of act 2) as well as admirable economy of theme. All Leonora's entries are in one way or another a continuation of her first aria, "Madre, pietosa vergine"; the physical connection is provided by a *scena,* rich in themes from the aria, that comes after it and before the aria opening the duet; the *scena* introduces the gatekeeper, Fra Melitone, who appears twice briefly during the duet. Also, at the end of the aria we hear a chorus, with organ, directly announcing the finale of the act, which follows the duet. The four numbers, aria, *scena, scena* and duet, Finale (13, 14, 15, and 16 in the 1862 score), are thus fused into one large block.

What is remarkable in this duet is its dramatic economy, that is, the practice of joining together the character's different melodic themes. The Padre Guardiano's music has a simple unity of tonality that gives all his entries the same solemn, straightforward, noble character. Leonora's melodic sphere is dominated by two great themes heard in her aria: the "destiny" theme that begins the opera (see ex. 7a above, p. 191), characterized by a vehement anacrusis and a shifting between the fifth and the minor sixth of the key, and a prayer theme, also heard in the overture, with its pattern of ascending sixths conveying fervent hope (see ex. 18 on p. 272).

The first theme, stated in the prelude to the aria "Madre, pietosa vergine," reappears in the aria's accompaniment (first section in G minor), in the embellishment of the fifth by the minor sixth (enriched with embroidery in the lower register); also, the harmonic linkage is the same and the crescendo very similar. In the duet, at 2, the voice reverses the melodic movement of the destiny theme (minor sixth, fifth, third, and tonic), while the words convey the idea of curse; at 7, the vocal line again has the double embellishment on the fifth of the key (A minor) that was already noted in the accompaniment to the aria and is taken from the elaboration of the destiny theme. Here, too, the text describes the danger that Leonora will

EX. 18

wander over hill and dale, pursued by the "force of destiny." An interesting detail is that this passage differs in the first version of 1862, where it is far less closely tied to this major theme, a sign that Verdi probably intended, and tightened, the economy of theme.

At 8, on the other hand, we have a clearly rising theme, resolute rather than actually free of anguish, that makes an excellent transition between the painful ascent of the hope theme peculiar to the aria (see ex. 18) and the jubilant serenity of the theme Leonora sings in the final cabaletta, also taken from the overture; in its unmistakable emphasis on the intervals of the perfect fourth and major sixth, this last theme tells us plainly that Leonora has at last reached port. At the point where these two poles meet, we find the phrase Leonora sings at 4, which seems to convey each of the feelings that obsess her. The voice climbs more confidently with its intervals of the fourth and the sixth (like the hope theme and the cabaletta) but fails to break loose and turns back on itself, like the destiny theme, and is then caught up and thrown into disarray by the memory of her father. Rarely has a twenty-measure melodic phrase succeeded in capturing so precisely the confusion of a soul trapped between contradictory forces. However, the revision of the 1862 version provided an opportunity to make even more fruitful use of this phrase: here, in contrast to the 1862 version, it comments on the short *scena* dividing the a due at 6 and the Andante mosso at 7.

In this duet Verdi thus achieves great structural coherence (by closely joining together the numbers of the setting) as well as thematic consistency (by linking the melodic themes as though they arose one out of the other). The technique is completely different from Wagner's, for, where the latter used themes the listener could easily recognize, combining and developing them, Verdi works by moving from one key to another, linking the keys through a hidden affinity of which the listener perceives only the overall effect. This thematic coherence doubtless was a conscious aim of Verdi's, for around this same time, in 1865, between the two versions of *La forza del destino,* he revised *Macbeth,* in particular the great act 1 duet between Lady Macbeth and her husband. Without oversimplifying, one might say that the revisions are essentially aimed, especially in the cabaletta, at reinforcing the thematic affinities of the two voices and the connections between Lady Macbeth's melody in that movement and the beginning of the Allegro.

This technique of giving the duet flexible articulation by means of short sections that can be integrated into the traditional parts reaches its climax in the love duet in *Otello.* Here, the parts or sections one can pinpoint are not so important as the perfect ease with which these different phases are joined as well as the constantly lyrical quality of the musical language: at this stage there is no need for any twist of plot, any revelation or coup de théâtre to launch a long crescendo of emotion that leads to the culminating point of the kiss and ends by dissolving into infinity.

The principle governing the development of the duet is in fact the same one Verdi followed in all areas of opera: to allow each situation to yield up its own form. Hence, he avoids systematically applying an imposed scheme, although he does not refuse one if need arises. A good example of how this principle encourages diversification is *Simon Boccanegra,* with its seven duets (in the numbering of the original version of 1857, one of these is called a *scena*). Another is *Aida,* with its six duets. If, in the case of the Amneris-Radames duet described above (act 4) or the Aida-Radames duet (act 3), we can clearly discern the traditional structure beneath the surface, elsewhere it is more difficult to perceive. Thus, the first Radames-Amneris duet (act 1) is based, after a *scena,* on a single spirited movement that also appears in the following trio with Aida. In the Amneris-Aida duet (act 2) and even more the one between Aida and Amonasro (act 3), free and formal phases are set side by side, justifying a joining by short sections. As for the final duet between Aida and Radames (act 4), one can no doubt view it as a cantabile in two sections followed by a slow cabaletta, but because of the fundamentally static nature of this moment—the two lovers' preparation for death—one is more inclined to see it as a single slow movement in three stages. In fact, the possibilities of cutting one or even two movements of the usual four, reversing the traditional dynamic, displacing the twists of plot that change the situation from one movement to the next, and expanding a movement as we have seen with the *tempo d'attacco,* all end up giving the composer great latitude.

THE DUET SCENA

What all the duets I have discussed have in common is that they are based at one moment or another on a stasis that is meditative or lyrical in character. But at times the situation is sufficiently tense to rule out these pauses and call for continuity in the dramatic confrontation. In these cases Verdi treats these moments as "scenes," with the freedom implied by the *scena* or using the relatively flexible technique of the parlante I have already described, which possessed a highly diversified structure.

In this other line of development, the Rigoletto-Sparafucile duet in act 1 marks a new epoch in every respect. Dramatically, for instance, we have noted how it "floats" between the two large blocks of the first act. Musically, this is not one of those rather free *duettini* one finds in other operas of the time but a true duet based on metrical verse, not on a mixing of meters, as is characteristic of the *scena;* yet it does not include strophes for the characters, instead reproducing the almost whispered conversation in which the assassin Sparafucile offers his services to Rigoletto. Only one part is treated as *parlante armonico* (the melody being entrusted to the orchestra while the voices weave freely in and out), and it is constructed on the ABA' pattern followed by a coda; B is treated freely, while A uses a regular sixteen-measure melody (a1 a1 b a2) partially repeated in A'.

The advantage of this use of parlante is not only that it allows the conversation to take place without restraint but also that, beyond the contrasts of the voices, it hands over to the orchestra the task of unifying the scene. This is the role of the sinuous, veiled principal theme given to a cello and muted double basses; the uniformly dark instrumentation (violas, cellos, double basses, clarinets, bassoon) reinforces this shadowy feeling.

In *La traviata* the fleeting encounter of Alfredo and Violetta (act 2, scene 6) is neither duet nor *duettino* and is labeled a *scena:* most likely Verdi did not want another duet after the grand duet with Germont. Besides, this passage could not include a lyrical stasis because of its tense, febrile quality: Violetta *must* leave because she has promised Germont that she will, and she can allow herself only a few words. Yet this is a high point of the opera, and Verdi gives it a superb emotional crescendo culminating in Violetta's explosive "Amami Alfredo," a slightly different reprise of the love theme.

The scene begins in an atmosphere of sadness and dejection as Violetta writes to Flora and prepares to write another letter to Alfredo: four measures in the traditional "death" rhythm followed by a melancholy theme for clarinet, its mournful character conveyed by stressed appoggiaturas, comment on the deadly calm Violetta is forcing on herself. Sudden starts in the orchestra warn us of Alfredo's unexpected arrival, and both characters are thrown into extreme agitation. The crescendo begins on an A-minor pedal as, in an attempt to evade her lover's questions, Violetta stammers a few words about a rosy future and a father's blessing. The melody is chopped up, disjointed, incoherent, the better to prepare for the magnificent outburst of the love theme that is intended as a farewell.

Verdi designated the great meeting of Philip II and the Inquisitor in act 4 of *Don Carlos* as a "scène" in his autograph score, but contemporary printed sources refer to it as "scène et duo" or "duetto." Here, too, the violence of the relations between the two characters precludes lyricism: rather than a meeting of equals we have a succession of invectives on the part of the Inquisitor, who is determined to bend the King's will, to make him deal firmly with his son and obtain the head of the Marquis of Posa, who has become Philip's friend. The duet therefore includes "outbursts" that are much like the movements of a conventional duet but that, unlike them, never crystallize: the A-minor arioso "Dans ce beau pays"/"Nell'ispano suol," a second arioso in E♭ major, "L'esprit des novateurs"/"Le idee dei novator," and a final explosion in B♭ minor that is as spirited as a cabaletta. Philip, crushed by the aged Inquisitor's strong personality, never achieves a true melodic utterance, and, when he expresses his discomfiture, "Pour traverser les jours"/"Per traversare i dí dolenti," it is a long descent in octaves in the orchestra, rather than his melodic line, that describes his deep-seated longing to escape the solitude of kingship. The dialogue, rendered freely and yet with constant tension, is flanked on either side by an effective theme at the beginning and close of the duet, suggesting the heavy, unsure gait of the old, blind Inquisitor: like that of Rigoletto's duet, to which it has been compared, this theme also suggests the devious maneuverings and sinister atmosphere surrounding the struggle for power.

For quite different reasons, my last example, Iago's conversation with Otello immediately following his Credo (act 2), cannot be ranked as a duet. The fact that Iago is working indirectly on Otello's suspicions regarding the possible relationship of Cassio and Desdemona, by allusions and hints, precludes any regular melody (which Verdi in any case scrupulously avoided for this character, except when he is dissembling). The

EX. 19

dialogue therefore has the complete freedom of a half-spoken conversation, and only Otello briefly comes close to melodic movement, in a short arioso described earlier (see ex. 10 above, p. 212).

Nonetheless, the coherence of this scene is ensured by the use throughout of a melodic motif (*x* in ex. 19) that is given various forms: characteristically, it has a narrow range (a minor third) and an easily recognizable rhythm: ♪♪♪ ♪. Small and cunning, the motif is actually highly ambiguous since it can be by turns amiable and threatening. It appears in the first act when Iago tells Roderigo he thinks it stupid to drown oneself "per amor di donna." It turns up again, in the same act, when Iago describes to Montano how Cassio has taken to drink ("Ogni notte in tal guisa"), whereas he was the one who made Cassio drink; here the phrase is clearly associated with Iago's malice. It leaves its stamp on the prelude to act 2, where it is repeated eight times alone, then linked to an elegant, almost affected figure (see ex. 19).

Later, the phrase forms the menacing prelude of Iago's Credo, where it recurs several times, transposed up a semitone, both in its complete form and reduced to a rhythm. At Otello's entrance it seems to vanish, as though Iago were donning a mask to face the general, but even here one is struck by the frequency with which Verdi makes use of the motif's characteristic minor third, either ascending or descending as well as filled in. It first appears in the accompaniment to the dialogue with Cassio ("Non ti crucciar . . . tu dêi saper, del nostro Duce, pregala tu"), recurring increasingly in the dialogue with Otello (see, e.g., the comments of the cellos and bassoons beneath "Nol credi onesto?"). The meaning of this furtive, insinuating presence becomes apparent when Iago explicitly speaks of jealousy in a phrase, "È un'idra fosca, livida," that the whole orchestra underlines in parallel octaves, and that juxtaposes two minor thirds (F♯-G♯-A and E-D-C♯). No better description can be imagined of

the delicate, suffocating web Iago is weaving to imprison Otello: the insidious nature of jealousy and the ensign's devious nature are merged in a
single formula.[12]

Form and Movement

In chapter 4 I described the difficulty composers sometimes had in combining form, as musical structure, and movement, as a dramatic dynamic.
We also saw how Verdi used various procedures to achieve two aims: to
avoid the slowing down of the drama that could result from the full-scale
deployment of a musical form and to reconcile the principle of action,
involving movement, with those of tension and contrast, which involve
the temporary suspension of action in order to reveal most vividly the
clarity of the fixed and often sharply contrasted affects.

In his early operas Verdi kept his eye riveted on dramatic movement,
but, challenged around the middle of the century by complex, elusive
works like *Lear,* he realized that he did not want to sacrifice lyrical formalization. After attempting to introduce forward movement into form,
he tried to preserve form in movement. This search for a balance between
two poles, stressing first one, then the other, resembles Verdi's approach
to conventions, which he rejected when they seemed all-powerful and
defended when they were being attacked on all sides. It may perhaps also
be a trait of the Italian tradition constantly to seek compromise between
those factors tending toward movement and continuity and those tending
toward formal regularity and tonal structure. Although Scott Balthazar
has suggested that opera from Rossini to the young Verdi incontestably
strives for the greatest dramatic continuity, it is also true that the growing
importance of "kinetic" phases *(tempo d'attacco* and *tempo di mezzo)* in
relation to those of a static nature is neutralized by Verdi's tendency to
build these kinetic sections into tonally and melodically stable movements, thus reducing their dynamic potential.

THE DEVELOPMENT OF THE SCENA

During the period under consideration, the term *scena* referred to the
introductory section of an aria or ensemble, generally written in unrhymed lines of seven and eleven syllables and not calling for regularity
of melody. Any aria that seemed unorthodox tended to be labeled *scena,*
as Bellini titled Elvira's mad aria in *I Puritani.*[13] Yet the very ambiguity

of the word, which has a general meaning peculiar to the theater and at the same time suggests metrical and musical choices, can lead to the idea of a larger unit embracing both the actual *scena* and an aria or ensemble. When Bellini used the word *scena* to describe the final scene of *Il pirata,* which includes Imogene's aria, he was suggesting not so much some irregularity of form as a desire to represent *all* the elements of the scene as parts of a single unit. He is telling us that the *scena* is no less important than the aria proper.

There was thus a trend toward homogeneity of musical treatment in spite of the diversity of procedures employed: a blend was created between the various movements of the musical number through the extension of the *scena* with its greater purely musical quality, bringing it to the same level as the aria or ensemble and making for greater dramatic continuity. This rapprochement had a precedent in French tragic opera, which sought to avoid breaks between the recitative and the aria, to the point where commentators repeatedly stressed how difficult it was to see any difference between them.[14] On the other hand French Romantic opera, whose development was greatly influenced by the Italian, for a time made a cleaner distinction between *scena* and aria.

Speaking generally, the *scena* (in this broader sense) is linked to the passage following it in the same number (scene and aria, scene and duet); there are few autonomous scenes.[15] *Macbeth* marks a milestone because (in the original version of 1847) it contains three autonomous episodes designated by the term *scena,* whether or not they include a formally structured piece. Thus, we have the *gran scena,* in which Banquo and his son enter the park where he, Banquo, will be assassinated (including the cantabile "Come dal ciel precipita"); the *gran scena delle apparizioni,* which describes the ghosts of the English kings in procession and contains the predictions made to Macbeth; and, finally, the *gran scena del sonnambulismo,* or sleepwalking scene. Two of these scenes at least (the apparitions and sleepwalking scenes) are of central importance in the organization of the opera.

Even in the classic case where the *scena* introduces a number, it can have no less importance than the set piece that follows. For example, the *gran scena* just before the duet between Macbeth and his wife in act 1 matches the monologue "Mi si affaccia un pugnale" in which Macbeth, in his fear and anguish, decides to murder Duncan, his king. He thereupon disappears into the King's bedchamber, and Lady Macbeth enters; not until Macbeth emerges does the actual duet begin ("Fatal mia donna"). It is in this monologue that Macbeth begins his descent to hell, and the writing is especially taut and intense; here, Verdi truly seeks a dark, veiled kind of style.

That the description *gran scena* can denote not merely an extended *scena* but, especially, the composer's wish that the aria be promoted to a single, greater unit comprising both the *scena* and the aria is demonstrated by the thematic affinities connecting *scena* and aria in the sleepwalking scene. The intervals of the semitone and minor third, the brilliant passages on diminished triads, the repeated fast, light notes, the chromatic passages—all these devices dominate the *scena* and at the same time connect it with the rest of the opera, where some of these techniques play a major role. Thus, when the actual aria "Una macchia è qui tuttora" begins, the orchestral accompaniment, where all these techniques are combined, is perceived not as a routine accompaniment but as the continuation of a symphonic discourse that began with the opening measures of the *scena*.

With the confidence born of experience, Verdi could then use the *scena* as the vehicle to describe a leading character. For instance, in *La battaglia di Legnano,* the *scena* just before the Rolando-Lida *duettino* "Digli ch'è sangue italico" describes the heroine's distress far more effectively than the preceding solos. Parlato, recitative, vehement declamation, cantabile, and arioso, vocal outbursts and a varied orchestral commentary, all lend intensity to this scene, in which for a brief moment Lida seems to foreshadow Verdi's great tragic heroines—Violetta, Amelia, Elisabeth de Valois, and Aida. Yet the best example of this upgrading of the *scena* is found in *Rigoletto.* Throughout the opera, the title role has only one aria, in the second act. His fatherly feelings can be felt in his duets with Gilda, but the depths of his bitter, tormented nature are entrusted to an extremely intense monologue just before he enters his house (act 1). Likewise, in the second act, when Rigoletto comes to court looking for his daughter, whom the courtiers have abducted, his search is depicted by a *scena* treated as a parlante. It is based on an E-minor theme that has enough ambiguity to convey the jester's falsely carefree manner (he chatters in a playful tone), his tension as he watches for any clue as to his daughter's whereabouts, and his suspicion of the courtiers, all of whom he regards as accomplices. When he becomes convinced that his daughter is at the palace and that everybody knows it, he explodes and hurls curses on the courtiers, and the aria proper begins.

The next stage in this development comes when the barriers between the *scena* and the aria collapse, even if they can still be discerned by analysis—the point at which the aria can appear to be a part of the *scena* rather than the *scena* appearing to be a preparation for the aria. This effect of a brief lyrical pause in the midst of a larger dramatic scene can be heard in Amelia's aria "Ma dall'arido stelo" in act 2 of *Ballo*. Amelia sings for only twelve measures before the melody is handed over to the orchestra, the voice accompanying in parlante; there is no cabaletta. The moment when Amelia thinks sadly of the emptiness that would afflict her heart if she gave up her love for Riccardo affords only a brief respite; this is a violently dramatic prelude and scene colored by the fear evoked by the gloom of her surroundings and the anguish of renunciation.

From *Ballo* on, all the great moments devoted to a character are based on an ever flexible, varied combination of *scena* and "aria." Let us take as an example Aida's act 1 aria (called *scena* in the original score), in which she describes herself as tortured by a conflict between her love for the Egyptian general, Radames, and her loyalty to her people, the Egyptians' enemies. There are five sections:

1. "*Ritorna vincitor.*" In this section of ten lines of seven and eleven syllables, Aida realizes that she has blasphemed by hoping that the Egyptians will be victorious over the Ethiopians. This passage is clearly treated as recitative.

2. "*L'insana parola.*" This is an arioso in E minor of four by four measures (six lines of *senari*). In a violently declamatory tone, Aida begs the gods to destroy the Egyptian army. A brutal four-measure transition (Aida is alarmed at her own violence) leads to the next section.

3. "*E l'amor mio.*" We are in the spirit of the *scena* again (eight lines of seven and eleven syllables), but by singing for the first time her identifying theme, which up to now has been left to the orchestra, Aida takes us into a more lyrical atmosphere: she realizes that by wishing victory for her own people she is hoping for the death of her lover.

4. "*I sacri nomi di padre.*" The regular (4 × 4 measures) A♭-minor melody resembles the first section of a romanza even though the text is still in lines of seven and eleven syllables: Aida realizes that her situation is hopeless.

5. "*Numi pietà.*" The melody, in A♭ major, remains regular (8 + 8 + 10 and coda), as befits the second part of a romanza, but the meter changes (four lines of *quinari doppi*): Aida asks the gods to have pity on her suffering.

It is easy to trace here the minor/major scheme of a romanza (4 and 5) preceded by a long *scena* (1 and 3), including an arioso (2). What ensures the unity of this passage is the homogeneity of the melodic style, which, although suggesting different emotions—anger, despair, prostration—

never departs from the tone of a great tragic monologue founded on an insoluble inner conflict. As a result, the change to melodic regularity does not give the impression of a rift between the dramatic situation and lyrical effusion. It is a confirmation that the "aria" is integrated into the *scena* conceived as an entity.

THE RESISTANCE OF FORM

We have seen how Verdi's evolution did not tend in the direction of "musical prose," which under the pressure of the drama would have shattered the traditional forms to ensure total continuity of the action. The composer never abandoned closed forms insofar as they fix a moment or "situation" conventionally because he never wanted to give up the clarity of gesture on which form is based. What we do find, on the other hand, are shifts of balance between the two poles of forward movement and lyrical stasis. For example, the aria, a bastion of convention, loses its monumentality in favor of the flexibility of the *scena,* while the Finale, at first distinguished by its dynamic rush toward the frenzy of the Stretta, grows ever broader, moving in the direction of a giant choral frieze.

Verdi's early operas show a tendency to upset the traditional forms lest they stand in the way of dramatic momentum. But, inversely, the composer would occasionally stress their monumentality, stretching them out into huge structures as in *Giovanna d'Arco* and *Attila* (see, e.g., Odabella's cavatina "Allor che i forti corrono" in the prologue to *Attila*). It is as though, alarmed by his own frenetic pace, the composer were restraining himself by striving for vast sonorous architectures. Between *Macbeth* and *Rigoletto* Verdi seems to have reached a maturity in his relation to form that led him to a double path: miniaturization and diversification.

Miniaturization consists in retaining the *pezzo chiuso,* the closed number, insofar as it "freezes" a moment, but making it lighter lest it hinder the unfolding of the action. The lightening of heavy forms, the excision of customary linkages, and the superimposition that we have already examined are all forms of miniaturization, as are the fragmentation of duet movements and the integration of arioso melody into a larger scene. In the late operas we find a striking example of this miniaturization, which retains the spirit of a closed form while owing nothing to any traditional arrangement. Otello's entrance "Esultate" is constructed like an extremely short solo—twelve measures that develop a phrase made up of unequal segments, with no reprise or symmetry—yet it still has the value of an aria, its position, panache, and heroic connotation. By contrast, Falstaff's aria "Quand'ero paggio del duca di Norfolk" is perfectly regular (a1 b a2 over 3 × 8 measures), but it lasts scarcely more than a minute (in old recordings the singer, frustrated by its brevity, would repeat it two or three times).

Diversification was manifestly a constant concern for Verdi, who, when writing to his librettists, never stopped calling for new, "bizarre," or "bold" forms. Alongside forms he had inherited, he developed others that were less current or belonged to other traditions. For instance, the strophic form, rare in his first works (but very common in French Romantic and comic opera), is more widely used from the time of *Luisa Miller*, with Rodolfo's aria "Quando le sere al placido": examples are the Duke's ballata and song in *Rigoletto*, the Andantes of Violetta's arias in the first and last acts of *La traviata*, Hélène's sicilienne and Henri's *mélodie* in *Vêpres*, Eboli's Veil Song and Elisabeth's romanza in *Don Carlos*, and so on. The dramatic importance of this form is obvious: it is employed in settings that would in any case call for a song (Iago's drinking song in *Otello*, the Veil Song in *Don Carlos*) or for storytelling (Ferrando's tale in *Il trovatore*) or else to express simple, elegiac feelings (e.g., nostalgia for past happiness in *Luisa Miller*) or a young woman's musings about her girlhood dreams (Violetta's "Ah fors'è lui"). Hence, the form is usually marked by a simple melodic style, with frequent repetition of melodic segments (a a vs. a1 a2), as in the Andante of Violetta's "Ah fors'è lui," which is based on the scheme a a b c c. It is a sign of a break away from a uniformly heroic tone and the quest for a more intimate style.

More ambitious is the French form of the ABA′ type, which consists of two regular sections wrapped around a freer middle section. This form appears in *Battaglia* in Rolando's romanza "Ah m'abbraccia d'esultanza," which follows the a1 a2 b a1 a2 scheme. Given prominence in the French operas, as in Procida's aria "Et toi Palerme" and Montfort's "Au sein de la puissance" in *Vêpres* or Elisabeth's act 5 aria in *Don Carlos*, it also appears in such Italian works as *Simon Boccanegra* (Amelia's aria in the first act). The finest example, Elisabeth's aria (which in fact is described as a *scène* in the various scores), demonstrates the dramatic advantages Verdi drew from this method of presenting an aria.

Elisabeth, wife of Philip II, comes at night to the monastery of St.-Just for a last rendezvous with her son-in-law and former fiancé, the Infante Carlos. But first she engages in a long meditation before the tomb of Charles V, to whom she addresses her aria. Her situation as Queen of Spain compels her to forget her love; her despair and the presence of the tomb fill her with gloomy thoughts, as does the monastery, where, three acts earlier, the monks chanted of the vanity of this world (on the theme that dominates the prelude to this aria). Still, Elisabeth cannot help being touched by the memory of past happiness, without, however, being able to overcome her desire to find peace in death.

While the libretto describes this situation in six strophes of alexandrines rhymed a a b b (with the last strophe repeating the first), the music completely overrides the monotonous metrical presentation. The first section (A), "Toi qui sus le néant"/"Tu che la vanità," consists of 5×4 measures on the scheme $a1$ $a2$ b $c1$ $c2$, using the minor-major shift peculiar to the romanza. It is a solemn invocation to the dead emperor, to whom Elisabeth confesses her suffering (strophe 1). The middle section (B) begins to enliven the gloomy, frozen landscape evoked in the prelude and the aria's opening section: the Queen's thoughts turn to her imminent meeting with Carlos (strophe 2), her homeland, France, and her betrothal to the Infante (strophe 3), then to Spain and again Carlos (strophe 4); finally, she bids farewell to her youth (strophe 5). This section is treated freely, alternating between recitative and parlante, but the importance of nostalgia justifies the orchestra's recollection of previously heard themes that constitute Elisabeth's emotional memory. Finally, section A is repeated in its entirety (with variations in the accompaniment): Elisabeth closes the parenthesis of memory and returns to her thoughts of death. Thus, the solid framework of two regular sections encloses within it one long section that has the freedom of the *scène*.

If one compares this scene with Aida's "Ritorna vincitor," described above, one can see how Verdi was able to reach his long-sought ideal, that the dramatic situation create its own form. Elisabeth's destiny is at stake, and now nothing more can rescue her from the inner death represented by the loss of all her hopes. Thus, a whiff of nostalgia, a moment of weakness, a return to a buried past, are locked, as in a clamp, by two more regular sections. Aida's destiny is more fluid and contradictory since she is being tossed from one extreme to the other in search of an unattainable balance, finally finding the sorrowful peace that the last part of her aria conveys in a beautiful expansion of the melody—whence the very different structure already summed up above.

The point of this formal diversification is therefore to establish, as often as possible, a musical form pertinent to the dramatic situation. This aptness is rarely achieved in the early operas owing to the limited number of forms used and because Verdi employed rather inflexible models of melodic segmentation. One of the first arias in which form has the power to characterize is the sleepwalking scene in *Macbeth* (dating from the first version of 1847). This is because, despite a regular structure, the links to the preceding *scena* and the skillful connections between the sections give the feeling of an uninterrupted cantilena that is both changing and monotonous, and because the melodic structure varies between brief, taut gestures and more broadly declamatory passages, always circling around the same neurotic abyss—the bloodstain that nothing will wash away.

From around 1850 on, form began to play an essential role in defining a character. In *Rigoletto,* each character is laid out in a different way: the Duke's numbers—a strophic ballata in the first act, a strophic song in the last, a double aria in the second—have an ironically conventional air about them, as befits a character lacking in mystery; Gilda's first aria, "Caro nome," is variegated in form, with many ornaments and trills to suggest an innocent, somewhat dreamy young girl; "Tutte le feste al tempio" (which, although integrated in the duet with Rigoletto, can be understood as a solo) creates the impression of an invented popular ballata, narrative in character, that clings to a basic innocence that will be shattered in the third act. As for Rigoletto, his presentation is, as we have seen, mostly given in *scene;* his one aria, in act 2, is totally atypical with its three "panels," an invective in C minor, an arioso in F minor, and a lyrical section in Db major.

From that point on, simply seeing the way an aria is organized gives an indication of the character and his or her state of mind: there is a huge distance between Radames's limpid romanza "Celeste Aida" and Aida's tormented "Ritorna vincitor." In *Forza,* Leonora is given three arias—a romanza in the first act, an aria in the second, and a *mélodie* in the fourth—three differently structured solos matching three situations that have nothing in common.

BLENDING

Transitions

One of the weak points of Italian opera is the blatant quality of the articulations announcing the beginning or end of a number. The fact that a cadence may have served to make the spectator pay more attention by signaling the end of the recitative or encouraged him to applaud at the end of an aria in no way excuses its often mechanical character. (Allowing for untimely applause may in fact explain the often rough quality of final cadences in the operas of the *Primo Ottocento.*) One of Verdi's first concerns was to disguise these "transition" areas so as to smooth the way for a more important scene. Consider, for example, the graceful way the

Duke's ballad rises out of the *Introduzione* of *Rigoletto:* a pedal on E♭ serves as a pivot to move from that key to A♭, the tonality of the ballad; during the ensuing conversation the *banda* gives way to the orchestra, the meter changes from a rather bland C to the swaying elegance of $\frac{6}{8}$, the E♭s shed their rough acciaccaturas, and, before anyone notices it, the aria has begun in an entirely different musical atmosphere. In the same way, the final A♭-major chord becomes the first chord of the minuet for the Duke and the Countess Ceprano.[16]

Also in *Rigoletto,* the so-called storm trio in act 3 begins in a way that is both unexpected and prepared—with a rhythmic crescendo leading to a dominant pedal that is not resolved until the first note of the trio. The storm divides the exposition from the reprise, and, with the latter, the final cadence is swallowed up by the storm at its height. In contrast, shortly before that, everything conspires to put in relief the Duke's song "La donna è mobile" since it is quite alien to the dark atmosphere of the act: the dominant chord followed by a long pause, then a second pause after the orchestral ritornello. The song having produced its surprise effect, Verdi blends the coda into the conversation between Sparafucile and Rigoletto. A final example taken from the same opera is Rigoletto's act 2 aria: if one compares this with a fairly similar example like Nabucco's aria from the Finale of act 2, one can see that in the latter the various sections are placed end to end, whereas in Rigoletto's aria they are fused through a recurring rhythmic figure of sixteenth-note sextuplets that ensures continuity.

Occasionally a phrase will lose its regular pacing, the accompaniment its regularity, and the aria or ensemble will gently glide into a *scena.* The final trio of act 3 of *La battaglia di Legnano* makes use of this procedure to describe the violent conflict between the three characters. The first movement, "Ah! d'un consorte o perfidi," disappears into the *scena* after Rolando's curse; the third movement, "Ah Rolando! il ciel ne attesto," no longer a trio now that Rolando has left the stage, is dissolved when Arrigo's pleading ends since the far-off sound of the approaching Company of Death leaves the characters no chance to end their cabaletta quietly. Likewise, in *Otello* Iago's drinking song (act 1), three couplets with refrain, is not allowed to continue smoothly on its way: the third couplet is interrupted by the increasing tipsiness of Cassio, whom Iago has tricked into getting drunk. These examples, like the counterexample of the Duke's song in *Rigoletto,* show that Verdi had to modulate the links between a "closed form" and the scenes before and after, depending on whether he wanted the effect of contrast or continuity.

Action within the Form

Arias and ensembles having traditionally been justified as providing moments of meditation outside the plot, composers from Rossini to Verdi strove to allow these forms to move the action along by means other than the *scena*. When, around the time of *Don Carlos* (1867), Verdi found himself accused of Wagnerism, he replied by quoting *Ernani* and *Macbeth*, singling out the final trio of the former as the source of a style used to the full in the later French opera.[17] The foundation of this defense is probably that the *Ernani* ensemble develops a dramatic conflict rather than pausing for an outpouring of pure emotion.

The situation at the start of this ensemble is highly dramatic. The aged Silva had wished to marry Elvira, his niece and ward, but she prefers Ernani; because of a pact of honor, Ernani had formerly given his feudal lord the right of life and death over him; now, on the lovers' wedding day, Silva comes to claim his due and savor his revenge. The trio "sings" throughout, their "singing" carried on a rocking $\frac{9}{8}$ rhythm, and each character is given a different vocal profile: vehement or pleading for Elvira, rebellious or resigned for Ernani, harsh and angular for Silva. Yet what strikes one is the trio's continuous melodic and tonal mobility and the ever-changing relations between the characters. What we have is actually a kind of negotiation—Elvira begs, waxes indignant and angry, Ernani is frozen in despair but, knowing rebellion is useless, tries at the same time to calm Elvira, while at every turn the surly Silva refuses to budge.

Twenty years later, during the laborious reworking of the denouement of *La forza del destino*, Achille de Lauzières suggested that Verdi end the work with a trio, but Verdi turned him down: "De Lauzières wanted to do a trio like the one in *Ernani*. But in *Ernani* the action continues during the entire trio, while here the action stops at the very moment the trio begins. Therefore it is of no use."[18] Yet *Forza* does end with a trio, one that includes the same voices as in *Ernani*: tenor, soprano, and bass. Leonora dies in her lover's arms—not before feverishly urging Alvaro to accept destiny, not before the Padre Guardiano has convinced the hero to give up his bitterness against God and Alvaro, tempted by rebellion, has finally bowed his head, transfigured by Leonora's serenity. Throughout, the action continues as dialogue and interaction between the characters.

Imbrications

One of the aims of Verdi's evolution was to try to make simultaneous what at first was in sequence, to superimpose what at first had been juxta-

posed. For instance, in the first act of *I Lombardi,* Verdi blends four contrasting emotional levels: the religious tone of a nuns' chorus, the impassioned fury of Pagano ("Sciagurata! hai tu creduto," the Andante of
Pagano's aria), the bloodthirsty determination of Pagano's hired assassins,
and Pagano's spirit of revenge (his cabaletta "O speranza di vendetta").
These elements are successive, the intercontamination, so to speak, practically nil. When similar contrasting elements reappear in the Finale 2 of
Trovatore, one notices first that the rather crude colors of *I Lombardi* have
been softened, making for quite a Mozartian lightness. Next one notices
that the levels have fused together: the assassins' rapid, furtive musical
entries contrast with the Count de Luna's passionate bravery and the calm
voices of the nuns, all mingled in the final concertato.

In this device is striking in the revision of the act 4 quartet of *Don Carlos*
between the first version (1867) and that of 1884. The second version,
which is slightly shorter (forty-six measures as against fifty-five), loses far
less time before mixing the voices, but the dramatic situation is the same.
Philip II has been abusing his wife out of jealousy, and he rebukes himself
for his rage; Rodrigue, the Marquis of Posa, comes to urge him to act
quickly to save the Infante and his ideals; Eboli, who has encouraged the
King's jealousy, sees the disastrous results of her intrigues; finally, Elisabeth, who has fainted, regains consciousness during the quartet and sings
of her distress as an unjustly suspected wife.

In the 1867 version, Philip II begins alone on a twisting, somber theme
(low strings, bassoons, timpani) and curses his suspicious nature (twelve
measures); he is followed by Rodrigue, alone (five measures), who tells
himself in a staccato style that he "must act," then by Eboli (six measures),
accompanied by Rodrigue and Philip. Finally, it is Elisabeth's turn (nine
measures); her sorrowful song is barely punctuated by Eboli. Four measures end this number, which is followed by a concluding phase in which
all four characters sing together.

The 1884 version includes undeniable improvements of detail. Eboli is
not so lyrical and more overcome as she expresses her remorse; the ensemble section is lighter; and, finally, Verdi makes more skillful use of Philip's
long, beautiful phrase conveying his melancholy grandeur (first presented
by the orchestra, it is repeated by Philip shortly after on "Non, la fierté
de cette femme"/"No, non macchiò la fe' giurata"), with the result that it
becomes the backbone of the whole quartet. What is important here is
that the presentation is much less meditative: Philip's solo goes from
twelve to eight measures, Eboli entering in the fifth, with chromatic sighs.
Rodrigue begins alone but is joined at the third measure by Eboli and

Philip, while Elisabeth's entrance is virtually unchanged. Fourteen measures thus suffice to present the characters, as against twenty-two in the first version. Clearly, Verdi was striving for a greater synthesis of vision in the situation.

If the aim was to "continue the action" in the course of an ensemble, without, however, sacrificing opera's lyrical dimension, a way had to be found to fuse the styles of dramatic dialogue and lyrical effusion, without letting one level damage the other. The duet in the first act of *Aida* presents a tense conversation, full of insinuation, during which Amneris interrogates Radames, whom she suspects of having a secret love, while he tries to conceal his passion for Aida. Treated as a parlante, the passage is supported by the regular development of a highly strung, vehement theme associated with Amneris's jealousy; both characters are given very brief musical entries. Enter Aida, quite unaware of the tension in the air, and the duet turns into a trio consisting of three asides: Amneris's suspicions, always on the same E-minor theme, crystallize and fasten on the slave girl, while Radames grows more and more fearful. In a counterpoint to this theme Aida deploys an intensely lyrical, ample phrase (16 + 20 + 11 measures) that is in complete contrast to the nervous interpolations of the other two characters.

The same technique can be seen in the quartet in act 2 of *Otello*. Unity is ensured by Desdemona's long, sinuous melodic line, which is spun from one end to the other, without once turning back or repeating itself, and is marked by the gentle expressiveness characteristic of the role. Realizing that her husband is troubled, she is sweetly submissive, inviting him to the consolations of love. Otello, declamatory and vehement, wonders if it is his age, his color, or his rough warrior's nature that is the cause of his adversity. Contrasting with both these vocal lines, the one lyrical, the other dramatic, is the animated argument between Iago and his wife, Emilia. In spite of her resistance, Iago insists on snatching Desdemona's handkerchief, which his wife had picked up from the floor; essentially, the exchanges consist of short sixteenth-note interpolations ("sospetto insano / dammi quel vel / né mi paventi . . . "), to the extent that, but for the gathering tension, one might imagine one was watching an opera buffa.

Moreover, this overlapping technique is employed here with consummate artistry; the composer kills several birds with one stone, mixing together Iago's drinking song and his sinister plots, Desdemona's extreme sweetness and the ensign's treacherous insinuations, Cassio's banter and Otello's ragings, Iago's fleeting triumph as he tramples the writhing Moor, and the offstage chorus acclaiming their great general.

TO RUN OR TO SING

The composer constantly had to decide whether, as Verdi put it, to run or to sing, to capture the movement of the drama or to suspend it for a lyrical pause. A few specific examples will show just how difficult these choices could be. The first concerns the Finale 2 of *Il trovatore*. Believing Manrico dead, Leonora decides to enter a convent; the Count de Luna, her unlucky suitor, sees that he now faces a more powerful obstacle than his former rival—the church!—and decides to carry off Leonora before she can take her vows. But Manrico is not dead and suddenly rushes in, to everyone's amazement. Seeing himself surrounded, the Count is unable to retaliate and watches, furious, as the troubadour leaves with Leonora.

Cammarano suggested breaking up this episode as follows:[19] (1) de Luna's aria, probably a romanza; (2) nuns' chorus; (3) entrance of Leonora, who is preparing to take the veil when the Count arrives, followed almost immediately by Manrico; (4) general astonishment, a concertato with soloists and chorus, the traditional stupefaction ensemble; (5) *tempo di mezzo,* during which Ruiz enters to announce that the military situation is turning in Manrico's favor and the Count yields; (6) a vehement Stretta, in which each character comments on the situation.

This is a classic Finale, but the coup de théâtre of Manrico's sudden appearance—on which Verdi insisted—is suspended by two consecutive ensembles. So a second version was proposed: (1) no aria for de Luna; (2) nuns' chorus; (3) short trio between the praying Leonora, the Count, intent on abducting her, and Manrico, still hidden, who is overjoyed to have arrived in the nick of time; (4) a scene in which Leonora comes forward and Manrico reveals himself and carries her off without giving de Luna time to react. This time the exploitation of the situation is somewhat rough, and Verdi most probably did not approve of the trio, which spoils the effect of the hero's sudden appearance.

We then come to the definitive solution: (1) Count's aria, with Andante, cabaletta, and soldiers' chorus (reintroducing a solo for de Luna—even expanding it into a complete aria—actually meets the demands of general concision since this is his first aria in the opera); (2) nuns' chorus, mixed with that of soldiers; (3) Leonora's arrival, the attempted abduction, the appearance of Manrico; (4) general concertato; (5) final scene in which Manrico leaves without a fight on the part of the Count. Verdi has thus rejected an orthodox version of the Finale (in Cammarano's first proposal), and he has also rejected a draconian condensation, instead opting for a middle path that reduces the Finale's usual two movements to one. The change was made all the easier because, as Verdi stressed, the concertato is midway between the spirit of the Largo and that of the Stretta.[20]

The Finale of act 4 of *Don Carlos* caused Verdi problems when he again took up the opera in 1882. It was a necessary stage in the plot but did not call for the ample development the composer had given it in the original version. How to treat it? Briefly, as a scene rushing to its conclusion? But then the episode would lose its spectacular dimension, which obviously attracted Verdi, as well the "situations" freely developed by the music.[21]

Let us sum up the Finale, recalling briefly the ample treatment Verdi had given its various elements in the first version (DC1) and the changes made in the Milan version of 1884 (DC2). The infante Carlos has been put in prison by his father; convinced that his trust has been abused, that his son is in fact innocent and that Rodrigue alone is to blame, Philip II comes to set him free. Carlos receives him angrily, telling him that Rodrigue deflected suspicion onto himself so as to save the King's son. DC1 treats this passage in sixty-six measures, with a long, heroic invective from Carlos, "De ce mort le sang a rejailli jusqu'à votre visage"; DC2 makes it only a brief outburst of eighteen measures. Philip is astounded since he had sensed Posa's integrity and generosity but has now turned him over to the Inquisition. DC1 here has an ensemble, "Qui me rendra ce mort," of fifty-eight measures, for Philip, Carlos, and the courtiers; the piece was cut before the first performance and so does not occur in DC2, perhaps because Verdi had used its main theme for the Lacrymosa of his *Requiem;* instead, only four measures are used to describe the King's regrets.

At this point a tocsin sounds, and a rebellion is announced: the people, urged on by Eboli, who is still in love with Carlos, are coming to free him; the King orders the gates to be opened to the crowd and boldly faces the rebels. This confrontation is given full treatment in DC1: 134 measures, reduced to fifty-eight for DC2; however, part of the rebellion was cut even before the first performance. The revolt is not quelled until the Grand Inquisitor appears, ordering the people to prostrate themselves before their King: the Inquisitor's entrance is hardly changed, going from forty-six to forty-three measures.

It is obvious that the double confrontation between the crowd and the King, then the crowd and the Inquisitor, was redundant and that Verdi preferred practically to eliminate the first confrontation so that the second would have greater impact. We thus go from a massive Finale to one fast, animated scene. Moreover, *Don Carlos* is an opera marked throughout by this same oscillation between French ceremonial spectacle and Italian concision, which explains the coexistence of several versions that revise but never quite replace each other.

The most interesting case is the third act Finale of *Otello*. In Boito's initial plan it was treated in traditional fashion:[22] Otello abuses and humiliates Desdemona, after which a great concertato describes the characters' reactions. This plan did not satisfy Verdi since the action unfolds *before* the ensemble, which immediately becomes static. The librettist found an elegant solution, suggesting that the Finale be organized around two poles, a lyrical pole centered on Desdemona, her suffering, and the compassion of the other characters, and a dramatic pole in the person of Iago. The latter sees his plans thwarted by Otello's recall to Venice and Cassio's nomination in his place: he must act quickly to precipitate the catastrophe, encourage the Moor to hasten his revenge, and make Roderigo get rid of Cassio.

The idea was brilliant, but realizing it was another matter. Verdi had given the lyrical part such a sweep that the dramatic side suffered and Iago's musical entries did not stand out clearly. Well after the first performance, this Finale continued to torment him. He suggested paring down the orchestra, grouping the choruses, and distancing them to give Iago prominence. A few days later he wrote: "Here too we can't achieve theatrical truth or effect unless we succeed in completely isolating Iago so that the eyes of the public are focused on him alone; so that his words, not his voice, dominate the entire scene. And underneath there must be a vague, indistinct noise, a wrong noise, if you will. Yes, wrong! This word makes a musician's hair stand on end, but that doesn't matter."[23] When the opera opened in Paris in 1894, Verdi finally had an opportunity to find a solution to his problems.

The 1894 Finale[24] is of approximately the same duration as that of 1887, although it is some twenty measures shorter on the page. Its chief interest is that it lets the character of Iago stand out prominently. The introduction of the 1887 Finale gave Desdemona a twenty-five-measure solo, "A terra! . . . sì . . . nel livido fango," which is followed by an a cappella quartet (Emilia, Cassio, Roderigo, Lodovico) and Desdemona's reprise of a phrase accompanied by the chorus and soloists. During these thirty-seven measures Iago and Otello are silent. In 1894, Desdemona's solo is modified and shortened and the a cappella quartet excised, saving twenty measures and allowing Iago to enter the ensemble much sooner. Furthermore, in the 1887 version, Iago's words can scarcely be heard against the dense choral background, whereas, in 1894, the lighter scoring of this middle section makes them far easier to apprehend. The concluding section (m. 72) begins, in 1887, with a reexposition of the introductory theme of the Finale, sung by the chorus and underlined by bursts of cornets and trumpets. In 1894, this is sung by Iago, whereas, in 1887, his voice was merged with the massed voices; here, he keeps the spotlight and, after expelling his poison first on Otello, then on Roderigo, ostensibly rejoins the choral group.

There is an unmistakable gain on the level of dramatic clarity, even if the composer may have regretted losing some fine passages. Verdi never specified that this Paris Finale should replace the original version, and we therefore have to adhere to the 1887 edition. Still, it would be extremely interesting to have it included as an appendix in some recording of the opera since a comparison of the two versions points up the problems of blending the lyrical and the dramatic spheres in a complex ensemble.

Melody

Verdi's attitude toward melody does not quite conform to the mental picture we have of him—more and more attentive to the drama, therefore less and less concerned with beautiful singing. Paradoxically, the opposite would seem to be the case. True, it is generally admitted today that he broke the last remaining links with bel canto and oriented vocal lines toward an essentially dramatic conception. As Rodolfo Celletti writes, "The principle to which Verdi strictly adhered was that the 'theatrical' moment, namely the psychological situation of a particular character and a particular scene, must always prevail over the 'vocal' requirements. This is true in the recitative as well as in the arias or ensemble pieces."[25] The attacks to which Verdi was subjected by the guardians of tradition[26] and the blame he received for corrupting bel canto only corroborate this break with the tradition of ornamented song.

As regards singers, he never made any secret of his preference for artists who combined a beautiful voice with great acting talent. He praised Adelina Patti's voice, but his memories of that singer are only of her acting! When he recommended La Piccolomini, La Spezia, or La Boccadabati, it was because they had "a small voice but great dramatic talent and a theatrical heart and soul." If he had qualms about the tenor Tamagno for Otello, it was because he feared that the singer would not declaim forcefully enough certain phrases that presented no particular vocal difficulty but called for great expressiveness. When he was casting *Falstaff,* his greatest concern was diction: "Our singers can generally only scream; they have no elasticity in their voices, they do not articulate clearly or easily and lack emphasis and breath."[27] Finally, even if, fairly late in his career, Verdi agreed to suit roles to particular voices, if certain roles bear the stamp of the singer who created them (e.g., Jenny Lind as Amelia in *I masnadieri,* Fraschini as Stiffelio and Colini as Stankar in *Stiffelio*), the fact is that he wrote the parts rapidly, as he heard them, independent of the artist provided in the casting. This method was to create problems for Varesi, the first Germont.

Yet what we see over the years is actually a revaluation of "pure" song. At first timidly, then more obviously in the case of *Luisa Miller,* Verdi rediscovered his liking for the melodic curve that charms the ear more by its quality as sound than by a strict adherence to the text. While he was writing *Otello,* he recalled that "melody is always Italian, essentially Italian, and can only be Italian, wherever it comes from."[28] And, in this violent, almost expressionist opera, he was careful to include one character who stood out constantly thanks to her lyricism and the quality of her song. Finally, he defended the Italian school of singing, which, he said, shaped its art on a tradition that was precisely that of bel canto.[29]

There is an explanation for this contradiction. In his youth Verdi found himself confronted with a genre that, despite the changes wrought by Bellini, Donizetti, and Mercadante, had a certain rigidity as well as a great feeling for lyrical exaltation. Because of his dramatic temperament, doubtless also out of reaction—rather as Bellini had at first reacted to Rossini's ornamented style by stripping melody of decoration—Verdi expressed himself in a vehement, tense melodic style, and the elegiac or pathetic moments in his youthful operas are not always of the best quality. Having achieved a superb mastery of his art around the 1850s and benefited from certain experiments (the expression of interiority and the exploitation of variety), he could abandon himself to the pleasure of song, even that of the voice itself. Added to that was his habitual spirit of contradicting himself: prompt to criticize melody as an obstacle to the affirmation of drama, he restored it to its rightful place as soon as he felt that it was less threatened by excessive dramatic tension.

EVOLUTION

Melody in Verdi's operas developed by means of the modification of certain habits that had restricted its flexibility and variety. Among those techniques were the prevalence of four-measure phrases, which called for a uniform breaking up of the melodic line; the tendency to center a vocal number on a simple, homogeneous register; and, finally, the habit of giving the orchestra the role of accompanist while leaving melodic invention to the voice alone. It was by changing these parameters that Verdi was able to gain greater flexibility of melodic expression.

Phrasing

The custom of composing a melody in groups of four measures (or any multiple of four) ruthlessly dominated the operatic world of the *Primo Ottocento*. Mozart respected regular phrasing less than did Rossini, who, in turn, was less loyal to it than Bellini or Donizetti. The practice was indissociable from the metric presentation of strophes: generally speaking, each melodic segment of four measures was matched by two lines of poetry, while the coda repeated lines that had already been used. Added to this isorhythm was the habit of melodic symmetry, particularly important in the so-called Bellinian model, where three of the four melodic segments had the same beginning: a1 (two lines of poetry), a2 (two lines), b (two lines), a2 or 3 (two lines), that is, sixteen measures followed by a coda. Librettists were sufficiently familiar with the melodic models to organize their texts according to the musical structure (e.g., by altering the mood of the text for segment b). This regularity of phrasing was also usually adhered to in purely instrumental melodies, for instance, those used to underline a parlante.

From *Luisa Miller* on the tyranny of periodic phrase structure became increasingly strained and attempts at asymmetry more and more frequent. The presentation of the various characters in the first-act Finale exploits these irregularities: old Miller's first solo is broken up vigorously as 3 + 2 (a1), 3 + 2 (a2), 4 + 3 + 4 + 4 (b); Rodolfo and Walter alternate in phrases of five measures, while Luisa's entry goes back to a four-measure unit. In the first act of *Rigoletto,* the Duke's ballad shows a slight departure from the symmetrical model that, added to the syncopated stresses, gives his song a carefree elegance. This characteristic did not escape the notice of Basevi, who gave the composer credit for it, taking the opportunity to deplore his contemporaries' *"manierismo,* which demands rigorous symmetry and periodicity of the rhythm."[30]

La traviata contains many instances of flexible phrasing, usually produced by an elision of melodic segments that does away with the regular pauses implied by the four-measure division. One of the best examples of this new melodic writing is the first phrase of the prelude. It consists of sixteen measures, but, if the B-minor beginning is regular, with its four measures arriving on the dominant, the next twelve measures (3 + 4 + 5) unfold without a break up to a blunt pause on a dominant chord announcing the E-major theme about to follow.

Once again, this trend should be taken not as an abandonment of the four-measure phrase but as a refusal to be tyrannized by it. The regularity implicit in periodic phrasing caused Verdi to rely on it throughout his operas because it was easy to comprehend and memorize, but as time went on it no longer systematically governed melodic development. After the trilogy, a melody often opens, like the prelude to *La traviata,* with a crisp and regular phrase that sets the tone, and then unfolds freely over a somewhat capricious curve.[31] This gradual freeing of melody is obviously designed to give it a wider sweep where formerly it was constrained by frequent pauses.

Unity of Tone

In traditional opera, melodic development tended to depict either a single passion or a conflict between two moods. States of uncertainty, hesitations, or reversals were reserved for the *scena.* Because, as we have seen, Verdi tended to narrow the gap between the spirit of the *scena* and that of the aria, it is logical that he would try to introduce psychological diversity into melodic development. The speed with which he moves from one mood to another is an important stage in his evolution, as we saw in the example of the Andante "Non sai tu" of the Riccardo-Amelia duet in *Ballo.* Verdi could now tackle unstable, tormented, contradictory characters that could not have been handled with the homogeneous traditional aria or ensemble.

Leonora, in *La forza del destino,* is an example. Her first solo, "Me pellegrina ed orfana," depicts a basic feeling, her sadness at leaving her birthplace to go off with her lover, and the metrical structure is fairly orthodox: three strophes of four *settenari.* Yet the feeling is a complex one, encompassing her sadness at leaving her parents' home like an orphan, the impression of being driven into exile by an obscure fate, and a strong sense of guilt that causes her to swing between remorse and the sensation of being under a curse. Verdi treats this passage as a romanza, but it greatly exceeds the relatively simple scheme of its two minor and major sections. True, the scheme is handled with relative melodic regularity from "Ti lascio, ahimè": (1) F minor, $a1 + a2$, 4 + 4 measures; (2) F major, $b1 + b2$ extended, 4 + 10 measures and coda on the same text, which is a sorrowful farewell to her birthplace. But the actual romanza is preceded by an "introduction" or first part that corresponds to the first two strophes of the text and is treated with the freedom of a *scena:* a peaceful cadence (2 + 2 measures: "me pellegrina ed orfana," the melancholy of exile), a long, tormented chromatic cadence (4 measures: "un fato inesorabile," the feeling of destiny), a crescendo that sweeps the voice up to high G, then descends on the dominant of the key (8 measures: "colmo di tristi immagini," the burden of remorse), a tortured vocal gesture on the dominant pedal repeated four times (6 measures: same text).

The first section is nonetheless firmly integrated into the romanza thanks to a number of elements: tonality (F major/minor); the importance of the initial cadential formula preceded and followed by a cello arpeggio, a formula repeated at the end of the romanza (as is the cello arpeggio at the end of the first part); this same arpeggio figure, melancholy in the cello but spasmodic in the accompaniment of the minor section of the romanza; the dominant pedal present in both halves; a semitone melodic figure that closes the first section in the voice (D♭, C: "pianto") but continues in the orchestra over four octaves and is heard again at the end of the aria ("addio"); as well as several other melodic links. Because of this echo effect, which I have merely hinted at, Verdi unifies the material of his aria while allowing himself a wide variety of moods: melancholy, resignation, anguish, distress, and so on.

Relation of Voice and Orchestra

Autonomy of orchestral discourse appears only gradually in Italian opera since it goes counter to a tradition limiting the orchestra to the simple role of accompaniment. Strange as it may seem, Rossini, Bellini, and Verdi were accused of "Germanism," that is to say, of thickening the texture of the orchestra—by doing which they were actually following a general trend found in much nineteenth-century music. Later in life, Verdi rejected the excesses of the symphonic style, but there is no denying that he had contributed to it.

In the preceding chapter we saw one of the reasons for the development of an autonomous orchestral discourse: the increasing complexity of the characters and especially the emergence of disturbed psychological dimensions that were not articulated, either because they were subconscious or because they could not be spoken about. Thus, it is not surprising that, when Verdi reworked a score, he often gave the orchestra an initiative he had formerly given to the voice since the moment called for the expression of a troubling inner state rather than a recognizable feeling.

A comparison of the apparition scenes in the first and later versions of *Macbeth* shows that both Macbeth and the witches have less to sing in the second version, where they are sometimes confined to a sort of *recto tono*. Why? Because an overly mobile vocal line would have destroyed the witches' aura of mystery and Macbeth's solemn but frightened tone, while the orchestral discourse, which is stranger and subtler in the later version, can better render the fantastic atmosphere of the scene as well as the contrast between Macbeth's soldierly bearing and his profound inner panic.

Otello's act 3 monologue is an admirable example of this modulation of the powers of voice and orchestra. Summed up briefly, Otello's arguments run as follows: (1) My God, if you had plunged me in the most extreme misery, I would have accepted the burden and resigned myself to heaven's will. (2) But why take away from me this vision of beauty where my soul found its peace? In the first part of the monologue, "Dio mi potevi scagliar," Otello is so overcome by the violence of the scene in which he and Desdemona have just confronted each other that he can scarcely articulate and his voice practically does not budge from the tonic A♭ except to fall heavily back on the dominant (of A♭ minor). It is not until the last measures, where he speaks of resignation, that his voice rises toward C♮ (harmonized by an E♭ dominant-ninth chord), with a striking effect of transfiguration. Thus, the orchestra describes the depths of Otello's despair: the ponderous chromatic descent of the strings from E♭ to A♭, the triplets in the violins, each time moving one step lower, and the heavy rocking of the cellos and bassoon. The effect is even more gripping when the voice collects itself in the second part of the monologue and, as Otello evokes his lost love (the word *love* is not pronounced, being replaced by metaphoric equivalents—*mirage, sun, smile, ray of light*), the hero recovers the grace of song and its lyrical sweep while the orchestra returns to its traditional role of accompaniment. But the respite is brief, and at the end of the monologue Otello once again gives in to violence.

TRANSFIGURATION OF THE PHRASE

Hard though it is to fathom a composer's melodic genius, one can begin to approach it through the distinction I suggested concerning the composer's attitude toward the text—semanticization of the music through an overall grasp of the text or musicalization of the word starting with the individual phrase of the text. Listening to the poetry, paying attention not only to its peculiar rhythm but also to the affective connotations it conjures up, is one of the sources of Verdi's melodic inspiration. For him, to listen to a phrase of text is to transform it into a musical gesture clear enough that it will appear as a "natural" musical equivalent. Hence Verdi's insistence on the *parola scenica,* already a rough sketch of that gesture. Certain Verdian lines impress themselves on the memory with the accuracy of their intonation: "tutto è finito," the words Macbeth speaks when he returns to the stage having murdered Duncan; "Elle ne m'aime pas," Philip II's refrain in his great act 4 aria; "Un bacio, un bacio ancora," Otello's last words; or Quickly's "Reverenza" and "Dalle due alle tre" in *Falstaff.*

The declamatory style of recitative, freer in the disposition of text, reproduces the way the poetry "breathes" more readily than full-fledged melody, which is hampered by the shackles of the meter and the symmetrical phrase structure. Many recitatives seem unremarkable until, for instance, a tragedienne demonstrates their economy and precision. Consider, for example, the one preceding Violetta's aria in act 1 of *La traviata:* the emphasis of the chromatic slide on *accenti,* the hesitant appoggiaturas on *sventura* and *amore,* the vocal run on *gioie,* the high A♭ of *follie,* all underline the heroine's troubled state of mind with admirable restraint.

Still, Verdi always knew how to get around too regular poetry when the sense of the text called for a setting that avoided melodic regularity. Consider, for example, the beginning of the quartet in *Oberto,* Nabucco's great aria when he is struck down by a thunderbolt in the Finale 2, or Rigoletto's act 2 aria, where the vehemence of the declamation breaks up the melody to convey the character's disintegration. One can scarcely make out the monotonous rocking motion of the arioso, "Marullo . . . Signore . . . dimmi tu . . . dove l'hanno nascosta? è là? . . . non è vero? è là?" Again, what better way to render the King of Spain's impatience and anger, at the beginning of the trio with Ernani and Elvira, when he suddenly sees Ernani standing before him, than by the simple phrase, "Tu se' Ernani! . . . me'l dice lo sdegno" (You're Ernani! so tells me the contempt) (see ex. 20).

The versification (two decasyllables) in no way hinders the expression of the King's contained fury, which is soberly underlined by a brief orchestral commentary. This dramatization of the text culminates in the cry—not the inarticulate cry Don Giovanni utters as he is swallowed up in hell, or that of Desdemona as she is smothered by Otello, but an explosion of joy or despair that, instead of expanding into a regular melody, is caught in a single sweeping phrase running the whole length of the vocal register. After *Ernani,* almost every opera contains one of these broad phrases that capture a destiny in a flash of blinding light. The most mov-

EX. 20

ing is without doubt Amneris's triple cry, during Radames's trial, when she rebels against a ruthless condemnation for which she herself is responsible.[32]

Verdi's musical transfiguration of the poetic phrase most often requires a melodic setting that excludes lyricism and approaches declamation. This occurs so frequently and obviously that it disguises an opposite but equally important phenomenon: the effort to give the phrase a lyrical dimension capable of conveying its affective meanings, which can be overpowered by too declamatory a setting. Here are two instances of both practices:

When Philip II is describing his authoritarian policies in his grand duet with Rodrigue (*Don Carlos,* act 2), he sings "too much," and, although his vocal line is beautiful, it is too melodious for such a gloomy theme. Hence, the same phrase is reversed and made more declamatory (in the "Neapolitan" version of 1872): the same descending motion is also found in the 1884 revision, but it has become more tired and somber, as befits a despot (see exx. 21a and 21b).

EX. 21a (1866–67)

EX. 21b (1883–84)

EX. 22   (1883–84)

By contrast, when Philip confesses his spiritual loneliness, in the original version the voice "freezes" on an E ("Tu m'as vu sur mon trône et non dans ma maison"), and the immobility of the vocal line fails to convey either the suffering this confession implies or the King's tortuous character; both are superbly expressed in the long, sinuous, far more lyrical phrase of the 1884 version (on a slightly different text) (see ex. 22).

Virtually throughout Verdi's career, lyrical effusion is conveyed in the *pezzo chiuso* or at least in those short ariosi often found in introductory scenes, which suggest a conventional musical form, yet without taking it to its conclusion. *Otello* is a different story. Especially in the role of Desdemona, which Verdi said should sing from beginning to end but which has no actual aria until act 3, this opera offers examples of what might be called the lyrical transfiguration of the phrase in a guise governed by the

EX. 23

principle of "continuous melody." Most of the duets, particularly the great love duet in act 1, are based on freely structured phrases. The choice of poetic lines of seven and eleven syllables appropriate to recitative clearly made the composer's task easier: the melodies gain a tighter grasp of the intonations of the text, its pauses, sallies, and salient words; they mimic the "natural" voice while at the same time giving it a constant vibration that reflects the character's emotions—in this case, the emotions of love and memory (see ex. 23).

DRAMATIC NUCLEI AND MELODIC ARCS

Working from what I have called the semanticization of the music, that is, from a musical intuition that subjects itself to the text, Verdi's genius is essentially one of synthesis, and he tends to fix a passion, a situation, even a drama, in a clearly perceptible melodic nucleus that seizes the listener's attention. Bellini's melody is a gradual revelation, an "epiphany of a truth," in Marzio Pieri's apt expression;[33] it slowly unwinds, loosening its long garlands with a natural grace. On hearing "Casta diva," or "Ah non credea mirarti," or "Qui la voce sua soave," the listener retains not a formula but a motion, an ascent toward an emotive apotheosis. In the case of Verdi's best-known arias, it is almost always the energy of the gesture that is engraved on the memory.

Sometimes there is a close link between the melodic pattern and the original text. For instance, the vehement rhythm of the Stretta in the Rodrigue-Eboli-Carlos trio (*Don Carlos,* act 3) owes much to the line's anapestic scansion (‿ ‿ ‿ –): "Malheur sur toi fils adultère, mon cri vengeur va retentir"/"Trema per te, falso figliuolo, la mia vendetta arriva già." Sometimes, and this is logically the case of those themes given to the orchestra, the theme is purely musical, and it is up to the text to adapt to it.

The problem is to ensure that the energy of the pattern does not become diluted in the orchestral development or in the organization of the vocal phrase. Owing to the nature of his melodic style, Bellini, for example, was probably less hampered by traditional structures since he needed that periodicity to be able to build up his long cantilenas; at most he had to see to it that the overall arc had continuity and unity. Verdi, on the other hand, intent on grasping the whole in one musical gesture, struggled to preserve this energy in the structure of the aria. The stunning success of famous arias such as "La donna è mobile" or "Di quella pira" comes from the fact that, by means of rhythmic devices and melodic inversion, the composer maintains the momentum that is already present, in its entirety, in the very first measures.

The overture to *Luisa Miller* shows the masterly way Verdi makes use of these vigorously synthesizing motifs that do not fade with repetition. The overture is in fact monothematic and is based on a motif with a simple rhythm: ♩. ♫ ♩. This is sounded throughout the overture, both in its first form and with variations, either elegiac or dramatic, given to a solo instrument or to the whole orchestra. The extremely stirring rhythmic pattern has the force of those destiny themes the most famous of which is heard in the opening measures of the overture to *La forza del destino.* It acquires enough importance from the very beginning so that, as the opera continues, many passages that have the same rhythmic pattern and describe the same relentless march of Luisa and Rodolfo's destiny are perceived as being linked to that first theme.[34] In this case the same single formula, charged with meaning, irradiates the whole work.

Verdi's evolution and the ever greater liberty he took vis-à-vis regular metric structure led him to preserve, and even strengthen, these melodic kernels that launch a solo and to develop them more freely (I have given several examples of this process at n. 31). The fact that a melody could begin in regular phrases (e.g., a1 a2 = 4 + 4), the better to fix the formula, and then expand more freely allowed him to affirm its gestural character and at the same time give it a breadth that a strict 4 × 4 division would have precluded. One notes here a certain parallelism with the composer's formal development, miniaturizing on the one hand and diversifying on the other.

The dual tendency toward contraction into a single strong motif and expansion of the same motif or its constituent elements is characteristic of the Verdian melodic style after the trilogy. We can see it, as I have described, in the way the first theme of *Forza* colors the whole scene of Leonora's conversion and in the Eboli-Carlos-Rodrigue trio in *Don Carlos*, which exploits the basic anapestic rhythm in a number of different ways. It is also to be found in the trio involving Amneris, Radames, and Aida, in act 1 of *Aida*, which is marked by a vehement motif associated with Amneris's jealousy: although this ensemble is highly orthodox in its presentation (3 × 8 measures, repeated a little further on), its essentially rhythmic nature lends itself to great melodic flexibility, which appears clearly at the end of the trio when Aida develops her great lyrical phrase.

● ● ● ● ● ● ●

Nevertheless, Verdi did not abandon pure lyricism or the looser adherence to the text and greater concern for the melodic curve that goes with it. Dramatic expression tolerates, and often requires, discontinuity and diversity of rhythm, whereas lyrical expression seeks fluidity of tone and continuity; the dramatic gesture tends toward autonomy, while the lyrical impulse is aimed at integration into a broader ensemble. From *Luisa Miller* to *Falstaff*, Verdi strikes this lyrically elegiac vein as soon as there is a weakening of tension.

In a general way, this mode of expression seeks melodic continuity by relying on relatively short units. Thus, "Quando le sere al placido," the first fruit of Verdi's elegiac lyricism, is constructed in an orthodox manner (a8 + b8 + 1) but is based on one-and-a-half-measure units. The first section of Amelia's aria in *Simon Boccanegra* (act 1) is based on a single twelve-measure phrase articulated in units of one and a half measures, all with the same rhythmic profile; Radames's romanza repeats, five times by groups of two measures, the same ascending gesture that takes up the whole of the first section, with the exception of a concluding phrase of four measures. The last movement of the Aida-Radames duet is constructed with the utmost simplicity, but it has the effect of an incantation, appearing as it does to repeat tirelessly the same melodic spiral consisting of three or four notes (see ex. 24).

The last products of this lyricism, Nannetta and Fenton's duet and

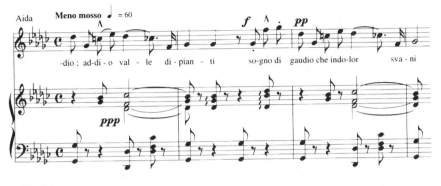

EX. 24

Fenton's sonnet in *Falstaff,* seem to return to traditional phrase structure; yet the melody is syllabic throughout and has acquired such ease that it never seems to be imprisoned in a mold, any more than does the "infinite" melody one can discern in certain passages of *Otello.*

The paths of Verdi's melodic genius are varied, but in all of them one can see a loyalty to the Italian melodic tradition, however much it may have been revised or modified. The composer never loses the sense of the vocal line; he always has the hidden hope of reconciling dramatic truth and purity of melodic design. There is no better example of this desire for reconciliation, surely, than the sleepwalking scene in *Macbeth,* one of the highest manifestations of the young Verdi's dramatic genius. Its strength is that it constantly moves on two planes—a melodic and lyrical plane and a dramatic, declamatory one. On the one hand we have a melody taut with anguish, broken up into nervous fragments, a mimetic discourse that encapsulates the inner disintegration of the character, and on the other hand a melodic arc that is light and of great beauty and whose continuity can be readily traced. Because of this solid structure the aria does not degenerate into verismo expressionism, just as the hidden presence of tradition more generally ensures the glory of Verdi's melodic expression.

Ambivalence of Form

Form, as a regular, symmetrical structure, possesses a power of objectivity because it offers a guarantee of impersonality as the composer builds a character. The monumental aesthetics of melodrama ensures that a character's moral attitude must be encapsulated in an exemplary gesture that can be fixed in song. Verdi's evolution led him to question the exaggerated clarity of this aesthetics, and his later, more complex apprehension had repercussions for form. Was it really appropriate for capturing a character, or did it offer only a false appearance that hid the character's true essence? The form that had once been synonymous with the character now resembled a judgment, perhaps imprecise and incomplete, that the creator made of his character. Form could appear as no more than an illusory order, an aspiration to a moral clarity that was now lost. The only form that escaped this fallibility was death, real or metaphoric; the only monumentality that was not suspect was that of the tomb. This ambivalence, which metamorphosed from an image of life organizing and building itself into an image of death, is illustrated in Verdi's darkest, most pessimistic drama, *Don Carlos*.

In his great act 4 aria, Philip II broods on the poignancies of his personal life: his wife's indifference ("Elle ne m'aime pas"/"Ella giammai m'amò"), the memory of their first meeting ("je la revois encore"/"Io la rivedo ancor"), his anguish and insomnia ("le doux sommeil a fui"/"Il sonno, oh Dio! sparì"), his anxieties as king ("si le roi dort, la trahison se trame"/"Se dorme il prence"). All these themes are conveyed in a free mixture of recitative and arioso. The actual aria, with its implicit regularity, corresponds to the moment the King sees himself dead, promised to eternal sleep, "sous les voûtes de pierre des caveaux de l'Escurial"/"sotto la vôlta nera, Là, nell'avello dell'Escurial"—as if to say that Philip II will find his "form" only when he sleeps eternally in his royal mantle.

Similarly, in Elisabeth's grand scene in the last act, the moving central section is devoted to a look back on her life; the most highly structured section is the invocation to Charles V, "Toi qui sus le néant des grandeurs de ce monde"/"Tu che le vanità," which is obviously an appeal for "the deep, gentle peace of death." In each case, life is but broken fragments, outbursts, reminiscences, the only grand gesture available to the character being death. The 1884 version only accentuates this obsessive presence of death since it opens and closes on the vision of the Emperor's tomb.

The character's "form" is therefore but a role of which he or she is prisoner. In fact, all the characters in this opera are stifled in their roles, and their deepest nature, if they have an opportunity to reveal it, consists of nothing but vertigo and confusion. This disintegration of the character's inner life and moral consistency creates a crisis in melody as the embodiment of a clear, defined psychological attitude. Certain passages of the opera illustrate this in remarkable fashion; for example, in the second duet between Elisabeth and the infante Carlos (act 2), we see two characters who are constantly struggling to assume an attitude but who fail, thrown back on their inner disarray.

Carlos asks to be allowed a meeting with Elisabeth, who is now his mother-in-law. A hesitant, sad musical phrase is heard, and we see him, melancholy and a little restrained in his sorrow and frustration. This facade cracks over the next twenty measures, which are highly chromatic and have no definite tonality ("L'air d'Espagne me tue"/"Quest'aura m'è fatale"), and he explodes in a great cadential phrase that leads to D minor. Elisabeth seems more self-composed, as is shown by her relatively balanced and obviously tonal solo; she agrees to intervene with her husband so that the Infante may become governor of Flanders. Stung by her coldness, Carlos is amazed and pleads with her, then explodes once again in a phrase leading to G minor. Elisabeth still resists, taking refuge in defense of duty ("Le devoir, saint flambeau"/"Il dover, come un raggio"), in Bb major, but this ten-measure rhetorical outburst dies down, exhausted, in the cadence.

The middle Andante in Bb major, "O bien perdu"/"Perduto ben," recovers some serenity in the parallel vocal lines of the two characters, who, as they remember their lost happiness, seem to find a unity of feeling in looking back at the past. Carlos breaks down again, however, although in a different way: he sinks into a strange dreamlike state ("O prodige" / "O prodigio"). Seeing Carlos in a faint, Elisabeth is terrified: she clings to the first theme of the Andante and repeats it in Eb but cannot carry it through to the end ("hélas! sa douleur me déchire"/"Ahimè, il dolor l'uccide"). From ecstasy, Carlos goes into a slight delirium and, oblivious to the present, loses himself in the flood of memories, causing the Queen to panic.

In the last movement of the duet, both characters try to compose themselves, but this final effort serves only to betray their inner confusion the more: Carlos relies on a traditional cabaletta rhythm ♩ ♫♫♫♫ ♪ ♩ ("Que sous mes pieds se déchire la terre" /"Sotto il mio piè"), but his melodic line is instantly stifled in a convulsive sob of love. Elisabeth, in four measures, sweeps across her range with an energy worthy of Elvira but in the following eleven measures becomes lost in her chaotic vehemence (see ex. 25). A noteworthy feature of the passage is the expansion of the melodic line, which, after a firm beginning, is thrown off balance by Elisabeth's turmoil. The same melodic pattern dominates the entire duet. At the very end of this passage, Carlos rushes off, and the Queen thanks God for having helped them both be faithful to duty.

EX. 25

This duet thus illustrates a crisis of the opera character, whose outward appearance is only a veil concealing a profound inner fragility—the torment and feeling of emptiness or failure we find in the most ambivalent characters of the work, Carlos, Philip, and Elisabeth. The character still erects his statue, but he can no longer inhabit it, and the statue crumbles to dust. From this time on, form—melodic regularity, isorhythm, tonal clarity, crispness of articulation—disintegrates, as does the character whose image form should sculpt. Unless, that is, form reflects the one stable image he can hope for, the eternal one carved of him by death.

CHAPTER EIGHT

Unity

More than any other genre, opera is under constant threat of bursting apart. So many elements play a part in its creation, so many people contribute to its realization and are tempted to steal the limelight, that the fragile balance it represents is upset time after time—to the singer's advantage in most cases, but occasionally also that of the librettist and composer, down the line to the conductor and even the stage director. Meanwhile, the public goes on applauding selected arias, deliberately ignoring their context. The scant importance given to dramatic logic in opera, the tendency of the music to strain the temporal and causal connection, the emotional impact certain singers knowingly create, all tend to favor an approach that stresses the highlights of a work rather than its continuity.

It is easy to understand why the problem of opera's coherence became a major concern for critics. If coherence was never in doubt for someone like Wagner, who was both a musician and an aesthetic thinker, it seemed far less certain in the case of other composers, until critical studies showed that in fact the problem affected all composers of opera. The tree that has sometimes hidden the forest is the conviction that unity and coherence had to follow certain procedures, which amounted to a denial of the variety of aesthetics that have governed the history of the genre.

It therefore seems prudent to take these aesthetics into account so as to appreciate how Verdi thought through the unity of his work. It is obvious that a baroque opera did not obey the same criteria as did one by Gluck or Wagner: the fundamental need for variety that baroque composers felt did not exclude a multiplicity of plots, characters, and passions typical of the chivalric poetry their librettists often took as their model.

The fortunate outcome of contradictory passions could take precedence over the logical coherence of a plot from the exposition to the final catastrophe. Volker Klotz and later Carl Dahlhaus have rightly insisted on the need to distinguish between "open-form" and "closed-form" dramas.[1] Baroque drama is obviously an open form that does not follow a strict dramatic logic but seeks opulence, even though it is based on closed elements like the aria, chorus, and sinfonia: therefore, the fact that a composer added or cut out arias, expanded or contracted, does not necessarily mean that he was harming the unity of the opera. Music drama, in contrast, is a closed form that follows a dramatic line from one end to the other and is based on structures that tend to open up in order to join together.

From this viewpoint, Verdi tends in general toward the closed form. From the first, he has his eye riveted on the "drama," and his method shows that he strictly observes the plot and eliminates anything that would impede its course. Later, he seems to regret the loss of the variety and abundance that were ingredients of opera throughout its history, and he tends to integrate subsidiary elements unconnected with the plot; yet this development is not so much a return to another aesthetics as the quest for a superior synthesis in which all the elements are thought of as integral parts of a whole.

Moreover, criticism has often made musical continuity an essential criterion, as though the unity of an opera would be the more perfect if the composer eliminated gaps and overly clear articulations and created a stream of sound interrupted only at the end of each act. Thus, in the case of classical composers, the critics have sometimes given too much praise to continuously connected numbers as compared with numbers separated by clear, sharply defined cadences or recitatives. This bias has worked to the detriment of the Italian tradition, with its long-held custom of separation by numbers. Because Rossini, Bellini, and Donizetti thought in terms of successive numbers, it does not follow that they conceived of them as isolated fragments to be juxtaposed within a more or less random plot. In this connection, it is striking that Verdi never confused the *pezzo staccato,* an isolated musical piece without a dramatic context, with the *pezzo chiuso,* a musical piece that, although characterized by articulations clear enough to enable it to be separated from the context, is integrated into a broader whole.

One last problem concerns the limits that can be set to this quest for unity. The search for coherence is confused with the Pythagorean principle of making the greatest possible whole depend on the smallest number of basic elements; the critics end up resembling those Buddhists of whom Roland Barthes speaks who, through asceticism, reach the stage where they can "see a whole landscape in a single bean."[2] With a little ingenuity, one can deduce an entire opera from one melodic formula, augmented or diminished, altered or reversed. But how would the ordinary listener be able to grasp this often complex system? Manfred Bukofzer used to make a distinction between "the audible form" and "the inaudible order," the effects of musical structure perceptible to the average ear and the system in which these effects can be integrated but that remains accessible only to study.[3] He hastened to add that the inaudible character of this order did not dispense with the need for critical study—but then one tends to lose the link with the drama, for the more one concentrates on a "deep" musical structure, the less one can grasp the connection to the "surface" of the plot, which relies on continuity but just as much on breaks and contrasts. It is probable that for composers such as Handel, Mozart, Verdi, and even Wagner, all of whom behaved above all as men of the theater, the audible effect that strikes the spectator and gives him *impressions,* to use Verdi's language, is more important than the exactness of the structure as it might appear on paper to the student.

The Desire for Unity

Verdi's quest for unity is inspired by emotion arising from a text. The first stage in the composition of an opera is therefore an encounter with a text that produces an "impression," and the dramatic coherence of the text arises from this vision of the whole. Every stage of the creation must reflect this "impression" with the greatest accuracy: the inner assimilation of the dramaturgy changes impression into "idea," that is, into a dramatic plan, a precise structuring of text and music. Unity of idea perforce engenders the continuity of the creative gesture; the staging must preserve the homogeneity of this gesture while preventing it from being impaired by the multiplicity of intervening elements (singers, conductor, stage manager).

In short, Verdi lays stress on the dynamic of "inspiration" rather than on "treatment." In a famous letter in which he contrasts these two terms, he states with the utmost clarity that, "if the opera is made all in one breath *[di getto],* there is only one main idea and therefore everything must come together to create that oneness."[4] The material evidences of unity—thematic and tonal coherence, homogeneity of color—are only

outcomes of this creative gesture. It is in this immediate synthesis of perception far more than in structural manipulations that we should seek
out the bases of the unity of Verdi's operas.

Verdi's refusal to pick up the pen except to transcribe a complete dramatic whole explains his well-known rejection of occasional pieces: "You
are demanding something I cannot do. A piece of music! I abhor those
isolated pieces that, artistically speaking, have no real purpose and no
reason."[5] From these refusals, both moderate and categorical, that dot the
composer's career, it is easy to tell that Verdi not only had no desire to
write "pure music" but also did not want to compose from librettos that
seemed merely to offer the possibility of a few beautiful pages: "I am more
and more convinced," he wrote in connection with Dumas *père's La Tour
de Nesle,* "that it would be possible to write magnificent pieces of music
but never an opera: at least, I wouldn't be able to do it."[6]

His insistence that a composition, even if expanded, should still give
the impression of a single gesture explains Verdi's aversion to what he
calls *mosaic* music, a term covering works written in a discontinuous way
or bearing the trace of several influences. Contentious toward the Opéra
de Paris, where, he maintained, too many people offered composers their
advice, he even attacked the major works of the repertoire: "Surely no
one can deny the genius in Rossini! Still, in spite of all his genius, we can
detect in *Guillaume Tell* this fatal operatic atmosphere and sometimes,
though not as often as with other composers, one finds some things that
are excessive and some deficiencies and one feels the musical character is
not as open and self-assured as in *Barbiere.*"[7] If we bear in mind that this
letter was written in 1869, that is, after the long, laborious genesis of *Don
Carlos,* we may wonder whether Verdi was not speaking as much of his
own experience as of that of his illustrious predecessor!

In the face of this hostility to "mosaic pieces," it is impossible not to
mention ballet, which was precisely one of the elements insisted on by the
Paris Opéra. In fact, Verdi did not show any opposition to ballet in principle, once he had found a way to integrate it into an overall conception.
While revising *Macbeth* for Paris in 1864, he was initially bothered by the
problem of a ballet, which he did not want to see become "an insanely
furious divertissement" given to the witches. In reply, the accommodating
Escudier asked him to supply only "two or three dance pieces" to be inserted in act 3. Yet Verdi would write a complete ballet, unasked, because
he managed to find "a little plot that ties in very well with the drama."
Thus, when preparations were being made to produce the new *Macbeth*

in Italy, Verdi wanted the ballet retained because of its "great importance."[8] In similar fashion, he would insist that the original version of *Don Carlos* be performed *in its entirety* in Italy, ballet included.[9]

He showed far more reluctance if he foresaw a problem integrating the ballet into the opera. When Vaucorbeil, director of the Opéra, requested a ballet for *Aida* in 1879, he resisted, saying, "It seems to me that *Aida* should stay as it is, and that by adding something one would spoil the architecture of the whole, if I can put it like that."[10] In 1887, when weighing the possibility of a ballet for *Otello,* he felt that, "artistically speaking, it's a monstrosity" and that, if it saw the light of day, it should not be published in the score.[11] Nevertheless, he would yield to custom for the Paris premiere of 1894!

The fundamental criterion was therefore the suitability of the part for the whole. Thus, in 1847, he justified replacing one cabaletta with another for the act 3 Finale of *Macbeth:* the first was good in itself but "intolerable" when it took its place in the general scheme.[12] For the same reason, he sometimes accepted the custom of substituting arias but wanted them eliminated once they had served a precise purpose because, as he wrote concerning *Nabucco,* "I like the score to stay as it was written."[13]

This aspiration to write in the white heat of inspiration, or, as he was fond of saying, *dans le mouvement,* caused him to make two requirements of himself: The first was to start composing only when he had in his hands, if not the complete libretto, then at least a very clear scenario; this was a method that he seems always to have applied and that in any case he was setting forth as early as 1843.[14] The second requirement was that he write quickly. The advice he gave the young Giordano in later years proves that this way of working was an act of will as well as a spontaneous inspiration: "Never correct what you wrote on the previous day—you will not like it any more and you will mistakenly destroy all that you have done. Compose the first act, without pausing, without corrections; when you have done this, put the sheet of music to one side and start the second act. Proceed with the second act in exactly the same way, and then continue with the third and fourth acts. Then rest. When you have recovered your strength, revise and correct everything; you can be sure that this is the only way of avoiding error."[15]

How, as a practical matter, did the compositional process work? We know, from reading his advice to Giordano, that the composer wrote rapidly. If we exclude *Otello* and *Falstaff* as well as the French operas, we see that Verdi wrote most of his works in a relatively short time: about a month *(Alzira, Giovanna d'Arco)*, forty days *(Traviata)*, between three and five months *(Ernani, Due Foscari, Luisa Miller, Simon Boccanegra,* etc.). His wife Giuseppina Strepponi confirmed Verdi's habit of taking up his pen at the last moment and abandoning himself to creation "with a feverish ardor." [16]

From *Luisa Miller* on we possess complete autograph sketches by Verdi. Usually, he wrote on three staves, noting down the vocal line or lines and a skeleton of the accompaniment (bass, accompaniment formulas, harmonic articulations) and sometimes indicating the instrumentation. The sketch of *Rigoletto,* published by Forni,[17] is undeniably written *dans le mouvement,* to judge from the rapid, feverish scrawl and the rare erasures or corrections. The fact that no sketches have been found prior to 1849 has led some to believe that Verdi changed his method at that time, but, on the basis of evidence in early operas of Verdi's practice of conceiving a work in toto, present-day criticism tends to think that Verdi always began with complete sketches.[18]

The speed of composition is nevertheless made relative by the often lengthy duration of the phase before that, which corresponded to the completion of the libretto and most likely, at the musical level, to a sort of rumination that allowed the composer to get a feeling for the *tinta,* the rhythm, and the dynamic of his work. During this phase, on which we have very little information, the plan must have gained sufficient inner consistency to explain the rapid writing that followed; this would explain, first, why Verdi did not necessarily follow the order of the numbers in the libretto[19]—the ensembles were often written before the arias and the purely instrumental pieces last—and, second, why he sketched the music of certain passages before he had the exact text.

The next phase was that of orchestration, which Verdi did in two stages: he set up what American criticism calls a "skeleton score," which included vocal lines, the bass, more or less developed, and the instrumental solos. This score provided the basis for the vocal parts needed to rehearse the opera.[20] The actual orchestration was completed later, usually during the piano rehearsals *(prove al cembalo).*

Orchestration generally did not take long, and the composer did not find it constricting.[21] He promised to orchestrate *Rigoletto* in less than a week, during piano rehearsals.[22] If we exclude the three last operas, this is the method he followed for all the others. The speed of working may be explained by the relative importance of the orchestral texture, at least in the early operas, but often also by Verdi's wish to see for himself the possibilities offered him by the theater for which he was composing. Still, he did say one day that he conceived, all at the same time, melody, accompaniment, and instrumentation:[23] thus, most of the time orchestration was merely the transcription of combinations already present in his mind.

This being so, one can readily understand how hard it was for Verdi to take up again an opera that had been finished long before. In 1864, he complained to Escudier of the difficulty he was experiencing in reworking *Macbeth:* "You cannot imagine how boring and difficult it is to work oneself up for something all over again, and to find a thread that has been broken for so many years. Doing it doesn't take long—but I detest mosaics in music."[24] Yet practically no opera escaped this work of revision. There are the revised operas like *Simon, Macbeth, I Lombardi,* and *Don Carlos,* the operas that were corrected with regard to important points like *Traviata* and *Forza,* those for which a performance provided an opportunity for more or less heavy alterations like *Trovatore* and *Otello* for the Paris versions, those he had long hoped to revise like *Battaglia,* and, finally, those that were improved on in some point or other for a second presentation, like *Aida* between Cairo and Milan.

Rehearsals were often the occasion for last-minute corrections, either because changes had to be made for a certain singer, or because the effect anticipated for a passage did not turn out as convincing as the composer hoped, or because he deliberately waited until the zero hour to write a certain aria.[25] It is then that the man of the theater appears, one who knows that the truth of an opera can be fully seen only in performance, and we see before us a composer who is both impulsive and meticulous, instinctive and perfectionist. The eruption of melody that so delighted Barilli could quite well be controlled when the time came. As Pierluigi Petrobelli has skillfully demonstrated, the revisions were intended for the most part not to change direction so much as to free the "spontaneous" musical idea from its mold and give it the greatest possible incisiveness.[26]

In general, the critics praised Verdi's efforts toward unity. In 1843, Michele Leoni, a journalist, man of letters, and translator of Shakespeare, paid him homage for *Nabucco,* in the inflated style of the period: "In this work it is fair to state that one fragment may prevail over another, but not that one can shine just as brightly without the other. This is so because the harmony among the various parts is deliberately so complete and continuous that, if only one point is lacking, the whole would suffer as a consequence. This happens in every opera which is coordinated toward a single end and authentically impregnated with the one concept that inspired it. Such examples have grown rare in our times, no less because those who listen are impatient in their anticipation of enjoyment than because those who write are eager to satisfy this impatience."[27]

The question remains whether the idea that Verdi may have had of the unity of his operas changed over the years. In this connection one can distinguish three stages, the first of which concerns the youthful operas up to around 1848–49.

"Let there be a lot of fire, a huge amount of action and brevity," Verdi wrote in 1843 to Domenico Bancalari, a librettist briefly considered for the opera that was to become *Ernani*.[28] These three specifications of fire, action, and brevity, to which we should add that of excess ("a lot of," "a huge amount of"), give a fairly good definition of the composer's needs at this point in his career and correspond to the aesthetics of melodrama that was analyzed in a preceding chapter. *Fire* refers to the force of the passions, the potency of characters and situations; *action* to the need that these passions not only declare themselves but be embodied in precise situations; *brevity* to the concern that no collateral consideration or diversion be allowed to hide the linearity of the dramatic action. At this stage, unity is achieved by following strictly, even ferociously, the unwinding of the plot and, as we have seen, ensuring that the lyrical pauses made by solos and ensembles hold up only very provisionally the dynamism of the drama, which nothing must be allowed to deflect.

Around 1848, Verdi came up with other demands such as originality, even oddity, and especially variety of style. By *originality* he meant not simply originality of plot but a freshness of poetic "presentation" since this presentation intimately affected the musical writing; thus, he continually demanded "new forms" from his librettists because in the final analysis the composer depended on his writers if he wanted to innovate. Also, this was the period when he was thinking of writing an opera on *L'Assedio di Firenze* of which, as we have seen, he sketched some highly contrasting scenes where the "comic" enhanced the effect of the "terrible," the period, too, when he wanted to give certain passages in *Luisa Miller* a comic tinge and when he chose Ariosto over Tasso and Shakespeare over Greek tragedy, that is, two writers who mixed tones and style to give an effect of detachment. The mixture of light and dark is one of the principles that Verdi would stress the most when defending himself against the censorship of the libretto of *Un ballo in maschera*.

In 1854, he wrote his friend De Sanctis deploring the lack of good Italian librettos: "When will we have a poet who will give Italy a vast, powerful drama, free of all convention, varied, combining the elements and above all new?"[29] The quotation mentions two of the composer's main concerns at that period—originality ("free of all convention," "new") and mixture of tones ("varied," "combining the elements").

It also refers to a need for fullness ("vast") and synthesis ("combining the elements") that was to dominate Verdi's aesthetic thinking in the 1860s. This need is to some extent the logical result of the requirements he voiced in the 1850s: that variety of colors and their necessary balance displace the drama's center of gravity from objectivity toward a focus that can only be the composer's gaze, the place where opposites meet. This viewpoint alone can ensure the coherence of formerly disparate elements. Thus, Verdi quickly arrives at the point where he contrasts operas "of duets and cavatinas" and those that form a whole: he speaks of *music drama,*[30] but more significant, it seems to me, than this term, which has such a loaded connotation in opera history, are the terms *idea* and *intention,* which crop up in Verdi's vocabulary around the 1870s and describe the synthesis working in the composer's mind.

The exhausting struggle with the Neapolitan censors over *Ballo* and then the Italian productions of *Don Carlos* and *Forza,* works of huge proportions, gave Verdi an opportunity to define his concept of intention: "You should know that there are operas of *ideas* (bad ideas if you like) and operas of cavatinas, duets, etc., etc. for which some of your celebrities might be good, since your public likes them, but as for me, God preserve me from having them, above all in *La forza del destino.* . . . At the San Carlo you have much that's good, that's excellent. Perhaps what you have is the best in the world but for these operas you want something else. You want ensemble, you want the whole. That is what makes operas, not the purely musical writing of cavatinas, duets, Finales, etc., etc."[31]

It does not follow that Verdi had abandoned fire, action, conciseness, originality, and the mixing of styles, or even cavatinas and duets, for his evolution proceeded in mounting layers. It is in fact possible to schematize his development by saying that he began by *identifying* with the drama, by insisting that its musical organization correspond exactly to the unfolding of the plot, and gradually came to *think out* the drama, that is, simultaneously represent it and include it in a wider vision that he aptly calls the *intention.* Note in this connection that over the years Verdi preferred the term *situation* to *position,* which he most often used at the start of his career. The latter word has a strong physical connotation that suggests a snapshot of the dramatic gesture, whereas the former carries with it the more abstract idea of a network of connections at the heart of the drama.

In concrete terms, the unity of an opera is hard to grasp since every element plays a part in achieving it. Still, for convenience one can single out, first, continuity of movement, which leads the spectator, with no idling time, from start to finish of the plot (in other words, its rhythm); second, the devices that ensure cohesion and balance of the opera's structure (its architecture); and, finally, the analogies of style that link the various passages (its color, which Verdi in his own words called *tinta*). These are three directions that we can explore, noting, however, that Verdi does not seem to give the same importance to each one: the reverse of voluble about his secret ways of working, he nevertheless often suggests corrections designed to improve the rhythm of an opera, to avoid useless effects and preserve the necessary rapid pace. Likewise, he considers the determining of the *tinta* of each opera to be a fundamental operation. On the other hand, he is discretion itself as to the architecture of an opera, insofar as it does not proceed strictly from its rhythm.

The Mechanics of Unity

RHYTHM AND STRUCTURE

One of the peculiarities of stage productions is that they impose their length on the spectator, who has no control over it as he does when he reads a book or looks at a painting: whence the formidable danger of tedious or awkward passages. Because it is based on such fragility of illusion, opera is the form most exposed to the risk of sudden drops in tension. This is doubtless one of the reasons Verdi more than once compared himself to a jester—someone who has to amuse the public. The opera composer and the clown are both obliged to keep the spectator in suspense, to sweep him along in one unstoppable movement. Still, it is obvious that the rhythm we are referring to cannot be reduced to a simple temporal dimension—short scenes and rapid transitions between them in the case of the text, concision of forms and fast tempo in the music—and that it implies meaning, the deployment in time of a certain dramatic logic. Hence, rhythm presents itself as a way of giving the listener a passage of time that is "full," with no idle periods that could produce boredom and no incongruities that the spectator would find unacceptable.

Rhythm represents the first and perhaps the most fundamental element in the way music takes over a text. It is the art of replacing the logic and dramatic rhythm suggested by the way the text connects the turns of the plot with a logic and rhythm imposed by the connecting of the musical forms and the kinds of forms employed. Normally, the latter grow out of the former in the sense that the musical organization is inspired by the textual organization, but the composer's option to make choices, to enhance a character, a feeling, or an action or relegate it to the shadows, gives a certain autonomy to the musical rhythm as opposed to that of the text. It can even happen that the first forces itself on the second so that the text takes on its meaning only when transmitted through a certain musical development.

For example, the opening scene of *Rigoletto* depicts a tense situation among the courtiers, Rigoletto, and the Duke that culminates in an ensemble centered on the malice and enmities of the court ("Ah sempre tu spingi lo scherzo"); the concertato ends in a short Stretta, "Tutto è gioia," in which the courtiers sing of the gaieties of court life. This linkage is absurd from the point of view of dramatic logic: the courtiers who were at each other's throats now find that their life is nothing but pleasure!

Although indefensible from the viewpoint of the logic of the text, this Stretta obeys a musical logic that integrates it into an overall "rhythm," for its purpose is to clearly pit the courtiers, as a group, against the formidable Monterone, the judge figure who now makes his entrance. Moreover, it takes place in a dramatic progression imposed by the music: the first ensemble stresses the autonomy of individuals who hate each other, which calls for independent voices, an effect achieved through polyphonic treatment. But these individuals all belong to a community united by frivolity—thus the second ensemble (Stretta) is harmonized simply, without contrapuntal parts. Monterone's musical entry with its curse shatters each man to the core, and the third ensemble is by contrast in unison, to portray the profound solidarity of the court in a collective guilt in the eyes of the law. The successive use of three different kinds of musical writing, contrapuntal, harmonic, and unison, has a musical logic that in turn carries within it a dramatic meaning.

Yet this notion of rhythm is very hard to grasp concretely. If, as Henri Meschonnic writes, rhythm is "an organization or configuration of the subject in his speech,"[32] then it is the very way the composer breathes, the way his imagination moves, and one can study it endlessly. On the other hand, one can try to approach it by way of the techniques a composer employs to organize his "speech" within time. Certain elements that we examined in the chapter on melodrama—the dynamic of the phrase, the lightening of traditional forms, the brevity of recitative—contribute to the establishment of dramatic rhythm. The architecture of opera itself plays a part since it is merely a greatly extended rhythm seized at a single glance: in fact, architecture itself has often been defined as the sudden freezing of a rhythm.

There is every proof that Verdi was extremely sensitive to these problems of rhythm. The preceding observations on his method of composition are evidence that he hoped that unity of the creative plan would engender unity of perception in the listener. Just as clearly, he realized that the traditional organization threatened this rhythm, both dramatically, owing to the tendency of particular numbers to draw the characters into themselves, and because of the breaks caused by overly sharp articulations and too conclusive cadences.

At first, Verdi responded to the challenge with fairly primitive methods—short librettos and fast music, which by 1870 had earned him the reputation of "maestro of fast tempos."[33] At the start of his career, the indications he gave his singers often emphasized the need for such tempos, as witness the remark he made to a correspondent during rehearsals for *Ernani* in Vienna in April 1844: "I just want you to know that I do not like broad tempos: it is better to have too much vivacity than to be too languid."[34]

Working within a tradition of operas of successive numbers, he soon, however, adopted the basic criterion for establishing dramatic rhythm, distribution of the numbers. A letter written at the time *Ernani* was being prepared is proof: "In spite of the limited experience I may have, I still go to the theater all year round, and I pay careful attention to everything. I could see with my own eyes how so many compositions could have been saved had there been a better distribution of the pieces, a more careful evaluation of the effects, a clearer expression of the musical forms."[35] The economy of the whole appears here as a more important factor than the quality of each piece taken separately: we are entering an area, that of the general organization of an opera, that is still far from having yielded up all its secrets.

When we catch Verdi hesitating over a number, it is usually for reasons concerning that number's fitness in the overall scheme of an act or an opera. His shilly-shallying over Aida's romanza in act 3 had to do with the poor quality of the "cold and ordinary" poetry, the problem of handling the prima donna, the reluctance to throw the act out of balance by giving too much importance to his heroine, but above all the determination to avoid monotony: "The first chorus is somber and so is the scene between the priest and Amneris, as the solemn chorus resumes. Adding another slow, somber scene and romanza would produce boredom."[36]

We may measure Verdi's efforts to make musical forms coherent and integrated in an overall rhythm by comparing operas separated by less than ten years. If we take *Oberto,* the first Verdian drama, we can sum up its structure by numbering the structural blocks as follows:

Act 1

    1. Overture, introductory chorus, aria (double) for Riccardo (tenor), aria (double) for Leonora (soprano), Leonora-Oberto (bass) duet.

    2. Chorus, Riccardo-Cuniza (mezzo) duet, Cuniza-Oberto-Leonora trio, Finale 1.

Act 2

    3. Chorus, aria (double) for Cuniza, chorus, aria (double) for Oberto, Leonora-Cuniza-Oberto-Riccardo quartet.

    4. Chorus, romanza for Riccardo, Adagio for Cuniza, *rondò* for Leonora.

It is easy to distinguish four sections corresponding to the four dramatic phases of our "grammar," suggested in the chapter "Melodrama": (1) exposition, (2) preliminary phase, (3) crux of the action, and (4) denouement. The first phase corresponds to the presentation of Riccardo the seducer, Leonora the heroine, and her dramatic encounter with her father, the judge. The second phase presents the other characters as individuals and corresponds to Oberto and Leonora's plea for help from Cuniza, whose fiancé seduced and then abandoned Leonora; the finale highlighting this peak moment of the plot is a classic instance of the second phase of the judge who summons the community as witness and asks for its aid.

In the third phase, Cuniza gives up the idea of marrying Riccardo while the ever-vengeful Oberto decides to fight a duel with Riccardo; Cuniza prevents the duel and, posing as arbiter (conciliatory judge), enjoins Riccardo to marry the woman he has seduced. We guess that this development is a lure when we see the fury of the judge, who has no intention of giving up his revenge. The real denouement is the fourth and final phase, when the duel has at last taken place: Riccardo kills Oberto and flees in despair, while Leonora, feeling partly to blame for her father's death, decides to end her days in a convent.

Each phase has its own dynamic. Each one begins with a static element, the chorus, continues with a number essentially lyrical in nature, and moves, in a dramatic crescendo, toward a high point of the opera: the Oberto-Leonora duet, the act 1 Finale, the quartet, the final *rondò*. However clear it may be, this construction is nevertheless ponderous because of the rather dragging start given to one chorus, the fourfold repetition of the same scheme, not to mention the massive scale of the forms used (double arias and three-part ensembles) and the clear-cut separation between the numbers, which lessens the effect of the crescendo. One can therefore guess which problems would call for the composer's attention: reducing the inertia of the openings and transitions (choruses and marches), lightening the forms and joining them in a less predictable way so that they will make the act seem more unified.

Seen from this viewpoint, act 1 of *Macbeth* is of the utmost interest because of the skillful way Verdi links together the various elements, which are not substantially different from those he used in *Oberto*. Let us recall its musical structure: prelude-introduction (opening witches' chorus, Macbeth-Banquo scene and duet, witches' chorus in the guise of a Stretta of the introduction); cavatina of Lady Macbeth; *scena* and march; Macbeth-Lady *gran scena* and duet; act 1 Finale.

From the point of view of our grammar, the exposition includes the introduction and Lady Macbeth's cavatina; the preliminary phase starts with the march marking Duncan's arrival, continues with the duet of the two protagonists, who plot and carry out their crime, and ends with the act 1 Finale (begun with an arioso for Banquo), in which the assembly learns of the murder and curses the murderer.

Insofar as the introduction and Lady's cavatina make up the exposition, while the end of the act describes the preliminary phase—with the grand duet reflecting the perspective of the "actors" and the finale that of the "spectator" characters—one is tempted to see a construction in three stages: A (introduction and cavatina: exposition), B (march and duet: preliminary phase), C (Finale 1: preliminary phase). Nonetheless, the introduction acts as a finished prologue, quite distinct from the cavatina that follows: the one ends in D major, and the other begins on the note E, a shift that with Verdi often implies a dramatic change of course; also, in the introduction Macbeth merely listens and meditates, while in her cavatina Lady Macbeth prepares to act. Thus, one can understand the structure suggested by Francesco Degrada: A (introduction), B (Lady's cavatina and march), C (duet and Finale), corresponding to the fatality of the action, the motivation of the action and the way it is carried out, and the actual deed and its consequences.[37]

At the same time, the march accompanying Duncan stands out against what comes before and after it with its extrovert, descriptive character. Tonally, it would seem allied to Macbeth's monologue (before the duet), with which it is directly linked. It is like a pivot separating the plan from its enactment, which leads Eduardo Rescigno to see the march as a dividing line between two major portions of the act, the first based on a triple meter and comprising the introduction and cavatina and the second on a duple meter and including the duet and finale.[38]

It is not essential to find out which is the better method: a famous analysis of Baudelaire's sonnet "Les Chats" by Jakobson and Lévi-Strauss teaches us that the perfect coherence of a text often arises from the interlocking of various systems of construction.[39] One would come to the same conclusion by analyzing act 2, which covers phase 3 of the action and Banquo's murder: it is distinctly homogeneous, although evidently based on separate numbers. We therefore move from a light but elementary pace in the case of *Oberto* to a more sophisticated arrangement that, through this interlocking of subdivisions, achieves the greatest possible continuity in an aesthetics founded on distinct numbers.

Macbeth is based on a system that Verdi would never abandon: a rigorous joining of forms at the level of each act, which take their place within a firmly controlled design. This design may be compared to a dramatic crescendo that moves, as it expands, from an individual lyrical pole toward a collective dramatic one (aria, duet, trio, quartet, and Finale); it is a design we find later in *Ballo* and *Foscari* but also in other composers' works, such as Spontini's *La vestale*. It often follows an arched structure, rising to an apogee and then returning to its starting point (we have seen an example of this in the inn scene in *Forza*). Within the design, arias and duets can be embedded in a continuous orchestral texture, as in the *Introduzioni* of *Rigoletto* and *Macbeth*.

Verdi would attempt to improve the fluidity of this system through devices that act like mortar binding stones: strict tonal connections and thematic reprises. In the *Introduzione* of *Battaglia,* the repeat of the opening march and the tonal homogeneity built around the key of E♭ major allow the composer to reinforce the cohesion of an episode that nonetheless includes a patriotic a cappella hymn in A♭ major, a tenor solo in D♭ major, another baritone solo in B♭ major after the reprise of the hymn, and, finally, an oath in E♭ major. In the first act of *Aida,* the perfect tonal merging of the numbers serves to underline the regularity of the progression: Radames-Ramfis scene, romanza of Radames, Amneris-Radames duet, Aida-Amneris-Radames trio, ensemble, *scena* and aria of Aida, consecration, dance, and final prayer. Aida's *scena* gives the impression of a lengthy aside and does not really interrupt the majestic progress of the Egyptian war machine.

Even when he abandons the principle of numbering the pieces, Verdi continues the practice of setting pieces in an overall design. We have a superb example in the Libera me, the last section of the *Requiem,* which is the main nucleus of the work and one of its most dramatic passages. Although the piece is continuous, it is possible to make out subdivisions that succeed each other to trace a highly significant curve. One can describe it as follows, on the understanding that the divisions are for the convenience of analysis only and are elided in the score:

1. *Libera me: scene, soprano (and chorus), C minor.* Confronted with the fear of death and the Last Judgment, the individual, briefly in relay with the chorus, vehemently describes his terror.

2. *Tremens factus: arioso, soprano, C minor.* The soul subdues its fear in a relatively regular melody whose reprise ends in a luminous cadence in the major key, as though the individual were reaching a relative equilibrium.

3. *Dies irae: chorus, G minor.* After a long pause, the music shifts violently from C major to G minor, with the soprano yielding to the orchestra, which repeats part of the Dies irae already introduced at the beginning of the work; the gale blowing through the strings and the undulations and gasps of the voices depict the panic of a populace awaiting a sovereign ten times more terrifying than Nabucco, Attila, or Barbarossa. As the chorus ends there is a gradual ebbing of the crowd while the soprano reappears and repeats, as in 1, the Dum veneris.

4. *Requiem aeternam: aria, soprano and chorus, B♭ minor and major.* This is a slightly different reprise of the *Requiem* appearing at the beginning of the work. Over a rich choral texture, the soprano offers a fervent prayer that ascends, soothed, to high B♭. After a long pause she sings, alone, a shortened reprise of the Libera me that brings us back to C minor.

5. *Libera me: fugue, chorus, C minor.* The chorus again takes the initiative in a solidly structured fugue on the same text as 1.

6. *Libera me: arioso, soprano and chorus.* The conclusion of the fugue alternates the contrapuntal style and a more obviously choral writing that allows the soprano to reemerge, this time on motifs derived from the fugue that form a kind of arioso suggesting a long, inexhaustible lament.

7. *Libera me: scene, soprano and chorus, C major.* Reprise of the soprano's opening declamation but an octave lower and in C major.

The text of the Libera me, the responsory of absolution from the Mass for the Dead, takes up several verses present in the preceding prayers. This allows Verdi to make a musical synthesis of the entire work, alternating the soloist, the personification of the solitary individual reduced to his own efforts, with the chorus, representing the community. The writing shifts between an extremely theatrical style and the severe style of the fugue: the first ranges from highly dramatic declamation, this side of song, to elaborate lyrical expression; the second suggests a formal regression, a return to the wellsprings of religious musicality, a withdrawal to the most solid bulwark for man's existential fear when faced with death, an act of allegiance to a past that is now long gone but still living.

These contrasts follow the structure of a magnificent arc, whose culminating point is the *Requiem* prayer, which unites the individual and the group (4) and culminates, in its turn, in the soloist's high B♭. The various sections are grouped around this extremely intense moment: the soprano's terrified declamation (1) is repeated at the very end (7). Both the soprano's solo (2) and her dialogue with the chorus (6) bring us close to the aria where the individual expresses his emotion in regular melody. The Dies irae chorus (3), like the fugue of Libera me (5), portrays the group in its various attitudes toward death—panic and religious fervor. Finally, the Dum veneris concluding the Dies irae parallels the Libera me preceding the fugue: both reestablish the contrast of the individual and the group before and after the synthesis embodied in the *Requiem* prayer.

If I have singled out this passage, an inner journey that, with its wide spectrum, illustrates humanity's diverse attitudes in the face of death, it is because it provides an admirable example of what I have called *rhythm,* as a dramatico-musical encompassment. The passage carries us along a curve that each of the elements plays a part in building up: the alternation of soloist and chorus, the meaning of the text as the passage proceeds, the choice of writing—as free as a scene or structured as an aria or a fugue— and the gradation of intensity of sound.

TONALITY

The study of tonality in an opera is a good example of the problem I described in the introduction to this chapter, that is, the difficulty of defining how far the critic can go in the search for coherence before it becomes a mere play of wits. Drawn by the attraction of the *reductio ad unum* and the hope of finding that an opera may have just as much coherence as a pure musical form like the sonata or the symphony, the critic sometimes tries to group the various tonalities into a single system, secretly hoping that he will discover that one tonality governs the whole. This viewpoint does have the merit of demonstrating the coherence of musical discourse underlying Verdi's operas.[40] Still, aside from the fact that the theory is at times based on expedients more ingenious than convincing and that it underestimates certain cyclic factors that I outline below, it does not take into account breaks that are imposed by the drama and that can lead the composer to make similar breaks in the music. To take a precise example, is it more correct to insist on the "dramatic" value of E major in *Rigoletto* (to which I will return later), as a rupture relative to the preceding tonal block, or on its possible integration, through the play of enharmonics, in a system where D♭ major would be the basic key and tonic and E/F♭ the mediant, as David Lawton suggests in his ingenious scheme?[41]

Furthermore, how far can one go in attributing a semantic value to a tonality? Here, too, the temptation to endow each key with an ethos is not new, even if it has encountered some strong counterarguments. Sometimes a recurring modulation seems to conjure up a character or situation; sometimes it seems merely to have an articulatory value between the moments of the plot, without suggesting a precise meaning. If the critic's search for tonal coherence entails undervaluing the influence of the text guiding the composer, then the search for a semanticization of tonalities may well come up against a harmonic logic that excludes it.

Finally, as I pointed out, Verdi never speaks of either of these problems in his letters, which does not preclude raising them but is nevertheless significant. Moreover, in his analysis of the operas, Budden stresses on several occasions how relatively unimportant the tonal level of an opera was in the minds of Italian opera composers: "The tonic-dominant polarity, so dear to the German composer," he observes, speaking of *Oberto,* "[meant little] to the Italians of that time—and still less the complex system of relationships erected on it. So there is nothing unusual in the procedure, unthinkable in Beethoven, Mozart or Weber, whereby Verdi ends his overture in D major and begins his introductory chorus a tone higher."[42] It is a fact that Verdi's early operas show frequent examples of relatively abrupt linkages, even juxtapositions pure and simple, as well as arias and ensembles whose different sections are not dependent on related tonalities.[43]

It is often thought that this minimal attention to tonal architecture came from the habit of writing for different voices and that choosing a key is, to a large extent, to define an ideal sound space for a particular voice. This may well have been the consideration that guided Verdi when he changed the tonality of a passage between the first and the last versions since so often these transcriptions do not seem to lend themselves to a musical explanation or to be justified dramatically. At times, the original key even seems to contribute more to the overall coherence, in relation to what comes before and what follows.[44]

It may be the same concern that sometimes caused the composer to be uncompromising over transpositions. For instance, he refused to set Radames's romanza, written in B♭ major, a semitone lower when tenors were having difficulty holding the final high B♭ pianissimo and morendo for two measures. He preferred to suggest a variant that shortened the high note and then returned an octave lower to finish pianissimo, repeating "vicino al sol." His justification for refusing the change was not tonal coherence, or the significance of the chosen key, but vocal reasons: "If we transpose it a semitone, it becomes an absolute baritone tessitura, and if we take out the As any baritone could sing it."[45] It seems, therefore, that Verdi's primary concern was to create an emotional space linked to a certain color that was connected, in turn, to a tessitura that implied a tonality.

These examples do not mean that Verdi did not respect tonal connections in the overall scheme or that he did not frequently make dramatic use of them: they simply mean that tonal organization is not always a determining criterion. One can rule out, straight off, the idea of an affective lexicon of tonalities: if a given key has a certain significance in one opera, if, for example, the love of Alfredo and Violetta, in *Traviata,* is linked to the key of F major,[46] that does not mean that this key will have the same semantic value in another work. When Wolfgang Osthoff insists on the importance of E (major and minor) for the character of Gilda in *Rigoletto,* one wonders whether he means that the importance lies in the value peculiar to that tonality, which had a pastoral, bucolic connotation in baroque music,[47] or in its value of contrast in the general organization. It seems to be more the second meaning that is suggested by Rigoletto's act 1 monologue, where the tonality appears fleetingly under the words "Ma in altr'uom mi cangio!" (But here I am changed into another man). Although Gilda is not named, she is suggested musically in that the solo instrument at that moment is the flute and the voice announces the theme of "Caro nome."[48] After the introduction and the duet with Sparafucile, massively dominated by flat-note keys, this opening to the key of E has the effect of a sudden burst of sunshine through clouds and a break with the dark atmosphere that prevailed before.

It seems, then, that it is the relative, differential value of tonalities that should be our concern. The custom of giving certain modulations a dramatic value was traditional, and Verdi took advantage of it: modulation by a semitone, usually up, corresponded in most cases to an increase in the dramatic tension of a situation, an emotional shift that the situation underlined. Modulation by a whole tone often is a sign, with Verdi, of a progression in the drama, but without the feeling of sudden urgency that the semitone shift creates. Finally, modulation by a major third (in general down) often serves to oppose two moods, two characters, two worlds, and has the advantage of contrast. Note, however, that in these cases the relation of one tonality to another has the purpose of abstract articulation (like a coordinating conjunction that launches the sentence in a certain direction) rather than a meaning peculiar to the opera.

Nonetheless, the recurrence of certain tonalities on a large scale has led critics to ponder their semantic value. *Macbeth,* the touchstone of Verdian dramaturgy, has logically claimed commentators' attention. Julian Budden, usually extremely prudent in this area, admits that the opera shows three principal tonal "areas of pitch," Db, F, and A, which are connected with the idea of murder, with Macbeth, and with the outer world.[49]

The three keys studied here are separated by a major third, and it is interesting to note that this triad recurs in several of Verdi's operas. *Traviata* gives great importance to the same three keys of Db, F, and A (major).[50] In *Rigoletto,* Monterone's C minor stands out against the Ab that dominates the Duke of Mantua's fete, while Gilda is associated with the key of E. In his analysis of *Simon Boccanegra,* oriented toward the tonal architecture rather than the semantic significance of the keys, Edward T. Cone stresses the importance of E, C, and Ab, which dominate, respectively, the prelude and the first and last acts. Daniel Sabbeth, for his part, insists, apropos of *Falstaff,* on the three principal keys of E, C, and Ab.[51] The triad based on two major thirds, Ab–C–E and Db–F–A, thus would seem to be the basis for several operas. It is a bit dangerous to attribute an indisputable significance to these tonalities and more reasonable to think of them as having a purpose of articulation by creating a contrast between homogeneous blocks that are opposed in the drama.

Can one go further? Speaking of *Macbeth,* Budden adds to the three principal keys two subsidiary ones, E and Bb, while Chusid adds two more, C and E, thus bringing the total to seven semantically definable keys. In his study of *Rigoletto,* Marcello Conati suggests no fewer than nine significant keys. The coincidences can be unsettling but not always convincing: the semantic equivalence of a key is often belied by another passage that uses the same tonality with a totally different value.[52]

To sum up, the balance sheet can only be uneven and encourages the pragmatism adopted by Carolyn Abbate and Roger Parker in their coverage of analytic methodologies in the realm of opera.[53] In the field of opera studies one finds different methods coexisting, all of them admissible so long as there is no illusion that an absolute coherence can be established according to firm outlines. Opera (like the relation between words and music more generally) always works in a somewhat empirical manner, being based on elements that are both autonomous and interdependent: it calls for on the one hand fragmentary analyses that complement one another and on the other hand examinations that, on one precise point, attempt to bring together the various overlapping systems.[54]

THEMES

One method that composers, especially those of the last century, adopt to ensure the unity of an opera is the device of recurring themes. Dominating this trend is the major and widespread use that Wagner made of the leitmotif, whether for purposes of dramatic definition or musical structure. The technique never tempted Verdi, and it holds an altogether minor place in his oeuvre.

Curiously, it is in *I due Foscari* (1844) that the composer comes the closest to a thematic definition of his characters by giving them a recurring motif: Jacopo Foscari is defined by a G-minor theme, which is introduced by the clarinet in the prelude and repeated three times during the opera; the same goes for his wife, Lucrezia Contarini, for the Council of Ten, and for the Doge Foscari.[55] This is far from the comprehensive use of the leitmotif to which we are accustomed with Wagner, nor does it have anything to do with Wagner's technique of elaboration, transformation, and combination of these motifs; the Verdian themes are generally repeated in the same key and without appreciable modification.

What Verdi uses more widely is the procedure Roncaglia has called the *pivot theme,* a bold theme that condenses a basic feature of the drama and hardly appears more than two or three times at key moments of the plot; one example is the horn theme that opens the prelude to *Ernani,* another the curse theme with which the prelude to *Rigoletto* begins. The latter is just a simple chord, but its harmonic versatility allows it to fit into several of the opera's principal keys: thus, the C that is prominent in the prelude refers us to Monterone and his curse, which for Verdi constituted the central axis of the plot. These strong themes can, between them, create a tension that in some way surrounds the sound space in which the drama unfolds, usually beginning with the overture: thus, Ernani's horn is contrasted with the same character's heroic love, just as Violetta's wasting away contrasts, in the prelude to *Traviata,* with the characteristic abandon of the great love theme; in the same way Aida's sorrowful chromaticism is set against the implacable, regular, descending motion of the priests' music in the prelude to that opera.

We do not need to dwell at length on reminiscences, which crop up frequently in Verdi's operas, as in those of his predecessors. The habit of writing the symphonic introduction last of all usually encouraged him to use this section to announce certain effective themes of an opera; it was a question not of making a dramatic synthesis of the work, as was the case with the pivot theme, but rather of a potpourri summing-up of its various colors. Likewise, reminiscences from one act to another are to be found, although they are neither numerous nor very significant.

At the most, we should note that Verdi tends to employ reminiscence progressively less rather than more. The 1881 version of *Simon* contains fewer than does the original version, mainly owing to the excising of the potpourri prelude of 1857. Similarly, reminiscences are less frequent in the *Don Carlos* of 1884, or even 1886, than in the Paris version of 1867, and the two last operas show extremely sparing use of anything resembling a thematic reprise.

How to explain Verdi's relative lack of interest in a technique that was to enjoy such emulation in Wagner's wake? It could not be out of any desire to break away from his illustrious contemporary since Verdi's practice hardly changed from the time of his first operas and the timid attempt in *Foscari* was not followed up. More probably the explanation is a certain distrust of an essentially symphonic technique that handed the elaboration of the drama over to the orchestra, whereas Verdi preferred to gather up its fruits in vocal melody. His loyalty to the Italian vocal tradition could only strengthen his convictions, and it was with a certain irritation that he noted the burgeoning development of the symphonic technique. In a letter apropos of Bruneau's *Le Rêve,* he expressed disapproval of "the fact that all the action is contained and strangled in the circle of three or four—I won't call them motives, but orchestral phrases that keep recirculating throughout the opera, without the relief of a little vocal melody."[56] The main reason for this objection seems to be, however, the preference Verdi shows for a more allusive, insinuating, and impressionistic use of thematic analogies: he is concerned not so much with entrusting the progression of a meaning to certain clearly recognizable themes as with using a succession of brush strokes to create a homogeneous atmosphere appropriate to each opera—in a word, a color.

COLOR

The study of color (*tinta,* in Verdi's language as in that of some of his predecessors) is, in contrast, one of the most fertile fields in the analysis of Verdi's operas. *Tinta* is based on the use of melodic, rhythmic, harmonic, and orchestral analogies specific to an opera and occurring frequently enough to be significant; these kinships are sufficiently clear to be discernible through analysis but not so close as to constitute recurring themes, especially since the procedures employed are often very brief (e.g., one melodic element or a rhythmic formula).[57] The technique is therefore completely different from that of the leitmotif, which functions only if, in spite of the changes it undergoes, it can be recognized and identified by the listener; the analogies that make up the *tinta* of an opera appeal to a memory that is indistinct, an emotional memory, one that associates different moments but without perceiving the reason for this association.[58]

To the extent that color is specific to a certain work, these procedures should not be confused with those that help form a common basis peculiar to a tradition or a composer. The triple repetition of a formula, whether in *Macbeth, Jérusalem, Don Carlos,* or *Aida* but also in *Les Pêcheurs de perles* or *The Magic Flute,* is one of the basic procedures for giving luster and solemnity to a dramatic moment. The semitone, in the melody or accompaniment, often expresses grief or confusion; the anapestic rhythm ‿ ‿ – signals death in *Trovatore* as it does in *Traviata* and *Vêpres.* Similarly, each composer attaches a certain value to particular formulas, as Verdi does with the *fortissimo* trill or the unison of voice and orchestra, both of which carry a negative connotation.[59]

Contrary to tonal coherence, which eludes the average listener (how many people notice the relation of keys at the beginning and end of an opera!), *tinta* can be perceived by everyone as a homogeneous impression, even if the listener cannot tell precisely how that homogeneity comes about.

True, the semantic value of these analogies is hard to explain: often their only purpose is to strengthen the coherence of the musical discourse by creating in the listener's mind a feeling of kinship between the various moments. In his study of *Don Carlos,* Frits Noske isolates three musical figures, providing some twenty-five examples for two of them, amply proving their importance. He also shows that the figures essentially concern Philip II, Elisabeth, and the Infante Carlos, characters who are incidentally, according to Noske, consumed by frustration. Should one therefore conclude that these characters, considered as a signifier, have frustration as their signified?[60] The perplexity that certain interpretations arouse does not, however, affect the pertinence of these thematic groupings.

In a general way, "color" is one of the most important elements in the domain of opera. All the great composers tend more or less explicitly toward a unity of color: the tragic intimism of Handel's *Tamerlano* differs widely from the pomp and variety of *Giulio Cesare* or the elegant frivolity of *Partenope*. There is one tint for *Così* and another peculiar to *Figaro,* a *Tannhäuser* color that is distinct from that of *Lohengrin.* Color is a little like what Weber called the "unified basic tone" *(einheitlicher Grundton),* it being understood that it is not so much a question of giving an opera a single tone as of using an array of tints that are combined in one common palette.

In any case, the notion of *tinta* has an essential place in Verdian aesthetics. When the censors threatened to proscribe the libretto Piave had drawn up from Hugo's *Le Roi s'amuse,* the composer declared himself at his wits' end: "Piave had assured me that there were no difficulties regarding the subject. Trusting the poet, I therefore started to study it intensely and deeply meditate it, so that in my mind I had already found the idea and musical *tinta.* I could say that for me most of the work was already done. If I were now compelled to seek another subject there wouldn't be enough time to study it, and I couldn't write an opera I couldn't be happy with."[61] Note that the "idea" and *tinta* are fixed during the preliminary "rumination" of the subject, therefore prior to the actual composition.

It is noteworthy, too, that Verdi refers to "subject," not "libretto." The "rumination" of the subject fixes the idea and color of the drama, while the libretto specifies the organization of details. We have a very clear example of this in Verdi's note to Piave in connection with the first act of *Macbeth,* the versified introduction of which he wanted Piave to send him as soon as possible: "Once the introduction is done, I'll leave you all the time you want. At this point I'm so familiar with the general character and the colors that it's as if the whole libretto were already done."[62]

For a precise example,[63] let us study the ascending scale through the interval of a sixth in *Aida.* The formula in itself is commonplace and frequent; as for the heroic connotation of the ascending sixth, it was solidly established by the Romantic tradition, Wagner included. In act 1, Radames employs the formula to express his hope of triumph (see ex. 26*a*). Here, we have the young hero, already radiating with the glory promised

EX. 26*a*

EX. 26*b*

by victory. During the ensemble that follows Radames's appointment as general in command of the Egyptian army, Amneris follows him and, over a dotted rhythm, solemnly wishes the man she loves his victory: at this stage, the motif describes the martial arrogance of the Egyptians (see ex. 26*b*).

With spirit—the rhythm is no longer staccato and the movement rapid—Aida repeats the motif at the beginning of her *gran scena,* but the minor (no longer major) sixth and tritone (instead of a major chord) betray a surge of panic and recoil: the young woman has understood that by wishing for her lover's victory she is wishing for her countrymen's defeat (see ex. 26*c*). At the beginning of act 2 Radames has triumphed, the women surrounding Amneris weave vocal crowns for the conqueror, and the successive rising major and minor sixths have a caressing touch; this is the time the warrior rests as a reward for his valor in the field (see ex. 26*d*).

Next, the ceremony of triumph begins, and the King receives his gen-

EX. 26c

EX. 26d

EX. 26e

eral with the same melodic acclaim, but this time on a more expansive, satisfied rhythm underlined by a perfectly regular harmony (see ex. 26e). The Ethiopian prisoners file past, among them Aida's father, Amonasro, leader of the Ethiopians. He reminds us, with the same triplet formula used by the King, that his people will respond in kind to Egyptian arrogance (see ex. 26f)—a "quotation" that is not lacking in irony!

Later, when Radames is being judged as a traitor to his country, when,

EX. 26*f*

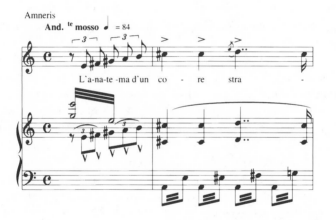

EX. 26*g*

EX. 26*h*

in short, the war machine recoils against the one who was to have been its chief hero, not surprisingly we find our melodic figure turning up again in Amneris's imprecation against the priest-judges, "Sacerdoti compiste un delitto": the rhythms of the King's speech and Amonasro's defiance (each follows the same steps) comment on "the anathema of a heart shattered" by the grief of knowing that Radames is doomed to die (see ex. 26g). The recurrence of the motif has poignancy here since the arrogant formula that Pharaoh's daughter used when addressing Radames now turns against her and depicts her unhappiness. It should be added that the theme accompanying the priests throughout their chant is in a way the reverse of this triumphant formula, being based on a descent by conjunct degrees usually no greater than a major sixth—this is the funereal reverse of Egyptian triumphalism (see ex. 26h)!

Here, we have a good example of Verdi's procedure. Overall, the formula used connotes Egyptian militarism, but it is enriched with different nuances depending on the context—triumphalist pride, Amneris's amorous hopes and despair, Aida's inner conflict, the victorious King's satisfaction, Radames's heroic illusions, the irony of the enemy who is vanquished but not brought low. In short, the color arises not so much from a predetermined plan as from the way it is used in a precise perspective and from the patina it acquires from the context in which it is employed.

In truth, all the elements of the work—overall structure, melodic style, libretto language, tricks of form, instrumentation—finally play their part in achieving the general color. If one wanted to find out what makes up the *tinta* of *La traviata,* given that Verdi conceived the opera as an intimate, sentimental drama with an average, almost colloquial style, one would cite (1) frequency of the strophic form, chosen for its almost popular simplicity; (2) the tendency to repeat the melodic segments without variation (aa instead of a1 a2) for the same reasons; (3) preference for triple meters, $\frac{3}{8}$, $\frac{3}{4}$, and $\frac{6}{8}$, because this rhythm is more popular than duple meters and suggests both the frivolity of the fete and the pathos of a love song; (4) the regular pace of the vocal line, often moving in equal note values to avoid the solemn, heroic connotation of dotted rhythms; (5) Verdi's tendency to let the voice proceed by conjunct motion, avoiding leaps of wide intervals; (6) the descending impulse of most of the great melodic themes; (7) the intimate orchestration that Boito described when he spoke of the "sad and tenuous, ethereal, almost disembodied" sonorities of the prelude;[64] and, finally, (8) the structure, already mentioned, which opposes boldly contrasting areas.

Conclusion

Ch'io sappia il mio destin,
se cielo e terra
Dovessero innovar l'antica guerra.

MACBETH

A few conclusions are in order as we come to the end of our long exploration of Verdi's universe. We have seen that the goal the composer constantly has before him is the theatrical fact, as a concrete totality covering words, gestures, sounds, and images, and that the recognition of the relative autonomy of the arts contributing to operas' creation, beginning with his own, does not exclude complete submission to the "drama," whether it concerns a particular situation or an overall conception.

In studying Verdi's development, one is struck by a strong concern for balance—balance between form and movement, sense of drama and love of song, innovation and tradition—which explains the very gradual pace of his evolution. Rather than reflecting a moderate, prudent temperament, this pragmatism bespeaks a vivid consciousness of the fact that opera is based on a set of conventions, that is to say, on a code common to both the artist and his public, and that the drama's truth is transmitted by means of stylization, which implies artifice. When the *avveniristi,* the champions of the music of the future, raged against "traditional forms," Verdi made this bitter comment: "It has now become fashionable to complain about the cabaletta and not to want to listen to them any more. This is a mistake as grave as of that time in the past when everybody wanted nothing but cabalettas. People protest as much as they can against conventions, and end up abandoning one just to embrace another."[1] Put differently, it is useless to launch into a priori arguments against convention because there is no escaping it; the essential thing is to change a convention when it is no longer capable of transmitting a discernible truth.

Along with his conviction that art rests on conventions that change over time, Verdi had an acute sense of the moral significance of form, as

337

the aesthetic filter of an artist's view of life. Here we see one of the most profound differences separating our composer from Wagner, whose violent repudiation of convention arose from a demiurgic ambition that art should be "nature" and possess more truth than the reality surrounding it.[2]

We have attempted to show that the motive force driving Verdi's development was the tension between two aesthetic poles corresponding to two ways of conceiving opera, hence also of viewing life: melodrama, an epic and synthetic vision, and music drama, a vision that is critical and analytic. These two views are in fact conflicting. The first seeks the transparency and sweep of moral attitudes, what one might call their unequivocal character, and represents the celebration of a reality, however painful it might be—the desire to transcend the ambiguity of everyday life. The second, in contrast, is examination and awareness, the pursuit of an ever-fleeting image of man and reality.

In the course of an evolution that takes us from one pole to the other, we find form changing not only in its modalities but also in its signification. At first, the conventionality of form also ensures a certain impersonality, a capacity for objectivization that this impersonality confers on it; then doubt creeps in: up to what point is form suitable for grasping a character or passion? Does it not merely "freeze" a pose, a purely theatrical attitude, a moment whose transparency may be false?

In his day Verdi stood apart from his cultural milieu, as we have seen from the reluctance of artistic circles to grant him the place he deserved. For a long time there floated about him an atmosphere of vulgarity, which still dogs him today—the impression of a rather perfunctory skill, a vigor effective but unpolished, a dramaturgy lacking in depth. Yet the very people who undervalued the composer sensed that his dramatic world resisted their view of him by its force and evocative power, the almost bald clarity of its outlines, its absence of indulgence and rhetoric.

This contradiction between the image of a composer who was "minor," provincial, and popular—not in the best sense of the word—and the reality of a success that spread to all parts of the world and all walks of life suggests that Verdi was in some way out of touch with the Romantic age. More than one observer has remarked on this, each one coming up with a different explanation. Alfred Einstein has noted the paradoxical nature of Verdi's Romanticism, which embraced its violent passions and larger-than-life excesses only to reduce the pretensions of Romantic subjectivity to absurdity and treat it with disenchanted humor.[3]

Alberto Moravia also points out the anachronism of a "sanguine, passionate, robust, explosive" personality in such a "mean and paltry" age: Verdi reminds him of one of those illustrious Renaissance palaces, now dilapidated, that still stand in many a middle-class city of provincial Italy. He sees the explanation for this lack of sympathy in cultural sociology: "What is this so-called vulgarity of Verdi? . . . It is the humanistic conception of our Renaissance that was forsaken and betrayed by the Italian ruling classes after the Counter Reformation but preserved by the common people and eventually left to degenerate into folklore."[4] This view of an artist who is both aristocratic and of the people, one might add, perfectly corresponds to Stravinsky's.

The most appealing interpretation of Verdi's alienation from his time comes from Isaiah Berlin.[5] The British philosopher takes up Schiller's contrasting of the naive poets, among whom he ranks Homer and Shakespeare, and the sentimental poets, who include, according to Schiller, the majority of his contemporaries. The first embody nature, while the second seek a vanished nature. "The value of the one consists in absolutely reaching a finite grandeur, while the value of the other lies in approaching an infinite grandeur." "The ancient poet's power stems from the art of something limited, the modern from the art of something infinite."[6] The faults of the naive poets are platitude and vulgarity, those of the sentimental poets excess, abstraction, and loss of the concrete.

In Berlin's view, Verdi looms as "the last of the great naive masters of Western music, in an age given over to the *Sentimentalisches*." The lengthy, nostalgic description Schiller offers of the naive poet conjures up—strikingly, it must be said—our composer's own personality: reserve, lack of familiarity, an impervious barrier between life and creative work, concealment of the springs of his art, the "dry, truthful way" in which he describes his object, "art of limitation." This "naïveté," moreover, is perceptible to the ear, and the difference in spirit between Verdi's music and the music of many Romantic composers is indeed that between "absolutely reaching a finite grandeur" and "approaching an infinite grandeur."[7]

This view is penetrating, but our study has led us to see how Verdi slowly grew closer to his own century, approaching the sensibility of the "sentimental" era. Verdi's forceful but provincial spirit became reconciled with the great currents of European culture, with its richness, its doubts, and its longings. The tension we have discerned between melodrama and music drama is the tension between a naive approach and a more shrewd and critical awareness of reality. In the young Verdi's world, what *exists* coincides with what *is;* after that, humor, alienation, and disillusion erode the solidity of the world, although without destroying it, and what *exists* is now no more than the trace of what *is* or aspires *to be.*

War of the Worlds

Can an artist who, as I said in an early chapter, makes his home, cuckoo-like, in others' nests be said to have a "conception of the world"? An opera composer's creative vision is displayed not so much in the subjects, characters, and ideas of his dramas as in the way he takes hold of a story and re-creates it—the stamp he leaves on it. Seen from this viewpoint, the dominant characteristics of the Verdian theater are excessiveness, the irreconcilable clash of opposites, the ineluctability of destiny.

From Romanticism, Verdi's characters inherit the absolute imperative of passion. In the case of the hero, this is expressed as libertarian protest, the refusal of any form of subjection, the claim to innocence and legitimacy; for the tyrant, it means a drive for power that brooks no obstacle, the smoldering fire that is all-consuming; and, for the judge, it is implacable loyalty to an order that must be upheld. Love is absolute, excessiveness is absolute, the desire for vengeance is absolute. Like some irresistible force, these imperatives are a call for mastery of man's fate. If Verdi remained indifferent to verismo, it was because verismo strips the character of his independence and makes him the helpless plaything of circumstances or his impulses, a determinism that was repugnant to Verdian morality.

Melodrama's larger-than-life passions would be mere grandiloquence if they did not require paying the cost, if the dynamism impelling the characters did not simultaneously entail their destruction. In fact, these passions immediately come up against others no less vehement and against the constraints of reality and the claims of the law; they refuse to coexist with others, preferring catastrophe to compromise and defeat to reconciliation. The real world, which is the arena in which these opposing forces confront each other, that is, the chain of actions and reactions that make up the plot, transforms these passions into destinies. Verdi portrays the inevitable enmeshment of his characters with an unbending sobriety. His plots are forced marches toward the outcome; nothing can prevent what must happen from happening. In this sense, his dramaturgy expresses the force of destiny as much as the destiny of force.

It is in this sense of the inexorable that the profound strength of Verdi's universal view is to be found. No matter how exaggerated or simplistic his characters may be, the whirlwind of their destiny sweeps away all traces in them of indulgence and rhetoric. Verdi confronts this cardboard theater, with its improbable, even absurd plots, with the detachment of the great realists. He clears away the romantic unreality of the "penny dreadful" to reveal the pathos, the drama, and ultimately the tragedy beneath.

Where is Verdi himself in this bitter struggle? It has been said that one of the characteristics of every great artist is to feel and represent contradictory forces with the same equanimity, and this holds perfectly true for our composer. It is also said that the man illumines the work, but the opposite is even more true since the work reproduces on a large scale tendencies that in life can only be expressed in attenuated form. Verdi was a man molded of contradictions and inner tensions; he behaved like a savage individualist, rebelling against any kind of subordination, intolerant of any dependence to the point of being unjust, haughtily claiming complete control of his life; and at the same time he was a man of fierce loyalties—to his fields, his country, and his tradition. He was a man of passion and discipline, tolerant and tyrannical, a calculating businessman and a sensitive, vulnerable artist; he believed in principles and liked to exercise his will, but he portrayed only individuals crushed by passion and often evinced a certain fatalism. These tensions, which would sometimes surface in a letter or an attitude, burst out with violence in each one of his operas.

In his works it is often hard to determine which side he is on, and it is symptomatic that he has been seen both as representing the world of fathers defending a repressive morality and as the spokesman for sons who revolt against their fathers. He likes rebels, outcasts, and pirates, but note how deferential he is toward those representing the established order, the judges who condemn those same rebels to death. There is no doubt that he sympathized with both sides: curiously, the most Verdian characters, like Azucena and Philip II, are often both executioner and victim.

In any case, he loves greatness, however it may be expressed. Yet he loves it as a moralist, not as an aesthete, for its celebration of human energy, not only for the beauty of the gesture. What he loves above all else is man's struggle against the world, the struggle that he knows is lost before it is begun but whose nobility and failure he wants to show at one and the same time. One way to look at his repugnance for the *pezzo staccato*—the isolated musical fragment—is to see it as Verdi's way of refusing to adopt a purely aesthetic view of a fine gesture or sentiment since these have meaning only when integrated in a story—the story of the struggle in which our destiny is played out.

* * * * * * * *

Certain observations are now appropriate. First of all, nothing evolves in the Verdian world. True, characters may be shown as changing and subject to contradictory impulses, since it is precisely one of the characteristics of the journey Verdi's characters make to move from a statue-like position to a situation that is far more mobile. Still, this change is not so much a metamorphosis as the surfacing in them of the ineluctable, the awareness that they are racing toward a failure their illusions had previously hidden from them. Revenge and the impossibility of forgetting are emblematic of the Verdian world. The world of men cannot forgive, and each creature can only persevere in his or her being. Peace and reconciliation are rejected into an indeterminate region that, dramatically, exists only as hope.

There is no evolution because there is no synthesis, no mediation, no dialectical relation between contradictory realities. Both the reconciling of opposites and redemption are foreign to Verdi's dramaturgy. Each character must pursue his course to the end; there is no remission other than the peace of death. He must stand tall, raising high his aspiration to freedom and fulfillment, until he falls victim to an unlucky fate, to chance, to others' passions or his own weakness. If one excepts the brief parenthesis of *Nabucco* and *I Lombardi,* where individual trials are transfigured by a messianic conception of history, there is no redemption to brighten the horizon, no mystic gleam that might give rise to a morality or simply a reason for hope, or any philosophy that might make it possible to end this logical, mindless succession of events.

In this, Verdi is no master thinker subordinating human beings and things to a higher order. The collisions of passion, reality, and the law have no meaning beyond being what they are. There is always an absolute primacy of the fact over any commentary or rationalization; the succession of events does not match any explanations that might make it bearable or possible to understand. It is a logic that we find again in the aesthetic domain, with what I have called the fatalism of sensation that takes precedence over any speech or justification. The world is absurd, incoherent, unfair, but he grants it supreme power and final judgment.

In this sense, it is appropriate to apply to Verdi's oeuvre what Adorno, taking up Nietzsche's parallel, writes about *Carmen:* "In Wagner, everything, every gesture, every motif and the overall interconnections—all are charged with meaning. In Bizet the inhumanity and hardness, even the violence of the form, has been used to obliterate the last token of meaning, so as to forestall any illusion that anything in life could have any meaning over and above its obvious one."[8] In Verdi's case the synthesis is not moral but artistic; the dialectic is in the style, not the thought. Every failure is a loss, all suffering useless and absurd. The sound and fury of things conduce to three attitudes, also present in Verdi's makeup: stoicism, which is the discipline of greatness; pity for the suffering; and humor, which is percipience and detachment.

It is this nakedness of the fact that makes Verdi's universe a tragic one. In *The Death of Tragedy,* George Steiner observes that Romanticism sought to rediscover the spirit of tragedy embodied in the Greeks and Shakespeare and that the attempt failed for two reasons: first, the ineluctable, unjustifiable nature of tragic reality could not stand up to the rise of historical optimism or the idea of redemption; and, second, egoism, as the exaltation of the self, which often becomes self-justification, destroyed the tragic spirit, which sanctifies what appears to be unjustifiable. Verdi, as we have seen, had nothing to do with these trends: however close his world might have been to Romantic theatricality, he remained fundamentally tragic through what I have called his sense of the ineluctable.

It is difficult at this point to avoid the problem of Verdi's religious beliefs, for they might be expected to provide the final explanation of the apparently inexplicable. Unfortunately, there is no sure reply to the question. That Verdi was anticlerical, as were in fact a good part of the ruling class in Italy at that time, is clear as daylight: in his operas "political" ecclesiastics are treated savagely, consoling priests with much benevolence.

Several of the composer's works, the *Pater noster,* the *Ave Maria,* the *Quattro pezzi sacri,* not to speak of the *Requiem,* clearly come from a religious vein of inspiration, but it may be that they derive from a questioning about death, destiny, and God, a search for peace of the heart, rather than from faith. Whether the composer was a believer is another matter. His occasional observance, his good relations with the clergy, the fact that his wife was a believer, the accounts of his last moments, which are far from clear,[9] hardly permit a satisfactory answer to the question. The most explicit testimonies, those of his wife, Giuseppina, point rather to atheism; contrasting Manzoni and Verdi, she wrote in 1872: "There are some virtuous natures that need to believe in God; others, equally perfect, that are happy not believing in anything, and simply observing rigorously every precept of strict morality."[10]

It may well be that, in a way that is hard for us to understand today but was no doubt common in his time,[11] Verdi coexisted with religion as a country landowner might coexist with a distant but powerful sovereign whom he has never seen but whose existence he would not dare deny. To feign familiarity with him would be quite out of place, while to state that he is merely imaginary is no less absurd. It is best to regulate one's existence by making an abstraction of this encumbering presence and keeping one's ideas about it to oneself. Did Verdi change at the end of his life? It is very far from sure, if one is to believe the letter Boito wrote Bellaigue after the composer's death: "He died magnificently, like a fighter, formidable and mute."[12]

The *Requiem,* which Verdi began before *Aida* and finished before *Otello,* does not alter the picture I have given of his vision of the world. In this work where, to paraphrase Giuseppina Strepponi, Verdi speaks to God in the language he always spoke in his operas, the individual kicks and struggles, cries and implores, passes from rebellion to appeasement and from prostration to hope, yet without shaking his prison walls or forcing open the bronze doors of the unknown.

ARIA   This is the staple of opera, a self-contained piece providing singers with an opportunity to shine. During the first half of the nineteenth century the aria was made up of two parts (deriving from the custom, already current in the previous century, of having the first, slow movement followed by a livelier one), which is the reason we often use the term *double aria*. With Rossini the use of the double aria became widespread, and by the time Verdi began his career the aria in its complete form was composed of the following sections: (1) *Recitativo* or *scena (d'attacco):* a more or less elaborate scene constituting the introduction of the aria; it can include an arioso or a little cantabile. (2) *Cantabile* or *Adagio* or *Andante* or *primo tempo:* this is the first part of the aria, lyrical in character and moderate in tempo. (3) *Tempo di mezzo:* the middle part, which is freer and often coinciding with a turn of the plot that justifies going from 2 to 4 and brings in other characters and/or the chorus. (4) *Cabaletta* or *Allegro:* second part of the aria, often lively and brilliant. Usually, it calls for a reprise after a ritornello, which is given either to the orchestra or to a soloist, possibly joined by the chorus and other characters who likewise take part in the concluding Stretta.

The term *cabalettismo* is used to describe the tendency toward a brilliant, energetic, or martial style, such as we find in Verdi's cabalettas. *Cavatina* denotes an aria of moderate tempo sung by a character at his or her entrance onstage, but the term also refers to the slow section of a double aria. The romanza is a simple aria, without cabaletta, made up of two sections, one minor and the other major; it therefore differs from the French song called a *romance.* The *rondò finale,* which was highly prized in the 1830s and 1840s, reflects the custom of ending an opera (or an act) with a grand aria for the protagonist that follows the pattern of the double aria. The preghiera, as the name suggests, is simply a prayer, without any precise formal implication. The arioso is a vocal form halfway between aria and recitative; it can be extremely flexible or perfectly regular. Finally, it should be recalled that contemporary terminology was fairly loose; thus, the forms described above could be subject to certain variations.

BANDA   The *banda* was a wind band including woodwinds, brass, and percussion; each sizable Italian city had its own, and some of them, such as Venice's Kinsky *banda,* enjoyed a wide reputation. In the first half of the nineteenth century it became fashionable to have every opera include a march or "display" music, given to the *banda.* The composer wrote the music on two or three staves, and the conductor of the *banda* orchestrated it according to the makeup of his group.

COMPRIMARIO   An intermediary category between the leading and secondary roles: in *Nabucco,* Zaccaria and Abigaille are leading roles *(primo baritono, primo basso, prima donna soprano),* Ismaele and Fenena are *comprimari (tenore comprimario,* etc.), and the High Priest of Baal, Abdallo, and Anna are secondary roles *(seconda donna soprano,* etc.). The *comprimari* took part in ensembles but might also have an aria (cf. Banco and Macduff in *Macbeth*).

CONCERTATO   Term used to designate any ensemble that groups together the soloists and possibly the chorus. However, it is generally used as a synonym for the great slow-tempo ensemble forming the high point of the Finale.

DUETTO   Another staple of Romantic opera. Perfected by Rossini, in its classic form it consists of five phases: (1) *scena:* an introductory episode, informal in character; (2) *tempo d'attacco* or *entrata:* a lively movement, often used for dialogue; (3) *Adagio* or *cantabile:* a central movement, moderate in tempo and more lyrical or reflective in character; (4) *tempo di mezzo:* an intermediate episode, fairly structured and lively; (5) *cabaletta* or *Allegro,* sometimes repeated, and ending in a Stretta. The term *tripartite duet* is often used, meaning sections 2, 3, and 5, which are the most important, 1 being introductory and 4 sometimes being omitted. According to Philip Gossett's terminology, 2 and 4 are kinetic movements, without a coda. Within each movement the singers can enter either together or one after the other (simultaneous or parallel presentation); their melodies can be similar (aside from transposition) or dissimilar; sometimes the presentation is in dialogue, with the melody shared between the two voices. Even in the case of parallel presentations on similar or different melodies, the movement often ends with an a due where the two soloists sing in unison. The *duettino* is a generally short duet, in one movement and freely structured.

ENSEMBLE   Used to designate a number that implies more than one soloist, with or without chorus. Ensembles composed of more than two soloists are relatively flexible in form, using that of either the finale or the duet, but usually tending to present the soloists separately before they join together in a concertante section.

FINALE   An ensemble placed, as the name suggests, at the end of an act; the most important one is positioned around the middle of the work, at the climax of the plot; it assembles all, or nearly all, the soloists as well as the chorus. The section derives from the Finale of opera buffa, from which it takes its two high points: the slow movement, an ensemble of stupefaction and confusion, and the Stretta, more or less frenzied. Rossini established it as a convention at the heart of opera seria. Customarily, it takes the following form: 1) introductory episode (chorus, hymn, march, soloist's aria, scene, etc.); (2) *tempo d'attacco,* very close in spirit to that of the duet; 3) *pezzo concertato* or *Largo:* a slow movement corresponding to a moment of meditation, terror, or reflection; (4) *tempo di mezzo* (or *materia di mezzo*), which is the occasion for coups de théâtre, unexpected entrances, etc.; (5) *Stretta,* characterized by a dynamic crescendo.

FORM   Since the term is apt to cause confusion, let us make clear that here it is used more or less systematically in the sense of a conventional musical unit; it typically has a regular structure tending to symmetry and reprises, while its closed character isolates it within the flow of the opera; finally, it is easily perceived by the audience and creates a feeling of relative predictability in the listener. The crisis these forms underwent from the 1850s on clearly does not imply any abandoning of the form as a musical elaboration.

INTRODUZIONE   The number or numbers that figure at the beginning of an opera or act. Sometimes it takes the form of a simple chorus *(coro d'introduzione),* sometimes one or more musical episodes (aria, *duettino*). In the latter case, the introduction ends in a *Stretta d'introduzione.* It can also give rise to a grand ensemble (the quintet of *I Lombardi* or the septet of *Stiffelio*) followed by a Stretta, by which it resembles the Finale.

OVERTURE   A symphonic number with which an opera begins. It can be a *preludio* (prelude), which is usually short and freely structured (often a potpourri of themes from the opera) and directly linked to the *Introduzione.* Another possibility is the sinfonia, which is longer, more solidly constructed, and clearly separated from the act that follows. In both cases, the themes are generally reused in the course of the opera.

PARLANTE   An intermediate technique between recitative and accompanied melody. Basevi distinguishes the *parlante melodico,* where the melody is entrusted to the orchestra and only partially used by the voices, the *parlante armonico,* where the voice is in free counterpoint with the orchestral melody, and the mixed parlante resulting from a blending of the first two forms.

PERTICHINO   Intervention of a character and/or chorus in an aria or ensemble, limited and perfunctory in character. Thus, one refers to an *aria con pertichini.*

PROGRAMMA or SELVA   A prose "scenario" in more or less detail that determines the overall scheme, structure, and articulations of an opera. Once the *programma* was accepted by the theater, the censors, and the composer, the librettist proceeded to the job of putting it into verse.

PUNTATURA Modifications, usually minor, made to a vocal line to adapt it to the needs of a certain singer.

SCENA This word gradually replaced the term *recitativo* to denote the sections that begin an aria or ensemble and are not subject to the criteria of metrical or musical regularity. The *scena* is very free in treatment: its style sometimes recalls the old recitative (declamation of the voice punctuated by chords, in the harpsichord and later the orchestra) and sometimes gives the orchestra more autonomy in the melody. The *scena* can include an arioso or contain purely instrumental passages.

SEASON Theater life was organized into seasons. The four chief ones were the season of Carnival (from 26 December to the week before the first Sunday of Lent), the spring season (from one week after Easter to the end of June), summer (July, August, and part of September), and autumn (from the end of September to mid-December). The most prestigious season was Carnival. Minor theaters could not guarantee performances every season. Singers were generally engaged on the basis of one season.

SEMISERIA Opera consisted of three genres: the seria genre, the most illustrious and the most expensive *(dramma [lirico], tragedia [lirica], melodramma [tragico]);* the buffa genre, which was less prestigious and less costly; and an intermediary genre, *opera semiseria* or *di mezzo carattere,* which combined domestic comedy, melodrama, and sentimental drama. Rossini, from *L'inganno felice* to *Matilde di Shabran,* Donizetti, from *Enrico di Borgogna* to *Linda di Chamounix,* and Bellini, with *Adelson e Salvini* and in a sense *La sonnambula,* all paid homage to the latter genre; it also tempted Verdi, although none of his operas can be placed in this category. The closest is *Luisa Miller.*

STRETTA Denotes the concluding section of a cabaletta where the movement gathers speed and the voices overlap. The term is also used for the entire rapid "cabaletta" movement of a finale.

VERSE Librettos were versified throughout, but custom decreed that the *scena* be written in *versi sciolti,* a free mixture of unrhymed lines of eleven and seven syllables, whereas the arias, ensembles, and choruses were written in *versi lirici* (the most common being five, six, seven, eight, ten or 5 × 2 syllables), partly rhymed and arranged in strophes.

Abbreviations

Analyzing Opera	*Analyzing Opera: Verdi and Wagner.* Edited by Carolyn Abbate and Roger Parker. Berkeley and Los Angeles: University of California Press, 1989).
Atti I	*Atti del I congresso internazionale di studi verdiani: Venezia, Isola di San Giorgio Maggiore, Fondazione Giorgio Cini, 31 luglio–2 agosto 1966.* Parma: ISV, 1969.
Atti II	*Atti del II congresso internazionale di studi verdiani: Verona, Castelvecchio; Parma, Istituto di Studi Verdiani; Busseto, Villa Pallavicino, 30 luglio–5 agosto 1969.* Parma: ISV, 1971.
Atti III	*Atti del III congresso internazionale di studi verdiani: Milano, Piccola Scale, 12–17 giugno 1972.* Parma: ISV, 1974.
Il melodramma italiano	*Il melodramma italiano dell'Ottocento: Studi e richerche per Massimo Mila.* Turin: Einaudi, 1977.
ISV; INSV	Istituto di Studi Verdiani (Parma) (until 1988); Istituto Nazionale di Studi Verdiani (1988 and after)
ISV Un ballo in maschera	*Verdi: Bollettino dell'Istituto di Studi Verdiani,* vol. 1, nos. 1–3. Parma: ISV, 1960.
ISV La forza del destino	*Verdi: Bollettino dell'Istituto di Studi Verdiani,* vol. 2, nos. 4–6. Parma: ISV, 1961, 1962, 1963–65.
ISV Rigoletto	*Verdi: Bollettino dell'Istituto di Studi Verdiani,* vol. 3, nos. 7–9. Parma: ISV, 1966–69, 1970–73, 1982.
ISV Ernani	*Verdi: Bollettino dell'Istituto di Studi Verdiani,* no. 10 *(Ernani ieri e oggi).* Parma: ISV, 1987.
Music in the Theater	*Music in the Theater: Essays on Verdi and Other Composers.* By Pierluigi Petrobelli. With translations by Roger

Parker. Princeton, N.J.: Princeton University Press, 1994.

Nuove prospettive   *Nuove prospettive nella ricerca verdiana: Atti del convegno internazionale in occasione della prima del "Rigoletto" in edizione critica, Vienna, 12/13 marzo 1983.* Parma: INSV; Milan: Ricordi, 1987.

WGV   *The Works of Giuseppe Verdi.* Chicago: University of Chicago Press; Milan: Ricordi, 1983–.

Chapter One

1. An idea of the situation is conveyed by the information that Paolo Mitrovich sent Verdi on 6 May 1857, concerning England: "There is no way to fill the house unless you schedule *La traviata, Il trovatore* or *Rigoletto,* and so your honored name will always figure on the playbill, to the dismay of the gentlemen of the press, who would rather see you torn to pieces. But no matter how stubborn they are with their ridiculous antagonism, the public pays no attention to them" (Franco Abbiati, *Giuseppe Verdi,* 4 vols. [Milan: Ricordi, 1959], 2:408).

2. Hans von Bülow had presented his letter as "the confession of a repentant sinner," and Verdi replied: "There is no trace of sin in you—and let's not talk about repentance and absolution! If some time ago your opinions were different from what they are today, you had every right to express them, nor would I ever have dared complain about them. Besides, who knows . . . perhaps you were right then! [1892]" (ibid., 4:438).

3. Harold Rosenthal, "The Rediscovery of *Don Carlos* in Our Day," in *Atti II,* 551.

4. Filippo Sacchi, quoted by René Leibowitz, in "Vérisme, véracité, et vérité de l'interprétation de Verdi," in *Atti I,* 145.

5. In *Encounters with Verdi,* trans. Richard Stokes (Ithaca, N.Y.: Cornell University Press, 1984), Marcello Conati quotes some significant statistics covering the period 1895–1912 in the great Italian opera houses (pp. 323–24nn).

6. Dino Buzzati, "Difficoltà di Verdi," in *Giuseppe Verdi* (Milan: Teatro alla Scala, 1951), 80.

7. In 1960, nine Verdi operas were still not included in the official discography, and, in 1961, several operas had received only one recording (*Luisa Miller, Ernani,* etc.), as against sixteen editions of *Aida.* See Giuseppe Pugliese's discographies in *ISV Un ballo in maschera,* no. 1 (1960), 159; and *ISV La forza del destino,* no. 4 (1961), 183.

8. Roland Mancini, "Y'a-t-il une renaissance Verdi en France," in *Atti III,* 258.

9. Rosenthal, "The Rediscovery of *Don Carlos* in Our Day," 551.

10. On all these problems, see Marcello De Angelis, *Le carte dell'impresario: Melodramma e costume teatrale nell'Ottocento* (Florence: Sansoni, 1982); John Rosselli, *The Opera Industry in Italy from Cimarosa to Verdi: The Role of the Impresario.*

(Cambridge: Cambridge University Press, 1984); John Rosselli, "Opera Production, 1780–1880," and Fiamma Nicolodi, "Opera Production from Italian Unification to the Present," both in *Opera Production and Its Resources*, vol. 4 of *The History of Italian Opera*, ed. Lorenzo Bianconi and Giorgio Pestelli (Chicago: University of Chicago Press, 1998), 81–164, 165–228; the testimonies of George Sand (*Lettres d'un voyageur [1837]* [Paris: Garnier-Flammarion, 1971]), Felix Mendelssohn *(Voyage de jeunesse: Lettres Européennes [1830–32])* [Paris: Stock Musique, 1980]), Hector Berlioz (*Mémoires* [Paris: Garnier-Flammarion, 1969], trans. [and ed.] David Cairns as *The Memoirs of Hector Berlioz, Member of the French Institute: Including His Travels in Italy, Germany, Russia, and England, 1803–1865* [New York: Norton, 1975]), and esp. Stendhal ([H. Beyle], *Vie de Rossini* [Paris: Editions d'Aujourd'hui, Les Introuvables, 1977], trans. Richard N. Coe as *Life of Rossini* [London: J. Calder; New York: Riverrun, 1985]); and *Giuseppe Verdi: Vicende, problemi e mito di un artista e del suo tempo: Palazzo ducale di Colorno, appartamenti del duca e della duchessa, 31 agosto–8 dicembre 1985* (Colorno: Edizioni "Una città costruisce una mostra," 1985). On the financial aspects of a composer's life, see Rosselli, "Verdi e la storia della retribuzione del compositore italiano," *Studi verdiani*, no. 2 (1983): 11–27.

11. Marcello Conati has calculated that between 1840 and 1860 in Emilia-Romagna, a region that includes Verdi's birthplace, Busseto, operas were staged in twenty-five communities, either in permanent seasons in large cities like Bologna, Parma, or Piacenza or in temporary seasons. Between 1830 and 1895, in the same region, forty-three communities were permitted to have regular seasons or occasional stagings of "serious" operas (Marcello Conati, "Mappe di rappresentazioni operistiche nell'Ottocento," in *Orchestre in Emilia-Romagna*, ed. M. Conati and M. Pavarani [Parma, Orchestra sinfonica dell'Emilia-Romagna "Arturo Toscanini," 1982], 29–31). A city like Milan, whose population around 1840 numbered about 150,000 inhabitants, had its three principal opera houses (La Scala, the Canobbiana, and the Carcano) and two where opera production was secondary (the Filodrammatici and the Teatro Re). In Venice, which had about 106,000 inhabitants in 1846, the famed La Fenice was joined by several active, although secondary, theaters like the Apollo, the Camploy, the Malibran, and the Gallo. Naples, with an 1843 population of 400,000, had five theaters devoted to opera, not to mention the other halls that occasionally put on opera productions. Stendhal, in his *Vie de Rossini*, was amazed to see operas springing up in small towns like Como and Varese.

12. In February 1846, the *Allgemeine musikalische Zeitung* calculated that in 1838–45 no fewer than 342 operas had their first performances, an average of forty-three productions per year. For a slightly later period, between 1842 and 1857, with the exception of the year 1849, Abramo Basevi gives the figure of 641 operas over fifteen years, i.e., an average of forty-three premieres per year (Abramo Basevi, *Studio sulle opere di G. Verdi* [Florence: Tofani, 1859], 58).

13. In 1840, at the very beginning of his career, Verdi's reactions in this re-

gard were significant: "I don't want to give impresarios bad habits." In the same letter he deplores the weakness of an impresario "who can't practice his trade." Indeed, the impresario "should never leave the choice of an opera to the singers" (*Carteggi verdiani,* ed. Alessandro Luzio, 4 vols. [Rome, 1935–47], 4:77).

14. On this point, see Marcello Conati, *La bottega della musica: Verdi e La Fenice* (Milan: Il Saggiatore, 1983). Conati's work on the genesis of operas that premiered at La Fenice in Venice gives an excellent picture of Verdi as manager of his own career, as much through the abundance of documents cited as through the relevance of the author's comments. At the other extreme of Verdi's long career, the *Verdi-Boito Correspondence* (ed. Mario Medici and Marcello Conati, English-language edition by William Weaver [Chicago: University of Chicago, 1994]) and the *Carteggio Verdi-Ricordi* (ed. Pierluigi Petrobelli, Maria di Gregorio Casati, and Carlo Matteo Mossa [Parma: INSV, 1988–] give proof of the meticulous care with which the composer supervised his creations.

15. Abbiati, *Giuseppe Verdi,* 3:324.

16. Ibid., 4:148 (letter of 14 April 1881). On the leitmotiv of the box office as the only barometer of success, see also *I copialettere di Giuseppe Verdi,* ed. Gaetano Cesari and Alessandro Luzio (Milan, 1913; reprint, Bologna: Forni, 1979), 722.

17. Abbiati, *Giuseppe Verdi,* 3:518. *Réclame(s)* is in French in the text.

18. Conati, *Encounters with Verdi,* 346.

19. Abbiati, *Giuseppe Verdi,* 2:311.

20. See François Joseph Fétis's entry on Verdi in *Biographie universelle des musiciens* (Paris: Didot & Frères, 1864).

21. Abbiati, *Giuseppe Verdi,* 1:364.

22. Ibid., 2:591 (November 1860). See also *Verdi intimo: Carteggio di Giuseppe Verdi con il conte Opprandino Arrivabene* (1861–86), ed. Annibale Alberti (Milan: Mondadori, 1931), 305.

23. Abbiati, *Giuseppe Verdi,* 2:448.

24. Letter of 1855 quoted by Ursula Günther, "Documents inconnus concernant les relations de Verdi avec l'Opéra de Paris," in *Atti III,* 571. Verdi also finds the character of Judith fascinating in general but condemns Scribe's *Judith* as "totally false" (ibid.). As for *La Tour de Nesle* by Dumas *père,* "it might yield some good pieces but not an opera" (Conati, *La bottega della musica,* 299). In *Stradella* he finds, in 1850, that "there is a lot of passion but the subject is skimpy and all the situations are old and very ordinary" (ibid., 197). And so on.

25. *The Letters of Mozart and His Family,* trans. Emily Anderson (New York: Norton, 1990), 847 (7 May 1783).

26. Ursula Günther, "La Genèse de *Don Carlos,*" *Revue de musicologie* 1 (1972): 22.

27. Günther, "La Genèse de *Don Carlos,*" 24ff., and "Documents inconnus," 572.

28. On Verdi's culture, see Luigi Magnani, "L' 'ignoranza' musicale di Verdi e la biblioteca di Sant'Agata," in *Atti III,* 250ff.

29. Peter Brooks, *The Melodramatic Imagination* (New Haven, Conn.: Yale University Press, 1995).

30. Quoted by Ildebrando Pizzetti, "Giuseppe Verdi maestro di teatro," *ISV Un ballo in maschera,* no. 2 (1960), 761.

31. If Arrigo Boito's memories are to be believed, the composer dreamed of writing a great symphonic poem! But the poem would have illustrated a well-known episode from Manzoni's *Promessi sposi,* the *Innominato*'s long night in the course of which that character is converted to religion. The attraction of symphonic music arises, therefore, from a powerfully dramatic scene. (See Wolfgang Osthoff, "Il sonétto nel *Falstaff* di Verdi," in *Il melodramma italiano,* 177).

32. Mozart to his father, 13 October 1781, *The Letters of Mozart and His Family,* 773; italics are mine.

33. Ibid., 853 (21 June 1783).

34. Carl Dahlhaus, *Wagners Konzeption des musikalischen Dramas* (Regensburg: Gustav Bosse, 1971).

35. Verdi heard the overture to *Tannhäuser* in 1865 in Paris; the first complete Wagner opera he attended, score in hand, was *Lohengrin,* in November 1871 in Bologna. The librettos of four operas, *Der fliegende Holländer, Tristan, Tannhäuser,* and *Lohengrin* (in an 1861 French edition), were in his library. As for Wagner's theoretical works, he asked Du Locle to obtain them in January 1870.

36. *Copialettere,* 641 (letter of 1870); *Verdi-Boito Correspondence,* 30 (letter of 1881) (*s'effacer* is in French in the text).

37. Among his criticisms of Jacopo's cavatina in *I due Foscari* (act 1), Verdi notes that, "once the cavatina is ended, Jacopo remains onstage and that's always bad for the effect" (*Copialettere,* 426).

38. Ibid., 678.

39. *Letters of Mozart and His Family,* 770 (26 September 1781).

40. Charles Osborne, *The Complete Operas of Verdi* (New York: Knopf, 1970), esp. 288.

41. *Letters of Robert Schumann,* trans. Hannah Bryant (New York: Dutton, 1907), 251 (22 October and 12 November 1845).

42. Abbiati, *Giuseppe Verdi,* 2:4.

43. Massimo Mila, *La giovinezza di Verdi* (Turin: ERI, 1974), 466.

44. Carlo Parmentola speaks ironically about the tendency to think of *Forza* as a "transitional work," claiming that it leads nowhere. The same goes for almost all Verdi's operas, he says ("Rataplan, confessioni sulla *Forza del destino,*" in *Il melodramma italiano,* 91). Similarly, René Leibowitz argues against the assumption that *Don Carlos* prepares the way for *Aida, Otello,* and *Falstaff,* noting aptly that "the subject matter of *Don Carlos* is unique in its genre" (*Les Fantômes de l'opéra* [Paris: Gallimard, 1972], 184).

45. Palmiro Pinagli collates many of these aesthetic opinions in *Romanticismo di Verdi* (Florence: Vallecchi, 1967). See also "Verdi's Own Words," in *The Verdi*

Companion, ed. William Weaver and Martin Chusid (New York: Norton, 1979), 144–92.

46. *Copialettere,* 90; *Verdi-Boito Correspondence,* 131.

47. Abbiati, *Giuseppe Verdi,* 3:579.

48. *Copialettere,* 432 *(Attila);* Abbiati, *Giuseppe Verdi,* 1:600 *(Corsaro),* 2:60 *(Rigoletto); Lettres inédites de G. Verdi à Léon Escudier,* collected by Jacques-Gabriel Prodhomme, *Rivista musicale italiana,* 35 (March 1928): 22 *(La forza del destino).*

49. *Copialettere,* 506; see also 511.

50. *Carteggi verdiani,* 4:233.

51. Ibid., 1:150.

52. In 1886, when asked by a French journalist whether he would write his new opera, *Otello,* in a new style or in that of *Les Vêpres siciliennes* or *Aida,* Verdi replied: "I cannot answer you. . . . I write as I feel, the method does not concern me; if I think a certain style conveys my thought, I use it, even if it means composing in a new style. That is the way I have always composed" (Conati, *Encounters with Verdi,* 169–70).

53. *Carteggi verdiani,* 4:231.

54. *Verdi-Boito Correspondence,* 269 (1899).

55. *Carteggi verdiani,* 4:85 (1883). Hence his praise for the gallery, i.e., for the masses who responded from the heart (see *Verdi-Boito Correspondence,* 179; and *Carteggi verdiani,* 2:156).

56. Leibowitz, *Les Fantômes de l'opéra,* 184.

57. In their introduction to the history of Italian opera, with its resolute multicultural viewpoint, Lorenzo Bianconi and Giorgio Pestelli recall that this unitary vision of opera marching, with all national traditions commingled, toward the goal of music drama is a specifically German view (*Storia dell'opera italiana,* vol. 4 [Turin: EDT, 1987], p. x (in the English translation, p. xii).

58. Mila, *La giovinezza di Verdi,* 469.

59. Conati, *Encounters with Verdi,* 125; Jean Malraye, *Verdi* (Paris: Seghers, 1965), 171.

60. Bruno Barilli, *Il paese del melodramma* (1930; reprint, Turin: Einaudi, 1985), 17, 92.

61. Mila, *La giovinezza di Verdi,* 7.

62. These periodizations are of ideological interest. But naturally there have been others far more technical in character, from the first, Basevi's *Studio sulle opere di Giuseppe Verdi,* published in 1859, in which the critic distinguished four successive styles (stopping, for obvious reasons, at *Aroldo*), to the most recent, such as that proposed by the excellent commentator Julian Budden in *The Operas of Verdi,* 3 vols. (London: Cassell, 1973–81; rev. ed., Oxford: Clarendon, 1992), 2:35. Budden distinguishes the "pioneering" from the "conservative" works (a classification valid for only part of the Verdian oeuvre).

Chapter Two

1. Giuseppe Mazzini, *Filosofia della musica*, ed. Marcello De Angelis (Florence: Guaraldi, 1977). The book also quotes extracts of theoretical works of the first half of the nineteenth century. See also Fabrizio Della Seta, "L'immagine di Meyerbeer nella critica italiana dell'Ottocento e l'idea di 'dramma musicale,'" in *L'opera tra Venezia e Parigi* (Florence: Olschki, 1988); Gilles de Van, "Plaisir ou liturgie," in *Sur l'opéra italien*, Textuel, no. 18 (Paris: UER "Sciences des textes et documents," 1986), 27–37.

2. The literature addressing this question is abundant: see, e.g., Marcel Beaufils, *Musique du son, musique du verbe* (Paris: Presses Universitaires de France, 1954); Vladimir Jankélévitch, *La Musique et l'ineffable* (Paris: Le Seuil, 1983); Eduard Hanslick, *The Beautiful in Music* (1854), trans. Gustav Cohen (New York: Liberal Arts Press, 1957); Marcello Pagnini, *Lingua e musica* (Bologna: Il Mulino, 1974); and Nicolas Ruwet, *Langage, musique, poésie* (Paris: Le Seuil, 1972).

3. Theodor W. Adorno, *Quasi una fantasia*, trans. Rodney Livingstone (London: Verso, 1992), 3.

4. See Jankélévitch's fine observations in the chapter of *La Musique et l'ineffable* entitled "L' 'espressivo' inexpressif."

5. Stendhal, *Life of Rossini*, 178.

6. On the gestural nature of musical expressivity, Robert Francès's formulation is noteworthy: "The relationship of the rhythmic and melodic scheme and the gestural schemes that accompany behavior represents one of the fundamental elements of music's expressive language" (*La Perception de la musique* [Paris: Vrin, 1958], 299).

7. "*Simon Boccanegra*," [*L'Avant-scène opéra*, 20; Budden, *Operas*, 2:269; Massimo Mila, *L'arte di Verdi* (Turin: Einaudi, 1980), 126.

8. A tendency solidly represented in the French literary tradition devoted to opera. See, e.g., Beaumarchais in the preface to *Tarare*, an opera by Salieri for which he wrote the libretto: "I think therefore that the music of an opera is, like its poetry, but a new art of embellishing the word, which one must not abuse" (quoted in *Théâtre* [Le Club Français du Livre, Paris] 2 [1960]: 226).

9. Basevi, *Studio*, 271.

10. Jean-Jacques Roubine, *L'Art du comédien* (Paris: PUF, 1985), 14.

11. John Black, *The Italian Romantic Libretto: A Study of Salvadore Cammarano* (Edinburgh: Edinburgh University Press, 1984), 263.

12. Mila, *L'arte di Verdi*, 217.

13. Charles Avison, quoted by Gary Schmidgall in *Literature as Opera* (New York: Oxford University Press, 1977), 374.

14. In "L'Expressionnisme allemand" (Paris: *Obliques*, 1981), 84.

15. Mila, *La giovinezza di Verdi*, 148.

16. Maria Rosaria Addamo and Friedrich Lippmann, *Vincenzo Bellini* (Turin: ERI, 1981), 518.

17. *Verdi intimo,* 297.

18. Modest Mussorgsky, quoted by Philippe Le Corf, "Boris Godounov," *L'Avant-scène opéra* 27 (May–August 1980): 37.

19. *Letters of Mozart and His Family,* 161–62 (26 September 1781).

20. Abbiati, *Giuseppe Verdi,* 4:356.

21. Luigi Rognoni, *Gioacchino Rossini* (Turin: ERI, 1968), 377; see esp. the whole chapter "L'ideale estetico di Rossini."

22. Ibid., 381, 330. See also a letter from the same year written to the critic Filippo Filippi (ibid., 374).

23. Giovanni Batista Rinuccini, *Sulla musica e sulla poesia melodrammatica italiana del secolo XIX* (Luca: Guidotti, 1843), 40, 16.

24. Carlo Ritorni, *Ammaestramenti alla composizione d'ogni poema e d'ogni opera appartenente alla musica* (Milan: Pirola, 1841). Basevi, *Studio,* 148, 47, 64, 124. See also several critics' opinions in Mazzini, *Filosofia della musica,* 79–132.

25. Rossini found that, in Bellini's *Il pirata,* the style was "carried to such a degree of philosophical reasoning that in places the music was lacking in brilliance" (quoted by Adamo and Lippmann, *Bellini,* 504). At the time of *Rigoletto,* Verdi was still being accused of "philosophizing" (see Marcello Conati, "Appendix to Bibliography of Critical Writings on *Rigoletto,*" *ISV Rigoletto,* no. 9 [1982], 1711, 1708).

26. Adamo and Lippmann, *Bellini,* 466–67, 473; see also Rodolfo Celletti, "La vocalità romantica," in *Storia dell'opera* (Turin: UTET, 1977), vol. 3, pt. 1, p. 198ff. Significantly, Celletti's history of bel canto stops at Rossini (*A History of Bel Canto,* trans. Frederick Fuller [Oxford: Clarendon, 1991]).

27. Rognoni, *Rossini,* 334.

28. Alberto Zedda suggests that this silence might be due to the composer's refusal to give up his idea of ornamented song, "whence an obvious clash between an orchestra that was thoroughly Romantic and a song that was still artificial" ("Alberto Zedda: Une vie pour Rossini" [an interview with Zedda], *Opéra International,* no. 115 [June 1988]: 19).

29. The composer of *Norma* believed that, "in music, the drama must make the audience weep, tremble, die through song" (Adamo and Lippmann, *Bellini,* 345).

30. William Ashbrook, *Donizetti and His Operas* (Cambridge: Cambridge University Press, 1982); see chap. 8, "Donizetti's Use of Operatic Conventions," and esp. pp. 246–49.

31. Adamo and Lippmann, *Bellini,* 494.

32. Abbiati, *Giuseppe Verdi,* 3:232 (1868).

33. *Verdi's "Macbeth": A Sourcebook,* ed. David Rosen and Andrew Porter (New York: Norton, 1984), 30.

34. *Copialettere,* 645.

35. Ibid., 61.

36. *Carteggi verdiani,* 1:30 (1855).

37. *Copialettere*, 624 (1876).

38. Conati, *Encounters with Verdi*, 345.

39. Abbiati, *Giuseppe Verdi*, 2:97; *Copialettere*, 665 (concerning *Aida*), 426 (concerning *I due Foscari*).

40. *Copialettere*, 441.

41. De Angelis, *Le carte dell'impresario*, 117, reproduces a letter on this subject written by the baritone Varesi, the original *Macbeth*; see also *Verdi's "Macbeth": A Sourcebook*, 33. On *Falstaff*, see a letter of Boito's of 9 May 1892 in *Carteggi verdiani*, 2:158.

42. *Verdi's "Macbeth": A Sourcebook*, 35.

43. Ursula Günther, "Zur Entstehung von Verdis *Aida*," *Studi musicali* 2, no. 1 (1973): 51.

44. *Verdi-Boito Correspondence*, 102–3, 115; see also the letters concerning *Otello* in the Verdi-Ricordi correspondence, *Giuseppe Verdi, Giulio Ricordi: Corrispondenza e immagini, 1881–1890*, ed. Pierluigi Petrobelli and Franca Cella (Milan: Teatro alla Scala, 1981).

45. *"Otello" di Giuseppi Verdi*, ed. James Hepokoski and Mercedes Viale Ferrero. Musica e spettacolo: Collana di disposizioni sceniche (hereafter "Otello": Disposizione scenica) (Milan: Ricordi, 1990), 27.

46. *Verdi-Boito Correspondence*, 196–97.

47. *Carteggi verdiani*, 1:244, 247, 252.

48. Ibid., 270, 274.

49. David R. B. Kimbell, "*Il trovatore:* Cammarano and García Gutiérrez," in *Atti III*, 34–45.

50. See the section "El trasfondo historico de El Trovador" in Carlos Ruiz Silva's introduction to the edition of *El trovador* (Madrid: Catedra, 1985).

51. Ursula Günther, "Der Briefwechsel Verdi–Nuitter–Du Locle zur Revision des *Don Carlos*," *Analecta musicologica* 15 (1975): 340.

52. Alberto Moravia, *L'uomo come fine* (Milan: Bompiani, 1964), 398.

53. *Carteggi verdiani*, 1:28, 30.

54. See Marcello Conati, "Ballabili nei *Vespri:* Con alcune osservazioni su Verdi e la musica popolare," *Studi verdiani*, no. 1 (1982): 41.

55. Abbiati, *Giuseppe Verdi*, 2:659.

56. Conati cites the testimony of a musician who came across Verdi in a hardware store in Parma and saw him feverishly scribble down the street cry of a seller of cooked pears who was passing by. Two years later, when he was playing in the orchestra at the first performance of *Aida,* the musician again heard the phrase, which Verdi had used for the priests' chant in act 3 (*Encounters with Verdi*, 87–88).

57. *Verdi-Boito Correspondence*, 224.

58. Carlo Gatti, *Verdi* (Milan: Mondadori, 1951), 427.

59. In "Ballabili nei *Vespri*," 44, Conati mentions concurrences noted by critics between Verdian themes and popular songs.

60. *Copialettere*, 268, 367; Abbiati, *Giuseppe Verdi*, 3:377, 379; Günther, "Zur Entstehung von Verdis *Aida*."

61. Jean Humbert, "*Aida* entre l'égyptologie et l'égyptomanie," *L'Avant-scène opéra* 4 ("*Aida*") (July–August 1976): 9ff.; Claudia Dolzani, "Elementi egittologici nell'azione dell'opera *Aida*," *Quaderni dell'ISV* 4 ("Genesi dell'*Aida*") (1971): 152–55.

62. Théophile Gautier, *Le Roman de la momie* (Paris: Gallimard Folio, 1986). J. M. Gardair's preface notes that Radames's triumph is derived from Gautier's work (p. 31).

63. Beaufils, *Musique du son, musique du verbe*, 157.

64. Ritorni, *Ammaestramenti*, 152.

65. Quoted by Francesco Degrada, "Prolegomeni a una lettura della *Sonnam-bula*," in *Il melodramma italiano*, 331. As Julian Budden puts it, "German audiences were prepared to be edified; Italians wanted to enjoy themselves" ("Verdi and the Contemporary Italian Operatic Scene," in *The Verdi Companion*, 69).

66. Beaufils, *Musique du son, musique du verbe*, 145ff.

67. Pier Jacopo Martello, "Della tragedia antica e moderna," in *Scritti critici e satirici* (Bari: Laterza, 1963), 273ff., trans. Piero Weiss as "Piero Jacopo Martello on Opera: An Annotated Translation," *Musical Quarterly* 66, no. 3 (1980): 370–403.

68. Ritorni, *Ammaestramenti*, 156, 154.

69. Michel Poizat, *L'Opéra ou le cri de l'ange: Essai sur la jouissance de l'amateur d'opéra* (Paris: Métailié, 1986), trans. A. Denner as *The Angel's Cry: Beyond the Pleasure Principle in Opera* (Ithaca, N.Y.: Cornell University Press, 1992), 31.

70. Quoted by Le Corf in "Boris Godounov," 55.

71. Gilbert Rouget, *La Musique et la transe* (Paris: Gallimard, 1980), trans. Brunhilde Biebuyck as *Music and Trance: A Theory of the Relations between Music and Possession* (Chicago: University of Chicago Press, 1985). See the curious (imaginary) letter in which an ethnomusicologist from Benin compares opera with his country's ceremonies of possession (pp. 337ff.).

72. Adorno, *Quasi una fantasia*, 66.

73. *Verdi-Boito Correspondence*, 7–8.

74. Abbiati, *Giuseppe Verdi*, 2:122; and Alessandro Pascolato, "*Re Lear*" e "*Ballo in maschera*": *Lettere di G. Verdi ad Antonio Somma* (hereafter *Verdi-Somma*) (Città di Castello: Lapi, 1902), 53.

75. *Copialettere*, 233 (1871). In his "Verdi, Ghislanzoni, and *Aida*: The Uses of Convention," *Critical Inquiry* 1 (1974): 291–334, Philip Gossett argues against those who glorify the destruction of tradition in Verdi's development and gives many examples showing how tradition persisted up to and including *Aida* (see, e.g., pp. 313ff.).

76. Abbiati, *Giuseppe Verdi*, 4:337 (1887). *Ricaner* is in French.

77. Gabriele Baldini, *Abitare la battaglia* (Milan: Garzanti, 1970), 193, trans.

Roger Parker as *The Story of Giuseppe Verdi* (Cambridge: Cambridge University Press, 1980), 174.

78. Theodor Adorno, "Reading Balzac," in *Notes to Literature* (New York: Columbia University Press, 1991–92).

79. Recall that Franz Werfel was one of the protagonists of the "Verdi Renaissance" in the 1930s in Germany. He is also the author of a curious novel in which he imagines Verdi going to Venice in 1883 to meet Wagner; but the trip is made too late, and Wagner is dead (*Verdi: A Novel of the Opera,* trans. H. Jessiman [New York: Simon & Schuster, 1925]).

80. Michel Leiris has rightly insisted on the use of sound space in this scene ("L'Arc," *L'Opéra* 27 [1965]: 7–12).

81. Ruiz, who in act 4, scene 1, accompanies Leonora to the entrance of the tower where Manrico is imprisoned, explains: "This is the tower where the state's prisoners sigh," and Verdi refers to the "song of the dying" (*Copialettere,* 120). The libretto simply mentions "songs in the wings," and the score offers no indications in this regard.

Chapter Three

1. Conati, *Encounters with Verdi,* 109.

2. Conati, *La bottega della musica,* 383–85.

3. We have seen an example of this in the sketch of the "Siege of Florence." Daniela Goldin quotes further examples in *La vera Fenice* (Turin: Einaudi, 1985), 304, 346 n. 49.

4. See Robert Anthony Moreen, "Integration of Text Forms and Musical Forms in Verdi's Early Operas" (Ph.D. diss., Princeton University, 1975).

5. *Verdi-Somma,* 75. That monotony of meter could have been one reason for the weakness of certain German operas was the conviction of Edward J. Dent, who remarked on it apropos of Spohr, Marschner, and even Schubert: "The weakness of *Alfonso und Estrella* is not dramatic but metrical. The poet cannot get away from the perpetual 8.7.8.7." (*The Rise of Romantic Opera* [Cambridge: Cambridge University Press, 1976], 137, 149).

6. Friedrich Lippmann, *Versificazione italiana e ritmo musicale* (Naples: Liguori, 1986).

7. *Copialettere,* 663.

8. See the examples in *Carteggi verdiani,* 2:115.

9. Lippmann, *Versificazione italiana,* 322; and Arnold Schoenberg, *Style and Idea* (New York, Philosophical Library, 1950), 72.

10. Commenting on Germont's cantabile in *La Traviata,* "Di Provenza il mar, il suol," where the musical phrase is based on repeated *ottonari* (eight-syllable lines), Verdi (*Copialettere,* 640) attributes its charm to the truncated syllable at the end of each line: "*suol, cancellò, sol. . . .*"

11. Abbiati, *Giuseppe Verdi,* 2:647ff.

12. Raffaele Colucci, quoted in Addamo and Lippmann, *Bellini,* 93.

13. Mario Medici, "Lettere sul *Re Lear,*" *ISV Un ballo in maschera,* no. 2 (1960): 776; *Verdi-Somma,* 64, letters of December 1853 and February 1854.

14. Abbiati, *Giuseppe Verdi,* 2:803. The laborious history of this denouement is told in detail by Edoardo Rescigno, *La forza del destino* (Milan: Emme Edizioni, 1981), 57ff. The correspondence relating to the episode is included in Abbiati, *Giuseppe Verdi,* vols. 2 and 3, as well as in *Copialettere,* 613 and passim.

15. For a recent portrait of one of the most celebrated of these, see Black, *The Italian Romantic Libretto.*

16. Felice Romani in 1839, quoted by Giuseppe Vecchi, "Il libretto di Giuseppe Verdi," *ISV Rigoletto,* no. 8 (1973): 881.

17. See the contract in Rescigno, *La forza del destino,* 31.

18. On this question, besides general books on Verdi's oeuvre, one can consult Frank Walker, *The Man Verdi* (Chicago: University of Chicago Press, 1982); Claudio Sartori, "*Rocester,* la prima opera di Verdi," *Rivista musicale italiana* 43 (January–February 1939): 97–104; David R. B. Kimbell, "Poi diventò *Oberto,*" *Music and Letters* 52, no. 1 (January 1971): 1–7; Pierluigi Petrobelli, program of *Oberto,* Teatro Comunale di Bologna, 1976–77 season.

19. *Carteggi verdiani,* 4:245. *Giovanna d'Arco* ends with the heroine's death, but this is an apotheosis and transfiguration.

20. Conati, *La bottega della musica,* 102.

21. Abbiati, *Giuseppe Verdi,* 1:477.

22. Conati, *La bottega della musica,* 91.

23. Abbiati, *Giuseppe Verdi,* 2:399, 412.

24. Note the tone of affectionate complicity of certain letters in Conati, *La bottega della musica,* 150, 152.

25. Baldini, *The Story of Giuseppe Verdi,* 127.

26. Conati, *La bottega della musica,* 53.

27. *Copialettere,* 118 (9 April 1851).

28. Abbiati, *Giuseppe Verdi,* 1:770; *Copialettere,* 71 (1848–49).

29. Abbiati, *Giuseppe Verdi,* 2:10, which gives a reproduction of the program.

30. Ibid., 18; and *Copialettere,* 274.

31. *Copialettere,* 118. Cammarano's *programma* is reproduced in John Black, "Salvadore Cammarano's *Programma* for *Il trovatore* and the Problems of the Finale," *Studi Verdiani,* no. 2 (1983): 78–108. Verdi's revised scenario is reproduced in *Copialettere,* 119. The Verdi-Cammarano correspondence, soon to be published by Carlo Matteo Mossa (*Carteggio Verdi-Cammarano, 1843–1852* [Parma:Istituto Nazionale di Studi Verdiani, in press]), as well as an introductory study by the same author in *Studi verdiani* no. 8, make it clear that the librettist was far from docilely obeying the composer's injunctions and that he energetically defended his conception of the drama. See also Mossa's essay, "The Genesis of the Libretto," within David Lawton's introduction to *Il trovatore* in *WGV,* Series I, vol. 18A (1993), xiii–xxii.

32. On this subject, see the *Verdi-Boito Correspondence;* and also "Il libretto di *Otello*" and "Il libretto di *Falstaff,*" in *Carteggi verdiani,* 2:95–142, 143–78.

33. *Verdi-Boito Correspondence,* 157 (17 March 1890), 158.

34. Ibid., 6 (October 1880), 18.

35. Edoardo Rescigno, *Macbeth: Guida all'ascolto* (Milan: Mondadori, 1983), 61.

36. Abbiati, *Giuseppe Verdi,* 1:691.

37. Francesco Lorenzo Arruga, "Incontri fra poeti e musicisti nell'opera romantica italiana," in *Contributi dell'istituto di filologia moderna* (Milan: Vita e pensiero, 1958), 234–90. See also Angelo Fabrizi, "Riflessi del linguaggio tragico alfieriano nei libretti d'opera ottocenteschi," in *Studi e critica testuale,* no. 12 (Bologna, 1976), 135–55; Fabrizi demonstrates Alfieri's importance in the elaboration of the style of Italian librettists of the early Ottocento, notably that of Cammarano.

38. Giuseppe Mazzini, *Moto letterario in Italia* (Imola: Edizione Nazionale, 1910), vol. 8, pt. 2.

39. Pierre Brunel quotes examples of extensive cutting of situations when C. R. Maturin's *Bertram* was adapted for Bellini's *Il pirata* or Soumet's tragedy became the same composer's *Norma* (*Vincenzo Bellini* [Paris: Fayard, 1981], 85, 255). Concerning the adaptation of foreign plays and especially Schiller's *Die Räuber* by Maffei, see also Frédéric Dutheil, "Le Livret d'opéra italien" (Ph.D. diss., Université de Bordeaux 3, 1985).

40. I have studied this profusion of sources in connection with two operas inspired by Schiller that have often been criticized for "betraying" the German dramatist, whereas the variations were simply taken from other sources, especially French ones: "*Guillaume Tell:* Les Sources du livret," in *Chroniques italiennes,* Université de Paris III, no. 29 (1992); *Le fonti del "Don Carlo" verdiano* (Milan: Teatro alla Scala/Rizzoli, 1992).

41. Jerome Mitchell, *The Walter Scott Operas: An Anthology of Operas Based on the Works of Sir Walter Scott* (Tuscaloosa: University of Alabama Press, 1977).

42. Markus Engelhardt, "Versioni operistiche dell'*Hernani,* " in *ISV Ernani,* 104–23.

43. Walter Toscanini, "Balli con titoli o soggetti di opere verdiane," *ISV La forza del destino,* no. 5 (1962), xciv–xcvii. See also Kathleen Kuzmick Hansell, "Il ballo teatrale e l'opera italiana," in *Storia dell'opera italiana,* vol. 5. Hansell lists a number of operas that were preceded by ballets very close in conception. Thus, in the early history of *Il corsaro* reference should be made to Giovanni Galzerani's ballet (1826). See also Rita Zambon, "Quando il ballo anticipa l'opera: *Il corsaro* di Giovanni Galzerani," in *Creature di Prometeo: Il ballo teatrale dal divertimento al dramma: Studi offerti a Aurel M. Milloss* (Florence: Olschki, 1996), 305–313.

44. Abbiati, *Giuseppe Verdi,* 3:8.

45. *Carteggi verdiani,* 4:217.

46. Ibid., 1:219.

47. Conati, *La bottega della musica,* 74 (letter of 5 September 1843).

48. *Copialettere,* 649.

49. *Verdi-Boito Correspondence,* 18; and Abbiati, *Giuseppe Verdi,* 3:246.

50. Abbiati, *Giuseppe Verdi,* 4:356.

51. *Copialettere,* 454. This quotation suggests that the composer could, in certain cases, give great importance to the psychological, and hence the semantic, quality of certain sounds of the language. Marie Pierre Lassus has studied the language of *Macbeth,* taking her inspiration from Imre Fönagy's psychophonetics, in "*Macbeth* ou l'anti belcanto" (Ph.D. diss., Conservatoire National Supérieur de Musique de Paris, 1990).

52. "Il libretto del *Ballo in maschera* massacrato dalla censura borbonica," in *Carteggi verdiani,* 1:241–76.

53. Hans Busch, *Verdi's "Aida": The History of an Opera in Letters and Documents* (Minneapolis: University of Minnesota Press, 1978); and *Copialettere,* 650.

54. Abbiati, *Giuseppe Verdi,* 1:474.

55. Abbiati, *Giuseppe Verdi,* 2:653, 370; *Carteggi verdiani,* 1:10.

56. Even though these documents show up in both Abbiati's *Giuseppe Verdi* and the *Copialettere,* errors of dating and attribution make it advisable to refer to *Verdi's "Macbeth": A Sourcebook,* 77–82.

57. Abbiati, *Giuseppe Verdi,* 1:643.

58. Patrick J. Smith, *The Tenth Muse: A Historical Study of the Opera Libretto* (New York: Knopf, 1970), 6.

59. Conati, *La bottega della musica,* 102. Although this tendency to reduce information to the very minimum is typically Verdian, it is echoed in a general tendency to shorten recitatives, which Black points out in *The Italian Romantic Libretto.*

60. Abbiati, *Giuseppe Verdi,* 2:71.

61. *Verdi-Somma,* 80 (1857); *Copialettere,* 641 (1870), 639.

62. *Copialettere,* 639 (14 August 1870).

63. *Verdi-Somma,* 80; Conati, *La bottega della musica,* 297.

64. *Copialettere,* 648.

65. The importance of *Macbeth* explains the number of studies devoted to the libretto and makes it possible to follow the adaptation of the English play: see Schmidgall, *Literature as Opera;* Goldin, *La vera Fenice;* Rescigno, *Macbeth;* and *Verdi's "Macbeth": A Sourcebook.*

66. Carlo di Stefano, *La censura teatrale in Italia* (Bologna: Cappelli, 1964); Ernestina Monti, "Contributo ad uno studio sui libretti nell'Ottocento," *Archivio storico lombardo* 17 (January–June 1939): 306–65.

67. Luigia Rivelli, "G. Gioacchino Belli 'censore' e il suo spirito liberale," in *Rassegna storica del Risorgimento* (Rome: Istituto per la storia del Risorgimento, 1923), 331.

68. Mario Lavagetto, *Un caso di censura: Il "Rigoletto"* (Milan: Il Formichiere, 1979).

69. On the vicissitudes of the libretto, see *ISV Un ballo in maschera,* nos. 1–3 (1960); cf. also Gilles de Van, "Le Travail du livret" and "Les Bals masqués," *L'Arc* 81 (1981): 14–25, 26–35.

70. *Copialettere,* 497.

71. Beaufils, *Musique du son, musique du verbe,* 74.

72. Luigi Dallapiccola, "Words and Music in Italian Nineteenth-Century Opera," in *The Verdi Companion,* 197–98.

73. Quoted by Budden, *Operas,* 1:129.

74. See Luigi Baldacci's penetrating study of the language of *La traviata* in *Libretti d'opera* (Florence: Vallecchi, 1974), 203–16.

Chapter Four

1. Basevi, *Studio,* 157.

2. A vast collection of contemporary criticism can be found in *Verdi: Bollettino dell'Istituto di Studi Verdiani,* Parma, devoted to particular works. See, e.g., vol. 3 *(Rigoletto),* nos. 7–9 (1969, 1973, 1982): 1634ff.

3. Rossini referred to Verdi as a "composer with a helmet"; Alphonse Karr saw him as "a man who writes down noises on paper and gives them to singers to bawl so that they quickly become hoarse and their voices crack"; and Scudo deplored "the violence of style, the disjointedness of ideas, the crudeness of colors" (Mila, *La giovinezza di Verdi,* 119; and Abbiati, *Giuseppe Verdi,* 2:406).

4. Barilli, *Il paese del melodramma,* 174.

5. *Carteggi verdiani,* 4:230.

6. Basevi, *Studio,* 157.

7. Georg Lukács, *Soul and Form,* trans. Anna Bostock (Cambridge, Mass.: MIT Press, 1980), 28–29.

8. Ibid., 29.

9. Ibid., 39, 159.

10. See Brooks, *The Melodramatic Imagination;* Paul Ginisty, *Le Mélodrame* (Paris: Michaud, 1910); Jean Follain, "Le Mélodrame," in *Entretiens sur la paralittérature* (Paris: Plon, 1970); "Le Mélodrame," ed. Jean-Marie Thomasseau, *Revue Europe,* nos. 703–4 (November–December 1987).

11. A!A!A! *Traité du mélodrame* (Paris: Delaunay, 1817).

12. Ibid., 47.

13. Brooks, *The Melodramatic Imagination.*

14. Mario Lavagetto, *Quei più modesti romanzi: Tecniche costruttive, funzioni, poetica di un genere letterario minore* (Milan: Garzanti, 1979). Philippe-Joseph Salazar's *Idéologies de l'opéra* (Paris: Presses Universitaires de France, 1980), 142, is also helpful.

15. Aldo Palazzeschi, *Stampe dell'Ottocento* (Milan: Treves, 1932), 152.

16. Luca Ronconi, quoted in *"Norma": Come nasce uno spettacolo* (Milan: Edizioni di Musica Viva, 1979), 57.

17. To be credible, a typology should be systematic and note anomalies in

order to reach a statistically reliable truth. Since such a study is necessarily dry and tedious, I have condensed it severely in the following pages and refer the reader to the complete version, my "Théâtre et musique dans les opéras de Giuseppe Verdi" (thèse d'état, Université de Paris III, 1990).

18. Georg Wilhelm Friedrich Hegel, *Hegel's Phenomenology of the Spirit,* trans. A. V. Miller (Oxford: Oxford University Press, 1977), 226.

19. Note, however, that in 1843, when preparations were under way for *Ernani,* the authorities at La Fenice wanted a vocal distribution that was beginning to be out of date: Ernani, contralto; Doña Sol (Elvira), soprano; Don Carlos, tenor, and Silva, baritone (see Conati, *La bottega della musica,* 81). Verdi, "the sworn enemy of having a woman sing dressed as a man" (ibid., 70), seemed to agree but finally insisted on the present distribution. When the opera premiered in 1844, the tenor had replaced the contralto as hero, but a certain flexibility was still allowed in the allotment of roles: thus, the contralto Marietta Alboni interpreted the part of Don Carlo (see *Verdi-Boito Correspondence,* 182; and *Copialettere,* 265).

20. *"Otello": Disposizione scenica,* 4.

21. Rodolfo Celletti points out that in the 1870s certain theorists of singing technique described the Verdian baritone as *mezzo-tenore* (half tenor), as one refers to mezzo-soprano ("On Verdi's Vocal Writing," in *The Verdi Companion,* 226).

22. It should be recalled that up to the 1870s the hierarchy of voices consisted of three categories: the premier role *(prima donna soprano, primo tenore),* the intermediary role, which might or might not have an aria but took a solo part in the ensembles *(soprano comprimario),* and the secondary role, which was usually very minor *(secondo tenore).* Merely adding a complete aria could be enough to move a singer up into a higher category.

23. *Carteggi verdiani,* 1:112.

24. Stephen S. Stanton, "English Drama and the French Well-Made Play, 1815–1915" (Ph.D. diss., Columbia University, 1955), 41–42.

25. Lavagetto, *Quei più modesti romanzi,* 78.

26. Milan Kundera, *The Art of the Novel,* trans. Linda Asher (New York: Harper & Row, 1988), 90.

27. Ibid. 88, 89.

28. Conati, *La bottega della musica,* 102.

29. Abbiati, *Giuseppe Verdi,* 1:731.

30. Luigi Dallapiccola, *Appunti, incontri, meditazioni* (Milan: Il Saggiatore, 1970).

31. Lavagetto, *Quei più modesti romanzi,* 34. See also William Weaver, "Aspects of Verdi's Dramaturgy," in *The Verdi Companion,* 141; Patrick J. Smith, *The Tenth Muse: A Historical Study of the Opera Libretto* (New York: Knopf, 1970), 244; André Tubeuf, "Verdi et le disque," *L'Arc* 81 (1981): 90.

32. *Verdi-Somma,* 46.

33. Gilles de Van, "Verdi et l'idéal chevaleresque: *Le Trouvère*," *L'Avant-scène opéra* 60 (February 1984): 13.

34. Budden, "Verdi and the World of the Primo Ottocento," in *Operas*, vol. 1, chap. 1. An aural illustration of this active period at the beginning of the nineteenth century, of which Rossini was the principal but not the only protagonist, can be found in the three recorded volumes that Opera Rara has devoted to it: "1800–1810," "Mayr," and "1820–1830."

35. *Verdi's "Macbeth": A Sourcebook*, 29.

36. Conati, *Encounters with Verdi*, 284.

37. *Carteggi verdiani*, 1:19 (1853). In general, it is this purely exterior quality of melodrama, denounced by Verdi, that gets the attention.

38. Barilli, *Il paese del melodramma*, 91.

39. Basevi, *Studio*, 29.

40. See pp. 19, 33, 145, 250, and 282 of the Ricordi piano-vocal score (*Ernani*, Milan: G. Ricordi [189-?], pl. no. 95095). In *Nabucco*, the feeling of decisive affirmation is captured by the octave leap, an interval that Verdi both uses and abuses in this opera. See pp. 43, 59, 80, 108, 112, 113, etc. of the vocal score (*Nabucodonosor*, Milan: G. Ricordi [c. 1920], pl. no. 42312).

41. See Massimo Bruni, "Funzionalità drammatica dell'accordo di quarta e sesta nello stile di Verdi," in *Atti I*, 36. The author comments at length on the "exclamatory value" of the Verdian six-four chord.

42. That is, the general use throughout an opera of a formula normally employed to suggest death. See Frits Noske, "Verdi and the Musical Figure of Death," in *Atti III* (reprinted in *The Signifier and the Signified* [The Hague: Nijhoff, 1977]).

43. *L'abbozzo del "Rigoletto" di Giuseppe Verdi*, with an introduction by Carlo Gatti (Bologna: Forni, 1978).

44. In his study of the genesis of *Ernani*, Philip Gossett gives very similar examples that illustrate Verdi's "systematic search" for a dynamic disequilibrium of the phrase. *ISV Ernani*, 60ff., esp. 64–65, 74–76.

45. Rodolfo Celletti, "Lo stile vocale di Verdi" in "La vocalità romantica," *Storia dell'opera*, vol. 3, pt. 1, 207ff. (See also the translation, "On Verdi's Vocal Writing," *The Verdi Companion*, 216–38.)

46. Letter to Leone Giraldoni, 9 December 1857, published in the *Gazzetta musicale di Milano*, 17 June 1860, no. 25, p. 199.

47. Basevi, *Studio*, 12.

48. See, e.g., Pagano's aria "Ma quando un suon terribile," which is integrated in a grand *scena* and constructed like a romanza *(I Lombardi)*; Giacomo's arias "Franco son io" and "Speme al vecchio" *(Giovanna d'Arco)*; Zamoro's arias "Un Inca . . . eccesso orribile" and "Irne lungi ancor dovrei" *(Alzira)*; Odabella's cavatina "Allor che i forti corrono" *(Attila)*; Francesco's aria "La sua lampada vitale" *(I masnadieri)*; etc. See also the last phrase, "E vincitor de' secoli," of Carlo's aria "Oh de' verd'anni miei" in *Ernani*.

49. Scott Leslie Balthazar, "Evolving Conventions in Italian Serious Opera: Scene Structure in the Works of Rossini, Bellini, Donizetti and Verdi, 1810–1850" (Ph.D. diss., University of Pennsylvania, 1985), 87 ff.

50. Abbiati, *Verdi,* 1:368.

51. Basevi notes the relative novelty of this duet: "This varied form is not new, but was little used before, when it was considered desirable to hear the same melody three times: first sung once by each singer and then by both together" (*Studio,* 15–16).

52. The trio and quartet of *I due Foscari* (act 2), the final quartet of *Attila,* and the final trios of *I masnadieri* and *Il corsaro* illustrate the same concern with characterizing the different voices by way of contrast.

53. Abbiati, *Giuseppe Verdi,* 1:469, 471.

54. See Balthazar, "Evolving Conventions in Italian Serious Opera."

55. Philip Gossett, "The 'Candeur Virginale' of *Tancredi,*" *Musical Times* 112 (April 1971): 326–29.

56. Conati, *La bottega della musica,* 74.

57. *Copialettere,* 430.

58. Abbiati, *Giuseppe Verdi,* 2:123. Black (*The Italian Romantic Libretto,* 190) notes that all Cammarano's librettos begin with a chorus, except for two comic works and *Il trovatore!*

59. Abbiati, *Giuseppe Verdi,* 2:124.

60. Jean Humbert, "Attribution à Auguste Mariette d'un scénario anonyme de l'opéra *Aida,*" *Revue de musicologie* 42 (1976): 244.

61. Some examples of overlapping for dramatic purposes: In act 2 of *I due Foscari,* the Jacopo-Lucrezia duet is linked virtually without transition to the trio between these characters and the Doge Foscari, a trio whose last prestissimo section becomes a quartet with the addition of Loredano. In *Giovanna d'Arco,* Giovanna's prologue cavatina "Sempre all'alba ed alla sera" has no cabaletta: the latter is to some extent recovered in the duet/trio with Carlo and Giacomo in the Finale of the prologue, which has the pace of a cabaletta. In *Luisa Miller,* the two sections of the last duet between Luisa and Rodolfo segue directly into the trio with old Miller that ends the opera. In his "*La solita forma* and the Uses of Convention" (in *Nuove prospettive*), Harold S. Powers analyzes interesting examples of telescoping: the superimposition of Giacomo's aria in act 2 of *Giovanna d'Arco* and of the Finale of the same act. He also draws attention to episodes that oscillate between two forms: e.g., the aria/duet of Luisa and Wurm in act 2 of *Luisa Miller* and the aria/duet of Amelia and Renato at the beginning of act 3 of *Ballo.* What we have basically is a sort of telescoping through the intercontamination of two forms.

62. For Verdi's predecessors, the cabaletta did not have to be vehement in expression or fast in its tempo, as Frits Noske aptly points out in "The Notorious Cabaletta" (in *The Signifier and the Signified* [The Hague: Nijhoff, 1977]).

63. In *I due Foscari,* Lucrezia's cabaletta "La clemenza! ... s'aggiunge lo

scherno!" (act 1) adopts the tonal scheme of the romanza (G minor then major); only the major section has a reprise. Verdi's recommendations to Varesi, who created the role of Macbeth, regarding his cabaletta at the end of act 3 in the original version (which would be replaced in 1865 by a duet with Lady Macbeth), are significant: "I urge you to pay special attention to the cabaletta; mark it well; it isn't in the usual form, because, after all that has gone before, a cabaletta in the usual mold and with usual ritornellos would sound trivial" (*Verdi's "Macbeth": A Sourcebook,* 36).

64. Two early examples: the cabaletta of Nabucco's aria "Dio di Giuda, l'ara, il tempio" (act 4) has no reprise because the Assyrian king is rushing to save his daughter Fenena. Nor does that of Macduff's aria "Ah la paterna mano" (*Macbeth,* act 4), for similar reasons. In each case the dramatic rhythm justifies shortening the aria.

65. The cabaletta of Carlo's aria "Urna fatal" in *Forza* (act 3) is partially repeated but varied by the addition of a final section followed by the coda etc.

66. A fairly rare example of a cabaletta without introductory Adagio.

67. See also Henri's aria in *Vêpres,* "O jour de deuil"/"O giorno di pianto," which is followed by a brief Allegro agitato that is explosive in effect, like a cabaletta. The first step of this process probably has to be to examine Carlo's aria "Oh de' verd'anni miei" (*Ernani,* act 3). Piave and Mocenigo's first scenario provided for a cabaletta, but Verdi preferred to treat this passage as a solemn meditation on the end of youth and the attainment of a maturity of power. Still, the ending "E vincitor de' secoli" is a valiant proclamation of imperial grandeur. Insofar as it follows a complete presentation (a1 a2 ba 2), it resembles not so much the second movement of the aria as an *appendice* (the term used by Basevi). Under this heading it illustrates a wish to integrate the spirit of the cabaletta into the aria without unfolding a complete melody.

68. *Verdi-Boito Correspondence,* 3–4 (August 1880).

69. Ibid., 7 (October 1880).

Chapter Five

1. Georg Wilhelm Friedrich Hegel, *Hegel's Aesthetics,* trans. T. M. Knox (Oxford: Clarendon, 1975), 1:560–61.

2. Stendhal, *Vie de Rossini;* Gilbert Maugain, *La Vengeance* (Paris: Les Belles Lettres, 1935). The spirit of revenge seems to be associated with patriarchal societies. Michelle Perrot points out that for nineteenth-century France it is possible to trace a "vengeance region" where demographers have identified a patriarchal structure ("Drames et conflits familiaux," in *Histoire de la vie privée* [Paris: Le Seuil, 1987], 4:279).

3. "Was there ever a composer so sensitive to criticism, so tenacious in rancour?" (Walker, *The Man Verdi,* 470).

4. Letter of 14 January 1848, Conati, *La bottega della musica,* 180.

5. When Boito challenged the publisher Sonzogno to a duel in 1893, Verdi,

who was then eighty, followed the affair closely, showing a keen sense of the etiquette, i.e., the necessity of defending one's honor (*Verdi-Boito Correspondence,* 210).

6. Max Gallo, *Garibaldi* (Paris: Fayard, 1982).

7. Giuseppe Mazzini, *Istruzione della giovine Italia,* quoted in "La giovine Italia," *Enciclopedia italiana* (1949), 276.

8. Abbiati, *Giuseppe Verdi,* 1:409.

9. Mary Jane Phillips-Matz, *Verdi: A Biography* (Oxford: Oxford University Press, 1993), 19.

10. *Copialettere,* 226.

11. Folco Portinari, *Pari siamo . . . : Storia del melodramma ottocentesco attraverso i suoi libretti* (Turin: EDT, 1981), 101.

12. Milan Kundera, *The Joke,* definitive ed. (New York: HarperCollins, 1982), 234–35.

13. It should be said in Verdi's defense that he had endless trouble with the censors, who took a poor view of a drama that featured a man of religion and ended with a scene in church. Is this why the last scene did not have the total desired dramatic force? The fact is that a year later Verdi considered reworking the scene, retaining the pastor hero.

14. *Verdi-Boito Correspondence,* 38.

15. *Carteggio Verdi-Ricordi, 1880–1881,* 72.

16. For a different interpretation, one that defends Verdi's evolution from a cruel, vengeful God to a God of love, see Marcel Moré, "A propos du *Requiem de Verdi,*" "Verdi et le sacré," and "La Foudre de Dieu," in *La Foudre de Dieu* (Paris: Gallimard, 1969).

17. Ottavio Barié, *L'Italia nell'Ottocento* (Turin: UTET, 1964), 168. See also "La Figure du père," in Perrot's *Histoire de la vie privée,* 121ff.

18. Edward Shorter, *The Making of the Modern Family* (New York: Basic Books, 1975).

19. Quoted in Dutheil, *Le Livret d'opéra,* 540. Shorter (ibid.) quotes a curious anecdote concerning an old Bavarian living in 1840: on learning that his daughter, who was pregnant but unmarried, could not marry her seducer, he tore his hair out, dashed his head against the walls, and died shortly afterward "of shock and dishonor."

20. Mitchell, *The Walter Scott Operas,* 20.

21. Baldacci, *Libretti d'opera,* 177–78.

22. In his study of Mozart's operas, Rémy Stricker similarly notes, apropos of *Idomeneo,* that Mozart avoided the confrontation of father and son, i.e., Idomeneo and Idamante: "If, in the end, their confrontation does not produce any great musical scene, except for the magnificent recitative of the first meeting and the tragic recognition (act 1, scene 9), the reason would seem to be that, inexplicably, Mozart shied away from the great tragic scene or scenes that could have

illumined the drama with regard to its deep, underlying meaning" (*Mozart et ses opéras* [Paris: Gallimard/Idées, 1980], 128). One might also point out that, in act 3 of Wagner's *Siegfried*, the relationship of Wotan and Siegfried has far less drama and emotional charge than that of the confrontation between Wotan and his daughter Brünnhilde in act 3 of *Die Walküre*.

23. Friedrich Schiller, *Intrigue and Love*, trans. A. Leslie and J. R. Willson (New York: Continuum, 1983), act 1, scene 7.

24. Mariá Rosa Alonso, "El tema de *Don Carlos* en la literatura," in *Atti II*, 16–59.

25. Friedrich Schiller, *Don Carlos*, trans. A. Leslie and J. R. Willson (New York: Continuum, 1983), act 2, scene 2.

26. Ursula Günther, "Scénario original de *Don Carlos* (1865)," *L'Avant-scène opéra*, nos. 90/91 (September–October 1986): 28ff.

27. *Don Carlos* and *Les Vêpres siciliennes* are French operas, but since they are chiefly known in their Italian versions I quote both languages.

28. Schiller, *Intrigue and Love*, act 5, scene 1.

29. Gilles de Van, "Pères et filles dans la dramaturgie verdienne," *L'Avant-scène opéra*, no. 19 ("*Simon Boccanegra*") (January–February 1979): 98, quoting from act 1, scenes 9–11.

30. The fact that this was a gradual process explains my disagreement with Luigi Baldacci's thesis (*Libretti d'opera*, 200ff.) that Boito was responsible for the collapse of the "taboo of the father and paternity" in Verdi's theater: by cutting out the Venice act in his adaptation of *Otello* the librettist eliminated the only father figure since Brabantio, Desdemona's father, who was opposed to the love between his daughter and the Moor, disappears from the drama. The fact is correct, but by the time Boito came on the scene the father figure had surely lost its prestige!

31. In his *Lettres européennes*, Mendelssohn describes a conversation on the shores of Lake Como in 1831 during which, to general approval, a doctor declared that Shakespeare's tragedies were of high quality but that the witches' scenes were "totally absurd and fit for children." On opposition to the fantastic in Italian culture, see Dutheil, *Le Livret d'opéra*, 770 ff. Muzio confirms the facile, popular interpretation of the fantastic in connection with the choruses in *Giovanna d'Arco*: "The demons' choruses are original, popular, truly Italian" (*Giuseppe Verdi nelle lettere di Emanuele Muzio ad Antonio Barezzi* [hereafter *Muzio-Barezzi*], ed. Luigi A. Garibaldi [Milan: Treves, 1931], 175; see also 195, 198). It should be recalled that Emanuele Muzio (1821–90) was Verdi's only pupil, from 1844 on, and his lifelong friend.

32. See "Il *Macbeth* verdiano: Genesi e caratteri di un libretto," in Goldin's *La vera Fenice*, 230ff.

33. *Verdi's "Macbeth": A Sourcebook*, 99.

34. The censors objected strongly to such an intervention, preferring the

clearer mechanisms of fault and punishment. G. Belli deplored the fact that what predominates in *Macbeth* is "the mysterious intervention of nonhuman forces and shadowy ideas of *fatum*" (Rivelli, "G. Gioacchino Belli 'censore,'" 389).

35. I do not include Azucena of *Il trovatore* because she is not a true witch: in García Gutiérrez's play she is presented as a gypsy, and, in the opera, only the popular superstition of Ferrando and the Count de Luna's soldiers makes her a witch, whereas the Count is not taken in and calls her simply a "base gypsy."

36. *Gustave III, ou Le Bal masqué* (Paris: Jonas, 1833).

37. Angel de Saavedra, duque de Rivas, *Don Alvaro, o La fuerza del sino* (Madrid: Catedra), 52, 54, 57.

38. In 1865, when a Paris production of *Forza* was being discussed, the director of the Opéra suggested that Verdi include the first scene of the Spanish play, in which Preziosilla appears, but Verdi was unenthusiastic and dragged his feet (see Günther, "Documents inconnus," 574, 575).

39. Conati, *La bottega della musica*, 53, 166 (June 1843, November 1845); Abbiati, *Giuseppe Verdi*, 1:665; and *Copialettere*, pl. XI (1846, 1849). In February 1850, Verdi sent Cammarano a scenario but did not follow it up (the scenario is reproduced in Abbiati, *Giuseppe Verdi*, 2:50). Between 1853 and 1855, after Cammarano's death, the collaboration with Antonio Somma produced two complete librettos, which are in the Verdi family archives, but an idea for the work is given in Verdi's correspondence with Somma. Luzio quotes extracts from Somma's second libretto in *Carteggi verdiani*, 2:58-79. *Lear* was still being discussed between April 1856 and October 1857, then again in 1865 (Günther, "Documents inconnus," 572).

40. See Schmidgall, *Literature as Opera*, 87.

41. *Verdi-Somma*, 58; Abbiati, *Giuseppe Verdi*, 2:283.

42. Osborne, *The Complete Operas of Verdi*, 77-82. But Osborne is wrong in believing that the composer was shifty in his negotiations with the San Carlo between 1856 and 1857, held back by a mysterious inner restraint. The negotiations were blocked on the question of casting, in particular for Cordelia, and there is no reason to suspect the composer of unconscious bad faith since Somma, his librettist, and Torelli, representing the San Carlo, themselves recognized the inadequacy of the *compagnia di canto* (see Abbiati, *Giuseppe Verdi*, 2:450, 457).

43. Like everyone else, Verdi had his "father problems." If his relations with Antonio Barezzi, his "adopted" father who contributed to his education and helped him in his studies before becoming his father-in-law, were apparently easy and harmonious, his relationship with his real father, Carlo Verdi, was far more tormented and went through some difficult phases. Nevertheless, we should bear in mind the social and moral position of the father in nineteenth-century culture and the crisis the father figure went through, which largely suffice to explain its role in Verdi's dramaturgy. On this subject, see, however, Jean François Labie's *Le Cas Verdi* (Paris: Laffont, 1987); and, more generally, for the composer's family relationships, Phillips-Matz, *Verdi: A Biography*.

44. Conati, *Encounters with Verdi*, 314. Verdi is far from being the only one to have found *Lear* frightening, as Gary Schmidgall recalls in "The Two Lears," in *Shakespeare and Opera* (Oxford: Oxford University Press, 1990). In fact, very few operas were derived from the play, these dating especially from the end of the century (Cagnoni, Gobatti, and Pedrell).

45. Opéra de Paris program for Aribert Reimann's *Lear* (1982).

46. Letter to Cammarano, 28 February 1850, Abbiati, *Giuseppe Verdi*, 2:51. See also the letter to Somma of 1853 in *Verdi-Somma*, 48; and Somma's letter in *Carteggi verdiani*, 2:65.

47. *Verdi-Somma*, 53.

48. See the pertinent observations in Leo Karl Gerhartz, "Il *Re Lear* di Antonio Somma," in *Atti I*, 110ff.

49. *Verdi-Somma*, 48; *Carteggi verdiani*, 2:66.

50. Edward J. Dent, "Verdi in inglese," *ISV Rigoletto*, no. 9 (1982): 1662.

51. Inès's entrance aria in *Inès de Castro* (Verona: Pietro Bisesti, 1836).

52. Quoted in Edward J. Dent, *The Rise of Romantic Opera* (Cambridge: Cambridge University Press, 1976), 180. Folco Portinari notes that in Italian novels in the first half of the century the hero is often "beautiful to the point of androgyny" (*Le parabole del reale* [Turin: Einaudi, 1976], 5)—an androgyny that was obviously not evinced by tenors, who were often stout and wore beards.

53. Palazzeschi, "Il Teatro Pagliano," in *Stampe dell'Ottocento*, 153.

54. Gallo, *Garibaldi*, 17 (Sand), 324 (Tennyson). Verdi's opinion was fairly close to Tennyson's, to judge from a letter of 1846 in which the composer asks Piave to come up with some lines for a romanza for the hero Foresto (in *Attila*): "I would recommend that you make them pathetic and whining: make this imbecile of a lover say that he would gladly have given up his place in heaven, but she rewarded him by making him . . . a cuckold" (quoted in David Lawton and David Rosen, "Verdi's Non-Definitive Revisions," in *Atti III*, 237).

55. Duque de Rivas, *Don Alvaro*, act 4, scene 1, p. 129.

56. De Van, "Verdi et l'idéal chevaleresque," 13.

57. Gilles de Van, "L'eroe verdiano," in *Opera e libretto* (Florence: Olschki, 1990), vol. 1.

58. Friedrich Schiller, *The Robbers*, trans. F. J. Lamport (New York: Penguin, 1979), act 5, scene 2, pp. 159–60.

59. *"Otello": Disposizione scenica*, 24ff.

60. Humbert, "Attribution à Auguste Mariette," 251–52.

61. "Come fu composta l'*Aida*,'" in *Carteggi verdiani*, 4:14, 15.

62. "Yes, yes, a few more years, perhaps only a few more months, and Italy will be free, united and a republic. What else should she be?" (Walker, *The Man Verdi*, 188).

63. Ibid., 221.

64. Ibid., 279. On his anticolonialism, see Conati, *Encounters with Verdi*, 351.

65. See Ursula Günther, "Giuseppe Verdis erster Erfolg in Paris," *Lende-*

mains (Cologne) 31, no. 2 (1983): 53–62 and Phillips-Matz, *Verdi: A Biography,* 220. However, this does not rule out the possibility that the liaison began in 1843, the hypothesis put forward by Phillips-Matz (p. 150).

66. Wolfgang Hildesheimer, *Mozart,* trans. M. Faber (New York: Farrar Straus Giroux, 1982), 329.

67. See, e.g., *Misérable et glorieuse: La Femme du 19ème siècle,* ed. Jean-Paul Aron (Paris: Fayard, 1980).

68. Christiane Issartel, *Les Dames aux camélias* (Paris: Chêne Hachette, 1981), 56. See also Jules Michelet, *La Femme* (Paris: Flammarion, 1981), 82 ff.

69. Jacques Lacan, *Ecrits* (Paris: Le Seuil, 1971), 2:239.

70. The new bourgeois morality established in Italy in the second half of the nineteenth century developed a veritable pedagogy of sacrifice. Intended for all, it was aimed particularly at women, with their essential qualities of submission, abnegation, and resignation. After the heroic passion of the Risorgimento, the minor literature of the last years of the century created an almost morbid atmosphere; the constant emphasis on sacrifice gave rise to a pleasurable delight in self-effacement, an almost sensual joy in renunciation.

71. Conati, *Encounters with Verdi,* 352.

72. See, e.g., Verdi's fine letter of 21 January 1852 to his father-in-law, Antonio Barezzi, in which he defends Giuseppina against the small-town gossip of Busseto (cited in Walker, *The Man Verdi,* 203–5).

73. Gino Monaldi, *Verdi: La vita, le opere* (Milan: Bocca, 1925–51), 153–54.

74. Phillips-Matz states that, according to the "oral tradition" of the Verdi family, the composer attended the first performance of Dumas's play in February 1852 (*Verdi: A Biography,* 303). However, insofar as Verdi was considering several librettos over the summer of 1852 and decided on Dumas's play abruptly and at the last moment, Conati contests this legend and suggests that Verdi became acquainted with *La Dame aux camélias* because Escudier had just sent it to him (*La bottega della musica,* 300ff.). See also Fabrizio Della Seta's introduction to the critical edition of *La traviata, WGV,* ser. 1, vol. 19 (1997), pp. xiii–xiv.

75. "I don't like whores on the stage," he stated in 1844, in connection with a libretto (see *Carteggi verdiani,* 4:79).

76. Roland Barthes, *Mythologies* (Paris: Le Seuil, 1957), 202.

77. *Copialettere,* 197. See also *Carteggi verdiani,* 1:37; and Conati, *La bottega della musica,* 315.

78. Conati, *Encounters with Verdi,* 51.

79. Abbiati, *Giuseppe Verdi,* 4:638 (27 February 1899). See also ibid., 517; and *Copialettere,* 390.

80. For a completely different interpretation of these alternating rhythms, see Daniel Sabbeth, "Dramatic and Musical Organization in *Falstaff,*" in *Atti III,* 415–42.

81. The composer considered "Di Provenza il mar, il suol" the best cantabile for baritone that he had written at that time (see *Carteggi verdiani,* 1:30).

82. See, e.g., *Copialettere*, 121 (1851); see also *Verdi-Somma*, 78 (1856).

83. Gilles de Van, "*La Traviata* ou la fin de l'idylle," *L'Avant-scène opéra*, no. 51 ("*La traviata*") (April 1983): 22ff.

84. Abbiati, *Giuseppe Verdi*, 2:122.

85. "Far more harmonically daring than anything Verdi had yet written" is Julian Budden's apt comment in *Operas*, 1:306.

86. *Copialettere*, 257.

87. Walker, *The Man Verdi*, 266 (15 November 1866).

88. See *Verdi-Somma*, 84, 85; and also *Carteggi verdiani*, 1:249.

89. See Conati, *Encounters with Verdi*, 306, in which G. Depanis gives an example of Verdi's deep-seated popularity.

90. Massimo Mila, "Verdi come il padre," in *Giuseppe Verdi* (Bari: Laterza, 1958), 300.

91. This transformation of the "outward crises of romantic melodrama" into "authentic conflicts of character and ideals" is described by George Steiner in connection with Schiller's *Don Carlos* and closely matches the process that took place with Verdi (*The Death of Tragedy* [New York: Hill & Wang, 1961], 175).

92. Massimo Mila describes it as "Verdi's only politically reactionary opera," the only one in which he sides with Caesar and not Brutus (*Giuseppe Verdi*, 227). J. F. Labie sees in it tangible proof of the composer's rallying to the Piedmontese monarchy (*Le cas Verdi*, 65ff.).

93. On suppressing the character, see Marcello Conati, "Verdi, il grand opéra e il *Don Carlos*," in *Atti II*, 277–78. Verdi is quoted in *The Verdi Companion*, 149.

94. Günther, "Der Briefwechsel Verdi–Nuitter–Du Locle," 340.

95. Steiner, *The Death of Tragedy*, 175. Borkman is the protagonist of Ibsen's play of the same name.

96. See Bernard Harris's preface to *Othello*, vol. 9 of *W. Shakespeare: Oeuvres complètes* (Paris: Le Club Français du Livre, 1959), 10.

97. I quote from the French version by Camille Du Locle and Arrigo Boito (Paris: Billaudot, 1983).

98. Pierre-Jean Rémy, "Othello et Otello," *L'Avant-scène opéra*, no. 3 (May–June 1976): 7–10.

99. "*Otello*": *Disposizione scenica*, 5.

100. Schmidgall, "Incredible Credo?" in *Shakespeare and Opera*, 241ff. The author reviews the numerous objections that have been raised to this "credo" and defends it as conforming perfectly to the spirit of Shakespeare's drama.

101. *Verdi-Boito Correspondence*, 75–76 (3 May 1884).

102. During the negotiations for *Otello*'s London premiere, scheduled for July 1889, the composer wrote Boito, imagining possible criticisms the audience might raise concerning both the dropping of the first act of the play and Iago's Credo. Although the letter was jocular in tone, Verdi did not quite equate the cutting of the Venice act, for which he took full responsibility, with the creation of the Credo, which he certainly accepted but for which he considered Boito

responsible (see *Verdi-Boito Correspondence,* 135–36). Luzio also relates an anecdote according to which the great Shakespearean actor Tommaso Salvini deplored, to Verdi's face, the discrepancy between the play and the libretto concerning Iago's diabolical nature, to which Verdi is said to have replied, with a shrug: "What else could you do?"—which, if the story is true, reveals a fairly tepid enthusiasm (see *Carteggi verdiani,* 2: 98n).

103. *Copialettere,* 693.

104. Ibid., 317 (24 September 1881).

Chapter Six

1. *Muzio-Barezzi,* 329.

2. Abbiati, *Giuseppe Verdi,* 2:391.

3. *Copialettere,* 532.

4. Erich Auerbach, *Mimesis: The Representation of Reality in Western Literature,* trans. Willard R. Trask (Princeton, N.J.: Princeton University Press, 1953).

5. We have seen how the libretto introduced a grand finale in act 1 that was intended to put a curse on Duncan's murderer but had no equivalent in the English play.

6. "Make it clear that there are two main pieces in the opera: the duet between Lady and her husband and the sleepwalking scene: if these pieces don't come across, the opera is done for," wrote Verdi to Cammarano (*Copialettere,* 62), an opinion that was restated several times.

7. "No matter what you do, you will never succeed in making it [the role of Macduff] very important. On the contrary, the more prominence you give it, the more it will show its insignificance. He does not become a hero until the end of the opera. He has, however, enough music to distinguish himself if he has a good voice, but he should not be given one note more" (letter to Escudier of 8 February 1865, *Verdi's "Macbeth": A Sourcebook,* 99).

8. This aria has in fact no equivalent in the play, but the composer could find justification for it in a tradition going back to the eighteenth-century actor David Garrick, who composed a speech for the dying Macbeth.

9. *Copialettere,* 62. Marianna Barbieri Nini, who created the part of Lady in 1847, recounted that many rehearsals were needed before the duet had the effect of being spoken rather than sung (Conati, *Encounters with Verdi,* 26).

10. See Pier Luigi Pizzi, "La Longue nuit de Macbeth," in *L'Avant-scène opéra,* no. 40 ("*Macbeth*") (March–April 1982): 99. As to Schlegel, Verdi read him assiduously around the time of *Macbeth,* in particular his *Lectures on Dramatic Art and Literature* (1811), trans. John Black, 2d ed. (London: George Bell & Sons, 1984).

11. In an early version of her dissertation (see chap. 3, no. 51 above), Marie-Pierre Lassus has aptly pointed out that certain phrases are identical in melody, rhythm, and harmony: e.g., Lady Macbeth's "Immoto sarai tu nel tuo disegno" before her act 2 aria (1865 version) and the witches' "Un'opra senza nome" at

the very beginning of the apparitions scene; both phrases are based on a plagal cadence and on the ascending melodic movement E-G♯ ("*Macbeth* de Verdi ou la mise en scène de l'inconscient" [Ph.D. diss., 1st phase, Conservatoire National Supérieur de Musique de Paris, June 1986], 91–92).

12. We should add the replacement of Macbeth's cabaletta at the end of act 3 by a duet between him and Lady Macbeth, the rewriting of the Scottish refugees' chorus at the beginning of act 4, and the replacement of the final sequence, which included a battle and then an aria for Macbeth, followed by a victory hymn.

13. *Copialettere,* 456.

14. *Simon Boccanegra* offers another example of these breaks in style that the composer accepted because they were in line with his dramatic vision. Verdi reworked several passages of the prologue, accentuating its nocturnal tonality, simplifying the vocal line to make it less mobile and singing, and darkening the accompaniment; but he did not touch the trivial little chorus in F major that concludes it and that has upset more than one commentator. The fact is that this piece, in which the people elect Simon doge and acclaim him, describes the external aspect of the action linking Paolo, Simon, and Fiesco, of which we have already seen the inner workings.

15. The opera actually premiered during the 1848 revolution, after the assassination of Rossi and Pope Pius IX's flight to Gaeta, before the ephemeral Roman republic was proclaimed. The first performance was greeted with great patriotic enthusiasm, and the fourth act was encored; later, certain rambunctious incidents, also inspired by patriotism, were reported in the press (see Monaldi, *Verdi,* 113).

16. *Carteggi verdiani,* 2:59.

17. David R. B. Kimbell, *Verdi in the Age of Italian Romanticism* (Cambridge: Cambridge University Press, 1981), 561 ff.

18. Mila, *La giovinezza di Verdi,* 374 ff.

19. *Carteggi verdiani,* 2:59; *Copialettere,* 60; Abbiati, *Giuseppe Verdi,* 1:770–81.

20. Budden, *Operas,* 1:414; see also Budden's "*La battaglia di Legnano:* Its Unique Character with Special Reference to the Finale of Act I," in *Atti III,* 71ff.

21. Abbiati, *Giuseppe Verdi,* 2:356, 369, 372, 449, 505, 511; *Copialettere,* 562; *Carteggi verdiani,* 1:26ff.

22. Karl Dietrich Gräwe, "L'uno e gli altri: Osservazioni sulla drammaturgia verdiana di conflitto interumano e della sua soluzione," in *Atti III,* 27–34.

23. Some nevertheless escaped this rule, such as *Macbeth, Lucrezia Borgia,* and *Belisario.*

24. See Hélène's Andante in G minor with its sudden outburst in the major at "Je t'aime"/"Io t'amo."

25. Black, "Salvadore Cammarano's *Programma* for *Il trovatore.*"

26. Wolfgang Osthoff connects her with the bucolic, pastoral tradition of the preceding century ("Musikalische Zuege der Gilda in Verdis *Rigoletto,*" *ISV Rigoletto* no. 8 [1973]: 950–80).

27. See, e.g., the coda of Giselda's prayer in act 1 of *I Lombardi*.

28. Francesco Orlando, *Ricordo di Lampedusa* (Milan: Scheiwiller, 1985), 46–48.

29. *Lettere inedite de Giuseppe Verdi,* ed. Giuseppe Morazzoni (Milan: Edizione della Scala, 1929), 29.

30. Abbiati, *Giuseppe Verdi,* 2:4–5.

31. *Copialettere,* 471–72.

32. *Verdi-Somma,* 46.

33. This idea of contrast perhaps owes something to Schlegel: in his *Lectures on Dramatic Art and Literature,* he considers one of the beauties of Romantic drama to be "the contrast of the jocular and the serious" (thirteenth lecture, 1811).

34. Andrea Della Corte, "Saggio di bibliografia delle critiche al *Rigoletto,*" *ISV Rigoletto,* no. 9 (1982): 1640 (printing a review of 12 March 1851).

35. Ibid., 1689.

36. Quoted by Rescigno, *Macbeth,* 62.

37. Abbiati, *Giuseppe Verdi,* 2:794, 3:743; *Verdi-Boito Correspondence,* 13; *Verdi intimo,* 286.

38. Daniela Goldin (*La vera Fenice,* 299) suggests, by contrast, that Verdi was not really ready to take on the mixture of genres in which he would engage five years later in *La forza del destino.*

39. Antonio García Gutiérrez, "Los hijos del Tío Tronerra," in *El trovador* (Madrid: Alhambra, 1979); Gilles de Van, *Riscritture parodistiche nell'Ottocento francese* (Florence: Olschki, 1993); Abbiati, *Giuseppe Verdi,* 2:199.

40. Baldini, *Abitare la battaglia,* 247. On the general problem of the mixing of genres, see Piero Weiss, "Verdi and the Fusion of the Genres," *Journal of the American Musicological Society,* 25, no. 1 (1982): 138–56.

41. Marcello Conati, "Appendix to the Bibliography of Critical Writings on *Rigoletto,*" *ISV Rigoletto,* no. 9 (1982): 1729.

42. Even without considering Rossini's and Donizetti's French operas, it is true that certain "French" traits had already penetrated Italian opera, as Philip Gossett has demonstrated apropos of Donizetti's *L'assedio di Calais* ("Music at the Théàtre Italien," in *Music in Paris in the 1830's* [New York: Pendragon, 1987]), but it was preferable to go to the source!

43. See Marcello Conati's excellent summing-up in "Verdi: Il grand opéra e il *Don Carlos,*" in *Atti II,* 242–80; see also Fabrizio Della Seta's "Verdi: La tradizione italiana e l'esperienza europea," *Musica/Realtà,* no. 32 (1990): 135–58, and esp. his *Italia e Francia nell'Ottocento,* vol. 9 in *Storia della musica* (Turin: EDT, 1993).

44. There is no reason not to believe Verdi when, on two occasions, he writes to the management of the Paris Opéra pointing out that he would earn as much in Italy as in Paris, and even more; he also claims that because Italy provides better protection of artistic property he derives more profit from his operas:

"With us, an opera produces five or six times more profit than it did a dozen years ago" (1854). See also the letter to Crosnier (1855). (*Copialettere*, 155, 160.)

45. "It would be far better for me to be *unknown* than to be *known the wrong way!* Now there's only one more move for me to make, to strike hard and decisively and appear on your stage with a Grand Opera: to succeed, or make an end of it" (ibid., 154; letter in French).

46. Abbiati, *Giuseppe Verdi*, 3:332; Conati, *Encounters with Verdi*, 344.

47. Fabrizio Della Seta, "L'immagine di Meyerbeer nella critica italiana dell'ottocento e l'idea di 'dramma musicale,'" in *L'opera tra Venezia e Parigi* (Florence: Olschki, 1988), 147–76.

48. Phillips-Matz, *Verdi: A Biography*, 51.

49. Apropos of *Robert le diable*, see his letter of September 1843, reported in Marcello Conati, *"Rigoletto": Guida all'opera* (Milan: Mondadori, 1983), 270.

50. *Muzio-Barezzi*, 180.

51. *Copialettere*, 139.

52. Andrew Porter, *"Les Vêpres siciliennes:* New Letters from Verdi to Scribe," *19th-Century Music* 2 (November 1978): 96.

53. He also liked Zorilla's play *El zapatero y el rey* because it would provide an opportunity for "some Arabian scenes either in the Alcazar in Seville or the Alhambra in Granada" (Günther, "La Genèse de *Don Carlos*," 24, 25, 30).

54. Abbiati, *Giuseppe Verdi*, 3:324; Monaldi, *Verdi*, 208.

55. *Copialettere*, 225.

56. Heine's volte-face is very significant in this connection. In 1837, he opposed Rossini's "individualist" and Meyerbeer's "socially modern" operas but, in 1847, saw them only as "machinery as artificial as it is expensive" (*Cronache musicali* [Fiesole: La Nuova Italia, 1983], 12–13, 20–21, 89).

57. *Copialettere*, 59, n. 3. Verdi almost always uses the French expression *mise en scène.* See the letter of 22 September 1847 about *Jérusalem* (*Copialettere*, 464) and that of 1855 concerning *Vêpres* (Abbiati, *Giuseppe Verdi*, 2:316).

58. Verdi knew Hayez particularly well because in the 1840s he was a fashionable portrait painter of high Milanese society and an habitué of the salon of Clarina Maffei, a great friend of Verdi's. There is also a head sculpted by Hayez in the composer's house at Sant'Agata. In addition, he was in charge of supervising the costumes for the Florence *Macbeth* (*Verdi's "Macbeth": A Sourcebook*, 33).

59. Conati, *La bottega della musica*, 74 (1843).

60. *Copialettere*, 437; and Conati, *La bottega della musica*, 143. Conati corrects the dating given in *Copialettere* from April 1844 to April 1845.

61. Maria Teresa Muraro, "Giuseppe Bertoja e le scene per la prima di *Rigoletto* alla Fenice," *ISV Rigoletto*, no. 9 (1982): 1584. Bertoja's sketches for the premiere of *Attila* are reproduced in "Le scenografie delle cinque 'prime assolute' di Verdi alla Fenice di Venezia," in *Atti I*, 328.

62. *Copialettere*, 439 (letter to Escudier of September 1845).

63. *Muzio-Barezzi*, 203, 234.

64. Abbiati, *Giuseppe Verdi,* 1:776.

65. Ursula Günther attributes this addition to the influence of a document describing an auto-da-fé at Valladolid in 1559 and a contemporary engraving by Franz Hogenberg illustrating the episode: in this precise case, the connection between the painting and the finale is strikingly confirmed ("La Genèse de *Don Carlos,*" 27, 28). Hogenberg's engraving is reproduced in *Atti III,* 564, and discussed by Günther in "Documents inconnus." But *Le Portrait de Philippe II,* a historical tale and "political drama" by Louis-Sébastien Mercier (1785), describes an auto-da-fé showing strong similarities to that of *Don Carlos* (de Van, *Le fonti del "Don Carlo" verdiano*).

66. *Verdi-Boito Correspondence,* 63; *Copialettere,* 339; Conati, *Encounters with Verdi,* 172.

67. Abbiati, *Giuseppe Verdi,* 4:463 (1892). Alberto Franchetti (1860–1942) was a composer of operas, among them *Cristoforo Colombo* and *Germania.*

68. *Copialettere,* 640. *Adresse* is in French in the text.

69. *Le Pasteur ou l'Évangile et le foyer,* by Emile Souvestre and Eugène Bourgeois, first performed at the Théâtre de la Porte Saint Martin in 1849.

70. Porter, "New Letters," 96 ff., esp. 106; *Copialettere,* 158.

71. *Carteggi verdiani,* 1:112 (1869).

72. *Lettres inédites . . . à Léon Escudier,* 22.

73. *Carteggi verdiani,* 1:111, 116.

74. Bob Rose in the sleeve notes for the recording of the 1862 version (Voce 72).

75. This does not rule out the possibility of connections between *Forza,* which, it will be recalled, was first performed in St. Petersburg, and an aesthetics that Mussorgsky was to realize in masterful fashion a few years later. Budden stresses the debt that *Boris* owes *Forza* with regard to the pilgrims' chorus and the characters of Melitone and Trabuco, models for Varlaam and the Idiot; he also points out the large number of "Russianisms" (*Operas,* 2:487, 499, 502, 520). Thus, Verdi could be said to have written a "Russian" opera in the spirit not of those already in existence, like Glinka's works, but of those that were to come.

76. Disguise is an important and symbolic theme in *Forza.* After her father's death, Leonora flees, disguised as a man, reaching the Hornachuelos inn and then the monastery of St. Mary of the Angels, where she finds refuge. At the end of the opera Alvaro is amazed to find a woman at the grotto where a mysterious hermit lives. Alvaro's own background is unknown, which is the chief reason for the Calatravas' hostility; in act 3 he goes off to war in Italy under the name Federico Herreros, later becoming Father Raphaël at the monastery of St. Mary of the Angels. In the inn scene Carlos passes himself off as Pereda, a student at Salamanca, and in the third act he is known as Don Felice de Bornos. Clearly, outside the "father's house," individuals have elusive identities! Hence the 1869 denouement, where the benevolent Padre Guardiano gives two of the three protagonists a religious identity.

77. Charles Osborne describes as "curiously playful" the Babylonian march that begins the first-act finale of *Nabucco* (*The Complete Operas of Verdi*, 56); describing the chorus of hired assassins that separates the two parts of Pagano's aria in act 1 of *I Lombardi*, Budden speaks of an "almost comic explosiveness" (*Operas*, 1:120).

78. *Copialettere*, 562. On the other operas inspired by Scribe's libretto, see Fedele d'Amico, "Il *Ballo in maschera* prima di Verdi," *ISV Un ballo in maschera*, no. 3 (1960): 1251–1328. See also de Van, "Le Travail du livret," and "Les Bals masqués."

79. *Verdi-Somma*, 84, 85.

80. Budden, *Operas*, 2:381.

81. Budden also notes that one section of Renato's melody is accompanied by a solo horn, an instrument that "has the ambivalence of Renato himself" (ibid., 380). The use of a "dark" rhythmic motif as a commentary on the word *splendido* (luminous) is a musical transposition of the oxymoron, of which the libretto offers many examples. The best known is in the chorus's exclamation, immediately after Ulrica's invocation, "come tutto qui riluce di tetro!" (lit., "everything here shines black"). On this subject, see Gilles de Van, "Notes sur Verdi humoriste," in *Omaggio a Gianfranco Folena* (Padua: Editoriale Programma, 1993), 3:1739 ff.

82. The use of the contrapuntal style to describe the final battle in the last version of *Macbeth* is another example of the ironic use of the form.

83. Pierluigi Petrobelli, "Aspects of *Falstaff*," BBC broadcast (1974).

84. See Massimo Mila's astute observations on this use of the perfect cadence in *Giuseppe Verdi*, 277.

85. Gilles de Van, "Mélancolie de Falstaff," *L'Avant-scène opéra*, nos. 87/88 ("*Falstaff*") (May–June 1986): 128.

86. Monaldi, *Verdi*, 291.

87. Alfred Einstein, *Essays in Music* (New York: Norton, 1962), 87.

88. Anne Ubersfeld, *Le Drame romantique* (Paris: Belin, 1993), 25–26.

89. Abbiati, *Verdi*, 2:62.

Chapter Seven

1. Lukács, *Soul and Form*, 28.

2. *Verdi's "Macbeth": A Sourcebook*, 12, 13, 19 (letters of Verdi), 321, 323–24 (text of the libretto with his rough drafts). See also Francesco Degrada, "Observations on the Genesis of Verdi's *Macbeth*," in ibid., 159–74.

3. Pierluigi Petrobelli, "Thoughts for *Alzira*," in *Music in the Theater*, 75–99.

4. Frank Walker, "Giuseppe Montanelli e il libretto del *Simon Boccanegra*," *ISV Un ballo in maschera*, no. 3 (1960): 1780.

5. *Verdi-Boito Correspondence*, 34. Fieschi is obviously Fiesco.

6. Basevi, *Studio*, 30.

7. Budden, *Operas*, 1:187–88.

8. The changes to this duet, which were added between 1853, the date of the

first performance, and 1854, when the opera took on its present form and was a huge success at Venice's Teatro Gallo a San Benedetto, are not pertinent to the following analysis.

9. *Carteggi verdiani,* 1:30.

10. Harold S. Powers, *"La solita forma* and the Uses of Convention," 90ff., 108.

11. Gossett, "Verdi, Ghislanzoni and *Aida."*

12. This element is linked to the motif that Frits Noske associates with Iago's plottings (see his extremely detailed study of the ensign's musical characterization, *"Otello,* Drama through Structure," in *The Signifier and the Signified,* 179).

13. Balthazar, "Evolving Conventions," 327 n. 14.

14. See the opinions of Goldoni and Quantz quoted by James R. Anthony in *French Baroque Music from Beaujoyeulx to Rameau* (New York: Norton, 1974), 82.

15. As exceptions one might cite Giacomo's *scena* in act 1 of *Giovanna d'Arco* or Pagano's *gran scena* in act 2 of *I Lombardi,* which in fact includes an Adagio in the form of a romanza.

16. Riccardo's solo "La rivedrà nell'estasi" rises with the same ease out of the introduction of *Un ballo in maschera.*

17. *Lettres inédites . . . à Léon Escudier,* 59.

18. Ibid., 37.

19. John Black, "Salvadore Cammarano's *Programma* for *Il trovatore."*

20. *Carteggi verdiani,* 1:14.

21. Verdi expresses his perplexity in a letter to Nuitter of November 1882, cited in Günther, "Der Briefwechsel Verdi–Nuitter–Du Locle," 372.

22. It is reproduced in part in *Carteggi verdiani,* 2:111 ff.

23. Abbiati, *Giuseppe Verdi,* 4:371–72. Toscanini scrupulously respected these indications in his recording, very obviously contrasting the reduced choruses with a noisy mumbling that is "indistinct" but not musically wrong. The effect is quite out of line with the usual interpretations.

24. Pending a critical edition, one can refer to the French version drawn up by Boito and Du Locle (Ricordi no. 51635).

25. Celletti, "La vocalità romantica," 211. See also Celletti's "On Verdi's Vocal Writing"; and S. Segalini, "Chanter Verdi," in *L'Arc,* no. 81 (January–March 1981): 36ff.

26. Celletti, "La vocalità romantica," 208–9.

27. Abbiati, *Giuseppe Verdi,* 4:444.

28. *Verdi-Boito Correspondence,* 63.

29. Conati, *Encounters with Verdi,* 113, 334–35.

30. Basevi, *Studio,* 186.

31. Examples of this procedure are the orchestral phrase in *Vêpres* accompanying the Eb-major parlante in the first part of the Montfort-Henri duet, act 1 (4 + 4 + 13); Montfort's attack in the Stretta of the same duet, "Téméraire!

téméraire!"/"Temerario! Qual ardire!" (4 + 4 + 18); in the first part of the Hé-
lène-Henri duet (act 2), Henri's entrance "Mais qu'un rayon d'espoir"/"Da tue
luci angeliche" (4 + 4 + 11); the first section of Montfort's aria in act 3, "Au sein
de la puissance"/"In braccio alle dovizie" (4 + 4 + 12); in *Simon Boccanegra,* in
the first part of the Amelia-Gabriele duet (act 1), Amelia's entrance "Vieni a
mirar la cerula" (4 + 4 + 11); Gabriele's largo in act 2 "Cielo pietoso" (4 + 4 +
4 + 16 with, it is true, internal reprises); etc.

32. Further examples: "Caro accento al cuor mi suona" in *Ernani,* just before
the Andantino of the Elvira-Ernani duet (act 2); Hélène's explosion of joy "O
transport, il respire" in *Jérusalem,* on learning that Gaston is still alive (act 2,
scene 1); Gulnara's rage as she tries to shake Corrado out of his torpor: "Non sai
tu che sulla tua testa" (*Corsaro,* Gulnara-Corrado duet, act 3); Azucena's cry of
despair in her trio with De Luna (*Il trovatore,* act 3) as she calls to Manrico for
help: "E tu non vieni, o Manrico"; etc.

33. Marzio Pieri, *Viaggio da Verdi* (Parma: La Pilotta, 1977), 11.

34. It occurs, e.g., in the opening chorus of the third act and in the duet that
follows, between Luisa and Miller. The rhythmic formula on which it is based
can be found in several motifs of the opera: in the little C♯-minor theme that
begins at Walter's entrance in the act 1 finale; in Luisa's entry in the act 2 quartet
and the orchestral motif opening Rodolfo's *scena* and closing aria in act 2; and in
the motif occupying the *tempo di mezzo* of the same aria. All these motifs linked
to the overture contribute powerfully to the color of the opera.

Chapter Eight

1. Carl Dahlhaus, *Wagner's Konzeption des musikalischen Dramas* (Regensburg:
Gustav Bosse Verlag, 1971), 18, with reference to Klotz.

2. Roland Barthes, *S/Z* (Paris: Le Seuil, 1970), 9.

3. Manfred Bukofzer, *Music in the Baroque Era* (New York: Norton, 1947),
365.

4. Abbiati, *Giuseppe Verdi,* 3:323–24. This letter is essential, being one of the
very few in which Verdi gives his ideas in matters of aesthetics.

5. *Copialettere,* 507 (1864).

6. Conati, *La bottega della musica,* 299 (1852). See also *Copialettere,* 508 (1871),
509 (1873).

7. Abbiati, *Giuseppe Verdi,* 3:323.

8. *Verdi's "Macbeth": A Sourcebook,* 75–76, 90, 123 (1865), 124 (1870).

9. Abbiati, *Giuseppe Verdi,* 3:109 (1866).

10. Günther, "Documents inconnus," 581 (letter in French).

11. Conati, *Encounters with Verdi,* 182.

12. *Verdi's "Macbeth": A Sourcebook,* 36.

13. Lawton and Rosen, "Verdi's Non-Definitive Revisions," 236.

14. Abbiati, *Giuseppe Verdi,* 1:472.

15. Conati, *Encounters with Verdi,* 374.

16. *Carteggi verdiani,* 2:8; see also Gustavo Marchesi, "Gli anni della *Forza del destino,*" *ISV La forza del destino,* no. 4 (1961): 41.

17. *L'abbozzo del "Rigoletto."*

18. Philip Gossett, "La composizione di *Ernani,*" *ISV Ernani,* 69.

19. David Lawton, "Observations on the Autograph of *Macbeth,*" in *Verdi's "Macbeth": A Sourcebook,* 210–27; see also 26.

20. See Martin Chusid's introduction to the critical edition of *Rigoletto, WGV,* ser. 1, vol. 17 (1983), p. xlvii; see also his "Editing *Rigoletto,*" in *Nuove prospettive.*

21. In 1861, he wrote the tenor Fraschini concerning *La forza del destino:* "I still have to orchestrate, but that's a small matter" (*Carteggi verdiani,* 2:19).

22. Conati, *La bottega della musica,* 250. According to Muzio, Verdi was reckoning on orchestrating *Alzira* in six days (*Muzio-Barezzi,* 205).

23. *Copialettere,* 559.

24. *Verdi's "Macbeth": A Sourcebook,* 83. On *Simon Boccanegra,* see also *Verdi-Boito Correspondence,* 16.

25. Apropos of *Macbeth,* see Lawton, "Observations on the Autograph of *Macbeth*"; the introduction by Chusid, whose critical edition of *Rigoletto* includes some last-minute corrections. On *Forza,* see Guglielmo Barblan, "Un po' di luce sulla prima rappresentazione della *Forza del destino* a Pietroburgo," *ISV forza del destino,* no. 5 (1962): 875ff. On *Falstaff,* see Barblan, "Spunti rivelatori nella genesi del *Falstaff,*" in *Atti I,* 16ff.

26. Pierluigi Petrobelli, "Remarks on Verdi's Composing Process," in *Music in the Theater,* 48–74.

27. Marcello Conati, *Verdi e il Teatro Regio di Parma* (Parma, n.d.), 51.

28. Abbiati, *Giuseppe Verdi,* 1:469.

29. *Carteggi verdiani,* 1:23.

30. In 1858, concerning *Ballo:* "And don't speak to me of success: if here and there one piece, or two or three, etc., etc. are applauded, that's not enough to make music drama. In questions of art I have my own very clear ideas, my convictions, which I cannot and must not give up" (Abbiati, *Giuseppe Verdi,* 2:472).

31. *Carteggi verdiani,* 1:111. See also ibid., 116; and the letter of August 1869 to Antonio Gallo, also concerning *Forza,* in *Copialettere,* 619.

32. Henri Meschonnic, *Critique du rythme* (Paris: Verdier, 1982), 70.

33. *Verdi intimo,* 116.

34. Morazzoni, ed., *Lettere inedite,* 27. See also, in connection with a performance of *Nabucco* in Venice, David Lawton and David Rosen, "Verdi's Non-Definitive Revisions: The Early Operas," in *Atti III,* 236.

35. Conati, *La bottega della musica,* 102.

36. *Copialettere,* 650, 653.

37. Francesco Degrada, *L'Avant-scène opéra,* no. 40 ("*Macbeth*") (March–April 1982): 25–77.

38. Rescigno, *Macbeth.*

39. Roman Jakobson and Claude Lévi-Strauss, "'Les Chats' de Baudelaire," *L'Homme: Revue Française d'Anthropologie* 2, no. 1 (1962): 5–21.

40. See, e.g., David Lawton, "Tonal Structure and Dramatic Action in *Rigoletto*," *ISV Rigoletto*, no. 9 (1982): 1559–81, and "Tonal Systems in *Aida* Act III," in *Analyzing Opera*, 262–75; and Martin Chusid, "Rigoletto and Monterone: A Study in Musical Dramaturgy," *ISV Rigoletto*, no. 9 (1982): 1544–58, which is further developed in his "The Tonality of *Rigoletto*," in *Analyzing Opera*, 241–61. Other studies are cited in the following notes.

41. See Lawton, "Tonal Structure and Dramatic Action," and "Tonal Systems in *Aida*."

42. Budden, *Operas*, 1:52–53.

43. See, e.g., Oronte's double aria in *I Lombardi*, act 2, in which each section is in A major, then A♭ major; or the Doge Foscari's last aria, whose movements are in E major, then E♭ minor/major; or in *Forza* Melitone's double aria, which is in A major, then E♭ major; etc.

44. Rodolfo's aria "Quando le sere al placido" (act 2), which was initially designed in B♭ major, then C major for the cabaletta, is lowered a tone (to A♭ and B♭). In the Violetta-Germont duet (act 2 of *Traviata*), the cantabile "Dite alla giovane" goes from E major to E♭ major. In *Forza*, Preziosilla's song in the second act was changed from B♭ major to B major and the baritone's aria (act 3), "Urna fatal," from F to E major. In the case of Preziosilla, B♭ major is more logical than B, and the transposition obviously makes the transitions more abrupt than in the 1862 version, where there is clear tonal continuity. Finally, the last two parts of the Elisabeth-Carlos duet, in the last act of *Don Carlos*, were transposed from C minor and B♭ major (1867) to C♯ minor and B major, but, in the latter case, Budden defends the dramatic appropriateness of the transposition (*Operas*, 3:144).

45. *Carteggi verdiani*, 2:42, which also reproduces the proposed variant. It will be noted, too, that, in 1881, Verdi had not the slightest intention of transposing Adorno's aria, in *Simon*, for Tamagno, preferring to add *puntature* (Abbiati, *Giuseppe Verdi*, 4:147). On the other hand, if one is to believe James A. Hepokoski, the quartet from act 2 of *Otello* was raised a semitone for Romilda Pantaleoni, who created the role of Desdemona ("Verdi's Composition of *Otello:* The Act II Quartet," in *Analyzing Opera*, 145).

46. Martin Chusid, "Drama and the Key of F Major in *Traviata*," in *Atti III*, 89–122.

47. Osthoff, "Musikalische Zuege der Gilda in Verdi's *Rigoletto*."

48. Conati, *Rigoletto*, 200.

49. Budden, *Operas*, 1:312. See also Martin Chusid, "Evil, Guilt, and the Supernatural in Verdi's *Macbeth:* Toward an Understanding of the Tonal Structure and Key Symbolism," and Daniel Sabbeth, "On the Tonal Organization of *Macbeth* II," both in *Verdi's "Macbeth": A Sourcebook*, 249–60, 261–69, the first

of which is devoted to the significance of tonalities, the second to tonal architecture.

50. In *La traviata,* the introduction is dominated by A major, F being linked with the love of Violetta and Alfredo (again, see Chusid, "Drama and the Key of F Major") and D♭ with the heroine's death: the opera ends in D♭ minor. This is the key of "Prendi, quest'è l'immagine" (final scene); "Gran Dio! morir si giovane" (duet with Alfredo in act 3) was in D before being lowered a semitone. At a crucial point in the duet with Germont (act 2), "Così alla misera," we are in D♭ minor. On *La traviata,* see Fabrizio Della Seta, "Il tempo della festa," *Studi verdiani,* no. 2 (1983): 108–47.

51. Edward T. Cone, "On the Road to *Otello:* Tonality and Structure in *Simon Boccanegra,*" *Studi verdiani,* no. 1 (1982): 72–98; Sabbeth, "Dramatic and Music Organization in *Falstaff.*"

52. In the case of *Macbeth,* the key of E plays more than a subsidiary role both because of its frequency (cabaletta of Lady's entrance aria "Or tutti sorgete," her act 2 aria "La luce langue," Macbeth's solo launching the Finale 2, witches' chorus at the beginning of act 3, and ballet) and its leading role in act 2. Does Budden's idea of power really take into account all the ways this key is used in the opera? B♭ is less significant and harder to interpret: Budden associates it with forward flight (escape) and Chusid with supernatural forces, which is not the same thing! Furthermore, if one assigns a meaning to D, why not to E♭, which is not much used but appears at a moment as important as Duncan's entrance? To take *Rigoletto,* if D is the key of the "felonious act" (Conati), why is it also that of the Duke in act 2, where that character suddenly appears as a smitten lover? If D♭ is the key of malediction, why does it predominate in Rigoletto's arioso "Culto, famiglia, patria" or in the Stretta of the Gilda-Rigoletto duet in act 1? Why is E♭, the tonality of fatherly love, also the key of the Finale 1 and of the furious chorus "Zitti, zitti, moviamo a vendetta"? In short, the more one tries to mend the net, the more Verdi seems to slip out of it, and one comes to doubt the very existence of a system of tonal significance.

53. See the introduction to *Analyzing Opera,* 1–24.

54. See Pierluigi Petrobelli, "Music in the Theater (apropos of *Aida,* Act III)," in *Music in the Theater.*

55. See the Ricordi vocal score of *I due Foscari* (Milan: G. Ricordi [c. 1912]), pl. no. 42307.

56. *Verdi-Boito Correspondence,* 184.

57. Péter Pál Varnai aptly observes that "Verdi's recurring themes are hardly ever concrete melodies, but rather, particular procedures of musical structure. If in spite of everything they are motifs, they seem 'masked,' that is, disguised within amply developed melodies" ("Dramma e musica nel *Nabucco,*" in *Atti III,* 453–64).

58. Gilles de Van, "La Notion de *tinta:* Mémoire confuse et affinités thématiques dans les opéras de Verdi," *Revue de musicologie,* no. 2 (1990): 187ff. I have

already described these thematic affinities in the preceding chapter, in connection with the duet between Padre Guardiano and Leonora.

59. Frits Noske, "Verdi and the Musical Figure of Death," in *Atti III*, 349–87; Péter Pál Varnai, "Contributo per uno studio della tipizzazione negativa nelle opere verdiane," in *Atti III*, 268–76.

60. Frits Noske, "*Don Carlos:* The Signifier and the Signified," in *The Signifier and the Signified*.

61. *Copialettere*, 106.

62. *Verdi's "Macbeth": A Sourcebook*, 8.

63. It is natural that, in one way or another, every Verdian critic should refer to this notion of color. So far as *Aida* is concerned, particularly valuable is Roger Parker's "Motives and Recurring Themes in *Aida*," in *Analyzing Opera*, 222–38.

64. *Carteggi verdiani*, 4:255.

Conclusion

1. *Verdi intimo*, 144.

2. On the Wagnerian claim that art should appear as true "nature," see Dahlhaus, *Richard Wagner's Music Dramas*, 69, 116–18.

3. Alfred Einstein, *Music in the Romantic Era* (New York: Norton, 1947), 286.

4. Moravia, "La volgarità di Giuseppe Verdi," in *L'uomo come fine*, 395 ff.

5. Isaiah Berlin, "The 'Naïveté' of Verdi," in *The Verdi Companion*, 1–12.

6. Friedrich Schiller, *On Naive and Sentimental Poetry*, trans. Daniel O. Dahlstrom (New York: Continuum, 1993), 202, 203.

7. Berlin, "The 'Naïveté' of Verdi," 7. At a conference at the Cini Foundation in 1979, in the paper "Verdi l'unzeitgemässe," Wolfgang Osthoff made some very illuminating comparisons between certain Verdi arias and Liszt's paraphrases of them, showing how the composer's harmony—dry, straightforward, *unzeit* in a certain way—had been corrected and made both more subtle and more *zeitlich* by the Hungarian composer.

8. Adorno, *Quasi una fantasia*, 69.

9. Testimony of Teresa Stolz, who watched over the composer in his agony (*Carteggi verdiani*, 2:313).

10. Walker, *The Man Verdi*, 282; see also 280–81.

11. See Labie's apt observations on this point in *Le cas Verdi*, 373ff.

12. Walker, *The Man Verdi*, 509.

BIBLIOGRAPHY

Note. Since the Verdian bibliography is considerable, only important works or those easily accessible are cited. The journal *Studi verdiani* lists, as systematically as possible, books and articles that have appeared since 1977.

Verdi Operas

Librettos. The Italian librettos of the operas (later versions) are to be found in *Tutti i libretti di Verdi,* with an introduction and notes by Luigi Baldacci and an afterword by Gino Negri ([Milan]: Garzanti, ca. 1975). The libretto of the first version of *Macbeth* is reproduced in Verdi's *"Macbeth": A Sourcebook,* edited by David Rosen and Andrew Porter (New York: Norton, 1984). The libretto of *Stiffelio,* with Julian Budden's translation, is published in the Royal Opera Texts series edited by Alison Latham (London: [1992]). The libretto of the first version of *Simon Boccanegra* is included in the Opera Guide series of the English National Opera and the Royal Opera (London: John Calder; New York: Riverrun, 1985). The libretto of the first version of *Forza* has not been published. The French librettos *(Jérusalem, Les Vêpres siciliennes, Don Carlos)* are published by Billaudot, Paris.

Scores. Verdi's operas are readily available in piano-vocal scores and, in some cases, orchestral scores from Ricordi, Milan, and other publishers. The University of Chicago Press and Ricordi are bringing out a critical edition under the direction of Philip Gossett (orchestral score and piano-vocal reductions): already published in full score are *Nabucco, Ernani, Alzira, Il corsaro, Luisa Miller, Rigoletto, Il trovatore, La traviata,* and the *Messa da Requiem;* in piano-vocal score are *Nabucco, Ernani, Rigoletto,* and the *Messa da Requiem.* Ursula Günther and Luciano Petazzoni have published a critical edition in piano-vocal score of all the versions of *Don Carlos* (Milan: Ricordi, 1974–80).

I. Correspondence and Biographical and Documentary Studies

A. CORRESPONDENCE

Note. Letters related to a particular opera appear under the relevant heading in section IV below.

Carteggi verdiani. Edited by Alessandro Luzio, Reale Accademia d'Italia, and Accademia Nazionale dei Lincei. 4 vols. Rome, 1935–47. Reprint, Bologna: Forni, 1993.

"Il carteggio di Giuseppe Verdi con la contessa Maffei." In *Profili biografici e bozzetti storici,* ed. Alessandro Luzio. 2 vols. Milan: L. F. Cogliati, 1927.

Dal carteggio inedito Verdi-Vigna. Edited by Gianetto Bongiovanni. Rome: Edizioni del "Giornale d'Italia," 1941.

Carteggio Verdi-Boito. Edited by Mario Medici and Marcello Conati. 2 vols. Parma, 1978. A one-volume English-language edition, with a new introduction by Marcello Conati, was prepared by William Weaver as *The Verdi-Boito Correspondence* (Chicago: University of Chicago Press, 1994).

Carteggio Verdi-Ricordi. Edited by Pierluigi Petrobelli, Maria di Gregorio Casati, and Carlo Matteo Mossa. 2 vols. to date: [1] *1880–1881;* [2] *1882–1885.* Parma: INSV, 1988–.

I copialettere di Giuseppe Verdi. Edited by Gaetano Cesari and Alessandro Luzio. Milan, 1913. Reprint, Bologna: Forni, 1979.

"Documents inconnus concernant les relations de Verdi avec l'Opéra de Paris." Assembled by Ursula Günther. In *Atti III* (1974).

Franco Faccio e Verdi: Carteggio e documenti inediti. Edited by Raffaele De Rensis. Milan, 1934.

Giuseppe Verdi, Giulio Ricordi: Corrispondenza e immagine, 1881–1890. Edited by Pierluigi Petrobelli and Franca Cella. Milan: Teatro alla Scala, 1981.

Lettres inédites de Giuseppe Verdi à Camille Du Locle. Collected by Jacques-Gabriel Prodhomme. *La revue musicale,* "10ᵉ année," no. 5 (March–April 1929): 97–112, and no. 7 (May–June 1929): 25–37.

Lettres inédites de Giuseppe Verdi à Léon Escudier. Collected by Jacques-Gabriel Prodhomme. *Rivista musicale italiana* 35 (March 1928): 1–23, (June 1928): 171–97, and (December 1928): 519–52.

Lettere inedite di Giuseppe Verdi. Edited by Giuseppe Morazzoni. Milan: Edizioni della Scala, 1929.

"Re Lear" e "Ballo in maschera": Lettere di Giuseppe Verdi ad Antonio Somma. Edited by Alessandro Pascolato. Città di Castello: Lapi, 1902.

Sei lettere di Verdi a Giovanni Bottesini. Edited by T. Costantini. Trieste: Schmidt, 1908.

Verdi intimo: Carteggio di Giuseppe Verdi con il conte Opprandino Arrivabene (1861–1886). Edited by Annibale Alberti. Milan: Mondadori, 1931.

B. BIOGRAPHICAL AND DOCUMENTARY STUDIES

Abbiati, Franco. *Giuseppe Verdi.* 4 vols. Milan: Ricordi, 1959. Essential because of the mass of unpublished documents.

Conati, Marcello. *Interviste e incontri con Verdi.* Milan: Il Formichiere, 1980. Translated by Richard Stokes as *Encounters with Verdi* (Ithaca, N.Y.: Cornell University Press, 1984). Articles by and interviews with Verdi's contemporaries.

————. *La bottega della musica: Verdi e La Fenice.* Milan: Il Saggiatore, 1983. Documentary study of the operas first performed in Venice.

Demaldè, Giuseppe. *Cenni biografici del maestro Verdi.* 1853. Edited and translated by Mary Jane Matz. *Verdi Newsletter,* no. 1 (May 1976): 6–10, no. 2 (December 1976): 8–12, and no. 3 (June 1977): 5–9.

Gatti, Carlo. *Verdi nelle immagini.* Milan: Garzanti, 1941. Iconography.

————. *Verdi* [1931]. Milan: Mondadori, 1951.

Giuseppe Verdi nelle lettere di Emanuele Muzio ad Antonio Barezzi. Edited by Luigi A. Garibaldi. Milan: Treves, 1931.

Günther, Ursula. "Giuseppe Verdis erster Erfolg in Paris." *Lendemains* (Cologne) 31, no. 2 (1983): 53–62.

Marchesi, Gustavo, and Gaspare Nello Vetro. *Verdi, merli e cucù: Cronache bussetane fra il 1810 e il 1839.* Expanded with documents discovered by Gaspare Nello Vetro; presentation by William Weaver. Busseto: Biblioteca della Cassa di Risparmio di Parma e Monte di credito su pegno di Busseto, 1979.

Matz, Mary Jane. "The Roots of the Tree." *Verdi: Bolletino dell'ISV,* vol. 3 *(Rigoletto),* no. 7 (1969): 333–64.

————. "The Verdi Family of S. Agata and Roncole: Legend and Truth." In *Atti I* (1969).

Oberdorfer, Aldo. *Giuseppe Verdi: Autobiografia dalle lettere.* Milan: Rizzoli, 1951. New ed., revised and corrected by Marcello Conati. Milan: Rizzoli, 1981.

Osborne, Charles. *Verdi: A Life in the Theatre.* New York: Knopf, 1987.

Phillips-Matz, Mary Jane. *Verdi: A Biography.* Oxford: Oxford University Press, 1993.

Pougin, Arthur. *Giuseppe Verdi: Vita aneddotica.* With notes and additional material by Folchetto (= Jacopo Caponi). Milan: Ricordi, 1881. A translation by Sibylle Zavriew of Pougin's *Verdi: Histoire anecdotique de sa vie et de ses oeuvres* (Paris, 1886). Reprint, with a preface by Marcello Conati, Florence: Passigli, 1989.

Verdi: A Documentary Study. Compiled, edited, and translated by William Weaver. London: Thames & Hudson, 1977.

Walker, Frank. *The Man Verdi.* New York: Knopf, 1962. Reprint, with a preface by Philip Gossett, Chicago: University of Chicago Press, 1982.

Werfel, Franz. *Verdi: Der Roman der Oper.* Berlin, 1924. Translated by Helen Jessiman as *Verdi: A Novel of the Opera* (New York: Simon & Schuster, 1925).

II. General Studies of Verdi's Operas

A. BOOKS

Baldini, Gabriele. *Abitare la battaglia: La storia di Giuseppe Verdi*. Milan: Garzanti, 1970–83. Translated by Roger Parker as *The Story of Giuseppe Verdi: "Oberto" to "Un ballo in maschera"* (Cambridge: Cambridge University Press, 1980).

Barilli, Bruno. *Il paese del melodramma* [1931]. Edited by Luisa Viola and Luisa Avellini. Turin: Einaudi, 1985.

Basevi, Abramo. *Studio sulle opere di G. Verdi*. Florence: Tofani, 1859. Reprint, Bologna: Forni, 1978.

Bellaigue, Camille. *Verdi*. Paris: Laurens, 1912–27.

Bonavia, Ferruccio. *Verdi*. London: Oxford University Press, 1930.

Bourgeois, Jacques. *Giuseppe Verdi*. Paris: Julliard, 1978.

Budden, Julian. *The Operas of Verdi*. 3 vols. London: Cassell, 1973–81. Rev. ed., Oxford: Clarendon, 1992.

Casini, Claudio. *Verdi*. 2d ed. Milan: Rusconi, 1981.

Della Corte, Andrea. *Verdi*. Turin: Arione, 1939.

Hussey, Dyneley. *Verdi*. London: Dent; New York: Dutton, 1940. Rev. ed., London: Dent, 1973.

Labie, Jean-François. *Le Cas Verdi*. Paris: Laffont, 1987.

Marchesi, Gustavo. *Verdi*. Turin: UTET, 1970.

Martin, George. *Verdi: His Music, Life and Times*. New York: Dodd Mead, 1963.

Mila, Massimo. *L'arte di Verdi*. Turin: Einaudi, 1980.

Monaldi, Gino. *G. Verdi: La vita, le opere*. Milan: Bocca, 1925–51.

Osborne, Charles. *The Complete Operas of Verdi*. New York: Knopf, 1970.

Pieri, Marzio. *Viaggio da Verdi: Discorso di un italianista intorno all'opera romantica*. Parma: La Pilotta, 1977.

———. *Verdi: L'immaginario dell'Ottocento*. Milan: Electa, 1981. Rich iconography.

Roncaglia, Gino. *Giuseppe Verdi: L'ascensione dell'arte sua*. Naples: Perella, 1914. Reprinted as *L'ascensione creatrice di Giuseppe Verdi* (Florence: G. C. Sansoni, 1940).

Soffredini, Alfredo. *Le opere di G. Verdi*. Milan: Aliprandi, 1901.

Tintori, Giampiero. *Invito all'ascolto di Verdi*. Milan: Mursia, 1983.

Toye, Francis. *Giuseppe Verdi: His Life and Works*. New York: Knopf, 1946.

See also Abbiati, *Giuseppe Verdi* (sec. IB).

B. ARTICLES AND COLLECTIONS

Abert, Anna Amalia. "Verdi." In *Die Musik in Geschichte und Gegenwart,* vol. 13. Kassel: Bärenreiter, 1966.

Della Seta, Fabrizio. "Verdi." In *Dizionario enciclopedico universale della musica e dei musicisti,* vol. 8. Turin: UTET, 1988.

"Giuseppe Verdi." *L'Arc,* no. 81 (1981). Special issue devoted to Verdi.

Giuseppe Verdi: Vicende, problemi e mito di un artista e del suo tempo: Palazzo ducale di Colorno, appartamenti del duca e della duchessa, 31 agosto–8 dicembre 1985. Colorno: Edizioni "Una città costruisce una mostra," 1985. Catalog of the 1985 Colorno exhibition.

Guide des opéras de Verdi. Series directed by Jean Cabourg. Paris: Fayard, 1990. Discography and bibliography.

Hanslick. Eduard. *Die moderne Oper.* Berlin, 1875–88.

Leibowitz, René. "Connaissez-vous Verdi?" In *Histoire de l'opéra.* Paris: Buchet Chastel, 1957.

Mila, Massimo. "Verdi." In *Enciclopedia dello spettacolo,* vol. 9. Rome: Casa editrice Le Maschere, 1962.

Parker, Roger. "Verdi." In *The New Grove Dictionary of Opera,* vol. 4. London: Macmillan, 1992.

Petrobelli, Pierluigi. "Verdi." In *Dizionario della musica.* Milan: Ricordi, 1959.

Porter, Andrew. "Verdi." In *The New Grove Dictionary of Music and Musicians,* vol. 19. London: Macmillan, 1980.

The Verdi Companion. Edited by William Weaver and Martin Chusid. New York: Norton, 1979.

III. Special Studies of Verdi's Works

A. BOOKS

Chusid, Martin. *A Catalog of Verdi's Operas.* Hackensack, N.J.: Joseph Boonin, 1974.

———, ed. *Verdi's Middle Period, 1849–1859: Source Studies, Analysis, and Performance Practice.* Chicago: University of Chicago Press, 1997.

Cisotti, Virginia. *Schiller e il melodramma di Verdi.* Florence: La Nuova Italia, 1975.

Della Corte, Andrea. *Le sei più belle opere di Verdi.* Milan: Istituto d'Alta Coltura, 1946.

Engelhardt, Markus. *Die Chöre in den frühen Opern Giuseppe Verdis.* Tutzing: Hans Schneider, 1988.

Gerhartz, Leo Karl. *Die Auseinandersetzungen des jungen Giuseppe Verdi mit dem literarischen Drama.* Berlin: Merseburger, 1968.

Godefroy, Vincent. *The Dramatic Genius of Verdi: Studies of Selected Operas.* 2 vols. London: Gollancz, 1975–78.

Hopkinson, Cecil. *A Bibliography of the Works of Giuseppe Verdi, 1813–1901.* 2 vols. New York: Broude Bros., 1973–78.

Hughes, Spike. *Famous Verdi Operas.* London, 1968.

Jürgensen, Knud Arne. *The Verdi Ballets.* Parma: INSV, 1995.

Kimbell, David R. B. *Verdi in the Age of Italian Romanticism.* Cambridge: Cambridge University Press, 1981.

Lavagetto, Mario. *Un caso di censura, il "Rigoletto."* Milan: Il Formichiere, 1979.

————. *Quel più modesti romanzi: Il libretto nel melodramma di Verdi, techniche costruttive, funzioni, poetica di un genere letterario minore.* Milan: Garzanti, 1979.

Lawton, David. "Tonality and Drama in Verdi's Early Operas." Ph.D. diss., University of California, Berkeley, 1973.

Mila, Massimo. *La giovinezza di Verdi.* Turin: ERI, 1974.

Moreen, Robert A. "Integration of Text Forms and Musical Forms in Verdi's Early Operas." Ph.D. diss., Princeton University, 1975.

Parker, Roger. *Studies in Early Verdi (1832–1834): New Information and Perspectives on the Milanese Musical Milieu and the Operas from "Oberto" to "Ernani."* New York: Garland, 1989.

Pinagli, Palmiro. *Romanticismo di Verdi.* Florence: Vallecchi, 1967. On Verdi's aesthetics.

Rinaldi, Mario. *Gli anni di "galera" di Verdi.* Rome: Volpe, 1969.

————. *Le opere meno note di Giuseppe Verdi.* Florence: Olschki, 1975.

Tarozzi, Giuseppe. *Il gran vecchio: La vita e le opere di G. Verdi del 1863 al 1901.* Milan: Sugar, 1878.

Travis, Francis Irving. *Verdi's Orchestration.* Zurich: Juris, 1956.

B. ARTICLES AND COLLECTIONS

Analyzing Opera: Verdi and Wagner. Edited by Carolyn Abbate and Roger Parker. Berkeley and Los Angeles: University of California Press, 1989.

Atti del I congresso internazionale di studi verdiani: Venezia, Isola di San Giorgio Maggiore, Fondazione Giorgio Cini, 31 luglio–2 agosto 1966. Parma: ISV, 1969.

Atti del III congresso internazionale di studi verdiani: Milano, Piccola Scala, 12–17 giugno 1972. Parma: ISV, 1974.

Baldacci, Luigi. "Padri e figli: Parole e musica, etc." In *Libretti d'opera e altri saggi.* Florence: Vallecchi, 1974.

————. "I libretti di Verdi." In *Il melodramma italiano* (1977; *see* sec. VA).

Berlin, Isaiah. "The 'Naïveté' of Verdi." In *Atti I* (1969). Reprinted in *The Verdi Companion,* ed. William Weaver and Martin Chusid. New York: Norton, 1979.

Celletti, Rodolfo. "Caratteri della vocalità di Verdi." In *Atti III* (1974).

————. "On Verdi's Vocal Writing." In *The Verdi Companion,* ed. William Weaver and Martin Chusid. New York: Norton, 1979.

"Colloquium Verdi-Wagner (Rome 1969)." *Analecta musicologica,* vol. 11 (1972).

De Van, Gilles. "Pères et filles dans la dramaturgie verdienne." In *L'Avant-scène opéra,* no. 19 *(Simon Boccanegra).* Paris: Éditions de l'Avant-scène, 1979.

————. "Appunti sull'evoluzione dell'eroe verdiano." In *Opera e libretto,* vol. 1. Florence: Olschki, 1990.

————. "Musique et narration dans les opéras de Verdi." *Studi verdiani,* no. 6 (1990): 18–54.

Engelhardt, Markus. *Verdi und andere: "Un giorno di regno," "Ernani," "Attila," "Il corsaro," in Mehrfachvertonungen.* Parma: INSV, 1992.

Fairtile, Linda B. "The Violin Director and Verdi's Middle-Period Operas." In Martin Chusid, ed., *Verdi's Middle Period,* 413–26 (1997; *see* sec. IIIA).

Kerman, Joseph. "Verdi's Use of Recurring Themes." In *Studies in Music History: Essays for Oliver Strunk,* ed. Harold Powers. Princeton, N.J.: Princeton University Press, 1968. Reprint, Westport, Conn.: Greenwood, 1980.

Jeuland-Meynaud, Maryse. "Le Théâtre espagnol et le mélodrame de Giuseppe Verdi." *Annales de l'Université de Lyon* 1 (1978): 127–68.

Lawton, David, and David Rosen. "Verdi's Non-Definitive Revisions: The Early Operas." In *Atti III* (1974).

Marvin, Roberta Montemorra. "Aspects of Tempo in Verdi's Early and Middle-Period Italian Operas." In Martin Chusid, ed., *Verdi's Middle Period,* 393–411 (1997; *see* sec. IIIA).

Moravia, Alberto. "La volgarità di Giuseppe Verdi." In *L'uomo come fine e altri saggi.* Milan: Bompiani, 1964.

Moré, Marcel. "À propos du *Requiem* de Verdi: La Foudre de Dieu, Verdi et le sacré." In *La Foudre de Dieu.* Paris: Gallimard, 1969.

Noske, Frits. "Verdi and the Musical Figure of Death." In *Atti III* (1974). Reprinted in his *The Signifier and the Signified* (1977; *see* sec. VB).

———. "Ritual Scenes in Verdi's Operas." In his *The Signifier and the Signified* (1977; *see* sec. VB).

Nuove prospettive nella ricerca verdiana: Atti del convegno internazionale in occasione della prima del "Rigoletto" in edizione critica, Vienna, 12/13 marzo, 1983. Parma: ISV, 1987.

Paduano, Guido. "Shakespeare e la parola scenica." In *Il giro di vite.* Florence: La Nuova Italia, 1992.

Parker, Roger. "*Insolite Forme,* or Basevi's Garden Path." In Martin Chusid ed., *Verdi's Middle Period,* 129–46 (1997; *see* sec. IIIA).

Petrobelli, Pierluigi. "Osservazioni sul processo compositivo in Verdi." *Acta musicologica* 43 (1971): 125–42. Translated by Roger Parker as "Remarks on Verdi's Composing Process," in Pierluigi Petrobelli, ed., *Music in the Theater* (1994; *see* sec. VB).

Pizzetti, Ildebrando. "Contrappunto e armonia nell'opera di G. Verdi." *La rassegna musicale* 21 (July 1951): 189–200.

Reading Opera. Edited by Arthur Gross and Roger Parker. Princeton, N.J.: Princeton University Press, 1988.

Roncaglia, Gino. "Il 'tema-cardine' nell'opera di G. Verdi." *Rivista musicale italiana* 47 (1943): 220–29.

Rosen, David. "How Verdi's Operas Begin: An Introduction to the Introduzioni." In *Tornando a "Stiffelio"* (1985; *see* sec. IV, s.v. "*Stiffelio*"). Reprinted in *Verdi Newsletter,* no. 16 (1988): 3–18.

———. "How Verdi's Serious Operas End." In *Atti del XIV congresso della Società internazionale di musicologia: Trasmissione e recezione delle forme di cultura musicale.* Turin: EDT, 1990. Reprinted in *Verdi Newsletter,* no. 20 (1992): 9–15.

———. "Meter, Character, and *Tinta* in Verdi's Operas." In Martin Chusid, ed., *Verdi's Middle Period,* 339–92 (1997; *see* sec. IIIA).

Rosselli, John. "Verdi e la storia della retribuzione del compositore italiano." *Studi verdiani,* no. 2 (1983): 11–27.

Savinio, Alberto. *Scatola sonora.* Turin: Einaudi, 1977.

Studi verdiani. Journal of the INSV. Ten issues published between 1982 and 1995. The journals (1–5 between 1963 and 1988) and newsletters (1–10 between 1960 and 1987) devoted to individual operas appear in section IV of this bibliography.

Tomlinson, Gary. "Opera and Drama: Hugo, Donizetti and Verdi." In *Music and Drama: Studies in the History of Music.* New York: Broude Bros., 1988.

Varnai, Péter Pál. "Contributo per uno studio della tipizzazione negativa nelle opere verdiane." In *Atti III* (1974).

Vaughan, Denis. "The Inner Language of Verdi's Manuscripts." *Musicology* (Sydney) 5 (1979): 67–153.

Verdi: Bolletino dell'ISV. Three volumes, each devoted to a single opera, and each subdivided into three numbers, published 1960–82 (vol. 1 = nos. 1–3; vol. 2 = nos. 4–6; vol. 3 = nos. 7–9). A tenth and last number was published in 1987 as *"Ernani": ieri e oggi.*

Verdi Newsletter. Published by the American Institute for Verdi Studies, New York, since 1976.

Vlad, Román. "Anticipazioni nel linguaggio armonico verdiano." *La rassegna musicale* 21 (July 1951): 237–45.

———. "Alcune osservazioni sulla struttura delle opere di Verdi." In *Atti III* (1974).

Weiss, Piero. "Verdi and the Fusion of Genres." *Journal of the American Musicological Society* 35, no. 1 (1982): 138–56.

See also Balthazar, "Evolving Conventions in Italian Serious Opera" (sec. VA); Chusid, *Verdi's Middle Period* (sec. IIIA); and, on forms and conventions, Gossett, "Verdi, Ghislanzoni and *Aida*" (sec. IV, s.v. *Aida*).

IV. Studies of Individual Operas

AIDA

"Aida." *L'Avant-scène opéra,* no. 4. Paris: Éditions de l'Avant-scène, 1976.

Aida. Edited by Nicholas John. English National Opera Guides, no. 2. London: J. Calder; New York: Riverrun, 1980.

Alberti, Luciano. "'I progressi attuali del dramma musicale' [1872], Note sulla disposizione scenica per l'opera *Aida*." In *Il melodramma italiano* (1977; *see* sec. VA).

Busch, Hans, trans. and ed. *Verdi's "Aida": The History of an Opera in Letters and Documents.* Minneapolis: University of Minnesota Press, 1978.

Conati, Marcello. "Aspetti di melodrammaturgia verdiana: A proposito di una sconosciuta versione del finale del duetto Aida-Amneris." *Studi verdiani,* no. 3 (1985): 45–78.

Erasmi, Gabriele. "*Norma* ed *Aida:* Momenti estremi della concezione romantica." *Studi verdiani,* no. 5 (1988–89): 85–108.

"Genesi dell'*Aida.*" *Quaderni dell'ISV* (Parma), no. 4 *(Aida)* (1971).

Gossett, Philip. "Verdi, Ghislanzoni and *Aida:* The Uses of Convention." *Critical Inquiry* 1 (1974): 291–334.

Günther, Ursula. "Zur Entstehung von Verdis *Aida.*" *Studi musicali* 2 (1973): 15–71.

Humbert, Jean. "Attribution à Auguste Mariette d'un scénario anonyme de l'opéra *Aida.*" *Revue de musicologie* 42 (1976): 229–56.

Immagini per "Aida." Catalog of an exhibition organized by R. De Sanctis and Pierluigi Petrobelli. Parma: ISV, 1983.

Jürgensen, Knud A. "Le coreografie originali di *Aida* (Paris, Théâtre de l'Opéra, 1880)." *Studi verdiani,* no. 6 (1990): 146–58.

Luzio, Alessandro. "Come fu composta l'*Aida*" and "Il trionfo di *Aida* all Opéra di Parigi." In *Carteggi verdiani,* ed. Alessandro Luzio, Reale Accademia d'Italia, and Accademia Nazionale dei Lincei, vol. 4. Rome, 1947. Reprint, Bologna: Forni, 1993.

Lawton, David. "Tonal Systems in *Aida,* Act III." In *Analyzing Opera* (1989; *see* sec. IIIB).

Parker, Roger. "Motives and Recurring Themes in *Aida.*" In *Analyzing Opera* (1989; *see* sec. IIIB).

Petrobelli, Pierluigi. "La musica nel teatro: A proposito dell'atto III di *Aida.*" In *La drammaturgia musicale,* ed. Lorenzo Bianconi. Bologna: Il Mulino, 1986.

ALZIRA

Castelvecchi, Stefano. Introduction to the critical edition of *Alzira. WGV,* ser. 1, vol. 8 (1995).

Conati, Marcello. "L'*Alzira* di Verdi attraverso le lettere e le cronache." In *Tre saggi su "Macbeth," "Alzira," "Manon" e "Werther,"* ed. Claudio del Monte, 33–114. Parma, 1980.

Mila, Massimo. "Lettura dell'*Alzira.*" *Rivista italiana di musicologia* 1 (1966): 246–67.

Petrobelli, Pierluigi. "Pensieri per *Alzira.*" In *Nuove prospettive* (1987; *see* sec. IIIB). Translated by Roger Parker as "Thoughts for *Alzira*" in Petrobelli, ed., *Music in the Theater* (1994; *see* sec. VB).

AROLDO (See STIFFELIO)

See also Conati, *La bottega della musica* (sec. IB).

ATTILA

Gossett, Philip. "A New Romanza for *Attila.*" *Studi verdiani,* no. 9 (1986): 13–21.

Mila, Massimo. "Lettura dell'*Attila* di Verdi." *Nuova rivista musicale italiana* 17 (1983): 247–76.

Noiray, Michel, and Roger Parker. "La Composition d'*Attila:* Étude de quelques variantes." *Revue de musicologie* 62 (1976): 104–23.

Smart, Mary Ann. "'Proud, Indomitable, Irascible': Allegories of Nation in *Attila* and *Les Vêpres siciliennes.*" In Martin Chusid, ed., *Verdi's Middle Period,* 227–56 (1997; *see* sec. IIIA).

UN BALLO IN MASCHERA

"*Un bal masqué.*" *L'Avant-scène opéra,* no. 32. Paris: Éditions de l'Avant-scène, 1990.

Un ballo in maschera. Edited by Nicholas John. English National Opera Guides, no. 40. London: J. Calder; New York: Riverrun, 1989.

De Van, Gilles. "Les Bals masqués." *L'Arc* 81 (1981): 26–35.

———. "Le Travail du livret." *L'Arc* 81 (1981): 14–25.

Hudson, Elizabeth. "Masking Music: A Reconsideration of Light and Shade in *Un ballo in maschera.*" In Martin Chusid, ed., *Verdi's Middle Period,* 257–72 (1997; *see* sec. IIIA).

Levarie, Siegmund. "Key Relations in Verdi's *Un ballo in maschera.*" *19th-Century Music* 2 (1978–79): 143–49.

———. "A Pitch Cell in Verdi's *Un ballo in maschera.*" *Journal of Musicological Research* 3 (1981): 399–409.

Parker, Roger, and Matthew Brown. "Motivic and Tonal Interaction in Verdi's *Un ballo in maschera.*" *Journal of the American Musicological Society* 36 (1983): 243–65.

Powers, Harold. "'*La dama velata*': Act II of *Un ballo in maschera.*" In Martin Chusid, ed., *Verdi's Middle Period,* 273–336 (1997; *see* sec. IIIA).

Ross, Peter. "Amelias Auftrittsarie im *Maskenball:* Verdis Vertonung im dramaturgisch-textlichem Zusammenhang." *Archiv für Musikwissenschaft* 40 (1983): 126–46.

Verdi: Bolletino dell'ISV, vol. 1 *(Un ballo in maschera),* nos. 1–3 (1960).

LA BATTAGLIA DI LEGNANO

Budden, Julian. "*La battaglia di Legnano:* Its Unique Character, with Special Reference to the Finale of Act I." In *Atti III* (1974).

Noske, Frits. "Verdi und die Belagerung von Haarlem." In *Convivium mu-*

sicorum: Festschrift Wolfgang Boetticher, zum sechzigsten Geburtstag. Berlin: Merseberger, 1974.

IL CORSARO

Hudson, Elizabeth. Introduction to the critical edition of *Il corsaro. WGV,* ser. 1, vol. 13 (forthcoming, 1998).

Mila, Massimo. "Lettura del *Corsaro* di Verdi." *Nuova rivista musicale italiana* 5 (1971): 1.

Quaderni dell'ISV, no. 1 *(Il corsaro)* (1963). Reprinted in 1972.

Town, Stephen. "Observations on a cabaletta from Verdi's *Il Corsaro." Current Musicology* 32 (1981): 59–75.

DON CARLOS and DON CARLO

Adams, Veinus, and John Clark. "*Don Carlo:* Problemi di rappresentazione e interpretazione." In *Atti II* (1971).

Atti del secondo Congresso internazionale di studi verdiani. Parma, 1971. Devoted to *Don Carlos.*

"Don Carlos." *L'Avant-scène opéra,* nos. 90/91. Paris: Éditions de l'Avant-scène, 1986.

Beyer, B. "Selbstverständigung und Verselbstverständigung: Eine Analyse von Giuseppe Verdis *Don Carlos.*" Ph.D. diss., Teknische Universität, Berlin, 1988.

De Van, Gilles. "Le fonti del *Don Carlo* verdiano." In *Don Carlo.* Milan: Teatro alla Scala/Rizzoli, 1992.

Günther, Ursula. "La Genèse de *Don Carlos.*" *Revue de musicologie* 58 (1972): 1; 60 (1974): 1–2.

———. "Der Briefwechsel Verdi–Nuitter–Du Locle zur Revision des *Don Carlos.*" *Analecta musicologica* (Cologne) 14 (1974): 414–44; 15 (1975): 334–401. The latter is written in collaboration with Gabriella Carrara-Verdi.

———. Preface to the piano-vocal score of *Don Carlos.* Milan: Ricordi, 1974–77.

Porter, Andrew. "The Making of *Don Carlos.*" *Proceedings of the Royal Musical Association* 98 (1971–72): 73–88.

Rosen, David. "The Five Versions of Verdi's *Don Carlos.*" Paper presented at the thirty-seventh annual meeting of the American Musicological Society, Chapel Hill and Durham, N. C., November 1971.

———. "The Operatic Origins of Verdi's Lacrymoso." *Studi verdiani,* no. 5 (1988–89): 65–84.

See also Degrada, *Il palazzo incantato;* Leibowitz, *Les Fantômes de l'opéra;* and Paduano, *Noi facemmo ambedue un sogno strano* (all in sec. VB).

I DUE FOSCARI

Biddlecombe, George. "The Revision of 'No, non morrai, chè i perfidi': Verdi's Compositional Process in *I due Foscari*." *Studi verdiani*, no. 2 (1983): 59–77.

Lawton, David. "A New Sketch for *I due Foscari*." *Verdi Newsletter* 22 (1955): 4–16.

Simone, C. "Per la cabaletta de *I due Foscari*." *Nuova antologia* 375 (September–October 1934): 327–34.

ERNANI

"*Ernani,*" *ieri e oggi*. In *Verdi: Bollettino dell'ISV*, no. 10 (1987).

Gallico, Claudio. Introduction to the critical edition of *Ernani*. *WGV*, ser. 1, vol. 5 (1985).

———. "Verso l'edizione critica di *Ernani* di Verdi." In *Nuove prospettive* (1987; *see* sec. IIIB).

Gossett, Philip. "The Composition of *Ernani*." In *Analyzing Opera* (1989; *see* sec. IIIB).

Spada, Marco. "*Ernani* e la censura napoletana." *Studi verdiani*, no. 5 (1988–89): 11–34.

See also Conati, *La bottega della musica* (sec. IB); Paduano, *Noi facemmo ambedue un sogno strano* (sec. VB).

FALSTAFF

Barblan, Guglielmo. "Spunti rivelatori nella genesi del *Falstaff*." In *Atti I* (1969).

Baumann, Thomas. "Rehearings: Late Verdi: The Young Lovers in *Falstaff*." *19th-Century Music* 9 (1985): 62–69.

"*Falstaff*." *L'Avant-scène opéra*, nos. 87–88. Paris: Éditions de l'Avant-scène, 1986.

Gerhartz, Leo Karl. "Versuch über *Falstaff*: Zu autobiographischen Aspekten von Verdis letzter Oper." In *Musik, Deutung, Bedeutung: Festschrift für Harry Goldschmitt zum 75. Geburtstag*, ed. Hanns-Werner Heister and Hartmut Lück. Dortmund: Edition V im Pläne-Verlag, 1986.

Girardi, Michele. "Verdi e Boito: Due artisti fra tradizione e rinnovamento." In *Arrigo Boito, musicista e letterato*, ed. Giampiero Tintori. Milan: Nuove edizioni, 1986.

Hepokoski, James A. *Giuseppe Verdi, "Falstaff."* Cambridge Opera Handbooks. Cambridge: Cambridge University Press, 1983.

———. "Under the Eye of the Verdian Bear: Notes on the Rehearsal and the Premiere of *Falstaff*." *Musical Quarterly* 71 (1985): 135–56.

———. "Verdi, Giuseppina Pasqua and the Composition of *Falstaff*." *19th-Century Music* 3 (1980): 239–56.

———. "Overriding the Autograph Score: The Problem of Textual Authority in Verdi's *Falstaff*." *Studi verdiani*, no. 8 (1992): 13–51.

Osthoff, Wolfgang. "Il sonétto nel *Falstaff* di Verdi." In *Il melodramma italiano* (1977).

Sabbeth, Daniel. "Dramatic and Musical Organization in *Falstaff*." In *Atti III* (1974).

Werner, Klaus-Günter. *Spiele der Kunst: Kompositorische Verfahren in der Oper "Falstaff" von Giuseppe Verdi.* Frankfurt am Main: Lang, 1988.

LA FORZA DEL DESTINO

"La Force du destin." *L'Avant-scène opéra,* no. 126. Paris: Éditions de l'Avant-scène, 1989.

The Force of Destiny. Edited by Nicholas John. English National Opera Guides, no. 23. London: J. Calder; New York: Riverrun, 1983.

Holmes, William C. "The Earliest Revisions of *La forza del destino*." *Studi verdiani,* no. 6 (1988): 55–98.

Nádas, John. "New Light on Pre-1869 Revisions of *La forza del destino*." *Verdi Newsletter* 15 (1987): 7–19.

Rescigno, Eduardo. *La forza del destino.* Milan: Il Formichiere, 1981.

Verdi: Bolletino dell'ISV, vol. 2 *(La forza del destino),* nos. 4–6 (1961–66).

UN GIORNO DI REGNO

Engelhardt, Markus. "Nuovi dati sulla nascita dell'opera giovanile di Verdi *Un giorno di regno*." *Studi verdiani,* no. 4 (1988): 11–17.

Parker, Roger. *"Un giorno di regno:* From Romantic Libretto to Verdi's Opera." *Studi verdiani,* no. 2 (1983): 38–58.

GIOVANNA D'ARCO

Chusid, Martin. "A Letter by the Composer about *Giovanna d'Arco* and Some Remarks on the Division of Musical Direction in Verdi's Day." *Studi verdiani,* no. 7 (1991): 12–56.

I LOMBARDI ALLA PRIMA CROCIATA and JÉRUSALEM

Quaderni dell'ISV, no. 2 *(Gerusalemme)* (1963).

Quattrocci, Arrigo. "Da Milano a Parigi: *Jérusalem,* la prima revisione di Verdi." *Studi verdiani* 10 (1994–95), 13–16.

LUISA MILLER

Kallberg, Jeffrey. Introduction to the critical edition of *Luisa Miller. WGV,* ser. 1, vol. 15 (1991).

MACBETH

Conati, Marcello. "Aspetti della messinscena del *Macbeth* di Verdi." *Nuova rivista musicale italiana* 15 (1981): 374–404.

Lassus, Marie-Pierre. *La Voix impure ou "Macbeth" de Verdi.* Paris: Klincksieck, 1992.

"*Macbeth.*" *L'Avant-scène opéra,* no. 40. Paris: Éditions de l'Avant-scène, 1982.

Macbeth. Edited by Nicholas John. English National Opera Guides, no. 41. London: J. Calder; New York: Riverrun, 1990.

Noske, Frits. "Schiller e la genesi del *Macbeth* verdiano." *Nuova rivista musicale italiana* 10 (1976): 196–203.

Osthoff, Wolfgang. "Die beide Fassungen von Verdis *Macbeth.*" *Archiv für Musikwissenschaft* 29 (1972): 17–44.

Verdi's "Macbeth": A Sourcebook. Edited by David Rosen and Andrew Porter. New York: Norton, 1984.

See also Degrada, *Il palazzo incantato* (sec. VB); Goldin, *La vera Fenice* (sec. VA); and Schmidgall, *Literature as Opera* (sec. VB).

I MASNADIERI

Marvin, Roberta M. "Artistic Concerns and Practical Considerations in the Composition of *I masnadieri:* A Newly Discovered Version of 'Tremate, o miseri!'" *Studi verdiani,* no. 7 (1991): 77–110.

NABUCCO

Cavicchi, Adriano. "Verdi e Solera: Considerazioni sulla collaborazione per *Nabucco.*" In *Atti I* (1969).

Lawton, David, and David Rosen. "Verdi's Non-Definitive Revisions: The Early Operas." In *Atti III* (1974).

"*Nabucco.*" *L'Avant-scène opéra,* no. 86. Paris: Éditions de l'Avant-scène, 1986.

Parker, Roger. Introduction to the critical edition of *Nabucco. WGV,* ser. 1, vol. 3 (1988).

Petrobelli, Pierluigi. *Nabucco.* Milan: Associazione Amici della Scala, 1966–67.

Varnai, Péter Pál. "Dramma e musica nel *Nabucco.*" In *Atti III* (1974).

OBERTO, CONTE DI SAN BONIFACIO

Giovanelli, Paola D. "La storia e la favola dell'*Oberto.*" *Studi verdiani,* no. 2 (1983): 29–37.

Kimbell, David R. B. "Poi diventò l'*Oberto.*" *Music and Letters* 52, no. 1 (1971): 1–7.

Sartori, Claudio. "*Rocester,* la prima opera di Verdi." *Rivista musicale italiana* 43 (1939): 97–104.

See also Parker, *Studies in Early Verdi* (sec. IIIA).

OTELLO

Della Corte, Andrea. *Le opere di Verdi: "Otello."* Milan, 1924.

Hepokoski, James A. *Giuseppe Verdi, "Otello."* Cambridge Opera Handbooks. Cambridge: Cambridge University Press, 1987.

———. "Verdi's Composition of *Otello:* The Act II Quartet." In *Analyzing Opera* (1989; *see* sec. IIIB).

"Otello." L'Avant-scène opéra, no. 3. Paris: Éditions de l'Avant-scène, 1976.

"Otello" di Giuseppe Verdi. Edited by James A. Hepokoski and Mercedes Viale-Ferrero. Musica e spettacolo: Collana di disposizioni sceniche. Milan: Ricordi, 1990. Production book drawn up by Ricordi, Verdi, and Boito.

See also Degrada, *Il palazzo incantato;* Kerman, *Opera as Drama;* and Schmidgall, *Shakespeare and Opera* (all in sec. VB).

RE LEAR

Gerhartz, Leo Karl. "Il *Re Lear* di Antonio Somma ed il modello melodrammatico dell'opera verdiana." In *Atti I* (1969).

Martin, George. "Verdi, *King Lear* and Maria Piccolomini." *Columbia Literary Column* 21 (1971): 12–20.

Medici, Mario. "Lettere sul *Re Lear.*" *Verdi: Bollettino dell'ISV,* vol. 1, no. 2 (1960): 767–78.

See also Schmidgall, *Shakespeare and Opera* (sec. VB).

MESSA DI REQUIEM

Messa per Rossini: La storia, il testo, la musica. Edited by Michele Girardi and Pierluigi Petrobelli. Parma: INSV; Milan: Ricordi, 1988. On the *Requiem* and the Mass originally intended for Rossini.

"Messa da Requiem." L'Avant-scène musique, no. 1. Paris: Éditions de l'Avant-scène, 1984.

Rosen, David. "The Genesis of Verdi's *Requiem.*" Ph.D. diss., University of California, Berkeley, 1976.

———. Introduction to the critical edition of the *Messa da Requiem. WGV,* ser. 3, vol. 1 (1990).

———. *Verdi, "Requiem."* Cambridge Music Handbooks. New York: Cambridge University Press, 1995.

Verdi, Giuseppe. *Libera me Domine; Messa per Rossini: Facsimile dell'autografo.* Parma: INSV, 1988.

RIGOLETTO

L'abbozzo del "Rigoletto" di Giuseppe Verdi [1941]. Facsimile edition of the autograph sketch, with an introduction by Luigi Gatti. Reprint, Bologna: Forni, 1978.

Chusid, Martin. Introduction to the critical edition of *Rigoletto. WGV,* ser. 1, vol. 17 (1983).

———. "Editing *Rigoletto.*" In *Nuove prospettive* (1987; *see* sec. IIIB).

———. "The Tonality of *Rigoletto.*" In *Analyzing Opera* (1989; *see* sec. IIIB).

Conati, Marcello. *"Rigoletto" di Giuseppe Verdi: Guida all'opera.* Milan: Mondadori, 1983.

———. *Rigoletto: Un'analisi drammatico-musicale.* Venice: Marsilio, 1992.

Danuser, Claudio. "Studien zu den Skizzen von Verdis *Rigoletto.*" Ph.D. diss., University of Bern, 1985.

De Van, Gilles. *"Rigoletto:* L'Introduction dans l'opéra italien comme forme musicale et prétexte dramatique." *Analyse musicale* 27 (1992): 25–29.

Gallico, Claudio. "Recognizione del *Rigoletto.*" *Nuova rivista musicale italiana* 3, no. 5 (1969): 855–901.

Lavagetto, Mario. "Quella porta, assassini, m'aprite." In *Opera e libretto,* vol. 1. Florence: Olschki, 1990.

Petrobelli, Pierluigi. "Verdi and *Don Giovanni:* On the Opening Scene in *Rigoletto.*" In *Music in the Theater* (1994; *see* sec. VB).

"Rigoletto." L'Avant-scène opéra, nos. 112/113. Paris: Éditions de l'Avant-scène, 1988.

Roncaglia, Gino. "L'abbozzo del *Rigoletto* di Verdi." *Rivista musicale italiana* 48 (1946): 112–29.

Verdi: Bolletino dell'ISV, vol. 3 *(Rigoletto),* nos. 7–9 (1969–82).

See also Conati, *La bottega della musica* (sec. IB); and Lavagetto, *Un caso di censura* (sec. IIIA).

SIMON BOCCANEGRA

Bogianckino, Massimo. *"Simon Boccanegra:* Il testo in prosa, i libretti etc." *Annali della Facoltà di Lettere e Filosofia dell'Università degli Studi di Perugia* 14 (1976–77): 297–359.

Budden, Julian. "The Vocal and Dramatic Characteristics of Jacopo Fiesco." *Studi verdiani,* no. 10 (1994–95), 67–75.

Busch, Hans, ed. and trans. *Verdi's "Otello" and "Simon Boccanegra" (Revised Version) in Letters and Documents.* Oxford: Clarendon, 1988.

Conati, Marcello. *Il "Simon Boccanegra" di Verdi a Reggio Emilia (1857): Storia documentata.* Reggio Emilia: Edizioni del Teatro Municipale "Romolo Valli," 1984.

Cone, Edward T. "On the Road to *Otello:* Tonality and Structure in *Simon Boccanegra.*" *Studi verdiani,* no. 1 (1982): 72–98.

Falcinelli, Sylviane. "Étude comparative des sources manuscrites milanaises du *Simon Boccanegra.*" Ph.D. diss., Conservatoire National Supérieur de Musique de Paris, 1980.

Kerman, Joseph. "Lyric Form and Flexibility in *Simon Boccanegra.*" *Studi verdiani,* no. 1 (1982): 47–62.

Osthoff, Wolfgang. "Die beide *Boccanegra* Fassungen und der Beginn von Verdis Spätwerk." *Analecta musicologica* 1 (1963): 70–89.

Puccini, Dario. "Il *Simon Boccanegra* di Antonio García Gutiérrez e l'opera di Giuseppe Verdi." *Studi verdiani,* no. 3 (1985): 120–30.

"*Simon Boccanegra.*" *L'Avant-scène opéra,* no. 19. Paris: Éditions de l'Avant-scène, 1979.

Simon Boccanegra: Disposizione scenica. Edited by Marcello Conati and Natalia Grilli. Musica e spettacolo: Collana di disposizioni sceniche. Milan: Ricordi, 1993. Production book drawn up by Ricordi and Verdi.

Varnai, Péter Pál. "Paolo Albiani: Il cammino di un personaggio." *Studi verdiani,* no. 1 (1982): 63–71.

Walker, Frank. "Verdi, Giuseppe Montanelli and the Libretto of *Simon Boccanegra.*" *Verdi: Bollettino dell'ISV,* vol. 1, no. 3 (1960): 1373–90.

See also Conati, *La bottega della musica* (sec. IB); Goldin, *La vera Fenice* (sec. VA); and Noske, *The Signifier and the Signified* (sec. VB).

STIFFELIO and AROLDO

Quaderni dell'ISV, no. 3 *(Stiffelio)* (1968).

Gossett, Philip. "New Sources for *Stiffelio:* A Preliminary Report." *Cambridge Opera Journal* 5, no. 3 (1993): 199–222. Reprint, in Martin Chusid, ed., *Verdi's Middle Period,* 19–43 (1997; *see* sec. IIIA).

Hansell, Kathleen Kuzmick. "Compositional Techniques in Verdi's *Stiffelio:* Reading the Autograph Sources." In Martin Chusid, ed., *Verdi's Middle Period,* 45–97 (1997; *see* sec. IIIA).

Tornando a "Stiffelio": Popolarità, rifacimenti, messinscena, effettismo e altre 'cure' nella drammaturgia del Verdi romantico. Edited, with an introduction by, Giovanni Morelli. Florence: Olschki, 1987.

LA TRAVIATA

Budden, Julian. "The two *Traviata*s." *Proceedings of the Royal Musical Association* 99 (1972–73): 43–67.

Chusid, Martin. "Drama and the Key of F Major in *La Traviata.*" In *Atti III* (1974).

Della Seta, Fabrizio. "Il tempo della festa: Su due scene della *Traviata* e su altri luoghi verdiani." *Studi verdiani,* no. 2 (1983): 108–46.

———. Introduction to the critical edition of *La traviata. WGV,* ser. 1, vol. 19 (1997).

Hepokoski, James A. "Genre and Content in Mid-Century Verdi: 'Addio del passato,' *La traviata.*" *Cambridge Opera Journal* 1 (1989): 249–76.

Issartel, Christiane. *Les Dames aux camélias.* Paris: Hachette, 1981. Rich iconography.

Parouty, Michel. *La traviata.* Paris: Aubier, 1988.

"*La traviata.*" *L'Avant-scène opéra,* no. 51. Paris: Éditions de l'Avant-scène, 1983.

La traviata. Edited by Nicholas John. English National Opera Guides, no. 5. London: J. Calder; New York: Riverrun, 1981.

IL TROVATORE and LE TROUVÈRE

Black, John N. "Salvadore Cammarano's Programma for *Il trovatore* and the Problems of the Finale." *Studi verdiani,* no. 2 (1983): 78–107.

Drabkin, William. "Characters, Key Relations and Tonal Structure in *Il trovatore.*" *Music Analysis* 1, no. 2 (1982): 143–53.

Chusid, Martin. "A New Source for *El trovador* and Its Implications for the Tonal Organization of *Il trovatore.*" In *Verdi's Middle Period,* 207–25 (1997; *see* sec. IIIA).

Greenwood, Joanna. "Musical and Dramatic Motion in Verdi's *Il trovatore.*" *Jahrbuch für Opernforschung* 2 (1986): 59–73.

Hepokoski, James A. "*Ottocento* Opera as Cultural Drama: Generic Mixtures in *Il trovatore.*" In Martin Chusid, ed., *Verdi's Middle Period,* 147–93 (1997; *see* sec. IIIA).

Il trovatore. Edited by Nicholas John. English National Opera Guides, no. 20. London: J. Calder; New York: Riverrun Press, 1983.

Lawton, David. "*Le Trouvère:* Verdi's Revision of *Il trovatore* for Paris." *Studi verdiani,* no. 3 (1985): 79–119.

———. Introduction to the critical edition of *Il trovatore. WGV,* ser. 1, vol. 18A (1993).

"*Le Trouvère.*" *L'Avant-scène opéra,* no. 60. Paris: Éditions de l'Avant-scène, 1984.

Mossa, Carlo Matteo. "La genesi del libretto del *Trovatore.*" *Studi verdiani,* no. 8 (1992): 52–103. An abbreviated version in English appears in David Lawton's introduction to the critical edition of *Il trovatore* as "The Genesis of the Libretto."

Parker, Roger. "The Dramatic Structure of *Il trovatore.*" *Music Analysis* 1, no. 2 (1982): 155–67.

Petrobelli, Pierluigi. "Toward an Explanation of the Dramatic Structure of *Il trovatore.*" Translated by William Drabkin. In *Music in the Theater* (1994; *see* sec. VB).

LES VÊPRES SICILIENNES

Budden, Julian. "Varianti nei *Vespri siciliani.*" *Nuova rivista musicale italiana* 6, no. 2 (1972): 155–81.

———. "Verdi and Meyerbeer in Relation to *Les Vêpres siciliennes.*" *Studi verdiani,* no. 1 (1982): 11–20.

Conati, Marcello. "Ballabili nei *Vespri:* Con alcune osservazioni su Verdi e la musica popolare." *Studi verdiani,* no. 1 (1982): 21–46.

Gerhard, Anselm. "'Ce cinquième acte sans intérêt': Preoccupazioni di Scribe e di Verdi per la drammaturgia de *Les Vêpres siciliennes.*" *Studi verdiani,* no. 4 (1988): 65–86.

Mila, Massimo. *Les Vêpres siciliennes.* Turin: UTET, 1973.

Noske, Frits. "Melodia e struttura in *Les Vêpres siciliennes* di Verdi." *Ricerche musicali* 4 (1980): 3–8.

Porter, Andrew. "*Les Vêpres siciliennes:* New Letters from Verdi to Scribe." *19th-Century Music* 2, no. 2 (November 1978): 95–109.

"*Les Vêpres siciliennes.*" *L'Avant-scène opéra,* no. 75. Paris: Éditions de l'Avant-scène, 1985.

Vlad, Román. "Unità strutturale dei *Vespri siciliani.*" In *Il melodramma italiano* (1977; *see* sec. VA).

V. General Studies

A. NINETEENTH-CENTURY ITALIAN OPERA AND CULTURE

A!A!A! [A. Hugo, A. Malitourne, and J. J. Ader]. *Traité du mélodrame.* Paris: Delaunay, 1817.

Adamo, Maria Rosario, and Friedrich Lippmann. *Vincenzo Bellini.* Turin: ERI, 1981.

Ashbrook, William. *Donizetti and His Operas.* Cambridge: Cambridge University Press, 1982.

Baldacci, Luigi. *Libretti d'opere e altri saggi.* Florence: Vallecchi, 1974.

Balthazar, Scott Leslie. "Evolving Conventions in Italian Serious Opera: Scene Structure in the Works of Rossini, Bellini, Donizetti and Verdi, 1810–1850." Ph.D. diss., University of Pennsylvania, 1985.

Barbier, Patrick. *La Vie quotidienne à l'opéra au temps de Rossini et de Balzac, Paris, 1800–1850.* Paris: Hachette, 1987. Translated by Robert G. Luoma as *Daily Life at the Opera, 1800–1850* (Portland, Oreg.: Amadeus, 1995).

Barié, Ottavio. *L'Italia nell'Ottocento.* Turin: UTET, 1964.

Berlioz, Hector. *Mémoires.* Paris: Garnier-Flammarion, 1969. Translated (and edited) by David Cairns as *The Memoirs of Hector Berlioz, Member of the French Institute: Including His Travels in Italy, Germany, Russia, and England, 1803–1865* (New York: Norton, 1975).

———. *Les Soirées de l'orchestre.* Rev. ed. Paris: Stock, 1980 [1968]. Translated (and edited, with an introduction and notes) by Jacques Barzun as *Evenings with the Orchestra* (Chicago: University of Chicago Press, 1973).

Blaze de Bury, Henri. *Musiciens contemporains.* Paris, 1856. Reprint, Editions d'Aujourd'hui, Les Introuvables, 1982.

Boito, Arrigo. *Opere.* Edited by Mario Lavagetto. Milan: Garzanti, 1979.

Brooks, Peter. *The Melodramatic Imagination.* New Haven, Conn.: Yale University Press, 1995.

Brunel, Pierre. *Vincenzo Bellini.* Paris: Fayard, 1981.

Carner, Mosco. *Puccini: A Critical Biography.* 3d ed. New York: Holmes & Meier, 1992.

Dahlhaus, Carl. *Musikalischer Realismus: Zur Musikgeschichte des 19 Jahrhunderts.* Munich: Piper, 1982. Translated by Mary Whittall as *Realism in Ninetheenth-Century Music* (Cambridge: Cambridge University Press, 1985).

———. *Die Musikdramen Richard Wagners.* Hanover: Friedrich, 1971. Translated by Mary Whittall as *Richard Wagner's Music Dramas* (Cambridge: Cambridge University Press, 1979).

———. *Wagners Konzeption des musikalischen Dramas.* Regensburg: G. Bose, 1971.

De Angelis, Marcello. *Le carte dell'impresario: Melodramma e costume teatrale nell'Ottocento.* Florence: Sansoni, 1982.

Della Seta, Fabrizio. "Italia e Francia nell'Ottocento." In *Storia della musica,* vol. 9, ed. Società Italiana di Musicologia. Turin: Società Italiana de Musicologia/ EDT, 1993.

Dent, Edward J. *The Rise of Romantic Opera.* Edited by Winton Dean. Cambridge: Cambridge University Press, 1976.

Dutheil, Frédéric. "Le Livret d'opéra italien (1825–1850)." Thesis, University of Bordeaux, 1985.

Einstein, Alfred. *Music in the Romantic Era.* New York: Norton, 1947.

Gerhard, Anselm. *Die Verstädterung der Oper: Paris und das Musiktheater des 19 Jahrhunderts.* Stuttgart: Metzler, 1992. Translated by Mary Whittall as *The Urbanization of Opera: Music Theater in Paris in the Nineteenth Century* (Chicago: University of Chicago Press, 1998).

Ghislanzoni, Antonio. *Gli artisti da teatro.* Milan: G. Daelli, 1865. Novel on the world of opera by the librettist of *Aida.*

———. "Storia di Milano dal 1836 al 1848." In *La chiave di baritono.* Milan, 1882.

Giazotto, Remo. *Maria Malibran (1808–1836): Una vita nei nomi di Rossini e Bellini.* Turin: ERI, 1986.

Goldin, Daniela. *La vera Fenice: Librettisti e libretti tra Sette e Ottocento.* Turin: Einaudi, 1985.

Il melodramma italiano dell'Ottocento: Studi e ricerche per Massimo Mila. Turin: Einaudi, 1977.

Join-Dieterle, Catherine. *Les Décors de scène à l'Opéra de Paris à l'époque romantique.* Paris: Picard, 1988.

Le Mélodrame. Centre Culturel International de Cérisy-la-Salle. Paris: Plon, 1970. *Revue Europe* (November–December 1987).

Lippmann, Friedrich. *Versificazione italiana e ritmo musicale: I rapporti tra verso e musica nell'opera italiana del'Ottocento.* Naples: Liguori, 1986.

Mazzini, Giuseppe. *Filosofia della musica: Della fatalità considerata come elemento drammatico, Moto letterario in Italia (1836–37).* Imola: Edizione Nazionale, 1910. *See esp.* vol. 8, pt. 2.

————. *Filosofia della musica e estetica musicale del primo Ottocento*. Rimini and Florence: Cuaraldi, 1977. With selected texts on the aesthetics of opera at the beginning of the nineteenth century.

Mendelssohn, Felix. *Voyage de jeunesse: Lettres Européennes (1830–32)*. Paris: Stock Musique, 1980.

Mitchell, Jerome. *The Walter Scott Operas: An Anthology of Operas Based on the Works of Sir Walter Scott*. Tuscaloosa: University of Alabama Press, 1977.

Mongrédien, Jean. *La Musique en France des Lumières au Romantisme (1789–1830)*. Paris: Flammarion, 1987.

Monti, Ernestina. "Contributo ad uno studio sui libretti d'opera in Lombardia e sulla censura teatrale in Milano nell'Ottocento." *Archivio storico lombardo* 17 (January–June 1939): 306–65.

Orchestre in Emilia-Romagna nell'Ottocento e Novecento. Edited by Marcello Conati and Marcello Pavarani. Parma: Orchestra Sinfonica dell'Emilia-Romagna "Arturo Toscanini," 1982.

Pizzetti, Ildebrando. *La musica italiana dell'Ottocento*. Turin: Palatine, 1947.

Portinari, Folco. *Pari siamo! Io la lingua, egli ha il pugnale: Storia del melodramma ottocentesco attraverso i suoi libretti*. Turin: EDT, 1981.

Rinuccini, Giovanni Battista. *Sulla musica e sulla poesia melodrammatica italiana del secolo XIX*. Lucca: Guidotti, 1843.

Ritorni, Carlo. *Ammaestramenti alla composizione d'ogni poema e d'ogni opera appartenente alla musica*. Milan: Pirola, 1841.

Rivelli, Luigia. "G. Gioacchino Belli 'censore' e il suo spirito liberale." *Rassegna storica del Risorgimento* (1923): 319–93.

Rognoni, Luigi. *Gioacchino Rossini*. Turin: ERI, 1968.

Romanticismo e musica: L'estetica musicale da Kant a Nietzsche. Edited by Giovanni Guanti. Turin: EDT musica, 1981.

Rosselli, John. *The Opera Industry in Italy from Cimarosa to Verdi: The Role of the Impresario*. Cambridge: Cambridge University Press, 1984.

Sala, Emilio. *L'opera senza canto: Il mélo romantico e l'invenzione della colonna sonora*. Padua: Marsilio, 1995.

Sand, George. *Lettres d'un voyageur (1837)*. Paris: Garnier-Flammarion, 1971.

Schlitzer, Franco. *Mondo teatrale dell'Ottocento*. Naples, 1954.

Serafin, Tullio, and Alceo Toni. *Stile, tradizione e convenzioni del melodramma italiano del Settecento e dell'Ottocento*. Milan: Ricordi, 1964.

Stendhal [H. Beyle]. *Vie de Rossini*. Paris: Editions d'Aujourd'hui, Les Introuvables, 1977. Translated by Richard N. Coe as *Life of Rossini* (London: J. Calder; New York: Riverrun, 1985).

————. *L'Opéra italien: Notes d'un dilettante (1824–27)*. Paris: Michel de Maule, 1988.

Véron, Docteur. *L'Opéra de Paris, 1820–1835*. Paris: Michel de Maule, 1987. Taken from the memoirs of Dr. Véron, director of the Paris Opéra.

Voix d'opéra: Écrits de chanteurs du XIX siècle. Paris: Michel de Maule, 1988.

Wagner, Richard. *Oper und Drama.* Edited by Klaus Kropfinger. 2d ed. Stuttgart: Philipp Reclam, 1984.

————. *The Art-Work of the Future, and Other Works.* Translated by William Ashton Ellis. Lincoln: University of Nebraska Press, 1993.

Weinstock, Herbert. *Donizetti and the World of Opera in Italy, Paris and Vienna in the First Half of the Nineteenth Century.* New York: Farrar Straus Giroux, 1979.

Zoppelli, Luca. *L'opera come racconto: Modi narrativi nel teatro musicale dell'Ottocento.* Padua: Marsilio, 1994.

B. OTHER WORKS

Bragaglia, Leonardo. *Storia del libretto nel teatro in musica come testo o pretesto drammatico.* Rome: Trevi, 1970.

Castil-Blaze. *L'Opéra italien de 1548 à 1856.* Paris, 1856.

Celletti, Rodolfo. *Storia del belcanto.* Paris: Fayard, 1987. Translated by Frederick Fuller as *A History of Bel Canto* (Oxford: Clarendon, 1991).

Clément, Catherine. *L'Opéra, ou la défaite des femmes.* Paris: Grasset, 1979. Translated by Betsy Wing as *Opera, or the Undoing of Women* (Minneapolis: University of Minnesota Press, 1988).

Dallapiccola, Luigi. *Parole e musica.* Milan: Il Saggiatore, 1980. A previous edition was published as *Appunti, incontri, meditazioni* (1970).

Degrada, Francesco. *Il palazzo incantato: Studi sulla tradizione del melodramma dal Barocco al Romanticismo.* Fiesole: Discanto, 1979.

Fubini, Enrico. *L'estetica musicale dal Settecento a oggi.* Turin: Einaudi, 1964. Translated by Michael Hatwell as *History of Music Aesthetics* (London: Macmillan, 1990).

Grout, Donald J., and Hermine Weigel Williams. *A Short History of Opera.* 3d ed. New York: Columbia University Press, 1988.

Hanslick, Eduard. *The Beautiful in Music.* Translated by Gustav Cohen. New York: Liberal Arts Press, 1957.

Jankélévitch, Vladimir. *La Musique et l'ineffable.* Paris: Le Seuil, 1983.

Kerman, Joseph. *Opera as Drama.* New, rev. ed. Berkeley and Los Angeles: University of California Press, 1988.

La drammaturgia musicale. Edited by Lorenzo Bianconi. Bologna: Il Mulino, 1986.

Leibowitz, René. *Histoire de l'opéra.* Paris: Buchet Chastel, 1957.

————. *Les Fantômes de l'opéra.* Paris: Gallimard, 1972.

Littérature et opéra: Colloque de Cérisy 1985. Papers collected and edited by Philippe Berthier and Kurt Ringger. Grenoble: Presses Universitaires de Grenoble, 1987.

"L'Opéra." *L'Arc,* no. 27 (1965).

Lukács, Georg. *Seele und Formen.* Berlin: E. Fleischel, 1911. Translated by Anna Bostock as *Soul and Form* (Cambridge, Mass.: MIT Press, 1974).

Nicolodi, Fiamma. "Opera Production from Italian Unification to the Present." In *Opera Production and Its Resources*. Vol. 4 of *The History of Italian Opera*, ed. Lorenzo Bianconi and Giorgio Pestelli, 165–228. Chicago: University of Chicago Press, 1998.

Noske, Frits. *The Signifier and the Signified*. The Hague: Nijhoff, 1977.

Opera e libretto. Vols. 1, 2. Studi di musica veneta. Florence: Olschki, 1990, 1993.

Paduano, Guido. *Noi facemmo ambedue un sogno strano: Il disagio amoroso sulla scena dell'opera europea*. Palermo: Sellerio, 1982.

Petrobelli, Pierluigi. *Music in the Theater: Essays on Verdi and Other Composers*. With translations by Roger Parker. Princeton, N.J.: Princeton University Press, 1994.

Poizat, Michel. *L'Opéra, ou le cri de l'ange: Essai sur la jouissance de l'amateur d'opéra*. Paris: Métailié, 1986. Translated by Arthur Denner as *The Angel's Cry: Beyond the Pleasure Principle in Opera* (Ithaca, N.Y.: Cornell University Press, 1992).

Regards sur l'opéra: Du ballet comique de la reine à l'opéra de Pékin. Paris: Presses Universitaires de France, 1976.

Rosselli, John. *Singers of Italian Opera: The History of a Profession*. Cambridge: Cambridge University Press, 1992.

———. "Opera Production, 1780–1880." In *Opera Production and Its Resources*. Vol. 4 of *The History of Italian Opera*, ed. Lorenzo Bianconi and Giorgio Pestelli, 81–164. Chicago: University of Chicago Press, 1998.

Ruwet, Nicolas. *Langage, musique, poésie*. Paris: Le Seuil, 1972.

Salazar, Philippe Joseph. *Idéologies de l'opéra*. Paris: Presses Universitaires de France, 1980.

Schiller, Friedrich. *Über Naïve und Sentimentalische Dichtung*. Vol. 5 of *Sämtliche Werke*. Munich: Winkler, 1972. Translated by Daniel O. Dahlstrom as *On Naive and Sentimental Poetry* (New York: Continuum, 1993).

Schmidgall, Gary. *Literature as Opera*. New York: Oxford University Press, 1977.

———. *Shakespeare and Opera*. New York: Oxford University Press, 1990.

Smith, Patrick. *The Tenth Muse: A Historical Study of the Opera Libretto*. New York: Knopf, 1970.

Sur l'opéra italien. Cahiers 34/44, no. 1 Textuel 18 (1986). Université de Paris VII. Paris: UER "Sciences des textes et documents."

Storia dell'opera. Edited by Guglielmo Barblan and Alberto Basso. 6 vols. Turin: UTET, 1977.

Storia dell'Opera Italiana. Edited by Lorenzo Bianconi and Giorgio Pestelli. Turin: EDT musica, 1987–. Three volumes of six (vols. 4–6) published to date; of these, vol. 4 has been translated by Lydia Cochrane as *Opera Production and Its Resources*, ed. Lorenzo Bianconi and Giorgio Pestelli (Chicago: University of Chicago Press, 1998). A complete translation under the series title *The History of Italian Opera* is planned.

INDEX OF NAMES